MIRACLE
MEDICINES

MIRACLE MEDICINES

SEVEN LIFESAVING DRUGS
AND THE PEOPLE
WHO CREATED THEM

Robert L. Shook

PORTFOLIO

PORTFOLIO
Published by the Penguin Group
Penguin Group (USA) Inc., 375 Hudson Street, New York, New York 10014, U.S.A.
Penguin Group (Canada), 90 Eglinton Avenue East, Suite 700, Toronto, Ontario, Canada M4P 2Y3
(a division of Pearson Penguin Canada Inc.)
Penguin Books Ltd, 80 Strand, London WC2R 0RL, England
Penguin Ireland, 25 St. Stephen's Green, Dublin 2, Ireland (a division of Penguin Books Ltd)
Penguin Books Australia Ltd, 250 Camberwell Road, Camberwell,
Victoria 3124, Australia (a division of Pearson Australia Group Pty Ltd)
Penguin Books India Pvt Ltd, 11 Community Centre, Panchsheel Park,
New Delhi – 110 017, India
Penguin Group (NZ), 67 Apollo Drive, Mairangi Bay, Auckland 1311,
New Zealand (a division of Pearson New Zealand Ltd)
Penguin Books (South Africa) (Pty) Ltd, 24 Sturdee Avenue,
Rosebank, Johannesburg 2196, South Africa

Penguin Books Ltd, Registered Offices: 80 Strand, London WC2R 0RL, England

First published in 2007 by Portfolio, a member of Penguin Group (USA) Inc.

1   3   5   7   9   10   8   6   4   2

Many of the designations used by manufacturers and sellers to distinguish their products are
claimed as trademarks. Where those designations appear in this book and the publisher was aware
of a trademark claim, the designations have been printed in initial capital letters (e.g. Tylenol).

LIBRARY OF CONGRESS CATALOGING-IN-PUBLICATION DATA
Shook, Robert L., 1938–
Miracle medicines : seven amazing drugs and the people who created them / Robert L. Shook.
p. cm.
Includes bibliographical references.
ISBN 978-1-59184-157-9
1. Pharmacy—History.   2. Drug development—History.   3. Pharmacognosy—History.   I. Title.
RS61.S39 2007
615'.1—dc22   2006052482

Printed in the United States of America

Set in Minion
Designed by Helene Berinsky

To Elinor
I love and adore you

CONTENTS

MIRACLE
MEDICINES

INTRODUCTION

While I won't promise that the miracles dealt with in this book are all of biblical dimensions, the millions who now continue to enjoy life because of these "miracle medicines" know firsthand that they save lives and reduce pain and suffering. These exotic man-made products were created and developed by the labor of tens of thousands of dedicated men and women working in the laboratories and manufacturing facilities of major pharmaceutical companies. And it's been only within the last fifty years or so that we've seen so many new and remarkable medicines that cure diseases and lessen chronic ailments.

It was heartening for me to learn that the individuals who devote their working lives to these scientific endeavors measure their worth by the good they do for others. It is rarely money that motivates them. Considering the contributions they make to humankind, and compared to the millions paid to entertainers, professional athletes, and senior executives, their paychecks are paltry. Physicians who have graduated with highest honors from our top medical schools and who work at these pharmaceutical labs could make far more money in private medical practice.

One astute Ph.D. cum laude graduate in chemistry said, "At a job interview with a pharmaceutical company, the recruiter told me, 'With your grades, you can make far more with a petroleum company. So then why are you interested in working for our company?' "

"I had to convince him that my interest was in the good I wanted to do," the chemist said. "The interviewer gave me a doubtful look, but he must have felt I was sincere because I got the job."

During my past twenty-five years as a writer, I have interviewed hundreds of successful people who were at the top in their fields. Never have I met, as a group, so many brilliant and dedicated professionals as I did while researching this book. I came away with deep respect and admiration for them.

Big Pharma is big business, and to many Americans most multibillion-dollar entities are faceless, monolithic corporations controlled by uncaring, mercenary managers. In this book, however, you will meet brilliant and indefatigable men and women who struggle for years to transform a strand of scientific theory into a new medicine. Dedicated scientists at such companies as Abbott, Johnson & Johnson, and AstraZeneca will come alive in their day-to-day labors and in their victories and defeats. As you will see, the failures far outnumber the successes. It's not unusual for chemists to work their entire careers in a laboratory and never have a discovery that makes it to the marketplace.

Within the confines of their laboratories, in their microbiologic worlds, these pharmaceutical adventurers trek to minuscule places, venturing into unknown territories, akin to the celebrated explorers of darkest Africa and Antarctica, and, more recently, the astronomers in outer space. Their discoveries can be equally exhilarating and also hugely beneficial.

In a November 2003 speech to the National Press Club in Washington, D.C., Sidney Taurel, CEO of Eli Lilly, told his audience about the tortuous coming-of-age of a new medicine: "The usual point of invention for pharmaceutical researchers is called the generation of a new chemical entity. Here, a molecule shows some desired activity against the target. We call these molecules 'leads.' A lead is no more a drug than an acorn is an oak tree. It is indeed something like a chemical 'seed' that must be tended and pruned and shaped through a very long and costly process. It has to be grown into a marketable medicine. Each stage of growth takes many years and requires a staggering investment.

"Once you have a lead, you have a molecule that has shown activity in a test tube. But you know next to nothing about how it will work in a living organism. Can the molecule be dissolved in a medium that can enter the body? After it enters the bloodstream, does it get to the target? What happens when the body tries to metabolize it? How does it interact with other chemicals in the body? What might its safety profile look like? There are a host of such questions you must answer and, based on the answers, changes you must try to engineer in the original molecule before you can begin to find out whether it will help patients in the real world. The key about this part of drug development is that it combines high costs with high technological risk.

"Moving a compound through these early stages of development takes six or seven years," Taurel continued. "It involves a lot of people putting in thousands of hours in many disciplines. By the time you reach the end of Phase I—the earliest phase of testing in human volunteers— when you include the cost of all the failures and the cost of capital, you may have more than $100 million invested in that compound. Yet 70 percent of the molecules that make it this far will never make to the market, and none of this work tells you what you most want to know: will it work in patients?

"To answer that question, you have to send the drug candidate through six or seven more years of very costly clinical trials, and the odds are still formidable. Somewhere between 40 to 50 percent of drug candidates that enter the third and final phase of trials fails to make it to market.

"Moreover, while all this development work is going on, and well before you have any assurance it will succeed, you have to make other heavy investments to develop the necessary formulations and processes to get ready to manufacture the drug, and to prepare to market it if and when it is finally approved."

A June 2005 *Fortune* article compared the job of Big Pharma researchers to juggling snakes. That's because they must ensure oral medicines can be readily formulated, remain stable when stored, resist destruction by stomach acids, get into patients' bloodstreams, and not break down into toxic compounds when metabolized.

Even when a new medicine does receive FDA approval, there is still no guarantee that it will succeed in the fiercely competitive marketplace. And while hundreds of patients might have been tested during the clinical trials, an approved medicine may be prescribed to thousands or even millions of patients. With these large numbers, there may be patients, over time, who experience certain previously unknown side effects that may cause the medicine to be withdrawn from the market. This is what happened to Merck's Vioxx and Pfizer's Bextra; both were multibillion-dollar Cox-2–inhibitor blockbuster drugs.

Consider, too, that a pharmaceutical company invests large sums of money, often hundreds of millions of dollars, in a manufacturing facility years prior to receiving FDA approval. Companies do this in order to have a lifesaving medicine immediately available upon its approval. The FDA requires companies to validate their capacity to supply a new medicine; otherwise, imagine how consumers would react upon being told their prescription could not be filled. Building a plant prior to a drug's approval is a huge risk—particularly with the number of drugs that fail prior to and during Phase III.

During my interviews with Big Pharma people, I observed a determined eagerness to do the right thing. I saw this in the course that Novartis took during the development of Gleevec, a breakthrough medicine to treat chronic myeloid leukemia (CML), a rare form of cancer that had a very low patient survival rate. There are relatively few CML victims in the United States—only roughly 6,650 Americans over age twenty are diagnosed each year. Compare this to the nearly 200,000 cases of prostate cancer, and 195,000 cases of breast cancer in the United States in 2001, the year Novartis had to decide whether to push forward with a new medicine that showed great promise for saving the lives of CML victims. Novartis's chairman and CEO, Daniel Vasella, M.D., explained his concerns: "Ultimately, we are a business, and business decisions are often based on some form of statistical analysis and the chance to make a profit.

"If it were purely a personal choice, we would ignore the questions that business professionals must ask. We would avoid asking how many patients suffer from CML. We would not ask whether we could supply the drug without charging a high price. We would not ask what would be the costs to the other parts of our business if we threw large amounts of capital and human resources into the development and manufacturing of this drug. We would skip all those questions. But we cannot, for, as I said, we are a business."

But when Dr. Vasella saw the favorable Phase 1 (initial clinical trials) results, he immediately gave the order for the company to move forward. "As a management team, when there is a fair chance that a product on the market will change the practice of medicine, we have a duty to put that product out there—even if it helps only a small number of patients. In that sense, we certainly do not function like many other corporations. I knew what we had to do, that we must not count pennies and must disregard costs. We would find the money. 'I don't care what it costs,' I told our head of global technical operations. 'Money doesn't matter. Let's just do it.' "

Following a 2004 survey of its readers, the *Financial Times* named Vasella the most influential European businessman of the past quarter century.

Vasella often makes the point that pharmaceutical companies, like all businesses, are held accountable to shareholders. With this in mind, I have included at the beginning of each chapter brief histories of each of the seven major pharmaceutical companies profiled in this book. These corporate backgrounds serve two purposes: First, they tell how each company started as a small enterprise with humble beginnings. Each one's ultimate success can be attributed to innovation, providing high-quality products, taking big risks, and overcoming insurmountable obstacles. At its best, this is how the free enterprise system works. Those who excel are rewarded. The fact that those featured in this book have become multibillion-dollar international companies is a testament to years of achievement and of making significant contributions to humankind. I mention this because for the past several years the pharmaceutical industry has been routinely panned by the news media. As a consequence, polls show that public opinion of drug companies has plummeted.

Second, these minihistories present the business side of these companies, in contrast to the research, development, and production side, where the focus is on the work done by researchers, chemists, physicians, and scientists. The company histories are told separately to avoid chapters that read as if this were a business book. They impart specific timelines without which the story about the medicine would be difficult to follow, primarily because events from the time of a molecule's discovery to when a medicine was actually launched in the market took place over periods of decades. During these long time frames, mergers, acquisitions, and corporate name changes often transpired. For example, one Astra-Zeneca scientist had originally worked for Atlas Chemical Industries, which was later acquired by Imperial Chemical Industries, PLC (ICI);

subsequently an ICI division changed its name to Zeneca, after which, in 1999, Zeneca purchased Astra and became AstraZeneca. Reading the business chronicle of these transactions is helpful in following the story of the drug Seroquel; as you will witness, some of the key contributors to the making of this drug worked for different firms prior to the formation of the corporation that is today AstraZeneca.

Similarly, early pioneers of Lipitor initially worked at Parke-Davis, a division of Warner-Lambert that was acquired by Pfizer in 2000. Similar mergers and acquisitions occurred after the early discovery work of Advair, Gleevec, and Remicade. GlaxoSmithKline and Novartis had not yet been formed when Advair and Gleevec were in their early stages of development. Likewise, Centocor, a start-up biotech company that launched Remicade, became part of the Johnson & Johnson family in 1999.

The fiercely competitive nature of the pharmaceutical industry led many companies to combine forces during the 1990s and early 2000s. This is why I recommend that you read the company history prior to reading the main part of the chapter. By doing so, you'll have a clearer understanding of the business climate that influenced certain decision making. I say this heedful of the fact that readers of science-oriented books may have a tendency to skim through these business segments.

A big challenge I faced with this book was: Could I write the stories of these miracle drugs so that a reader without a technical background could understand them? Would the scientists and chemists in the laboratories be capable of articulating technical and scientific findings in laymen's terms? With this in mind, I would preface each interview by emphasizing, "If my book sounds like a college chemistry textbook, people won't read it." Also, mindful of the need to hold the reader's interest, I explained to each interviewee, "It serves little purpose to write a book that bores people." So I've made it a point to convey the high-stakes nature of the risks and races these companies run to receive FDA approval before another pharmaceutical firm gets its competing product approved. And of course the most important race is the one to make a life-saving product quickly available to those victims stricken by terminal illness and crippling disease.

My goal is also to reach the people who take these medicines. They deserve to learn how an ongoing battle is raging within their blood-

streams, and how man-made molecules placed in their bodies are vigorously engaged to ward off their disease. I believe that proactive patients
do better than those passive patients who say to their physicians, "Here's
my body. Do with it what you have to do to make it well again." Uninformed patients are likely to feel helpless and often hopeless, conditions
not conductive to recovery. Informed patients are able to make optimal
choices. By proactively participating in getting well, they increase their
chances of having their good health restored. They are also more likely
to comply with the requirements of the medicines that their physicians
prescribe.

This is a book about lifesaving breakthroughs, about the men and women
who discover and develop miraculous medicines that reduce pain, cure
disease, and stave off death. It's about the pharmaceutical companies that
provide the funds and the unique environments that make it possible for
this extraordinary work to go forward.

Unfortunately, pharmaceutical companies that ranked as America's
most admired corporations in the 1990s have since lost favor with the
general public. It is not uncommon for the news media to portray these
companies as corporate villains, on a par with the tobacco companies.
For example, I recently read an article that made an issue of how the cost
of raw materials for certain medicines was only pennies, yet prescription
prices ranged from several dollars to hundreds of dollars. The article asserted that several popular medicines were priced so high that large
numbers of our senior citizens had no alternative but to purchase lower-
priced drugs in Canada. While the price of raw materials may indeed be
pennies, the article failed to mention the enormous cost of research and
development, the hundreds of millions of dollars spent for clinical trials,
and the huge up-front investment made to manufacture a new medicine.
It was an unfair assessment, tantamount to comparing the cost of the
raw materials that go into creating a masterpiece oil painting (canvas and
paint) to its million-dollar price tag!

Certainly not all pharmaceutical companies are perfect, but then,
what companies are? In considering the major contributions the drug
companies make to humankind, no other industry has contributed so
much. Their scientists are committed to the noble cause of relieving
suffering and prolonging life. They are doing their job well, making

tremendous strides. Yet public opinion is at an all-time low. If this trend continues, a public uproar could lead to the passing of legislation that curtails the industry's progress. If pharmaceutical companies are forced to operate under adverse conditions that constrain their productivity, where are we to turn for our new medicines? To academia? To the government? No way. It is imperative that our pharmaceutical industry remain healthy. *Our* health depends on it.

Only a few decades ago, physicians treated ulcers with milk and cream, and if that didn't work, they performed surgery. Antacids then came to replace dairy products, and with the introduction of a class of drugs called proton pump inhibitors, surgery for ulcers was vastly reduced. Advances like this in medicine on all fronts have been made. The death rate for heart disease has been cut by more than 50 percent during the past half century. As recently as the 1980s, HIV/AIDS carried an automatic death sentence; now, thanks to the ingenuity of scientists and the investment of pharmaceutical companies, we are benefiting from an 80 percent decrease in the U.S. death rate from AIDS.

The period between the 1940s and the 1990s has been hailed as the golden era of miracle drugs, but experts predict that those advances will be dwarfed by even greater achievement during the next twenty-five years. Such prophecies are premised on a flourishing, unencumbered pharmaceutical industry, not one that operates in an unfriendly environment with one arm tied behind its back.

I invite you to join me and come behind the scenes of seven of the world's leading pharmaceutical companies. Meet the men and women who make miracle medicines. Once you do, I feel certain that you will come away with an appreciation of how their work enriches our lives. And if you or a loved one currently uses one of the seven medicines featured on the following pages, this book may very well make a significant difference in your life.

1

ABBOTT COMPANY PROFILE

Born on a rocky farm near Bridewater, Vermont, in 1857, Wallace Calvin Abbott dropped out of school at fourteen to work full-time on his father's farm. Six years passed before his mother was able to convince him to go back to school. At twenty-three he earned his high-school diploma and enrolled at St. Johnsbury Academy to prepare to study medicine. Graduating in premedicine from Dartmouth at twenty-six, he enrolled in the University of Michigan medical school. In 1885, at twenty-eight, he received his M.D. degree.

Abbott returned to Vermont to practice medicine in West Rutland. That same year a family friend informed him that the man's brother, Dr. William Dodge, wanted to sell his practice and drugstore on the North Side of Chicago. The asking price was $1,000. Borrowing money from his family for train fare, the young doctor traveled to Chicago. A deal was consummated and, again with borrowed money, he bought both the medical practice and the drugstore. Abbott and his wife Clara moved into a two-room apartment behind his newly acquired business, People's Drug Store.

Making house calls on his sturdy Beckley-Ralston bicycle, Dr. Abbott typically charged one to two dollars per visit. In his drugstore, he created a line of products that included: Dr. Abbott's Tooth Ache Drops, Rock Candy Cough Syrup, Blackberry Balsam, Tonic Laxative Pills, Laxative Lozenges, Worm Medicine, Spring Blood Purifier, and French Dental Cream. His big seller was Anodyne Liniment, which was said to relieve both internal and external pains.

Dr. Abbott had become acquainted with Dr. Adolphe Pierre Burg-graeve, a distinguished Belgian surgeon practicing in Paris, who had formerly served as chief surgeon at the Civil Hospital in Ghent. Burggraeve pioneered the use of alkaloidal extracts, which he'd found could decrease bodily temperatures without interfering with circulation and nutrition. Burggraeve gave his patients doses of various alkaloidal pills that he made himself. The success of his treatments was impressive, and although there were many who criticized his work, Burggraeve attracted many followers, Abbott among them.

Burggraeve's experimentation led the way in the field that the physician called "dosimetry." His method was a radical departure from the then-common use of entire plants or of their crude water or alcoholic extracts as medicines. Large doses, nauseating taste, the likelihood to spoil and spill, and the curative uncertainty of these fluid-extract types of medications were all good reasons to seek a better way. Burggraeve instead used only the parts of drug plants that provided real remedial action—the active part, or "alkaloid," which he compressed into a tiny granule or pill. A big advantage was that this form was easy to consume, while fluid extracts were less reliable or controllable. Also, extracting alkaloids from such sources as herbs, plants, roots, or flowers, and preparing the granules in pure, measured forms provided an exact quantity of medicine. Dosimetry thus allowed a physician to give small, frequent doses of the pure, isolated alkaloid until the desired effect was achieved. Simply put, mathematical measurements removed much of the guesswork out of administering medicines formerly in liquid form.

Abbott had learned about Burggraeve's theories while attending a lecture series at the University of Michigan. Exasperated with the uncertainties of fluid-extract types of medications, he became an ardent believer in remedies in pill form. A year later, he decided to make his own alkaloidal granules.

The year was 1888, and it marked the founding of the Abbott Alkaloidal Company. Dr. Abbott started manufacturing his granule products in the kitchen of the small apartment in the rear of his drugstore. Sales in his first year totaled $2,000, a sum that included the earnings from his medical practice. They jumped to $4,500 in 1889. Abbott's quality control methods were the same as those that he applied as a pharmacist. Instead of pouring elixirs from one flask to another, he used molds of hard rubber and a spatula to convert moistened masses into tiny granules. His production guides were old copies of *Dosimetric Medical Review* and Dr. Burggraeve's *New Handbook of Dosimetric Therapeutics*. He also incorporated innovations he discovered through his own experimentation.

Abbott was quoted as saying, "I now have granules which are accurate ... the solubility rapid and perfect ... and the keeping quality assured without gum or any other material that will harden with age and render the granule worthless."

By 1890, annual sales had shot up to $8,000. To expand his manufacturing operation beyond his own practice, Abbott placed ads for his products in *Medical World*, a magazine read widely by physicians. The headline of an early ad read, in bold print: DOCTOR, WE'VE A NUGGET OF GOLD FOR YOU! It was quite a deal. With every order, he threw in a free copy of his self-published 100-page booklet on alkaloidal therapy, and with every $5 worth of orders for granules and an additional $1 for pills, he gave away 1,200 of Waugh's Laxative Granules, which came with the claim "the complete and radical cure of chronic constipation." Quite the promoter, Dr. Abbott's sales in 1891 hit the 5-figure mark—$10,000. The following year, the company moved from Abbott's apartment to an old frame home purchased by his parents, who had moved to Chicago from Vermont. The Abbott Alkaloidal Company was on its way.

Initially, Abbott's products were sold to physicians through *Medical World*, *Alkaloidal Clinic*, and other magazines addressed to doctors. In addition, Abbott mailed out catalogs to sell his wares. He also sent a copy of his *Helpful Hints for the Busy Doctor* to practically every physician in the United States and Canada. In 1891, he purchased the physician's journal *Alkaloidal Clinic* and that same year formed the Clinic Publishing Company. By 1894, annual sales were $29,000.

Dr. Abbott believed in creating a supportive work environment for his employees, and took measures to help them stay healthy. He encouraged his staff to follow his lead and ride bicycles to and from work. In addition to arranging substantial discounts from bicycle manufacturer Beckley-Ralston, he established a payroll deduction plan that took one dollar a week from employee paychecks until their bicycles were paid for. To discourage employees from chewing tobacco, he gave gold watches as Christmas presents to anyone who kicked the habit. (Fast-forwarding to the present, Abbott is consistently recognized as a premier employer. *Working Mother* magazine counts Abbott as one of the ten best employers for working mothers, and the company has become a perennial on *Fortune* magazine's annual list of "50 Best Companies for Minorities.")

Dr. Abbott had his share of detractors, however. There were those who frowned upon dosimetry, calling it quackery. Some claimed that his granules were too expensive, and still others believed that a doctor who sold his own medicines was no different than a common peddler. The American Pharmaceutical Association went so far as to rebuke doctors who bought directly from Abbott and other granule makers. But their criticisms were ignored, and the company prospered. By the turn of the century, annual sales were $100,000. The company incorporated in 1900, with many doctors among its first investors. In 1901, Abbott built a four-story 32,000-square-foot brick building that housed his publishing ventures. The manufacturing facilities remained in the frame house formerly owned by his parents. He was still seeing patients but spending far more time running his businesses.

In the beginning, almost all sales were generated through advertisements. Dr. Abbott advocated this method by saying in his publications: "We have no salesmen, therefore we cannot camp at your door with long-winded talk and a bag of samples. We haven't the time to do it, it isn't our way; and, when you come to think of it, this way by mail suits you better too."

But when faced with competition, he realized that he needed a sales force after all. In 1906, after 18 years in business, he hired his first sales manager. Initially all his drug reps had backgrounds as pharmacists or drugstore clerks. To Dr. Abbott, these men were more than run-of-the-mill salesmen; he referred to them as "Abbott Missionaries." After a 3-day training session, the first group of 7 was sent out with their wares to crisscross the country, traveling by horse-and-buggy and by train, calling on physicians, veterinarians, and druggists, selling alkaloid pills. The sales force soon paid off. By 1910, revenues crossed the magic half-million-dollar threshold to reach $546,000, and the customer list totaled 50,000 of the country's 130,000 physicians, plus 1,000 in Europe and 500 in Latin America.

In 1910, Joseph Beihn, previously director of the Chicago Health Department laboratories, joined the company. Put in charge of the company's biological laboratories, Beihn set up a veterinary department and then headed the medical department.

During World War I, many essential drugs manufactured exclusively by German companies became unavailable in the United States. Abbott concentrated on finding ways to synthesize medicines that were formerly made by the Germans. Now renamed Abbott Laboratories, the company became vital to the medical community with its local anesthetic procaine, a substitute for the German novocaine. The German remedy for gout, lumbago, neuralgia, and rheumatism, called Atophan, became Abbott's Cinchophyen. With German pharmaceuticals no longer in the picture, Abbott was within a year able to sell its similar medicines for less than half the price in the American market.

In 1918, Dr. Roger Adams, a brilliant consultant to Abbott who had been studying at the Kaiser Wilhelm Institute in Berlin, joined the company. The Harvard-educated chemist hired Dr. Ernest Volwiler, a promising Ph.D. chemist from the University of Illinois. Volwiler would later head Abbott research and go on to become the company's president and chairman.

In 1921, Abbott established a laboratory in Rocky Mount, North Carolina, to develop new drugs, including sedatives, tranquilizers, and vitamins. That same year, at 61, Dr. Abbott passed away. Dr. Alfred Burdick, who had joined the company in 1904 as associate editor of the *Alkaloidal Clinic* at $40 a week, was elected by the directors to succeed the founder as its chairman and president.

In 1923, Abbott entered the baby food business; one of its earliest milk products was Lactigen. That same year, the Moores and Ross Milk Company in Columbus, Ohio, introduced Similac infant formula, still one of the leading infant formulas. Abbott acquired Moores and Ross in 1964, and the business eventually became known as Abbott's Ross Products Division. Abbott's acquisition of Ross followed the company's entry into intravenous (IV) solutions in the 1930s and continued its strategy of diversifying into multiple segments of the health-care industry.

Seven months prior to the stock market crash in 1929, Abbott had become a publicly traded company. The stock originally offered at $32 rose to $40.50 its first full day of trading. Today, that same share of stock would be worth more than $250,000.

In 1930, under the direction of Dr. Volwiler, the company introduced Nembutal, a medication to be taken before surgery. It provided excellent sedation before a long-lasting anesthetic was administered, and patients were found to recover faster with less hangover and nausea. The drug came to be used later to ease childbirth, control convulsions, relieve insomnia, and alleviate disorders ranging from seasickness to delirium tremens. Nembutal became one of Abbott's best-known and longest-lived products. In 1933 the company introduced sodium thiopental (Pentothal), which marked the beginning of Abbott's long-term leadership role in the field of anesthetics—a role that continues today with their induction agent, sevoflurane.

During World War II, Pentothal performed excellently for wounded troops. Abbott also provided Allied forces with Sterilope envelopes, small sealed packages with an inner envelope that had a sifter top containing sulfa powder. When spread over a wound, this powder substantially reduced the danger of infection. The company also supplied troops with Halazone tablets, which purified contaminated water, and processed dried blood plasma, which helped save the lives of thousands of wounded soldiers. Abbott was also one of the pharmaceutical companies that produced lifesaving penicillin, establishing the company's long-term leadership position in anti-infectives.

By 1945, sales had grown to $37.9 million. That same year, a breakthrough medicine, Tridione, was introduced to treat children with petit mal epilepsy. This drug enjoyed a success rate of 30 percent in decreasing seizure attacks.

In 1950, Abbott launched Sucaryl, a cyclamate compound 30 times sweeter than sugar. It was discovered in 1937 when a young graduate student at the University of Illinois lit a cigarette, laid it on a lab bench heavily stained with salts of sulfamic acid, and, on his next puff, noticed the sweet taste. Sucaryl became Abbott's first major mass-market consumer product. Initially marketed to the medical profession and distributed only in drugstores, within a few years more than four hundred food manufacturers were selling cyclamate compound products. These included low-calorie soft drinks, jellies, jams, frozen fruits, and baked goods, as well as an array of other products in stores across the country.

In 1969, a scientific study showed that rats given extremely high doses of Sucaryl for an extended period of time had an increased incidence of bladder cancer. The information from this study was presented to the FDA and, while more than two dozen other studies on the safety of cyclamates did not confirm these findings or indicate any other safety concerns, the FDA banned the sale of cyclamates in the United States. Abbott no longer owns Sucaryl, but the product continues to be used today in food products in more than fifty-five countries.

In the 1970s, the company's management determined that 65 percent of all hospital patients suffered from some form of malnutrition. As a result, Abbott increased its activities in hospital nutritionals, which later moved the company into the lucrative home-care market.

During this time, Abbott began to see promise in a new area—one that would place a focus on disease prevention instead of treatment. In 1973, the Diagnostics Division was created, joining all of the company's efforts in biologics, radiopharmaceuticals, and clinical instrumentation together to provide physicians with accurate, advanced testing capabilities. Abbott's introduction of many first-of-a-kind products and significant technological advancements—such as highly sensitive tests for diagnosing hepatitis and clinical laboratory systems that greatly improved laboratory efficiency and accuracy—helped transform the practice of medical diagnosis and created the modern diagnostics industry.

Today, with its broad range of laboratory diagnostic equipment, Abbott is a global leader in diagnostics. The company's expertise in infectious disease research helped it develop and introduce the first FDA-approved test in 1985 to detect the human immunodeficiency virus (HIV), which causes acquired immune deficiency syndrome (AIDS). By the end of the 1980s, sales of blood analysis devices and tests alone had grown into a billion-dollar-plus business.

On June 30, 1999, Abbott received FDA approval for Norvir, a protease inhibitor used in combination with other antiretroviral medications for the treatment of HIV infection. The story of this truly miraculous discovery is in the chapter that follows.

In 2005, Abbott's annual sales totaled $22.3 billion, and, with a staff of more than 65,000 working at more than 100 different locations, the company serves people in 130 countries. Abbott has come a long way since its humble beginning, when Dr. Wallace Abbott started his practice on the North Side of Chicago.

The Fight Against AIDS

ABBOTT'S MIRACLE MEDICINES:
NORVIR AND KALETRA

"PATIENT ZERO" was a young, male airline attendant from Canada. While he wasn't the first person in North America to contract AIDS and die from the disease, he was an early case and the unknowing root of infection for a network of gay men in the United States.

No one knows where Patient Zero picked up HIV. But researchers are now convinced that the disease first entered humans in the Western African country of Cameroon. It is now generally accepted that HIV-1 is a descendant of a simian immunodeficiency virus (SIV) found in the chimpanzees indigenous to certain parts of Cameroon. SIV was passed to the chimpanzee from a lower order of primates. The first humans to be affected may have been hunters who killed chimpanzees to eat their meat, and while the exact timing remains unknown, recent research suggests that human infection first occurred in the early to middle part of the twentieth century. Another theory is that an infected chimpanzee's blood could have entered a hunter's bloodstream through a wound such as a scratch or a cut—and the virus mutated into human immunodeficiency virus (HIV).

This now-human virus, however, remained largely under cover until a series of curious ailments popped up in New York City in 1981. First, eight young, gay men contracted Kaposi's Sarcoma (KS). KS was then very rare in the United States, and when it did appear, the patient was usually an older man of Mediterranean or Jewish heritage, or an organ transplant recipient with a weakened immune system. The cancer was also typically not life threatening. So doctors were startled when a more aggressive form of KS struck young men. Somehow these men's immune systems had become too weak to beat back the growing tumor cells.

In the same year, the Centers for Disease Control and Prevention (CDC) catalogued an unusually large number of cases of a rare, but serious, form of pneumonia called pneumocystis carinii pneumonia (PCP) that occurs when a fungus infects the lungs. A healthy immune system can effectively fight off this fungus, so when PCP killed five gay men in Los Angeles, doctors knew that these men, too, had suffered a blow that crippled their immune systems.

The medical community concluded that a new—and devastating—disorder of impaired immunity was now spreading in the homosexual community, leaving once vibrant and healthy young people prey to all manner of microbes and mutant cells that usually caused no harm. The underlying immune disorder still had no name. The CDC categorized its victims by the symptoms they suffered when a pathogen or other problem overwhelmed their body's defenses, such as lymphadenopathy (swollen glands), PCP, or KS. These are so-called opportunistic infections.

The CDC also formed a task force, and, in July 1981, the centers' internationally renowned epidemiologist, James Curran, asserted that there was no apparent danger of contagion for nonhomosexuals. "The best evidence against contagion," he said, "is that no cases have been reported to date outside the homosexual community or among women."

When other cases of KS and PCP were traced to gay bathhouses in California, heterosexuals felt secure that these lethal illnesses were being transmitted only by homosexual activity. Religious extremists pronounced the disease to be a punishment from the Almighty for sinful behavior. Others tagged homosexuality as a "death style," calling the epidemic a "gay cancer," or the "gay plague." For a while, the CDC called the disorder GRIDS (gay-related immune deficiency syndrome).

But in August 1982, the official name became acquired immune deficiency syndrome (AIDS), underscoring that the basic problem was an immune deficiency that could result in any number of ailments—that is, a syndrome. The name also emphasized that the problem was something people acquired or contracted later in life rather than an inherited defect, although nobody yet knew what it was that people were contracting.

Officials had gotten rid of the term GRIDS just in time. Later that year, the virus turned up in children and in transfusion recipients. In

1983, it was found that the disease could be passed on heterosexually from men to women. Suddenly, AIDS was no longer a gay disease; the population at large felt vulnerable. In San Francisco, where AIDS was most prevalent, people panicked. The police department equipped patrol officers with special masks and gloves for dealing with suspected AIDS patients. The officers were concerned they could bring the bug home to their families. Landlords evicted individuals with AIDS. The Social Security Administration began interviewing AIDS clients by phone rather than meeting them face-to-face.

In a groundbreaking experiment published in *Science* in 1983, Dr. Luc Montagnier and his colleagues at the Pasteur Institute in Paris finally isolated from an AIDS patient the apparent culprit in all this misery—a virus that was similar to a family of human leukemia viruses. Shortly after that, Dr. Robert Gallo of the National Cancer Institute and his colleagues also isolated the virus and found a way to make it grow in a lab. Their work enabled the development of diagnostic tests for infection by the AIDS virus, soon to be named HIV. By culturing the virus in laboratories, they made it possible to create antibodies against parts of it. Antibodies are protein molecules produced by the immune system that recognize and fight specific foreign invaders, such as HIV. Since the structure of an antibody echoes the structure of the invader, diagnostic tests can reveal the presence of a particular invader, such as HIV, by detecting the antibodies the body produces in response to it.

By the end of 1984, the United States had 7,699 reported AIDS cases on its hands, more than double the 3,064 cases reported in the previous year. AIDS deaths had similarly skyrocketed from 1,292 in 1983 to 3,665 by the end of 1984. Disease specialists could read the handwriting on the wall. With no known cure, AIDS was a calamity waiting to happen. Unchecked, it threatened to reach catastrophic proportions.

DETECTING THE DEVIL

The first hope for curtailing the growing epidemic lay in the diagnostic tests set in motion by Montagnier's and Gallo's work. By this time it had become widely known that, along with unprotected sex, blood transfusions were a primary means of contracting HIV. Officials quickly realized that screening blood donors for HIV infection was crucial for reducing the risk to transfusion recipients.

Gerald Schochetman, Ph.D., now Abbott's director of infectious disease diagnostics research and development, was with the Centers for Disease Control and Prevention in Atlanta, Georgia, in 1985. "Once the virus was discovered," Schochetman explains, "it was apparent that something needed to be done to protect the safety of the blood supply. Tests were needed to detect infected people to prevent HIV from transmitting through blood transfusions." Already a leading manufacturer of blood screening and monitoring equipment, Abbott developed the first FDA-approved test to detect HIV.

With HIV-infected blood samples provided by the NIH, Abbott developed tests that detected antibodies to the virus. This meant not only that infected blood could be detected before it entered the blood supply, but also that people could find out early from their doctors whether they were infected with HIV, before they developed symptoms. A local physician would draw a patient's blood and send it to an independent laboratory that used Abbott diagnostic tests and equipment. Within a few days, the lab would convey the results to the patient's doctor, who would then inform the patient. With today's tests, results can appear within as little as fifteen minutes.

KNOW THY ENEMY

At the same time, several research-based pharmaceutical companies began racing to find a cure for this plague. Doing so required getting to know the enemy, HIV, in all its molecular detail. Only by decoding the molecular machinery the virus needed to survive could scientists design drugs that would put kinks in that machinery.

Finally, a group of researchers took a huge step forward when they published an article in *Science* in 1985 detailing the entire genetic makeup, or genome, of the AIDS virus. These scientists had identified every chemical building block in the long molecular chain of genetic material that resides inside the virus. Unlike the human genome, whose genetic material is made up of DNA (deoxyribonucleic acid), the HIV genome is made up of a related chemical called RNA (ribonucleic acid). Within the genome, the researchers identified important genes, or segments of genetic material that serve as templates for protein molecules. These proteins perform crucial activities in the life of the virus—activities that might be disrupted with drugs. In this way, work with HIV was one of the first applications of modern genomics, using techniques derived from our knowledge of genetic material.

Drug researchers were particularly interested in an HIV protein called a protease, which is like a small molecular scissors that chop a big protein into smaller pieces called peptides. HIV makes many of its proteins in one long piece, with several proteins strung together. HIV protease cuts the big protein strip into its components, a job that turns out to be necessary for the virus to mature inside a human cell and to infect new human cells. If researchers could interfere with the action of this protease, they could kill the virus by preventing it from maturing into its infectious form.

But HIV protease was not the only drug target buried inside the HIV genome. The first drugs manufactured to fight HIV were aimed at another HIV protein called reverse transcriptase (RT). When HIV infects a human cell, it inserts a copy of its genome inside the cell's genome—the action that defines it as a retrovirus. Doing so, however, requires a complex chemical step because the virus's RNA genome does not match the DNA of the human cell. To merge the two genomes, the RNA must first be converted into DNA—and that is the job of RT. Only after RT does its job can the virus insert its genetic material into the cell's genome and instruct the cell to make more copies of HIV.

THE FIRST AIDS DRUG

In 1987, Wellcome (now part of GlaxoSmithKline) received FDA approval for the first HIV drug. Retrovir, also known as zidovudine or AZT, attempted to stop the virus by blocking the actions of RT. In so doing, Retrovir reduced the ability of the virus to infect healthy human immune cells. These cells then failed to produce new viruses, decreasing the amount of virus in the body.

AZT was originally designed in the 1960s for the treatment of leukemia. The drug not only gummed up the workings of RT but also those of other proteins needed to synthesize DNA. Since DNA synthesis is required for cell division, scientists had hoped that AZT would prevent cancerous, rapidly multiplying blood cells from replicating. However, it was abandoned because of its toxicity and ineffectiveness in animals.

But AZT was reintroduced for AIDS in light of extreme public demand. Pharmaceutical manufacturers were under immense pressure from a frightened American public to fast-track anti-AIDS drugs to market. The demand had become a political issue, causing angry demonstrators to protest at rallies, chanting, "Give us the drugs NOW." With strong NIH backing, the drug went through regulatory procedures from test tube to patient in a record nineteen months.

Retrovir was able to ward off some of the effects of AIDS. On occasion, immune systems would show a modest improvement, helping deflect some of the opportunistic infections that plagued AIDS patients. One study demonstrated that AZT would prolong life for the sickest people with AIDS. Unfortunately, AZT's benefits were short-lived; the drug couldn't keep the virus down for long. So while AZT served as a stopgap and provided a ray of hope to AIDS victims, the drug failed to curtail the inevitable—the automatic death sentence that accompanied AIDS. Bristol-Myers and Hoffman LaRoche soon came along with related compounds, but, in addition to their toxicity, they were not effective at changing the progression of the disease.

PICKING ON PROTEASES

In 1987, British researchers Laurence Pearl and William Taylor declared in *Nature* that they had solved an important mystery surrounding the protease encoded in the HIV genome. Previously, researchers had noted that only part of this enzyme appeared to be present. But Pearl and Taylor studied the sequence of amino acids for the protease piece encoded in the HIV genome and figured out how it could form an enzyme. Two copies of this piece would be made, they determined, and then the two pieces would join together to form the full protease. The protease was thus a "dimer," a molecule composed of two subunits linked together. Their important research established a foundation by identifying this sequence in the HIV genome as a protease.

Meanwhile, a young organic chemist, Dale Kempf, had joined Abbott. Kempf had received his Ph.D. at the University of Illinois and had completed two years of postdoctoral research at Columbia University in New York City. "Having been trained to make molecules," the slim six-footer explains, "my initial assignment here at Abbott was to work on agents that would influence blood pressure." These blood-pressure agents are called renin inhibitors because they block the actions of an enzyme called renin (a protease). Kempf's job was to make a new type of antihypertensive, or blood-pressure-lowering agent, by finding a new way to interfere with the action of renin.

One day while Kempf was working in his lab, his boss at the time, Jake Plattner, head of infectious diseases research, said to him: "Dale, we think HIV makes a protease. We'd like to borrow some of your compounds to see if they can inhibit that protease."

"Of course you can," the good-natured Kempf volunteered, "but I think I can make better ones for you." Kempf started "submarining"— that is, doing some work on HIV on nights and weekends while continuing his work on the blood pressure protease during his regular workdays.

Soon Kempf requested a transfer to the infectious disease area. "The HIV epidemic had become front-page news, and if there was a way that I could somehow contribute to stopping it," he explains, "that's what I wanted to do."

Before long, Kempf was deeply immersed in his quest to find a molecule that could inhibit the dreaded, deadly disease. Having grown up on a family farm in Nebraska, hard work and long hours were no strangers to the young chemist. To those who knew him, he tackled every endeavor with relentless passion. A music major in college, Kempf possessed both vocal and guitar-playing skills, but once he took a course in chemistry, he switched majors. Dressed in his white lab coat, it is hard to imagine this mild-mannered chemist in his former life as a singing guitarist.

Kempf hired two chemists, and for the next eighteen months he and his colleagues tinkered with sophisticated computer graphics programs, creating detailed diagrams of the HIV protease to get clues about what sort of molecule might interfere with its function. Making these molecular pictures required shooting X-rays at tiny crystals made up of the protease and mathematically interpreting how the X-rays scattered. The result was a model of the protein's structure—the way its atoms are configured in three-dimensional space.

"With this technology we could conceptualize that the molecular scissors of HIV had a unique structure," Kempf explains, "and its key attribute was that the enzyme consisted of two parts that acted like two clasping right hands. Imagine that instead of a right and left hand clasping each other, you had two right hands and could turn one of them 180 degrees so that it could shake the other one."

With a picture of the protease in hand, Kempf started trying to build a compound that would block it. First, he envisioned his compound as a group of atoms positioned in a very specific order with a very specific geometry. Then he developed a strategy for building that compound using chemicals he had in the lab, or could easily get.

Strategy in mind, he mixed various stock lab chemicals in flasks, heated them or cooled them, and hoped they'd react to form bigger chemicals that might be like the one he envisioned. Once he and his team of molecular architects had made a promising compound, they purified it and then had to determine in atomic detail what compound they had actually made.

Molecules are too small to see with microscopes, even electron microscopes, so chemists typically determine the structure of their molecules using something called nuclear magnetic resonance (NMR), a technique developed back in the 1960s. The output of an NMR machine is a series of peaks from which chemists can deduce the presence of different atoms, and even how they are connected, revealing the complete geometry of that molecule. Kempf, an eternal optimist, made and tested hundreds of compounds, each one requiring days or even weeks of effort. Most of them failed to block HIV in the test tube.

But even that was just a first step. Many compounds that work in test tubes don't perform as expected in animals—and those that do work in animals often don't in humans. Drug developers might work on a project for many years, only to find that they don't have anything marketable. "Even though all your work theoretically might have made some scientific contributions, your effort will be for naught from a medical and commercial viewpoint," says Dan Norbeck, Ph.D., Abbott's vice president of pharmaceutical discovery. "To many people, that's hard to take."

Norbeck joined the company as a young research scientist in 1984 after receiving a doctorate in organic chemistry from California Institute of Technology. Originally a literature major while attending undergraduate school at Wheaton College, he too switched fields after taking a course in organic chemistry. "I was in graduate school in California," he recalls, "when I started reading about this new disease. The media gave it so much coverage that it grabbed everyone's attention. People kept asking, 'What's the cause?' 'Is there a cure?' 'How severe is this epidemic going to be?' It was exciting to come here and work on something so important."

Norbeck eventually joined Kempf and his small cadre of chemists working on something to block HIV protease. "What we did was atypical,"

Kempf recalls, "because scientific management tends to say, 'Well, this is a reasonable area to be in. Let's put our resources here and see what we can do.' What we did was the antithesis to that approach. It was a very small project that grew on its own through the years."

All the while, the potential competition loomed large. Kempf remembers going to scientific meetings and listening anxiously while a scientist from another drug company gave a presentation, hoping that the compounds being described differed from those that he and his Abbott colleagues had discovered.

FINDING THE ONE

After many long hours of building molecules, Kempf's small team found that one of them seemed to inhibit HIV protease; at least, it prevented the virus from growing in the test tube. Although huge hurdles remained before such a chemical could prove its worth as a drug, the early success convinced management that he and the other two chemists might be on to something significant. More chemists and assistants were added to his group, which then included eleven scientists.

But when it came to testing the compound in lab rats, big problems emerged. After the rats swallowed it, it was digested in the intestine but poorly absorbed into the bloodstream. And once in the bloodstream, it was quickly eliminated by the liver.

Kempf and his team spent the next few years attempting to design a molecule that would be easily absorbed into the bloodstream but not easily removed by the liver. They would change one aspect of the molecule, test it, and see what effect the modification had. They repeated this process hundreds of times until, in 1991, a major breakthrough occurred.

They had designed two separate compounds that appeared promising, but neither was quite potent enough. Kempf decided to introduce two modifications simultaneously to create yet another new compound. "As soon as we put it into rats for the first time, we knew we had something very special," Kempf recalls, "because, instead of rapidly disappearing, it stayed in the blood for more than eight hours! We were elated." The compound, labeled ABT-538, was eventually called ritonavir.

Meanwhile, John Leonard, M.D., a molecular virologist with credentials from Johns Hopkins University and Stanford and now Abbott's head of global pharmaceutical research and development, joined the company in March 1992 to head the HIV team. He had firsthand appreciation for the devastation caused by HIV/AIDS, having treated AIDS patients in San Francisco in the 1980s, at the height of the epidemic. At six feet four inches, a handsome man with a full head of dark blond hair, Leonard looks like somebody that central casting would have sent over to audition for the leading role as a doctor in a prime-time television series. "It was an exciting period because the biotech industry was getting started," he says, "and I decided that I could best serve others by figuring out how to make new medicines." Shortly after Leonard arrived at Abbott, he was talking with a colleague—a nurse—in his office. At one point, the nurse quipped: "Where I used to work, we always looked for something to celebrate to liven things up. We should do that here too."

"What do you mean?" Leonard asked.

"It doesn't matter what," she replied. "It's just a way of celebrating our successes."

"Well, I'll tell you what," Leonard answered. "You know how the football players celebrate a touchdown by spiking the ball? Maybe we should do that!"

A few days later, the nurse handed Leonard a gift-wrapped box. It was a nerf football. "Okay, it goes on my windowsill," he recalls laughing, "and we'll use it on special occasions."

A REASON TO BELIEVE

The next major step was to test the new medicine's effectiveness in humans, the only species to be infected by this particular virus. This was a big unknown. After all, the drug could cause severe side effects that no one anticipated. One explicit worry was that it would, like HIV, kill the immune cell in its own right. Another concern was that the human body would chew up the drug before it could do any good, so that even high concentrations of the medicine would plummet when they entered the body, or that, for other reasons, the drug just might not get to most of the HIV-infected cells.

For all these reasons, Norbeck, Kempf, and their colleagues were plagued by doubts. "There were times when we'd ask ourselves, 'Do we really have the skills to be competitive in this area?' " Norbeck recalls. "And there were people within the company who criticized, 'How can we possibly compete with companies that have been in antivirals for so many years?' " But the pressure only served to strengthen the HIV team's resolve. "As the stakes got higher, our team grew stronger," Norbeck says.

In the beginning stages of development, the medicinal chemists made only minute quantities of the drugs, but substantially larger quantities are required for clinical trials, and the drug would have to be affordable to AIDS patients. The first kilogram of ritonavir cost Abbott over $500,000. A patient would have to take 0.4 kilograms in a year, at a cost of $200,000—just for the raw material. "At that price," Leonard quips, "Warren Buffett and Bill Gates would be the only two people who could afford it, and they don't have AIDS." The company had to reduce the cost of the medicine a hundredfold or more.

And it had to do so amid its own mounting costs for development. According to Norbeck, the cost of the discovery phase alone for a candidate drug ranges between $10 million and $70 million. Added to that is the cost of all the failed drug candidates, which vastly outnumber the successes. Only about one in ten thousand compounds screened makes it all the way through the process, receives approval, and can be prescribed to patients. And costs accelerate sharply as drugs enter clinical trials. The doctors and nurses who administer the drug in the trials have to be paid, and massive amounts of data have to be collected in accordance with FDA regulations.

An AIDS program entailed far more risk to Abbott than, say, developing diagnostic equipment or nutritional products such as Ensure or Similac. "This was a time when many experts were declaring that AIDS was not solvable," says Leonard. "I was on the committee that presented our case to go forward with Norvir [ritonavir's eventual trade name]. Imagine going to a group of businessmen and telling them, 'We want to cure AIDS.' It's akin to Christopher Columbus going to the queen and telling her, 'I believe there is land over there.' You can imagine what the queen must have told him. 'Okay, good luck and have a nice trip, but take a lot of food and prepare for a long journey, because I don't share your certainty.' "

When speaking about the risks that a company takes on a new drug, Leonard compares them to the movie industry. "Movie studios want to produce blockbusters, and they are going to make the kinds of movies they believe the public wants based on previous returns," he asserts. "Based on the success of one movie, a number of studios may decide it's worth the investment to produce similar films that follow the same formula. This doesn't mean all their bets will pan out. The public will eventually tire of certain stories; the movie industry will have its share of failures. But by taking a careful approach to the way they invest their money in certain types of films, the studios will get their share of blockbusters, while others will provide only modest returns. It's the mix of those movies over a period of time that makes the likelihood of success materialize."

One day, Leonard met with Tom Hodgson, Abbott's president and chief operating officer at the time, on the progress of the HIV research. Hodgson listened intently. Leonard says he didn't know what to think, and for a moment feared that Hodgson would can the whole thing. Finally, Hodgson said, "I want us to succeed with this. I don't know how we're going to get there. So meet with me monthly and show me your progress. We'll decide together what we should do." Leonard breathed a sigh of relief.

The monthly meetings were intense. "I can say that there were times when this program hung by the thinnest of threads," Leonard says. "I can recall meetings with Hodgson when he seemed to be asking for a reason to believe. You open the newspaper and you read about a breakthrough medicine, and people on the outside think all of this is automatic. A new drug seems inevitable. But being on the inside, I can say that sometimes the destiny of a new medicine depends on the outcome of a conversation between two people."

SPRINT TO THE FINISH

The first human studies of ritonavir were done on healthy volunteers who were not infected with HIV, primarily to calibrate the proper dosage based on the amount of drug that actually made it into the human bloodstream. Leonard and his team tried to find a dose that was not so high as to cause serious side effects, but high enough to fight the virus effectively. Most important, after the pill was swallowed, the body had to absorb the medication through the intestines to get it into the bloodstream in sufficient concentrations to have potent activity. One obstacle to accomplishing this was the rapid metabolism many drugs experience when they reach the liver. In the case of a previous compound that was structurally similar to ritonavir and had been studied in human trials by the team, the liver changed the drug's chemical structure to a form that was not effective. As a result, Kempf and his team had to determine what parts of their molecules were subject to those changes. Once he identified the problem, Kempf chemically modified the two ends of the molecule—and voila! The liver no longer rejected it. Now the real challenge loomed: testing ritonavir in AIDS patients.

In 1994, Abbott researchers began that test. They were about to find out if the previous seven years of work in the laboratory had actual application. AIDS patients received one of several doses of ritonavir over a period of several months and were regularly examined to determine the drug's effect on the virus and on their overall health. "What we saw was something we did not expect," Leonard says. "The virus had fallen to levels that were less than 1 percent of what had been in their blood." The researchers showed these results to the leading AIDS scientists; nobody had ever seen the likes of them. They and Abbott executives were elated. The next step was to try the drug in much larger numbers of patients, a Phase III trial. Only then would researchers know that it really worked and did not have side effects serious enough to derail it.

In the summer of 1995, the development of Norvir was in high gear. Abbott's HIV team had caught up with the competition, such as Roche and Merck, that had entered the HIV protease inhibitor race even earlier than Abbott. One day, Andre Pernet, who headed Abbott's R&D, stood in the company cafeteria to address a large group of Abbott scientists, including many not involved in HIV work. "Okay, guys," he said, "we have a fantastic drug on our hands that has now entered critical Phase III trials. We need to sprint to the finish line. We need all hands on deck. This is our number one, two, and three priority. Everything else is secondary."

When Pernet said, "I need people," he meant everybody, and many in the room volunteered to join the HIV team. One was Eugene Sun, an Asian American who had graduated from Harvard and went on to receive his medical degree from New York University. Before joining Abbott, Sun had been an attending physician in the infectious disease service at the University of California at San Francisco Medical Center. Having lived in two AIDS hotbeds—New York City and San Francisco—Sun, a medium-built man with thick salt-and-pepper black hair, had been inundated with HIV and AIDS cases. "It was as if I had been following HIV around," Sun says. Probably for that reason, he says, he avoided working on the virus at Abbott until Pernet called him to duty.

It was late spring, and the big trial was just beginning. Usually, such a trial takes two years to finish, but Pernet declared they would have to be done by the end of the year, just eight months hence. To do that, Abbott rented a nearby office building, leased one hundred copying and fax machines for transmitting, copying, and receiving data from the trial sites, and hired or redeployed hundreds of employees to work on the project. "We essentially lived at our workplace for the duration," Sun recalls.

Despite the resources thrown into the AIDS project, the enterprise was chaotic at first, with recruits who did not know one another suddenly asked to work together on assignments that did not match their backgrounds, Sun says. He was asked to do a task that was largely administrative, reviewing the forms that described individual patients and their experiences with the drug. He felt his skills were being wasted.

So Sun went up to one of John Leonard's staff who was in charge of the trial and asked if there was anything more scientific he could be doing. The staff member assigned him to write one of the major sections of the New Drug Application (NDA), a document submitted to the Food and Drug Administration when a company wants to get a new drug approved for sale and marketing in the United States. It includes the masses of data gathered during the animal studies and human clinical trials. Sun was assigned to write the Integrated Summary of Safety (ISS)—the section that tells the whole story about the drug's safety and its efficacy, and which typically runs several hundred pages. He had never done anything like it before.

THE UNDERDOG

The results of Abbott's heated race with Roche and Merck to be the first to bring a protease inhibitor drug to the marketplace were sure to get big play by the media. Abbott was the smallest of the three companies and the last to enter the race. "We were the underdog," Sun articulates straightforwardly, "and we wanted to show that we could compete with the big boys."

Roche's protease inhibitor entry was Invirase (saquinavir), and it had enough of a head start that it was the favorite to first receive FDA approval. In November 1995, the FDA did approve saquinavir. Patients needed to take eighteen very large saquinavir capsules—along with other HIV medicines—daily. It was soon discovered that an enzyme system in the liver called cytochrome P450 removed saquinavir rapidly from the body to such low levels in the blood that it ultimately compromised the activity of the drug.

Meanwhile, a landmark study of Abbott's Norvir was well underway. In this trial, patients who were in the end stage of their disease and who were normally excluded from participation in clinical trials were given either Norvir or a placebo in addition to the combination of drugs they were already taking. Patients were randomly assigned to one group or the other, and the study was blinded, meaning even the researchers did not know which group was receiving Norvir and which was simply continuing with its previous treatment regimen.

Several months later, the blind was lifted, revealing the results. The patients on Norvir had considerably fewer AIDS-like symptoms and fewer had died. It was the first time an HIV protease inhibitor had been shown to reduce mortality. While the first AZT drugs, which had come out eight years previously, did reduce mortality, their good effects were eventually lost. Norvir made HIV all but disappear from the bloodstream for an extended period of time. Norvir was not a cure for AIDS, but it did hold the virus at bay, thereby prolonging life for otherwise dying AIDS victims. It did far more than any previous drug—and far more than anyone had anticipated.

One of the major reasons for Norvir's success, according to Sun, is its dual pharmacologic action. Like a Swiss army knife with a knife at one end and scissors on the other, Norvir has a "knife" that inhibits HIV protease, and "scissors" that disable cytochrome P450, the enzyme system in the liver that disassembled Roche's saquinavir. Its action on cytochrome P450 was the reason that Norvir stayed in the bloodstream at high concentrations far longer than its competition.

In late December 1995 a truck filled with files of papers drove through the night from Abbott Park, Illinois, to the nation's capital. Its mission was to deliver the NDA for Abbott's long-awaited HIV medicine to the Food and Drug Administration. An FDA advisory meeting was held on February 29, 1996. The meeting was so important and so visible that the commissioner of the FDA at the time, David Kessler, attended the entire twelve-hour session. In preparation for the meeting, at which the Abbott team would present Norvir data to a group of advisers who would make a recommendation either for or against the drug's approval, the team had assembled more than three thousand slides in anticipation of any questions the group could ask. The following day, March 1, 1996, Norvir was approved in record time, and the era of protease inhibitors began. That same day, Dale Kempf walked into John Leonard's office and picked up the dust-covered nerf football that sat on the windowsill. "I've been waiting a long time for this moment," he said to his friend, and he spiked the football.

"Nine years had passed since we started working on an HIV medicine," Kempf says, "so getting Norvir approved was deserving of a celebration. But I knew our work still wasn't over."

An unassuming, dedicated scientist, Kempf is content with the satisfaction of knowing that his laboratory work has made a contribution to humankind. This inner reward and recognition from his peers means more to him than the accolades of multitudes. Knowing this about Kempf helps one to understand his reaction, about a year before Norvir's approval, when a woman in new product development at Abbott asked him, "Dale, what's your middle name?"

"Why do you want to know?" he questioned.

"I'm trying to combine your name with Dan Norbeck's for our new drug's brand name."

Kempf politely replied that he thought they should name it something that sounded good. Hence the name Norvir—as in Norbeck.

A NUMBERS GAME

In the mid-1980s, prominent AIDS virologist David Ho, who later headed the Aaron Diamond AIDS Research Center in New York City, had helped usher an enormously productive shift in the treatment of AIDS away from the later stages of illness to the early days of infection. Previously, researchers had believed that the virus remained dormant for several years, and then something—no one knew what—spurred the microbial invader to awaken. Ho and his colleagues demonstrated that there was no initial dormant phase of infection—that the body and the virus are, in fact, locked in a pitched battle from the very beginning.

After testing AIDS patients, Ho determined that, in the earliest weeks of infection, millions of viral particles course through the bloodstream—as many as can be found in someone with a full-fledged case of AIDS. Within weeks, the viral load plunges to low, and in some cases undetectable, levels as HIV retreats to the lymph nodes. The patients recover and seem healthy. But HIV is still very active. In the lymph nodes, it produces thousands or millions of copies of itself every day. As a result, the immune system has to continually clear those infectious particles as quickly as they are formed. "It's like a person running on a treadmill," Ho explains. "It doesn't matter how fast a person runs. To an observer, the person appears to be staying in the same place."

Not even the greatest marathoner could keep up that pace forever. The virus eventually exhausts the body's defenses, and blood levels of HIV increase over time. So how do you stop the treadmill?

Ho felt that one protease inhibitor might not be enough. What was needed, he theorized, was a combination of drugs taken during the first few weeks of infection, before many billions of viral particles had formed, before the virus mutated to avoid immune assault, and before many billions of immune cells had died in the body's defense. "You could use drugs one at a time, but the virus is inevitably going to win because it has such a great propensity to change, to mutate," Ho says. "It became a numbers game with HIV."

Ho and Leonard had even gathered data for this idea. The researchers saw that only when protease inhibitors were used in combinations would viral levels truly plummet. As Leonard explains, "We could then say that to treat HIV successfully, you need to have this quantitative effect." Adds Ho: "It also taught us how long we need to treat an AIDS patient—and that's forever." Their results appeared in 1995 in *Nature*; the article received the highest number of citations in a single year in the history of the magazine. Ho was *Time* magazine's "Man of the Year" in 1996.

Taking Ho's work to heart, the Abbott team got the idea to test Norvir in combination with saquinavir. Abbott chemists believed that the combination would amplify the effect of saquinavir by fifty- to a hundredfold. Once saquinavir was available in the fall of 1995, Eugene Sun sent an assistant to Walgreen's to pick up a prescription. Then he could test the saquinavir-Norvir combination on HIV patients. The results showed, as the Abbott chemists predicted, that the combination therapy boosted the concentration of the drug in the blood by the expected amount, thereby greatly increasing its effectiveness.

"It was like a nuclear explosion," Sun says. After seeing these results, Roche agreed to collaborate with Abbott to study the combination therapy in HIV-infected patients. This therapy showed the best-ever results for treating AIDS patients. Now, doubling- or even tripling-up on protease inhibitors as a way to supercharge them is common practice in AIDS therapy. It is called pharmacokinetic boosting.

The protease inhibitors contributed to the "cocktail" of drugs—some forty to fifty pills a day—that an AIDS patient has to take for the rest of his or her life. Norvir accounted for twelve of those daily pills. Many of the other drugs are treatments for the opportunistic infections that plague AIDS patients. Others are to treat the terrible side effects caused by Norvir and other primary anti-HIV medications, including vomiting, diarrhea, and weight loss. The regimen is relentless. An AIDS patient who stops it is certain to see HIV come raging back, leaving him or her with a defenseless immune system.

INSPIRATION AND SUCCESS

But even this exhaustively researched therapy won't work forever. Viruses constantly mutate, or change. Over time, they change in ways that render them indestructible by drugs, and they survive. These hardy mutants eventually dominate, such that the formerly successful drugs no longer work. This is known as drug resistance. Abbott scientists were acutely aware of this looming danger.

At a medical meeting, Dale Kempf and Eugene Sun heard scientists paint a gloomy picture of AIDS patients who were taking protease inhibitors but were no longer doing well. HIV was becoming resistant to their drugs. And drug resistance wasn't the only problem. Unlike treatments for other diseases, AIDS treatment requires medication levels to be high all the time. HIV, after all, is an infectious machine capable of cranking out millions of viruses a day. The two men discussed this problem. "In order to win against HIV," Sun said, "we must come up with a way to maintain an effective dose of HIV drugs inside the body twenty-four hours a day. Current drugs are too weak to do that." Soon the two men were jotting down notes on napkins and formulating an idea for a new pill that would function as a much stronger brake on the virus.

To combat both the inevitable drug-resistance problem and the undesirable side effects patients experienced, Kempf and his colleagues had been slaving away in their laboratory making new compounds, even while developing Norvir. "All of us were determined to find another compound that would be the next, improved generation of Norvir,"

Kempf says. Although the odds were against them, he was optimistic that they would ultimately succeed.

Using three-dimensional imaging technology, Abbott scientists were able to create a map of the HIV protease to determine the location of the mutation that would ultimately allow the virus to become resistant to Norvir. Having that visual image would provide the team with critical information that would help them create the next-generation compound.

In 1995, a laboratory colleague, Hing Sham, Ph.D., synthesized a compound that the team called ABT-378. It bound to the HIV protease in a slightly different location than did ritonavir, avoiding the location where the mutation had occurred, thus making it a promising replacement for that drug when resistance reared its head. Indeed, in the test tube, ABT-378 effectively killed HIV strains that had already become resistant to ritonavir.

In addition to fighting resistance, the Holy Grail of HIV drugs also needed to stay in the body at high levels. That's where ritonavir came in. Ritonavir, Abbott scientists had come to realize, could stay in the body at high concentrations because it clogged one of the metabolic drains to the liver, something like a sock stuck in a sink drain. This is not generally a good thing, particularly for an AIDS patient who needs many drugs, but the researchers theorized that a very small dose of ritonavir might plug up the drain just enough to keep levels of ABT-378 in the body high.

Indeed, when researchers gave healthy people ABT-378 plus Norvir, the levels of ABT-378 in their blood were 77 times higher than those for people who received ABT-378 (later called lopinavir) alone. That experiment, among others, led to the idea for Kaletra, which is a combination of ritonavir and lopinavir.

Eugene Sun headed the clinical trials for Kaletra that began in November 1996. The trial compared two groups of patients: those assigned to receive Kaletra and those who took existing AIDS drugs. "There was no placebo," Sun points out. "We had no intention of using a sugar pill on an AIDS patient, who will die without medication." As in other large clinical trials, these were blinded, with the investigators unaware which patients were getting which medicine.

One trial of 653 HIV-infected adults compared Kaletra to Viracept (nelfinavir), a protease inhibitor manufactured by Pfizer, and found Kaletra to be superior. For example, after 11 months of therapy, viral levels dropped below a critical point in 75 percent of the patients on Kaletra but in only 63 percent of those taking Viracept.

In another study, one hundred HIV patients who had never taken medicine to fight their infection were given Kaletra. Such patients respond particularly well to drug treatment, because the HIV infecting them has not had a chance to develop resistance to any medication. In almost all of the patients who completed the seven-year trial—which continued for a number of years beyond FDA approval of the medicine—the virus was undetectable in their blood.

Sun vividly recalls an incident that occurred early during this trial, which was being conducted by Robert Murphy, a physician at nearby Northwestern University Hospital. "At the time, we weren't sure about the exact doses to give, so we tested a few doses," Sun explains. "Murphy recruited a dozen HIV patients. His clinic was off and running. A few weeks later he called me.

" 'I have some interesting news to tell you,' Murphy said. 'I'm getting calls from patients in these trials who are concerned because they think we are giving them a placebo.'

"There is no placebo, Rob," Sun replied. "We're testing several different doses of Kaletra, but everyone is getting Kaletra. No one is getting a placebo. You know that."

" 'Yes, but they're convinced they must be getting placebo because there are no side effects from the new drug,' Murphy replied.

"Back then HIV drugs were like poison and made patients sick, much as chemotherapy does. They'd have diarrhea, vomit, lose weight, and feel terrible," Sun adds. "That's because HIV drugs were poorly absorbed, and in order to get any to stay in their bodies, patients received big doses of these drugs and had to put up with their side effects. HIV patients were used to getting horrendous side effects, and were willing to put up with them because their lives were on the line. So now they were thinking, 'Something is wrong here. This can't be right. I've got a fatal disease and I'm not getting my drugs. I don't want to be in this trial.' Of course, we thought this was great news because we had a drug that didn't cause a lot of side effects—it was working. Looking back, it's been working for seven years and still counting.

"The big question when we went into this trial was: Are people going to throw up? Are they going to feel sick and nauseated? Are they going to have rashes? So when we heard this news, we knew this medication was going all the way. It was just a matter of executing the trials. We were at the point where the intellectual uncertainty was gone. This was a great spot to be in and admittedly unusual in this field. Generally in drug development there is a fair amount of attrition at each step of the way. The industry average for getting a drug from Phase I to approval by the FDA is one in ten. A drug will fail after Phase I because people can't tolerate it, and in Phase II you lose drugs because they don't work as well as was hoped. Or they work but have a bad side-effect profile. Or, while the drug seemed to work, it was tried with relatively few patients. Phase III consists of a larger number of patients and many different doctors so that there is more to compare the drug to, whether it is compared to a placebo or another drug, whatever the standard of care is. It can even be a specific drug for which the FDA requests a comparison. For example, we compared Kaletra to Pfizer's Viracept. Near the end of '96, when we got that call from Rob Murphy, we knew there wasn't a safety problem, and from an efficacy standpoint, we knew it was going to work. We were done!"

The FDA approved Kaletra on September 15, 2000. For Eugene Sun, this was a definite spiking moment. In front of other scientists during a meeting in John Leonard's office, Sun removed the nerf football from the windowsill and hurled it to the floor. It inspired a round of high fives.

LIVING WITH HIV/AIDS

In 1990 Alan Jones and his fiancée took blood tests to apply for their marriage license. Shortly afterward, Alan returned to the doctor for his test results. The doctor informed Alan that he was HIV-positive with a T-cell count of 400.

"Back then I had no idea that a T-cell count referred to the number of helper T-lymphocytes in a person's blood, the number of cells per cubic millimeter," Alan says. A normal count is usually over 1,000. If the number drops to 200 or below, you are considered to have AIDS, according to the CDC. My first thought was a picture of Rock Hudson and how he looked before he passed. I envisioned myself wasting away and dying. I was twenty-nine years old and I thought my life was over. I was completely devastated."

Alan recalled how he worked in a hospital laundry in 1984 and 1985, and had grabbed a bag of laundry from a conveyor belt that came from the operating rooms: "I felt a sharp stab and I hollered," he tells. "When I opened the bag, I found a dirty, *bloody* needle that had not been properly disposed. I was sent to the emergency room, given a tetanus shot, and I went back to work.

"I am convinced it was the needle that initially infected me," he continues. "At the time I found out, we also had to worry about my fiancée. As it turned out, she had not been infected. Her reaction was, 'You didn't know about this and everything that happened was before we knew each other. I love you, so let's get married and see how life [goes for] us.' So we married. It is a blessing that she has never tested HIV-positive."

For the next eleven years, life was good for the Joneses. Alan's wife had several jobs, including her current managerial position with a life insurance company, and Alan worked in the telecommunications and customer service field. An ordained minister since age twenty-four, he began his public ministry at age sixteen. He is also a professional gospel singer and a founding member of The Gospel Family, a group formed in 1995 in Pittsburgh. Alan has been on many European tours, with more on the agenda in the near future. The couple leased a lovely three-bedroom home in a subdivision in Duluth, just outside Atlanta. The thought of his HIV diagnosis was seldom on his mind. They prospered and enjoyed good health. While Alan was aware of his health status, he took no medicine for his HIV. He was symptom-free:

"I attributed my survival and good health to the fact that I am into holistic health, and to my faith in God. I took different herbs that are good for one's immune system plus I ate a lot of fruit and vegetables," he explains. "I also went to the gym and did vigorous workouts that sometimes lasted as long as two hours five or six times a week. Keeping in excellent condition was good for my immune system, and I never got sick—that is, until 2001 when I had an appendectomy. When I was rolled into the operating room, the doctor said to me, 'Mr. Jones, do you know that you have thirty T cells?' I didn't know what that meant, so I casually replied, 'No, I didn't, but thanks for telling me.' I had no idea of the severity of having thirty T cells. I didn't pursue medical attention to see where I was in the progression of my HIV. After the surgery I went on with my normal life."

In late September 2002, Alan developed walking pneumonia, and this time, his immune system shut down. Consequently he spent nine days in the hospital, five of which saw him close to death. He was heavily medicated with antibiotics and anti-inflammatory drugs but nothing worked. "My sister came in from Nashville and stood by my bedside praying. I'm a firm believer in the power of prayer. It worked, and four days later, I walked out of the hospital. After recovering two months later, I took a provider inquiry position with Affiliated Computer Services starting in early January 2003. In my initial training class, I came in contact with another trainee with a bad case of bronchitis. I was infected and kept the virus for a year. My immune system was shot. I was put on steroids and anti-inflammatories. Nothing worked."

Alan lost his endurance and was unable to do his daily exercises. Soon he was in a state of exhaustion and had a constant cough that he describes as sounding "like a bag of marbles rattling in my chest." In January 2004, he woke up one morning unable to get out of bed. He took a leave of absence from his job, and in early February, at the behest of an urgent care physician, Alan went to see an infectious disease doctor. He returned three weeks later to get the his results: he had 16 T cells and his viral load was 536,000—an AIDS diagnosis. "My doctor and I discussed treatment options, and he recommended Kaletra and Combivir, two very powerful antiretroviral medicines. The side effects were explained, and they were minuscule compared to what could otherwise happen to me."

Within three weeks, Alan's T cells were up to 25. He was elated. Three weeks later, his T cells went up to 55. During his next visit to the doctor, the nurse told him, "You have 75 T cells."

"I was so happy that when she left the room, I broke down and cried. My medicine was working and I was getting better. The numbers kept climbing. At the next visit they were at 101. By the end of the summer in 2005 my T-cell count was 585. I was 569 T cells above the 16 mark I had dropped to. I was elated.

"At first I was taking three gel capsules twice a day. The morning doses were easy to take, but the evening doses were more inconvenient, particularly during the hot summer months, when I was out and about during many of the outdoor festivities here in Atlanta. On one occasion, while in Montgomery, Alabama, I had the medicine packed in an insulated lunch bag with ice in my trunk, but due to the 100-plus-degree weather, the medication melted. This meant I had to be extra careful how I stored my medicine while I was out, so that this would not happen again. I've since switched to tablets that I can just stick in my pocket and they're there whenever I need them. I now take two Kaletra and one Combivir in the A.M. and again in the P.M. I can even do it on an empty stomach. A piece of cake. Like brushing your teeth."

Alan's positive attitude has helped him with his recovery. He downplays the tough times and his struggles, but there were many. When he was too weak to work, he and his wife were forced to move from their house and move in with friends for six months. A hardworking man who took pride in being the family's breadwinner, it hurt his self-esteem. The stress caused by his illness was a major factor that led to a separation. The couple remains separated to this day.

How does Alan alleviate the stress? He does it by helping other HIV/AIDS patients. He constantly speaks to HIV support groups, and he has served as a mentor to many HIV patients who, like he once was, are uneducated about the disease and don't know where to go for advice. Once, upon finding out that a stranger, whom he befriended while jump-starting his car, had AIDS, Alan gave him a pep talk on the importance of complying with his medicine schedule. For months he called the man every day to make sure he was taking his medications. "How bad do you want to live?" Alan constantly asked him. "Okay, this is what you have to do," he'd say. Then, he'd call him in the morning and later in the evening, always asking, "Did you take your meds today?" Eventually, the man was compliant and didn't need to be reminded. "I'm always telling HIV/AIDS patients, 'My medication determines how I live, the quality of my life, and if I die. Since I have no desire to die, I take it every day when I get up and when I go to bed. Don't ever try to cycle on and cycle off.' "

As a lay minister, Alan is articulate and a baritone. He has a wonderful speaking voice. With his passion to contribute to the fight against the disease, he regularly volunteers to speak to various audiences, ranging from high-school students to HIV/AIDS patients. As an HIV patient, they know where he comes from. Once, at a patients' clinic sponsored by Abbott, Alan spoke for seven minutes on the same podium as Magic Johnson, the famous ex–NBA basketball player who was also diagnosed with HIV. Upon being introduced to the audience, Magic said, "This Alan Jones is so positive and so full of energy that when I was standing behind the curtain, he made me feel so energized I wanted to run out here to join him onstage." Speaking with conviction, Alan has that effect on people who hear him.

Through his work with the church, Alan has observed what he believes is a stigmatization of people in African American churches. "There is an assumption that you are gay or have been engaged in a homosexual act to get the disease. They don't seem to understand the dynamics on how people get this disease today. They tend to categorize HIV/AIDS patients and congregants are made to feel uncomfortable talking about it. As a consequence, people are not receiving proper treatment. By my speaking out, I feel that I can create awareness in this area, and by doing so, more people will receive early treatment.

"I've had people say to me, 'God dealt you a bad hand,' " Alan concludes. "I don't look at it that way. I believe God provided me with an opportunity to serve others, and in this way, turn something bad into something good. If during my journey I can help just one other person to live and regain his or her lost zest for life, then I've already served my purpose that I was called to this place for."

There was a time when HIV/AIDS patients had no hope. Today they do.

SPREADING HOPE

Today, Kaletra is the leading protease inhibitor in the United States and throughout the world. HIV patients take as few as four Kaletra pills per day. While HIV patients are required to take this medication on a daily basis for the rest of their lives, with Kaletra they can live without constant fear of an anguishing death. But many challenges remain. There are an estimated 1 million AIDS patients in the United States and 37 million worldwide. In 2004, there were 3.1 million deaths caused by AIDS; 16 percent of these deaths were children under age 15.

Abbott is committed to the continual war against this disease and has expanded its efforts to confront the pandemic in the developing world. Throughout Africa and the world's poorest countries, the company provides Norvir and Kaletra at significantly reduced prices that are less than one-tenth of those in the United States. In addition to medicines, Abbott has provided more than fifty million rapid diagnostic HIV tests at no profit to diagnose HIV infection in needy countries.

Abbott also donates the same easy-to-use tests to help prevent mother-to-child transmission of HIV. This is the main cause of childhood HIV infections in the developing world. Testing is the first step in prevention; once an expectant mother finds out she is HIV-positive, she can access free and convenient treatment to effectively prevent transmitting the virus to her child. Germany-based Boehringer Ingelheim provides its drug, Viramune, to HIV-positive mothers during labor and to their newborns within seventy-two hours after delivery, reducing transmission rates by 50 percent. (Without such treatment, about one quarter of all infants born to HIV-positive mothers become infected.)

In addition to providing medicines and tests, Abbott has aligned its philanthropy to help address key barriers to testing, treatment, and care services for people affected by AIDS. This includes a program to help children affected by HIV/AIDS in several developing countries hit hard by the disease, including Tanzania, India, Malawi, and Romania. Efforts include a program to improve the treatment of children with HIV, as well as outreach to help orphans who have lost their parents to HIV and other children affected by the disease. The company also has made a significant investment in a countrywide initiative in Tanzania to modernize infrastructure and systems to improve services and access to care for the two million Tanzanians living with HIV/AIDS as well as those suffering from other serious illnesses. At Muhimbili National Hospital in Dar es Salaam, the nation's largest city, a new outpatient facility recently opened that is serving hundreds of patients a day, including many patients with HIV. Previously, HIV patients were seen in a tiny clinic that contributed to the stigma and discrimination of HIV sufferers by separating those with HIV from other patients. Abbott also built a state-of-the-art laboratory on the grounds of the hospital, and is helping eighty-four regional Tanzanian hospitals set up voluntary counseling and HIV testing services. Another focus is on training of hospital management and health-care workers to provide a sustained response to AIDS in the years to come.

Meanwhile, the scientific war against AIDS continues. Back in 1983, Robert Gallo optimistically announced, "We hope to have a vaccine [against HIV] ready for testing in about two years." His statement concluded with, "Yet another terrible disease is about to yield to patience, persistence, and outright genius." Nearly a quarter of a century later, no AIDS vaccine exists. Neither does a cure. But, thanks to scientists at Abbott and at other labs around the world, HIV has yielded to scientific ingenuity, and it is not so outrageous to assume that it will again.

2

ASTRAZENECA COMPANY PROFILE

"We are starting a new company!" declared AstraZeneca CEO Sir Tom McKillop in a live 1999 global satellite teleconference to the 40,000 employees of Swedish Astra AB and British Zeneca Group PLC. It was the marriage of equals: two mature, well-bred pharmaceutical giants committed to maintaining a tradition of deft management, far-sighted business acumen, and brilliant science.

In an increasingly competitive worldwide marketplace, pharmaceutical companies are judged not by the grandeur of the past but strictly on the merits of the present. Yet within a company's history can be found stories of triumph over challenges, stories that form the signature of great corporate character.

AstraZeneca PLC provides an ongoing chronology of such character and pharmaceutical greatness. The Astra AB/Zeneca PLC marriage has roots tracing back nearly a century to Sweden and Great Britain; to fully grasp the diversity and depth of this conglomerate requires a closer look.

ASTRA AB

Prior to 1913, Swedish law limited the manufacture of pharmaceuticals to only registered apothecaries, but a 1913 amendment to the law allowed industrial companies to manufacture drugs. Following the lead of Swedish physician and businessman Dr. Sven Carlsson, a consortium of four hundred Swedish physicians and druggists combined to form Astra

AB, an industrial pharmaceutical venture. All four hundred participants were the original stockholders in the company.

Astra's principals were an impressive and experienced group, including Professor Hans von Euler-Chelpin (who would receive the Nobel Prize in chemistry in 1929), Dr. Adolf Rising (Astra's first production manager and a former executive with Ciba, the Swiss pharmaceutical firm), and of course Dr. Sven Carlsson, Astra's first chairman. Their first products were Digitotal, a heart medication, and Glukofos, a nutritional supplement.

They prospered quickly. In 1915 they were joined by the successful Swedish apothecary Hjalmar Andersson-Tesch, who brought with him several of his own medications. Tesch's arrival quickly expanded Astra's product line, and when Tesch assumed the presidency of the company, rapid growth followed. Over the next several years Astra developed and acquired an impressive array of medicines. The company also developed production equipment for acetylsalicylic acid (the chemical base for aspirin) and artificial sweeteners (a very successful and profitable product during World War I). Astra also expanded operations by purchasing several factory buildings.

But Astra also faced difficulties during this era. The executives at Swedish chemical giant AB Svensk Fargamnesindustri, incorrectly assuming that war shortages in raw materials would persist for years, bought the entire capital stock of Astra. However, war shortages soon ceased and prices of raw materials dropped dramatically. The prices that Astra could charge in the market were far less than manufacturing costs and the company faced imminent bankruptcy.

Sweden's new socialist government stepped in and acquired Astra in order to create a nationalized pharmaceutical monopoly. Within months, however, the government collapsed and the new regime wanted to immediately dissolve the monopoly. Though it took four years, Astra was sold to a private group of investors in 1925.

The new owners were visionary Swedish businessmen Erik Kistner, Richard Julin, and Borje Gabrielsson. Their first step left an indelible mark on the character of their company: they created Astra's own worldwide distribution network. In just a few years' time the company was profitable again and poised for rapid growth.

By the 1930s, Astra had created advanced research and development facilities and was thus fully ensconced as a major player in the European pharmaceutical industry. This permitted Astra to develop many new and useful medications. These included Hepaforte for pernicious anemia and Nitropent, a medication for angina pectoris. While the company was pursuing the more advanced aspects of drug creation, it also pursued an impressive corporate expansion and acquisition strategy. By the end of World War II it had established subsidiaries in Finland, Denmark, Argentina, and the United States.

This growth and acquisition was further fueled by what would become Astra's best-known and most lucrative product: the local anesthetic Xylocaine. The discovery of Xylocaine might never have happened had it not been for the company's close relationship with the academic and research communities. In 1943, two chemists from the University of Stockholm (Nils Löfgren and Bengt Lundqvist) approached Astra about a discovery they believed was of great interest. Though they'd approached several other companies and had been rebuffed, Astra offered to underwrite the development. After five years of clinical trials, Xylocaine appeared on the market and was an instant hit. Its quality was recognized worldwide and Astra's reputation as one of the world's most important pharmaceutical manufacturers grew exponentially (by 1983, 80 percent of Astra sales were overseas.)

Further growth through excellent science and savvy alliances fueled Astra's development. By the 1970s Astra had formed separate divisions for its diverse activities: a pharmaceutical division for its array of drugs; a chemical division that produced agricultural products, nutritional products, cleansers, and recreational items; and another division that was responsible for medical equipment and rust prevention products. By the end of the decade, however, Astra announced that it would concentrate solely on the production of pharmaceuticals, and the company sold all of its other holdings.

By the mid-1980s Astra's financial success, driven primarily by new treatments for viral infections, gastrointestinal ailments, and central nervous system dysfunction, was gaining worldwide attention. However, the core group of investors in the company (most notably the famed Wallenbergs, one of Europe's most prominent families, who owned a 12 percent stake) was dissatisfied and they launched a search for a replacement of the CEO.

The unlikely choice was a forty-four-year-old Swedish chocolatier named Hakan Mogren. Once in charge, Mogren turned the marketing program on its ear. He rescinded license agreements, added subsidiaries where there had previously been licensees, and added nearly one thousand salespeople worldwide by the end of 1990. Under Mogren's leadership the sales force expanded from three thousand in 1990 to more than seven thousand by 1995. The company's sales and profits grew at a truly astonishing rate, quadrupling in six years.

On the products side, Astra had many successes, including Toprol-XL, a medicine for the treatment of hypertension and angina, and Losec, a "proton pump inhibitor" for the treatment of ulcers and other stomach acid–related diseases.

Mogren's most notable gambit was taking Losec head-to-head with Glaxo Pharmaceuticals' bestselling Zantac. To make this a profitable venture, Astra needed U.S. representation. This was accomplished through a partnership with Merck & Co., forming Astra-Merck Inc. (AMI). This 50/50 joint venture was instrumental in helping Astra gain FDA approval for Losec in the United States, where it was marketed under the trade name Prilosec. The Merck partnership was one of Mogren's most fruitful ventures; sales doubled in his first two years at the helm, driven primarily by Prilosec sales.

In 1998, the AMI joint venture was restructured into a limited partnership known as Astra Pharmaceuticals LP, the U.S. subsidiary of Astra AB. The restructuring was just one of many precursors that set the stage for a merger between Astra and a British company that, in many respects, had developed in a similar way. The company was Zeneca Group PLC.

ZENECA GROUP PLC

Across the North Sea, far from Swedish shores, the roots of Zeneca Group PLC were beginning to take hold in post–World War I Great Britain. By 1926, American DuPont and the German conglomerate IG Farben dominated international chemical commerce. The repercussions were strong, especially in Europe, where many smaller companies were completely squeezed out of the business. Survival meant rising to this imposing challenge. In response, Imperial Chemical Industries (ICI) of Great Britain was formed by the merger of four British chemical concerns: Nobel Industries Limited; Brunner, Mond and Company; United Alkali Company Limited; and British Dyestuffs Corporation Limited. The upstart merger plunged into research, began aggressively recruiting chemists, engineers, and managers, and, simultaneously, began forming alliances with universities and research centers.

The ICI group became a formidable force and competed on an equal footing with the chemical giants. Between 1933 and 1936 at least eighty-seven new products were created, including a remarkable new plastic known as polyethylene. By the early '30s ICI had also made a significant investment in pharmaceutical research, creating a division to synthesize medically active compounds. ICI started with seven chemists and soon expanded the staff with eight biologists dedicated to drug development.

On the pharmaceutical front, ICI researchers created a host of history-making medications. Among them was sulfamethazine, the first sulphur antibiotic for the routine treatment of infection; the antimalarial Paludrine; Hibitane, the most widely used antiseptic in the world at the time; and Halothane, the first commercially successful inhalation anesthetic since chloroform and ether.

In 1967, ICI established a U.S. presence with offices in Stamford, Connecticut. A year later, the company created a U.S. business unit that would become ICI Americas. ICI also acquired Atlas Chemicals, which had itself purchased The Stuart Company, best known for several pharmaceutical products that included the first chewable vitamins and the first effervescent laxatives.

ICI remained one of the major players in the exploding global bulk chemical business as well, and maintained a competitive position for decades. But post–World War II economics shifted the balance of power in the industry, and by 1980 sales were sagging and stock value was suffering. To meet this challenge the company appointed John Harvey-Jones—who later became a famed corporate turnaround specialist—to breathe life back into its sagging financial performance.

Harvey-Jones immediately recognized the difficulty in building ICI in the mature and stable bulk chemicals industry, so he restructured the organization to focus on its high-margin products, namely pharmaceuticals, specialty chemicals, and pesticides. All of these businesses remained under the ICI umbrella until 1993 when ICI formed a separate company, Zeneca. Headquartered in London, Zeneca was a global bioscience company engaged in the research, development, manufacture, and marketing of pharmaceuticals.

At its peak ICI had employed 120,000 employees in 130 countries globally. When Zeneca formed it had approximately 30,000 employees and a worldwide network of research facilities in twenty-five countries. By the end of its first year of operation Zeneca had catapulted into the top twenty pharmaceutical companies worldwide. Throughout the '90s Zeneca focused its business growth on providing treatment for disorders of the respiratory, cardiovascular, and central nervous systems. It released several notable products during this time, including Accolate, Merrem I.V., and Zomig.

Zeneca also introduced several new cancer medications. These included Casodex, Zoladex, Arimidex, and Nolvadex. Zeneca reinforced its commitment to cancer therapy when it acquired Aptium Oncology (formerly Salick Healthcare Inc.), a leading cancer treatment organization with cancer centers located throughout the United States. The relationship continues today as the company works to develop a new generation of cancer treatments.

Although Zeneca remained involved in the agrochemical industry, it was becoming clear by 1996 that further growth in the pharmaceutical business would require renewed focus. During 1999, Zeneca took the actions necessary to optimize the future development of each of its businesses. Zeneca Specialties was sold in a buyout jointly financed by Cinven and Investcorp, putting that business in a better position to achieve future growth within its own sector. Plans were announced to spin off and merge Zeneca Agrochemicals with the agrochemicals and seeds business of Novartis to form Syngenta. And that same year, Zeneca had finalized another merge—this one with Astra AB—to form one of the largest pharmaceutical organizations in the world.

ASTRAZENECA PLC

In 1999, Astra AB and Zeneca Group PLC completed their $34.6 billion merger, joining two global pharmaceutical heavyweights into one company: AstraZeneca PLC, headquartered in London, England. Stock values soared, employee morale was at an all-time high, and overnight AstraZeneca became the number three player in the entire industry.

One of the new company's first successes was Nexium, its next-generation proton pump inhibitor. Nexium addressed a medical need that remained unmet even by Prilosec. For many patients with gastroesophageal reflux disease (GERD—frequent and persistent heartburn), Nexium offered faster resolution of their heartburn symptoms and faster and improved healing of erosive esophagitis, or damage to the lining of the esophagus for patients with chronic acid reflux. Nexium was released in 2001, and by October 2002 it accounted for 20 percent of new prescriptions in the U.S. proton pump inhibitor market. By 2004 annual sales had risen to $3.9 billion.

AstraZeneca demonstrated success in other therapy areas as well. In the same year that it launched Nexium, the company introduced Zomig-ZMT, a formulation of its migraine medication that would dissolve easily on the tongue. In 2001, the FDA approved a new heart failure indication for Toprol-XL. And in 2003, Crestor entered the $20 billion statin market as a product that could both lower LDL (or "bad") cholesterol and raise HDL (or "good") cholesterol.

Sales of these and other medications created a sound financial footing for AstraZeneca. The company parlayed this success by making significant investments in research and development, technology, community development, and prescription drug programs for the needy.

In 2005, AstraZeneca employed more than 65,000 worldwide with over 12,000 of those jobs in the continental United States. With worldwide sales of $23.95 billion, AstraZeneca has committed $3.4 billion to 2005–2006's research and development budget, thereby truly becoming a world leader. Globally, nearly 12,000 employees work in AstraZeneca's research and development organization, which is housed in 11 R&D centers in 7 countries: Canada, France, India, Sweden, Japan, the United Kingdom, and the United States. The company balances this R&D workforce with 14,000 employees who actually produce the company's medications at 27 manufacturing sites in 19 countries.

AstraZeneca has invested heavily in facilities, equipment, and personnel for the development of the next generation of pharmaceuticals. In 2002, its state-of-the-art, 170,000-square-foot R&D facility opened in Waltham, Massachusetts, near Boston. A year later, this facility expanded again with the addition of 80,000 square feet of new laboratory and office space. Similar investments were made to other R&D facilities worldwide. Notable among these was the opening of four automated compound management facilities. These facilities have the robotic capability to access and process tens of thousands of compounds on a daily basis, making it easier to locate those few molecules that have demonstrated biological activity.

AstraZeneca doesn't just look internally for promising new compounds. It also investigates strategic licensing opportunities with external biotechnology companies. For example, AstraZeneca partnered with Abgenix in 2004 to develop antibody-based therapies to target cancer cells. To further foster the drug-discovery-to-marketplace journey, a variety of programs and processes have been established to increase communication and cooperation between AstraZeneca's drug discovery and clinical development organizations.

This investment is paying off; technological innovation continues to fill the AstraZeneca pipeline. In general terms, 10,000 new ideas are needed to create 10 workable trial drugs that will yield 1 that gets successfully to market. As of this writing, AstraZeneca has 70 investigational compounds in its pipeline, and more than 20 are now in preclinical trials for disorders as diverse as cancer, asthma, pain, schizophrenia, rheumatoid arthritis, diabetes, acid reflux, and Alzheimer's disease.

AstraZeneca invests its resources in its employees as well as its customers. In 2005 the company was recognized by *Working Mother* magazine for the fourth year in a row as one of the top 100 best companies for working mothers. The company also made *Fortune* magazine's 2004 list for the 100 Best Companies to Work for in the United States. AstraZeneca also works to ensure access to lifesaving medication for the underprivileged. In 2005, AstraZeneca provided more than $751 million in savings through its assistance programs to more than 712,000 patients without drug coverage throughout the United States and Puerto Rico.

A New Lease on Life

ASTRAZENECA'S SEROQUEL TREATS
SCHIZOPHRENIA AND BIPOLAR MANIA

FOR CENTURIES it was believed that mentally ill people were possessed by evil spirits. To be cured, the demons had to be exorcised by various treatments—some mild, some severe. One of the mild treatments was the playing of reed-pipe music to heal the body and mind, a remedy of the ancient Phrygians and Mysians in Asia Minor. The ancient Greeks had also used music for healing. Pythagoras (580 B.C.–500 B.C.) believed music was an expression of the harmony of the celestial spheres, and the heavenly music soothed the human soul. Likewise, according to the doctrine of ethos, Plato and Aristotle asserted that music influenced human character. While we don't know how many patients were cured by music, it was said to have a calming effect.

One severe treatment was to drill a hole in a person's skull to release evil spirits. Mental patients were also locked in dungeons and lunatic asylums. (Well into the twentieth century the mentally ill were called lunatics and idiots, monikers today that are thankfully no longer used.)

With the spread of Christianity, some religious leaders took the view that mental illness was punishment for one's sins. During the medieval era, it became the church's responsibility to care for the mentally ill. In the twelfth century, the first hospitals for the insane opened in Sweden. The Helgeandsorder (the Order of the Holy Ghost) operated lodging houses built to provide shelter for mental patients. In 1247, the Bethlem opened its doors in London under the direction of the sisters and brethren of the order of the Star of Bethlehem. The first residents weren't admitted until 1403. The colloquialism for the institute was Bedlam, and in 1547, Henry VIII handed the facility over to the city of London as a hospital for lunatics.

Over time, the hospital's reputation for its callous treatment became widespread. Interestingly, in the eighteenth century, Bedlam was a tourist attraction. Visitors came from afar to walk the halls and peer into cells, observing the behavior of the inmates. It was akin to today's stroll through the zoo. To those who came, the antics of the mentally sick were a source of laughter and amusement. In 1814, an average weekly crowd of two thousand sightseers purchased tickets to tour the premises of Bedlam in anticipation of a mirthful day.

So famous was the institution that the word "bedlam" has become part of our language, synonymous with confusion. Begging licenses were issued to the more fortunate inmates who had been released. With these, they received a tin badge to wear on their arms; these poor souls were known as Bedlam Beggars, or Bedlamers.

Throughout most of Christian Europe during the Middle Ages, it was the family that cared for a mad member. Lunatics and "village idiots" typically remained in the family's domestic care subject to neglect or cruelty, frequently hidden away in a cellar or caged in a pigpen. Or they were sent away to wander and beg for their food. Mental illness was deeply shameful to a family because it had overtones of diabolical possession or bad stock.

Most individuals who migrated to the New World brought with them the beliefs, traditions, and practices common in England. Madness there was a term that conjured up supernatural, religious, astrological, scientific, and medical elements. The boundaries between them were virtually nonexistent, and those who wrote about madness could integrate themes and explanations from all these elements to explain mysterious phenomena. Cotton Mather, an eminent Puritan minister who played an important role in late-seventeenth- and early-eighteenth-century Massachusetts, emphasized that Satan could tempt individuals into madness by exploiting their moral weaknesses. Sin, after all, was at the heart of the human condition, and one of its consequences was madness.

EARLY MEDICAL TREATMENTS

It wasn't until the late 1800s that the experts of the day broke away from the belief that mental illness stemmed from religious and supernatural causes. German psychiatrist Emil Kraepelin (1856–1926) classified specific symptoms of mental disorders by studying and recording hundreds of clinical histories of patients. Starting in 1896, Kraepelin took ten years to complete his studies. His findings revealed his concept of dementia praecox, which he defined as the "sub-acute development of a peculiar simple condition of mental weakness occurring at a youthful age." Kraepelin postulated that there is a specific brain or other biological pathology underlying psychiatric disorders. Just as his laboratory had discovered the pathologic basis of what is known as Alzheimer's disease today, Kraepelin was confident that it would someday be possible to identify the pathologic basis of psychiatric disorders.

One of the cardinal principles of his method was the recognition that any given symptom may appear in virtually any one of a number of disorders; for example, there is virtually no single symptom occurring in dementia that cannot sometimes also be found in manic depression. What distinguishes each disease symptomatically (as opposed to the underlying pathology) is thus not any particular (pathognomonic) symptom or symptoms but a specific *pattern* of symptoms. In the absence of a direct physiological or genetic test or marker for each disease, it is possible to distinguish them only by their specific pattern of symptoms. Thus, Kraepelin's system was a method of pattern recognition rather than a grouping by common symptoms.

Later Kraepelin collaborated with Alois Alzheimer of Alzheimer's disease fame. Having been hailed as the founder of biological psychiatry, Kraeplin suggested that psychiatric diseases are principally caused by biological and genetic disorders. His psychiatric theories dominated the field of psychiatry at the beginning of the twentieth century and are widely accepted today. He vigorously opposed Freud's premise that regarded and treated psychiatric disorders as psychological rather than biological in origin.

Medications for mental illnesses in the twentieth century ran the gamut, including the use of alcohol, alkaloids, chloral hydrate, and opium. When used in high doses these remedies were sometimes able to provoke a psychotic-like state, reducing anxiety and inducing sleep; however, they did not eliminate hallucinations and other psychotic symptoms. These medications did help provide a calming atmosphere in the asylums, however. Other means to restrain patients included straitjackets, shoes with locks, dresses that were locked at the bottom, and gloves that were tied around the wrists to prevent patients from injuring themselves or others.

In the late 1920s, fever therapy became the first real cure for a mental illness. Observing that mad persons often improved after a fever disease, Julius Wagner von Jauregg, an Austrian neurologist, induced malaria infection in mentally ill patients. His discovery earned him a Nobel Prize in 1927.

In the middle of the 1930s, convulsion therapy was used with schizophrenic patients, who were injected with camphorated oil and cardiazol to provoke seizures. This practice was prompted by the observation that schizophrenia and epilepsy rarely occurred together, and when they did, the psychotic symptoms usually decreased after an epileptic attack. Following an injection of cardiazol, the patient would suffer a series of repeated cramps that often caused fractures of the vertebrae, especially with older patients, and heart problems. While curare, a muscle relaxant, relieved the vertebrae fractures, patients frequently had strong periods of anxiety following the injections.

Perhaps the most notorious treatment in the twentieth century was the lobotomy. Here, the performing surgeon cut off, from the frontal lobe, the nerve fibers to deeper brain regions—locations for the patient's emotional life. The general idea was to reduce anxiety and uneasiness. Egas Moniz, a Portuguese physician, developed this procedure and received a Nobel Prize in 1949 for his work. Following a lobotomy, many patients did indeed become less anxious and aggressive, but they also became indifferent and blunt.

Around the same time, Walter Freeman, an American neurologist, came up with an alternative surgery whereby he placed an ice pick in the upper part of the eye and knocked it with a hammer until it had penetrated five centimeters into the brain. To generate interest in his technique, Freeman performed free operations at hospitals across the country, inviting surgeons and journalists to observe his work. Many patients who underwent lobotomies and ice-pick surgery died or contracted infections and epilepsy. An estimated forty thousand Americans were lobotomized during the 1940s and 1950s; the number of lobotomies was appreciably reduced with the introduction of new antipsychotic drugs in the early 1950s. Today, stereotactic capsulotomy, an operation much improved over the lobotomy, is never performed against the patient's will.

Electroconvulsive therapy (ECT), known as shock therapy, was first used in the early 1940s. An electric shock treatment, it induces a grand mal seizure in the brain, one that is similar to an epileptic convulsion. It fires up the brain's electrical pathways. The seizure alters many chemical aspects of the brain during and following the seizure activity. To be effective, ECT requires a series of treatments, typically three times a week for two to four weeks. ECT causes changes to occur in the brain that relieve depression; this has been confirmed by before-and-after CT scans and MRI scans.

During the early use of ECT, the strong electrical currents caused severe muscular contractions that resulted in broken bones and dislocated joints. Patients were awake during the procedure, making it a frightful experience. ECT received additional bad press after the release of *One Flew Over the Cuckoo's Nest*, the 1975 Academy Award–winning movie based on Ken Kesey's novel. This big box-office film portrayed shock treatment for schizophrenia as a nonlethal punishment akin to being strapped in the electric chair. Today, the ECT patient is put to sleep with a very short-acting barbiturate and is temporarily paralyzed with a drug to prevent muscles from contracting. The patient sleeps restfully through the duration of the 30- to 120-second procedure, awakes fifteen minutes later, and typically is discharged from the hospital shortly afterward. Patients have described it as milder than a trip to the dentist. The treatment has significant side effects, however, and a high relapse rate, but it does serve as a viable option when a patient fails to respond to medication.

CHLORPROMAZINE: THE FIRST ANTIPSYCHOTIC DRUG

In 1952, Henri Laborit, a surgeon in Paris, discovered that by using a lesser amount of anesthesia on his patients he could reduce surgical shock and hasten recovery. Knowing that shock was the result of changes in certain brain chemicals, and aware that the central-depressant side effects of antihistamines reduce the effect of allergies, Laborit experimented with these drugs on mental patients. One drug in particular, known as chlorpromazine, had very noticeable effects. Laborit observed that, when used as a presurgical sedative, the drug produced mood-altering side effects. His patients had less anxiety about their upcoming surgery, and some of them conveyed indifference. Laborit's findings prompted psychiatrists to prescribe chlorpromazine for their most needy patients.

Pierre Deniker, a Canadian psychiatrist, administered the drug on his most despairing patients. The outcome was astonishing. Patients who had stood in one spot in a mental institution for weeks and others who were violent and had to be restrained both were able to communicate with other patients. These same patients no longer required supervision. It was an awakening among the psychiatry community. As a consequence, chlorpromazine developed into the first antipsychotic.

Smith Kline, a company low on funds for research, purchased the rights to chlorpromazine from the European company Rhone-Poulenc in 1952 to market it as an antipsychotic medicine. Chlorpromazine was the first antipsychotic drug used to treat schizophrenia, although its biological effects remained a mystery.

SCHIZOPHRENIA: THE MOST DEBILITATING MENTAL ILLNESS

Schizophrenia, the most serious, complicated, and disabling of all mental illnesses, is a brain disorder that severely hampers an individual's ability to think clearly, make decisions, and separate reality from delusion. It is also the most misunderstood mental illness; it is not a split personality, a character flaw, nor a condition caused by poor parenting. It is a biological disorder due to subtle abnormalities in the brain. When Eugen Bleuler named the disease from the Greek word *schizophrenia* (*schizo*—split; *phrene*—mind), his intent was to describe the fragmented thinking of people with the disorder, not a person with a split or multiple personality. The multiple personality image is a very rare form of the disease, one that has been grossly exaggerated over the years in literature and film.

The evidence that schizophrenia is a biologically based disease of the brain accumulated rapidly in the past half century. The 1950s discovery that schizophrenia responded dramatically to drugs such as chlorpromazine indicated that the cause of the disease might be biological. More recently this evidence has been supported with dynamic brain imaging systems that show precisely the wave of tissue distribution that takes place in the brain of a person with schizophrenia.

Individuals with no apparent family history have about a 1 percent chance of developing schizophrenia; however, the chances increase to 10 percent for those with a parent or sibling who has it. The chances increase to 40 percent if both parents have it and 30 percent in the case of an identical twin. Doctors treat 3.2 million people in this country suffering from schizophrenia.

In a study in the early 1990s funded by the National Institute of

Mental Health and by the Department of Veterans Affairs, patients with schizophrenia were 2.4 times more likely, and those with bipolar disorder 1.6 times more likely, to be homeless than those with major depression. Even with treatment, 85 percent of schizophrenics were unemployed, most never married, and 10 percent had taken their own lives.

While the antipsychotic drugs produced in the 1950s improved lives, they had severe neurological side effects such as restlessness, muscle rigidity, and tremors (extrapyramidal side effects, known as EPS). One of the most severe was tardive dyskinesia (TD), characterized by involuntary movements of the extremities, trunk, tongue, lips, and face—symptoms similar to acute Parkinsonism. Not only could these side effects be debilitating, patients often felt self-conscious and consequently tended to be withdrawn. These symptoms usually began after several months of treatment and were sometimes irreversible.

These medicines had other side effects. For example, they increased prolactin, a hormone produced by the pituitary gland. Women with raised levels of prolactin experienced menstrual irregularities, while male patients could have galactorrhea, a condition that caused their nipples to secrete fluids. The drugs were also associated with osteoporosis as well as sexual dysfunction. It's no wonder doctors had difficulty keeping their patients on first-generation antipsychotic drugs or that noncompliance rates ran as high as 50 percent.

The next major advance in the treatment of schizophrenia was clozapine, which was discovered in the 1960s and introduced in the 1970s. Patients on clozapine didn't tend to have the involuntary movements characteristic of earlier drugs. However, 1 to 2 percent of those who took it developed agranulocytosis, a condition where the white blood count drops dramatically and affects the immune system's ability to fight infections. As a consequence, clozapine was taken off the market in the mid-1970s in the United States and many other countries. It was reintroduced in the United States in the 1990s, subject to close patient blood monitoring.

ASTRAZENECA THROWS ITS HAT IN THE RING

These are the events that shaped the discovery and development of AstraZeneca's Seroquel. It's a story that began decades ago and involved a small, but dedicated, team of scientists. Cyrus Ohnmacht was one of the members of that team. After graduating from Muhlenberg College, a small coed school in Allentown, Pennsylvania, with a degree in chemistry in 1961, Ohnmacht spent the next four years at nearby Lehigh University in Bethlehem earning a Ph.D. in organic chemistry, followed by three years as a postdoctoral fellow at Lehigh and at the University of Virginia. In 1970, he joined Atlas Chemical Industries in Wilmington, Delaware.

Atlas was a small company whose philosophy was to compete with the big companies in their disclosed areas of intellectual property (i.e., patents, publications, etc.). It made novel chemicals and focused its pharmacology efforts in the areas of anti-inflammatories and analgesics, tranquilizers and muscle relaxants. Ohnmacht made compounds in several of those areas. A year after he joined the company, Atlas was purchased by Imperial Chemical Industries PLC, the giant British company, as part of ICI's expansion strategy in the United States. At the time, ICI was a shadow of the powerhouse it had once been. (In the 1930s ICI was arguably the largest, most prestigious company in the U.K.) Like Atlas, ICI was interested in making novel drugs, and with the change in management came a different research philosophy. At the smaller Atlas, the mind-set had dictated that the company keep its distance from any competitor's patented compounds to avoid going head-to-head with the industry leaders. But ICI was big enough that it didn't shy away from such competition, and like a handful of other companies, it recognized there could be a golden opportunity in making a compound that could replace clozapine.

In the 1970s, two other scientists interested in developing antipsychotic drugs joined ICI. Dr. Ed Warawa was one of them. He earned his Ph.D. at Stanford and did postdoctorate work at Columbia. Prior to joining ICI, Dr. Warawa had worked as a chemist at Abbott Laboratories researching antipsychotic drugs. The other man who joined Ohnmacht at ICI was Dr. Bernie Migler. He received his Ph.D. from the University of Pittsburgh and was a pharmacologist who had worked on antipsychotic drugs at Squibb. Migler brought with him to ICI a wealth of knowledge about animal testing used to screen for potential antipsychotic drugs. And during the research that led to Seroquel, he developed animal tests that were even good predictors of antipsychotic activity and of potential adverse effects.

In 1976, Jeff Goldstein, who had a degree in veterinary sciences, master's degrees in neurophysiology and business administration, and a Ph.D. in neuroscience from the University of Delaware, joined the group.

Around that time, ICI formed an antipsychotic project team whose goal was to discover an effective atypical antipsychotic. The team consisted of Ohnmacht, Warawa, Migler, Goldstein, and others, including Mort Goldberg, who was head of biomedical research at the time, and Andre Salama, a research pharmacologist. For the next several years, the group conducted experimental work in ICI's labs, but none of their initial efforts resulted in a marketable drug.

One of the obstacles that limited the group was the fact that ICI was a chemical company. Its pharmaceutical research efforts were limited to just a few therapy areas. So while the endeavors of the Central Nervous System (CNS) group, formerly the antipsychotic project team, at ICI showed promise, their work didn't receive nearly the attention given to other research conducted in areas where the company had a history of successes. Propranolol, for example, was one of the first beta blockers, and it represented potentially a big discovery in the area of hypertension medicines. It was no surprise then that management looked more favorably at Propranolol, with its bigger market, than at the work of the CNS group. Still, the company knew there was opportunity in the CNS area, but one that would require more investment.

When a company attempts to develop a drug, it must consider the risk-benefit analysis. The hope is that the drug will work and be safe and tolerable. ICI knew that the first generation of antipsychotic drugs definitely worked. The problem was that they had safety profiles that made the drugs difficult to tolerate. The side effects, and in particular the motor side effects, were often as bad as the actual disease. Anyone who saw a patient on one of these drugs was able to tell immediately that the patient was on neuroleptics or major tranquilizers. Neuroleptic by definition means to seize or take. These drugs not only seized the brain, they paralyzed it. A patient with schizophrenia would hallucinate and become delusional, but he didn't stand out much. A person who was paralyzed or who had these abnormal muscular movements, weird facial expressions, and uncontrolled muscle spasms definitely got your attention. It wasn't the disease, however. What people were seeing were the side effects of the drug.

The situation was hard on the patients. If they were confined in a hospital, they were not ridiculed or stared at. But they did not lead a normal life. If they tried to reenter society by taking a drug that controlled their hallucinations and psychotic behavior, they had to cope with side effects that attracted attention. It wasn't fair to them that their caregivers didn't know which way to go.

The ICI scientists looked at the marketplace, at the disease, and at the patients, and said, "Let's see if we can do something here." By the early 1980s, the antipsychotic project team had defined what type of medicine they would try to develop—a medicine that would deliver benefits similar to clozapine but with reduced adverse side effects.

The lab work that was needed to come up with the right molecule was challenging, and the scientists were uncertain they would succeed. The team feared that clozapine was so unique that a similar drug might never be found. There was also the possibility that management might lose faith and pull the plug—a worry of every pharmaceutical scientist who fears that his or her project may be canceled when little or no progress is being made.

AN EARLY BREAKTHROUGH

After several years of effort, the team finally discovered what it was looking for. After rounds of experimentation, Dr. Warawa devised a compound that in biological testing performed by Dr. Migler was found to produce biological effects similar to clozapine with reduced dyskinetic symptoms. The chemical was Seroquel, although at the time, it was known by its chemical name, quetiapine.

Wayne Macfadden M.D., a psychiatrist from the University of Pennsylvania Health System, where he did clinical studies on both inpatients and outpatients, joined AstraZeneca in 2001. He had also done clinical trial work at GlaxoSmithKline. As AstraZeneca's U.S. medical director for Seroquel, MacFadden explains how it works: "Roughly speaking, a high degree of dopamine in the brain often leads to bad things. Dopamine is a neurotransmitter in the brain, and there are others, such as serotonin and norepinephrine. Broadly speaking, an excess of dopamine is believed to cause psychosis in people—they hear voices and have hallucinations and strange beliefs and delusions. Why do certain people have an excess? The short answer is that no one knows exactly why. It's something that has been observed in various imaging studies, and then by trial and error and serendipitous discoveries with this type of medication to address that kind of problem. So while it is not a cure, by normalizing the dopamine in the brain, people generally improve."

The Seroquel molecule is complicated. It interacts with a lot of different receptors—not only dopamine, but also serotonin and norepinephrine and other neurotransmitters and chemicals in the brain. Seroquel helps to partially block these receptors, which causes a reduction in the level of psychosis. This helps people return to normalcy.

"Think of a receptor as if it were a lock and a key," Jeff Goldstein explains. "The lock is the receptor, and the transmitter, the chemical, is the key. Only one key is going to fit the door lock, only one chemical fits in that receptor. We knew about the receptors and how to look at the effects that drugs have on them. We just didn't know what it all meant." Ultimately ICI's team developed a drug that had low affinity, meaning it would produce low effects at the receptors. "When our management first saw what we were doing, we were told, 'We're not going to pay for the development of a drug that has low effects on receptors. Go back and give us a drug with high effects on receptors.' We had to convince management that we should make a low-potency pill when they were leaning toward a high-potency pill. Now potency has to do with the pill's size— the smaller, the higher the potency. Management opposed a low-potency drug, but we kept repeating, 'Potency and efficacy. Potency and efficacy.' That is, the team wanted a drug with low potency and high efficacy that functioned like clozapine, the gold standard at the time."

It was not only an uphill battle in the lab. The research team was continually being challenged by management about the wisdom of making a CNS drug. Georgia Tugend, who served as marketing brand director at AstraZeneca prior to her retirement in 2005, recalls that there was a lot of apprehension around Seroquel in the early stages of development. "When we were Zeneca before the merger, Seroquel was in a drug class that we weren't familiar with because we were mainly an oncology and cardiovascular company," Tugend explains. "We were also a true hospital products company. We had a major anesthetic and some hospital anti-infective products. These are the areas where our research was strong. This was where we had expertise. We didn't treat serious mental illnesses."

To complicate matters more, several other companies were already active and recognized in the market. "It was a crowded field," says Jim Minnick, director of brand communications. "We were stepping in with some giants, and it made some of our people around here concerned."

Tugend emphasizes that in the early stages of Seroquel development there was a constant debate with management to get financial resources allocated for the drug. "We were competing with other drugs within the company," she recalls, "and one was Accolate, an asthma drug. We sold drugs in the primary care area, and the company was well entrenched in that marketplace. At the time, Accolate was being billed as a future block-buster drug with the potential of significant sales. Plus, it was in an area where the company had a solid track record. Seroquel's comparable future in sales, on the other hand, had more modest forecasts. Consequently, Seroquel was treated like a stepchild within the company."

At one point, the company investigated licensing the product out to another company with expertise in this class of drug. "We soon found out there weren't any takers," Tugend says. "At the time, it looked as if we only had a weak dopamine blocker. Furthermore, most of the companies already had an antipsychotic product in development and they showed no interest in talking to us. We even talked to other drug companies about a joint venture in comarketing Seroquel, and again there was no interest. Nobody was interested in this little antipsychotic we were working on. So the company had to ask itself a difficult question: could it be successful with a product that didn't fit into its book of business or its therapeutic portfolio at the time? The one thing we had going for us was that our people in discovery were passionate about this molecule."

It was this passion that helped the team stay focused and motivated through the long journey required to bring the drug to market. After Seroquel was discovered, another full year of pharmacology work was needed. As Goldstein explains, "When you have a drug to treat a disorder of the brain, you have to make sure it doesn't adversely affect other body systems. The drug is not isolated in the brain. The patient has other body parts—he has a heart, lungs, kidneys, and so on. In what's called secondary pharmacology, we looked at the cardiovascular system, the renal system, the pulmonary system, etc. It took us about a year to complete this work, making sure that Seroquel didn't pose unacceptable risks."

INITIAL INTERNAL RESISTANCE

Fortunately it didn't. In late 1985, the team went back to senior management and presented its case. "Picture a group of business executives sitting around the table, having a discussion about how to spend X hundreds of millions or X billions of dollars," explains David Brennan, AstraZeneca's CEO. "They have many agendas and they must decide what things are most worthy, knowing there isn't enough funding for everything. In our business, and I'm sure the same is true in every business, there are many choices. So the decision about risk is based on what you think the opportunity is. We look at a product and try to decide if it is going to be good for somebody, and if so, we figure out a business model and work around it. And when we find a drug that has the potential to treat people in a superior way to existing medicines in the marketplace, we back up and say, 'We need to figure out how we are going to actually do this because it's the right thing for us to do.' "

For Seroquel, this decision-making process was particularly arduous, but in the end, management gave its consent for Seroquel to move forward into development.

Reflecting on this decision, Brennan says: "In the case of Seroquel, we weren't in the area of central nervous system disorders. However, when we were hearing in our pipeline that this miracle drug was coming through, our marketing and sales people quickly got behind the product with their full support. And that process continues today; if the research people come to us next year, and say they have something for glaucoma, we've got to figure out how to make it work for that drug. This is opposed to the marketing people telling the research people to find a cure for such-and-such disease. Here, it's our research people who tell the marketing people about what they're working on in the laboratory, and they reply, 'Yes, we can sell that.' "

"This is an organization that really gets excited about the opportunity to get into a new therapeutic area," Brennan continues. "This business involves risk taking. One of the challenges that my management team and I face is that our internal people want us to extend ourselves by going further and faster and be willing to take on even more risks.

"With a product like Seroquel, we had to go a bit more on faith because we recognized it was a new class of compounds, and as it turned out, it would be years before its value became apparent and we'd know how far advanced it was over older treatments."

GOING FROM DISCOVERY TO DEVELOPMENT

At this still-incipient stage, only a handful of scientists had worked on Seroquel, and the company had spent an estimated $3 million. This is a relatively small amount compared to what must be spent in development, especially with the clinical trials. Taking the drug up to the next level is where a company's investment skyrockets. At each such costly step up, there are challenges posed by management to determine if the drug warrants additional funds. It must be tested by a team of toxicologists, and if it passes these tests, the next team will do the clinical tests. At any time, something can go wrong and the program could be scrapped. Once a drug moves into the development stage, there is no guarantee it will ever reach the marketplace. The odds remain stacked against it.

The toxicology tests on Seroquel confirmed that the drug was safe in animals. Starting in 1986 and continuing for nearly two years, Phase I clinical trials were conducted on humans—one hundred volunteers who did not suffer a mental disorder. They were healthy people who received the drug to determine if it was safe and tolerable for humans. They experienced no extrapyramidal symptoms or increased prolactin levels. Nor did anyone contract agranulocytosis. They were carefully monitored; Seroquel seemed to be safe when administered to humans. Phase II and, later, Phase III clinical trials began. During the Phase II trials, tests on schizophrenic patients demonstrated that Seroquel had antipsychotic activity, meaning it appeared to work on schizophrenia. And, most important, it continued to seem safe and tolerable.

Jeff Goldstein now became involved with the clinical tests, as well as with presenting the company's results to the FDA. The Phase II trials involved approximately two hundred people, and the results were presented to the FDA in 1993.

Goldstein left research and worked in the clinical group, spending most of his time talking about Seroquel to doctors: "At the time, the company wasn't well known in the CNS area," Goldstein explains, "so we wanted to establish relationships with people in the field prior to the actual launching of the drug upon receiving FDA approval. The company had to give me training on how to make my presentation to the FDA, and I was a nervous wreck, knowing that all the time and effort that our team put into the drug was now in the hands of the FDA review board. I made my presentation and answered their questions to the best of my ability, but I wasn't able to ascertain what they were thinking. Afterward, when I got back to the office, my colleagues wanted to know how it went, and I could only answer, 'I think it went well,' but I really didn't know. For the next couple of weeks I was on pins and needles. Then one day, one of our regulatory guys came running down the hall. 'Hey Jeff, we got the letter from the FDA,' he shouted. 'We can now enter Phase III.' "

An estimated two thousand people enrolled in the Phase III clinical trials that began in 1993. As a worldwide program, the company sought approval from the FDA, the European Regulatory Agency, and the Japanese Regulatory Agency. All in all, Phase III took three years, ending in 1996. The tests documented that Seroquel had an excellent side effect profile. (Concurrently, the company was seeking approval for Accolate, then its highest priority drug, and one with a budget far larger than that allocated to Seroquel.)

Also in 1993, ICI spun off its pharmaceutical division, which became known as Zeneca. To the members on the Seroquel team, the "demerger" was welcome news. No longer were they working for a drug division of a chemical company—Zeneca was a bona fide pharmaceutical company. The company would now be governed by decision makers who were only in the pharmaceutical business.

With Accolate receiving the lion's share of funds for its costly Phase III trials, Seroquel was designated a relatively minor drug. Despite the passion and belief of the Seroquel discovery team, it did not fit in the company's therapeutic portfolio at the time, so the company projected moderate revenues for it and only gave it a modest budget for its clinical trials.

In hindsight, the company should not have limited its initial clinical studies to schizophrenia. A broader clinical study program could have included treatment for bipolar mania and bipolar depression. However, the drug did receive a budget to cover the costs of a clinical study program in schizophrenia. Throughout the trials, there were few or no hitches, and in mid-1996, the company filed its New Drug Application (NDA) with the FDA. Jeff Goldstein recalls the day. "It was one of the most historic days of my life," he reminisces. "When two vans pulled up to the front of the building to pick up the boxes containing all the data, a group of us had a small celebration outside and I took pictures. The vans pulled away and that was it. However, when the Accolate NDA was filed, that was a major event. There was a lot of hoopla within the company, and the company gave away a memento, a glass picture frame with the word ACCOLATE inscribed on it. I took a photo of those two vans pulling away, and I now have it in the Accolate frame on my office wall. Watching the departure of the vans, we had a feeling of confidence, knowing we put together an excellent package. We were confident enough that we were already thinking ahead to after the approval for schizophrenia and planning clinical trials for bipolar disorder, both mania and depression. The FDA approval letter came at the end of 1996. I was on an all-time high. 'But will it be successful?' I kept asking myself."

BIG-TIME UPFRONT EXPENSES

In addition to the hundreds of millions that clinical trials can cost, there are also other major expenses incurred in anticipation of FDA approval—expenditures that must be made even before the drug is approved. The FDA mandates that a pharmaceutical company must demonstrate its capacity to produce at least 10 percent of what it forecasts will be its commercial production. "No longer can a company make small quantities of a medicine in a petri dish during the clinical trials and then, if it's approved, set up a facility for mass production," explains Ken Murtha, the company's vice president of operations. "Now a company is required to validate that it will have a robust and reliable process to deliver medicines to patients when they need it. The FDA wants confirmation that a company can manufacture its product in large quantities before it approves the drug. To comply, Zeneca made an investment of an estimated $50 million in equipment, materials, chemicals, and packaging materials throughout 1996."

This was spent before Seroquel was approved—with no assurances it would ever make it to the marketplace. A clinical trial could have revealed any number of problems or concerns that would have put the new drug on hold or led to its being rejected.

"We also spent $93 million in the formulation," Murtha continues, "before the product could officially be made. We stocked an inventory of Seroquel prior to approval, which meant we faced another risk that if the FDA turned it down, or they told us to take another year or two to do such and such, we'd lose expiration dating. That would require that we throw the inventory out. It's a double whammy. At the end of the day, it's about our integrity. When we say we have a product available for human consumption, we must make sure that it is there."

To stock such an inventory, hundreds of people had to be hired and trained in the manufacturing plant in Newark, Delaware, prior to Seroquel's approval. In addition to their salaries, there was the cost of covering these workers and their managers with fringe benefits, and all the while, Seroquel had yet to generate a single dollar of revenue.

In preparation to launch Seroquel, the marketing team worked over-time trying to get a feel for the marketplace. Team members conducted interviews with physicians and psychologists as well as with schizo-phrenic patients, their family members, and caretakers. Jeff Goldstein spent much of his time during the clinical trials on the road, making pre-sentations to scientific and medical groups. And so did Georgia Tugend, who conducted interviews with 240 physicians, one at a time, over a twelve-month period. She also conducted one-on-one interviews with 50 patients and caretakers, asking questions such as, "What are your unmet needs?" "What do you need going forward?" "What is important to you?"

There are strict FDA regulations that a pharmaceutical company can-not market or promote a drug prior to its approval. This means a com-pany is not permitted to make any sales calls to talk about the product, nor is it allowed to distribute promotional literature in advance. And ad-vertising is strictly forbidden. Pharmaceutical companies, however, are permitted to present certain scientific information to various medical as-sociations and other professional groups in the health field.

"While a pharmaceutical company can't sell or promote a drug prior to FDA approval," David Brennan states, "it does make preparations for its marketing and sales organization to be in place so it can be off and running on day one."

This was easier said than done with Seroquel. "At first, the company wasn't sure how to categorize Seroquel," Georgia Tugend says. "We didn't know which of our reps should sell it. Initially it was agreed that Seroquel would be a product of our hospital group, the logic being that these reps called on hospitals [where] it was probable that a hospital either had a psychiatric ward or was an actual mental health hospital. But after a few rounds of debate, there was a change of plans. Management decided that if the regular hospital sales force carried this drug, its efforts would be di-luted because Seroquel would be sold among several other brands."

Gradually, the solution became clear. Brennan explains: "Generally speaking, a company already has a sales force in place. With Accolate, for example, our existing sales force called on pulmonary and primary care physicians—an audience we knew well because of our leadership posi-tion in respiratory medicines. On the other hand, our target market for Seroquel was psychiatrists, and since the company was not established in the field of antipsychotic drugs, Zeneca was an unknown name to many of them. While we had the option to give Seroquel to our existing sales organization, we elected to build a new one from scratch to sell this particular product."

According to Georgia Tugend, it was a decision that made a lot of sense. "The decision was based on how this drug works on sophisticated mechanisms of action within the brain, which meant we'd have to train reps to be specialists in this area of medicine. What's more, while psychiatrists are physicians, they tend to behave like pharmacologists. They are very analytical in how they determine which drugs to prescribe to their patients. I attribute this behavior to the nature of their knowledge about the brain itself. For the most part, the psychiatrist's approach to understanding antipsychotics is different from other physicians' approach to understanding other medicines. These differences, coupled with the fact that Seroquel was unique, led us to start a specialty sales force to sell this product."

BUILDING A SPECIALTY SALES ORGANIZATION FROM SCRATCH

To build this specialty sales organization, an all-out effort was made to hire and train people from the outside rather than convert sales reps from within. "We wanted experienced people," explains Michael Hickey, vice president of sales, "but we didn't just hire people with sales backgrounds. Nor for that matter did we hire recent college graduates. We recruited licensed clinical social workers, consultant pharmacists, psychiatric nurses, and general nurses, as well as people who worked as caregivers in support groups. We were looking for individuals who had a passion from the consumer's viewpoint, individuals who could say, 'I see these patients and I understand that there is an unmet need.' "

When it came to calling on psychiatrists or institutions that treated schizophrenia, Zeneca started from square one. This meant its marketing and sales staff would have to establish relationships with doctors to whom the company had never previously sold its products. In an industry where sales reps establish long-term relationships with their customers, this was a difficult challenge—especially when psychiatrists and other physicians are so busy treating their patients that they have little time to spare to meet with drug sales reps. It should also be noted that the competition—companies such as Pfizer and Merck—had been calling on psychiatrists for decades and had established deep-rooted relationships.

In 1996, Zeneca hired 13 district sales managers, 12 of whom came from other companies. Some of these had experience in antipsychotic medicines. The initial sales force consisted of 110 new specialty sales reps who were hired predominantly to call on office-practice psychiatrists. They had a daunting task. There were 50,000 to 60,000 registered psychiatrists in the United States, 40,000 of whom were actively practicing. In addition to the new specialty sales reps, the Zeneca sales reps who called on hospitals also carried Seroquel in their portfolios.

"This was a risky and expensive venture," explains Jim Blessington, a company marketing and finance executive, "because we had to create a new infrastructure as opposed to utilizing an existing sales organization. The nature of the pharmaceutical business is that you're doing a lot of risk management. We are continually making decisions on how far out do we go on a new product that exposes the company to a downside. We're used to taking risks and it starts in the lab when our scientists do their work on molecules. We're looking at many, many compounds, constantly testing them, in our attempt to get one to succeed. We do this knowing that the odds are so great against having one of them see the light of day or generate one sales dollar. I don't know of any other industry that has this level of risk."

Don Beamish, the company's executive director for emerging brands, emphasizes that, like all well-managed businesses, a pharmaceutical company establishes appropriate targets for a newly launched product: "We set financial targets," he explains, "that were based on how much we estimated Seroquel would sell annually and then we put a resource plan in place to meet those objectives. Early on, the sales expectations were modest. This meant the resources that we could put in the product were also modest because resource allocation is commensurate with sales expectations. When we launched Seroquel, the competition had much more [in] marketing and sales resources committed to their schizophrenia drugs, and we found ourselves in a David versus Goliath position. Our competitors had far more salespeople in the street making calls than we had, and by sheer numbers this gave them a major competitive advantage. On any given day, they could make more calls than our reps. In Seroquel's first year, one of our reps was able to see a targeted group of physicians seven or eight times a year, whereas the competition's rep might make twenty calls on the same doctors in a year's time."

With so many drug reps trying to get their foot in the door, doctors cannot see each and every one of them. Still, conscientious doctors recognize the importance of hearing about the latest medical information; turning a deaf ear on all unknown drug reps would be an injustice to their patients. Hence they pick and choose which drug reps are granted an audience. To succeed, a sales rep must get in front of enough physicians to tell his or her story. That the job entails a lot of rejection is one of the challenges that confronts every drug rep. It is particularly challenging when selling a new drug and representing an unfamiliar company.

Despite their underdog status, the Seroquel sales reps possessed a quiet air of self-confidence. These were men and women who believed in their product—and it came through. They were on a mission. Their enthusiasm was contagious. As a result, they were able to convince the gatekeepers at doctors' offices to give them appointments, and with their foot in the door, slowly but surely, they convinced doctors to give Seroquel a try.

When a breakthrough drug is being launched, there is always reluctance to accept it. Physicians, like the rest of us, resist change. "Our salespeople were true believers," Georgia Tugend says, "and this helped them to keep making calls when it was difficult to get appointments. We anticipated there would be resistance. Still, we insisted on no high-pressure tactics. We were in this for the long haul and wanted to build solid relationships. We trained our reps to use a soft-sell approach. Our goal was for each sales rep to build long-term relationships with their customers. [But] while they used a low-key sales approach, it was important for them to ask for the order. Our reps would suggest to a physician that if he or she had a patient whose schizophrenia was not being controlled, a patient who was suffering from significant side effects or tolerability issues on his current medication, perhaps that one patient should be started on this product."

Progress came slowly, but it did come. "We were making progress one patient at a time," Tugend remembers. "That's because doctors eventually consented to give it a try on one patient who wasn't doing well on other medications, and if the results were favorable with ours, they'd try it on another and then another patient. As more and more patients responded positively, their doctors observed that Seroquel did work. These results led doctors to prescribe the drug to still other patients. With many of these physicians, it became the preferred treatment for schizophrenia. Later, through word of mouth, one psychologist told another, and the number of patients on Seroquel grew exponentially."

"It's not uncommon for a pharmaceutical company to experience a slow start with a new drug," explains Tony Zook, president and CEO of AstraZeneca U.S. "At any given time, we are trying our best to manage a portfolio of products in sync with how we manage the investment and risk across an entire portfolio. It's difficult to accurately forecast how a new drug will be received. Seroquel started off slowly, but it was such a good product that its momentum kept building and building. As a consequence, we regrouped and elevated Seroquel as one of our high-priority products."

Henry Nasrallah, an internationally renowned psychiatrist who served as chairperson of psychiatry at Ohio State University, worked with the company during its clinical trials. He also sat on a national advisory board with other outside experts who worked closely with the company. "Back in 1997, Seroquel's market share was barely 1 percent," Nasrallah says. "It was so low, there was talk about discontinuing it. The advisory board kept telling management, 'This is an excellent drug. It has so much potential. Put more money into it. Give it a chance.' Fortunately the company did. Over time, the real test was [whether] the patients showed solid benefits. Patient acceptance in my opinion is always the most important ingredient for a medicine to succeed and, of course, having doctors being so impressed with a drug's efficacy and safety, which was the case with Seroquel."

David Brennan concurs that the key to a good marketing plan is customer acceptance. "There's a lot of competition out there," the CEO explains, "and over time, the product has to prove itself as something of value in order to succeed. Good products work, and when they work, people realize it. When Seroquel was first introduced, it encountered an initial challenge because it had FDA approval for lower doses, and the doctors would gradually increase a patient's doses over a period of time. Our competitors' drugs didn't have as much titration, and consequently, physicians were not seeing their patients realize significant benefits. Only later when the drug's dose was increased for treatment did it work exceptionally well with few side effects. It took a while before we learned this, and it contributed to our slow start."

THE MERGER OF ASTRA AND ZENECA

This was the scene in 1999 when Zeneca Group PLC and Astra AB merged to become AstraZeneca, one of the world's largest pharmaceutical companies. As in any merger, there is always concern among employees that there will be changes. The Seroquel group had long been treated as a low-priority drug team. Its members were conditioned to having lesser status. With the merger, the company would be considerably larger and might therefore give Seroquel even less attention. So even while sales were brisk, there was apprehension. As it turned out, Astra had a strong commitment to CNS medicines, and the combined sales forces enhanced Seroquel's presence in the marketplace. Now, an army of six thousand AstraZeneca reps call on doctors around the globe.

Following the merger, Tom McKillop, a thirty-year Zeneca veteran and a chemist with a Ph.D., became the newly appointed CEO, a position he held until he retired in December 2005. McKillop was an ardent believer in the drug.

There was a very definitive statement made by senior management. David Brennan says of the 1999 merger: "It was made clear not to have one company be dominant in any significant way. This principle guided a lot of the decision making going forward. It wasn't 'our way is better than your way.' We asked each other, 'How did you go about doing this?' 'Let's see if we can come up with a third way that takes the best of both worlds and creates another way of doing it.' Culturally it was acceptable because it's not authoritarian. It was more, 'We can do it this way and it doesn't matter who wrote it.' It was a bit more time-consuming, but we invested the time to make sure we had support from our employees. It was a cultural issue—about the company's values and what we stand for—and how that is translated across the United States, the United Kingdom, Sweden, and worldwide."

THE PROOF IN THE PUDDING

There is a story about a dog food manufacturer that was coming out with a new product. The company had an elaborate and expensive marketing plan. It had a huge budget for advertising, and it secured excellent shelf space in the supermarkets. Large quantities of merchandise were shipped out to its wholesalers and in turn to retail outlets across the country. The new product was launched with a major campaign. A month or so later, crates of the dog food were returned to the manufacturer. The product was a bomb.

"Why did we fail?" the company's chairman demanded of his board members. "We did everything right. Our marketing plan was superior to the competition's. Our packaging was superior. We sent merchandise to the leading retailers. We ran wonderful commercials on national TV. Every one of you here in this room loved this product. Our salespeople loved it. Our distributors loved it, and the retailers loved it. Why didn't it sell?"

Everyone remained silent with their eyes cast down. Finally, one director said in a whisper, "The dogs didn't like it."

Not the case with Seroquel. The product's success was premised on both doctors and patients liking it. As Don Beamish points out, "What it all boils down to is customer satisfaction. When doctors prescribe it, they see the effect that it has on their patients. They get feedback from the patients themselves. Over time, the foundation of the product is that it works. Seroquel does what it's supposed to do."

Generally a psychiatrist spends an average of fifty minutes per week visiting with a patient, and it could be more frequently with those in analysis. Due to the nature of the job, a psychiatrist is apt to spend more time listening to patients than other doctors, and it's probable that he or she will develop a close relationship with a patient. So when patients suffering schizophrenia began reacting positively to Seroquel, their psychiatrists were quick to notice. Patients on Seroquel were coming back to see their doctors only weeks later with visible improvements, and in a matter of a relatively short period of time, many were able to reenter the mainstream. To these dedicated doctors, witnessing this type of recovery was most rewarding. Patients were getting back to having a normal life—patients who had formerly been withdrawn from society were able to function. The stories of these patients were quite emotional—doctors were seeing firsthand what this new drug had done. They were impressed and they began to put other patients on Seroquel, and they spread the word to their colleagues.

The patients on Seroquel also spread the word. Unsolicited testimonial letters came pouring in from patients and family members raving about the drug's remarkable results. "In all my years in this business," says Tony Zook, "I've never seen anything like it. Patients and family

members were incredibly proactive in letting us know the positive impact this drug had on their lives. They were even willing to share their stories with our employees, so that they could personally thank them for bringing Seroquel to market and making their physicians aware of its benefits. When they shared their stories, tears were running down everyone's cheeks. It was an amazing thing to witness."

"Patients' testimonials inspire us," David Brennan stresses. "When we get an acknowledgment about how Seroquel changed their lives, it has a profound effect because it reminds us that what we do is so important and meaningful."

Patients were also invited to visit the plant in Newark, Delaware, where Seroquel is made. "It's important for the men and women who work at these sites to hear patient stories," Ken Murtha explains. "Working at a plant or a supply site can be somewhat challenging because the work is repetitive. So my job as vice president of operations is to bring energy and life to what they do. I'm constantly telling them how they affect lives. 'You don't move boxes. You don't make pills,' I tell them, 'you advance life.' I'd have a patient speak to a group of our workers so they could identify with an individual. This made it personal. 'You gave him back his life,' I emphasized. 'You gave that person the ability to earn a decent wage.' "

Another time, Dr. Henry Nasrallah said that he would give Seroquel to his own son or daughter if the child was schizophrenic. "If you cannot give a drug to a family member," he emphasized, "you shouldn't give it to a patient." Nasrallah was highly respected within the company, and when his words were repeated and ultimately spread to the workers in the manufacturing facility and to the sales force in the field, they served to boost morale.

TWO HEARTWARMING STORIES

The patient stories continued to pour in. John Cadigan chronicled his daily battles with schizophrenia over a period of ten years and made a video documentary of his life. The first documentary filmed and directed by someone living with the disease, his film, *People Say I'm Crazy*, made with his sister Katie's assistance starting in 1992, tells how Cadigan experienced his first psychotic break at age twenty-one during his senior year at Carnegie Mellon University, when he was living "like a mole" in a

basement apartment. "I had stopped going to classes because I was too afraid," he says in the film. "I thought they were all out to get me, all out to mess with my mind and drive me crazy." He explains that the documentary was a way "to force me to examine my life, and maybe accept what was going on with me." Together with his sister and award-winning documentarian Ira Wohl, Cadigan photographed his routine activities in and around Palo Alto, California. In 1997, Cadigan got his own camera and took over the principal photography. The result is a portrait of a brilliant but tormented man pursuing his life as an artist despite ongoing battles with his inner demons. *People Say I'm Crazy* captures intimate moments in his life—setbacks and triumphs both personal and creative.

From 1991 to 1994, Cadigan's doctors had tried every antipsychotic, antidepressant, and mood-stabilizing drug on the market, as well as electroconvulsive therapy, but nothing worked. In 1994, another doctor put him on Clozaril, the brand name for clozapine, and while he did become more functional, he gained more than one hundred pounds. Cadigan gives credit to Seroquel for saving his life. (It should be noted that Astra-Zeneca helped fund *People Say I'm Crazy*, which won several prestigious awards as a documentary.)

Geri Hanson's battle with schizophrenia began much earlier than Cadigan's. Her symptoms appeared in early childhood, but until 1994, at age fifty, she had never been given a correct diagnosis. "I've heard voices ever since I was a little girl," she says, "but I thought everyone heard them, so I didn't think there was anything wrong with me. The voices kept me up at night, keeping me from getting a good night's sleep. I had trouble concentrating in school, and even when I'd watch television, I couldn't focus. The voices kept telling me how ugly I was and that I was such a bad person. It's no wonder my self-esteem was low."

Although an intelligent girl, Hanson's inability to focus made her a poor student. Frustrated, she dropped out of high school at sixteen and afterward was unable to keep steady employment. She jumped from one low-paying job to another, such as waiting tables and clerking in retail stores, until she was fired due to tardiness. Married at eighteen and a mother at twenty-one, Hanson got divorced at age twenty-five. A year later, she met Don Hanson, an automotive parts salesman and father who had custody of four young children. In 1973, the Hanson family moved to Tamarac, Florida; today Geri and Don reside in nearby Margate. She continues her story:

"Somehow, and don't ask me how, I was able to raise five kids," she says, "in spite of my schizophrenia that kept getting worse and worse. The voices started to get louder and come more frequently. They would also give me commands. For instance, I was commanded to take walks in the middle of the night down the highway. I'd do it, hoping that a truck would run me over. It's a miracle I didn't get killed. The police would take me home and tell my husband, 'Don't let this woman out of the house.'

"The voices instructed me to be self-destructive. I'd break my dishes, cut up my clothes, and even worse—I'd cut myself, putting deep gashes in my arms and legs. I attempted to commit suicide on several occasions. My mother was so supportive even through all the grief I caused her. I'd make long-distance calls to her in Stuart, Florida, about seventy miles north of here, telling her, 'Mom, I'm just calling to say good-bye because I'm going to die.' Then I'd give instructions on how my possessions were to be distributed after my death. What a terrible ordeal to put a parent through. Still, she never abandoned me.

"Incredibly, I was a stay-at-home mom. I baked cookies and cakes, made Halloween costumes, and I was once the editor of one of the kids' school newspapers. I did all those things while I was fighting those demons in my head."

The voices became so intense that Hanson told her husband, "There is something seriously wrong with me. I've got to get help." Then, one day out of the blue, she checked herself into a clinic. This was in 1990, and for the first time she was diagnosed a schizophrenic. Many more visits to hospitals would follow, and Hanson began taking one medication after another:

"I couldn't go on living with the schizophrenia," Geri explains, "but the medicines they gave me were putting me through a different kind of hell. I had EPS and TD, and the tremors and the uncontrollable shaking were horrendous. One medicine locked my jaw shut, and I was unable to open my mouth. Practically every hospital stay was a nightmare of its own. Sometimes I'd sleep in a dormitory-style room, and other times, I had my own room—if you could call it a room. It was more like a jail cell with barely enough space for a metal bed. The door was always locked so I couldn't get out unless they unlocked it. In other institutions, I felt threatened when I'd walk among the general patient population. I'd look at them and say to myself, 'This can't be me.' But it was me. I was definitely one of them."

When Hanson was not confined in hospitals, she was trying different doctors. "Once I went to this far-out guy who was a self-proclaimed medical guru. I'm not sure why but he wore a turban as if it was proof he was a guru. He kept giving me these terrible medications. While I was seeing him, I spent nearly an entire year holed up in my bedroom eating nothing but M&Ms."

After years of ineffective medications, Humana, her health-care provider, gave her a list of doctors, instructing her to select one to treat her. She chose Ely Pelta, a physician in nearby Coral Springs. "During my first visit with him," she says, "all I did was cry like a baby. He was extremely patient and understanding. Dr. Pelta recommended that I go on Seroquel, a new drug that he really liked. I was willing to try anything, so I did as he instructed. After two months, I started to see some real progress. The voices disappeared, I didn't have any side effects, and I was feeling really good."

Dr. Pelta wanted to make sure Hanson stayed on her new medication. He'd frequently call to ask about her supply of Seroquel and later helped her get prescription drug assistance under AstraZeneca's patient assistance program.

"I'm blessed to have two saints in my life," she says. "Dr. Pelta is one of them. My husband Don is another one, and I don't know how he put up with me for all these years. Today, in our retirement, Don and I work three days a week, running our own condo-cleaning service. Along with his social security and my disability benefits, we're able to live comfortably."

Not long after starting Seroquel, Hanson was able to do things that she hadn't done in years—little things like going to the supermarket and attending services at church. In early 2006 she flew to Boston to visit her son Steve and his family: "My biggest thrill was walking through the airport by myself. Now that's something I could not even imagine I'd be capable of doing by myself. I looked around the airport and saw all the other people, and I said to myself, 'I'm just like everybody else. Nobody's looking at me and thinking what's wrong with that woman.' What a liberating feeling. I felt wonderful.

"My son Steve is the love of my life, and he was so proud that I was able to travel from West Palm [Beach] to Boston by myself. And I have the world's best daughter-in-law. Josée Marie has always showered me with love and affection, even during my darkest times. The two of them

were so excited with the 'new me.' While I was in Boston, I got to know my grandchildren, ten-year-old Matthew and eight-year-old Stephanie, and now we stay in touch by phone and e-mail. I love hearing their sweet voices and excitement when they call: 'Hi Grandma, we love you.' I am so blessed to have so much today—things that I missed for so many years."

Hanson recently made another trip, to Chicago for a family reunion. "I got to see loved ones I hadn't seen for years. And I met nieces and nephews that I didn't even know existed. Now we call and e-mail back and forth, exchanging photos, jokes, news, and so on. And my sister Joan and I have become close again. Next month she's coming to Florida to spend a week with me."

Hanson is doing wonderfully, but is she 100 percent cured? "Let's say I'm 99 percent better, because when I'm really stressed out, I'll hear a voice or have a bout with depression," she explains. "When I do, I curl myself up in a blanket and I hide under my covers, or Don takes me down to the beach to watch the tide come in, and I soon get over it. One thing is for sure—I take my medicine every day, 300 milligrams in the morning and the same dose again in the evening. I understand that I'll never be completely cured, but as long as I take Seroquel, I feel confident that I'll have a lot of the happiness that I missed out on for so many years."

She concludes her story with, "I am so grateful to the people at AstraZeneca. I would love to have the opportunity to meet the ones who figured out how to make Seroquel. If I could, I'd give each of them a big hug and let them know how much I appreciate what they have done for me."

FOR SCHIZOPHRENIA ONLY

Once Seroquel had proved itself, psychiatrists who were having success with the drug for schizophrenia started to prescribe it to their patients with bipolar mania and depression. Because the FDA had approved Seroquel only for schizophrenia, the company could not market it for these conditions. This meant its marketing and sales force could not mention it as a treatment for anything other than schizophrenia. "Once you go out there with your label," David Brennan explains, "and the FDA says, 'Here's what you are allowed to say based on what you studied,' you are bound by the decisions that you made ahead of time. If you want to change that label, you have to do the studies. We have to do studies and then, only after the FDA has given its approval, can we sell it for that indication."

Despite the company originally limiting its clinical trials to the treatment of schizophrenia, this did not prevent psychiatrists from prescribing the drug to their patients for other disorders. No such restrictions are imposed on physicians by the FDA. And in an area of medicine where many questions about the human brain remain unanswered, there is abundant conjecture on how the brain functions as compared to other organs. As a consequence, psychiatrists tend to experiment with medications they prescribe.

When working on the Phase III clinical trials, the company's scientists did realize that there were other potential indications. An advisory board consisting of practicing physicians had talked about such experiences with their patients. Articles in medical journals had been written. But without an approved indication on the label, a sales rep could not mention a word about how the drug could be prescribed as a possible treatment for any condition other than schizophrenia.

MAKING WAY FOR OTHER INDICATIONS

As Seroquel was being marketed for its first indication, the company began making plans to conduct other clinical trials to receive approval for indications in addition to schizophrenia. Bipolar disorder was chief among the indications the company hoped to pursue. This brain disorder causes unusual shifts in a person's mood and energy, making it difficult to function. These mood swings are not like the ups and downs that affect most of us from time to time. They are acutely more severe. They distort moods and thoughts, bring about disturbing behavior, devastate rational thought, and often undermine one's will to live. The mood shifts are dramatic, going from excessively high periods that are accompanied by excessive irritability and distractibility to desperately low periods that bring on feelings of hopelessness and despair. Bipolar mania describes the high periods; bipolar depression describes the low periods. Each can be treated as a separate condition.

"When we started preparing to submit the data for the NDA for Seroquel back in 1996, the wheels were starting to turn about other indications down the road," Wayne Macfadden says. "We nicknamed our first bipolar depression trial 'BOLDER,' from the term "BipOLar DEpRes-sion," which was really meant to be an exploratory study. The results were so robust that we got really excited. This opened a lot of people's eyes around here about Seroquel's potential in treating depression and anxiety. When we saw these results, we started looking at four, five, and six years down the road because we recognized its potential to someday be a megabrand."

"While we were waiting for the FDA to give its approval for schizo-phrenia," explains Jeff Goldstein, "we started to plan our clinical trials to get an indication for bipolar mania and depression. When we filed our NDA for bipolar mania, it was the identical medicine that was approved in 1996 for schizophrenia."

Don Beamish points out that with the schizophrenia indication, physi-cians were given some guidance, but it was up to them to determine the dosage and titration (the period it takes to reach the optimal dose of the medication): "The physicians had to figure out how fast they had to in-crease the dosage for their schizophrenia patients. But this time around, with mania, the trials were conducted with a fixed-dose regimen which led to much greater dosing and titration specificity in our product label. This meant that our sales reps could say, 'It's 100 milligrams for the first day, and day two it's 200, day three it's 300, day four it's 400, and day five it's 600.' That's what it is: 100, 200, 300, 400, and 600. This was a major improvement in terms of titration clarity versus our indication for schizo-phrenia. This also meant that our sales reps could make recommenda-tions to a physician: 'Doctor, don't forget to make sure you use Seroquel at 400 milligrams and above for mania.' Sometimes, doctors would start patients on a lower dose, intending to increase it, but then forget and just leave them there."

"Certain medications have a more pronounced dosage relationship to side effects," Beamish continues. "The higher the dose, the more side ef-fects. And not all side effects are the same. In this class of medications, there are dose-related extrapyramidal symptoms. With Seroquel, a doc-tor could give a higher dosage and efficacy could increase, without neces-sarily increasing side effects. We used to say, 'Start low and go slow.' Our thinking has since changed. We now realize that it's important to have a patient feel better and stay on his medicine, and this frequently means going fairly rapidly with upping the titration so he can get to the right dose, and the sooner, the better."

David Brennan observes that Seroquel's developmental path is not that unusual in the industry. "There is a tendency to underestimate a new drug, and early on, we weren't thinking about bipolar disorder or other psychotic disorders. Then when the drug came to market and psychiatrists saw how safe it was, they started to use it for milder psychoses. They used it by trial and error and, upon our seeing their results, we decided to do the studies to find out if it really was working. When a company enters a new category of medicine, it's just the beginning of a long learning process. When we brought Seroquel forward, we started to develop it for other indications."

FDA APPROVES SEROQUEL FOR BIPOLAR DISORDERS (MANIA AND DEPRESSION)

Following a vast and expensive clinical trial program, the largest in the history of the company at the time, the FDA approved Seroquel to treat bipolar mania in January 2004. Following FDA approval for bipolar mania, the company conducted Phase III clinical trials to test Seroquel's effects on bipolar depression, and on October 20, 2006, the drug was approved to treat this indication.

With an indication for bipolar mania, Seroquel sales reached $2.1 billion in 2004, elevating it to AstraZeneca's second bestselling drug, behind Nexium, the famous "purple pill" that treats acid reflux disease. In 2005, Seroquel sales increased to $2.8 billion, but it still has a way to go to catch up with Nexium. With sales of $4.6 billion in 2005, Nexium is one of the world's bestselling medicines. Seroquel's approval for treatment of bipolar mania, however, has increased the prospects that it will continue to be a blockbuster drug. The total population for bipolar disorder is between 3 to 4 percent as compared to 1 percent of the total U.S. population for schizophrenia. If approval for Seroquel for bipolar depression is granted by the FDA, the patient population will be even greater. It is estimated that 15 percent of the total population will be affected at some time in their lives with the illness.

INFORMING THE PUBLIC

"One of the biggest challenges with bipolar disorder," Johan Hoegstedt, vice president of specialty care, explains, "is the number of misdiagnosed and underdiagnosed patients out there. It is estimated that only about 25 percent of the U.S. population with bipolar disorder are actually diagnosed with the illness. So our work is cut out for us. First, we are working to educate psychiatrists on bipolar disorder, and second and more important, we are reaching out to supporters of primary-care patients. Although they don't necessarily treat bipolar disorder, through our efforts they may be able to better diagnose these patients. Fortunately, there is more understanding about people being misdiagnosed due to the lack of results from regular antidepressants. In another area, we are educating patients and their family members via the Internet on what to look for when someone is inflicted with bipolar disorder to hasten quick treatment with correct medicines."

According to Jim Blessington, AstraZeneca marketing/finance executive, patient education is critical: "Many bipolar disorder patients self-medicate. They medicate themselves through the use of alcohol or drugs. Then, to support those kinds of habits, antisocial behavior escalates. This increases crime and homelessness that is directly related to this disease state. I don't think people fully comprehend how much society saves when those with these diseases are properly medicated.

"We're also working on educating people with schizophrenia or bipolar disorder to stay on their medication. The problem is, once they feel well they think it is okay to stop taking their medication. It's part of our job to educate these people so they understand that they have a chronic disease. Anyone who has ever lived with someone with any of these diseases knows immediately when their loved one has gone off the drug. Like someone with diabetes or HIV, a patient is never cured, but with medication, the disease can be controlled."

Even with patient education efforts, Seroquel, like all antipsychotic drugs, has a high noncompliance rate. Many stop taking their medication due to the stigma that's associated with mental disorders. The stigma traces back to medieval times, and it has become engrained in cultures over the centuries. Patients as well as their family members feel shame and guilt and are humiliated to admit there is mental illness in the family. Consequently, they are slow to acknowledge that treatment is needed, and they are quick to believe they are rid of their problem when their medication shows signs of working. They fear being perceived by others as crazy or weak. Fortunately, our society has become better educated and the stigma of mental illness is slowly being eradicated. Individuals suffering mental illness, as well as their parent(s), are now realizing that it is not their fault.

Back in 1972, when George McGovern was the Democratic candidate for president, his running mate was U.S. senator Thomas Eagleton from Missouri. When it was disclosed that Eagleton had been hospitalized for depression on several occasions, he was dropped from the ticket. The media gave so much coverage to Eagleton's illness that it served as a wake-up call to the nation. Some people believe it was a moment of truth, calling for America to recognize mental disorders for what they are—illnesses.

Seven years later, in 1979, the National Alliance of the Mentally Ill (NAMI) was founded as an organization dedicated to destigmatizing the illness. NAMI is a nonprofit, grassroots, self-help support and advocacy organization of consumers, families, and friends of people with severe mental illnesses. Today NAMI has hundreds of thousands of volunteers who participate in more than one thousand local affiliates and fifty state organizations to provide education and support, combat stigma, support increased funding for research, and advocate for adequate health insurance, housing, rehabilitation, and jobs for people with mental illnesses and their families. The organization enables people to receive access to the kind of help they need, including medication. NAMI recognizes the role that caregivers play and invites them to participate in helping a loved one by providing meaningful support.

AstraZeneca supports NAMI and vice versa. When Georgia Tugend started a program called Caring, Outreach, Partnership, and Education (COPE), brochures and booklets were published and distributed to patients, mainly through doctors' offices and social workers, to provide information on coping with mental disease. The AstraZeneca literature was not product specific, meaning it did not promote Seroquel, and it was endorsed by NAMI. This series of booklets provided everyday practical information for patients, ranging from how to interview for a job to how to get housing. Readers were informed about various state agencies in their area to contact for assistance on how to receive housing and transportation. (It is estimated that as many as half the people in the United States with mental illness are on some form of public assistance.) Individual booklets covered specific subjects. For instance, a book on interviewing for a job provides guidance ranging from proper grooming to résumé preparation. The advice is applicable for a variety of jobs, including clerical worker, dishwasher, or cook. Other brochures focus on what a caregiver should know. Published in several languages, the booklets are read

by millions. COPE provides a valuable service to the mental health community and has given credibility to AstraZeneca, a newcomer in the field.

The message of organizations like NAMI is being heard, and as a result, many people with mental disorders are openly discussing their personal illness. As they do so, the stigma is quietly fading as doors open for
others to seek help. Many courageous and high-profile people, such as
Mike Wallace of *60 Minutes*, have talked openly about their personal battles with depression. Newswoman Jane Pauley has discussed her bipolar
disorder in the presence of a national audience. Movie actresses such as
Patty Duke and Carrie Fisher have served as poster girls for mental illness. Television actresses like Brooke Shields and Lorraine Bracco have
been open about their bouts with depression. These people understand
the power and influence of their celebrity and how it can help others to
not feel so alone.

AstraZeneca actively supports the Depression and Bipolar Support
Alliance (DBSA). This organization fosters an understanding about the
impact and management of these life-threatening illnesses by providing
up-to-date, scientifically-based tools and information written in language
the general public can understand. DBSA supports research to promote
more timely diagnosis, develop more effective and tolerable treatments, and
discover a cure. The organization works to ensure that people living with
mood disorders are treated equitably. DBSA has a grassroots network of
more than one thousand patient-run support groups across the country.

The company has helped fund and develop a DBSA program, Sleepless in America (www.sleeplessinAmerica.com). A visit to this Web site
explains that sleep restores brain chemicals and rests the body. Some researchers believe that the brain organizes and stores memories during
sleep. Lack of sleep cán affect our daytime functioning, hormonal balance, appetite, and immune system. Adults require seven to eight hours
of sleep, but some may need as few as five or as many as ten. The site explains how various brain chemicals are involved in sleep. For instance,
serotonin affects mood, emotion, sleep, and appetite. Serotonin, as well
as the brain chemicals noreprinephrine and adenosine, can be affected
when a person starts a new antidepressant, which can lead to experiencing more drowsiness than usual.

Sleepless in America's Web site also provides information for anyone
having sleep problems. So why does AstraZeneca support this program?
It's a way to reach out to people who are unaware they have a psychotic

disorder. They may be in denial and heretofore have refused to accept that they may have a mental disease. A visit to the Web site may furnish otherwise uninformed individuals with information about bipolar disorders. Likewise, a visit to this site can alert a spouse or a parent about signs exhibited by a loved one in denial. It also has a survey that can be taken to provide feedback that can help identify indicative signs of a bipolar disorder.

The nation's oldest and largest nonprofit organization is the National Mental Health Association (NMHA). Its roots trace back to 1908 when Clifford W. Beers, a former psychiatric patient, founded the organization. After having been institutionalized and experiencing horrible abuse, Beers set out to seek reform in the treatment of people with mental illnesses. NMHA addresses all aspects of mental health and mental illness. It is devoted to improving attitudes toward mental illness, boosting services for the mentally ill, working for the prevention of mental illness, and promoting mental health. This organization achieves its goals through various programs to educate the public on both national and local levels. In addition to its educational, research, and advocacy efforts, the NMHA provides services via its 340 affiliates across the United States.

Two other programs that AstraZeneca supports are Celebration Recovery and Brighter Beginnings in Mental Health, both of which have "feel-good" events that demonstrate that psychotic disorders can be overcome—they offer hope, as witnessed by people who attend and have triumphed over their diseases. These gatherings create awareness that there is no disgrace in suffering from a mental disorder, and that those who do can survive and enjoy a good, productive life.

With the widespread awareness of mental illness in America that has occurred as a result of the good work of these nonprofit organizations— as well as many others—the stigma is fading. Today psychiatrists and primary-care physicians are no longer apprehensive about prescribing antipsychotic drugs to their patients. Similarly, patients are more willing to accept treatment. The public is recognizing that there is no disgrace in having a mental illness—no more than a physical debilitation. All this means earlier detection and more rapid treatment. And with more knowledge about the disease, it is probable that compliance will be increased. If so, it will be a win-win for everyone.

With a foothold now in CNS medicines, AstraZeneca is also working on drugs that may someday lead to a major breakthrough in treating dementia. There are many exciting venues on the drawing board in the CNS world of medicine. CEO David Brennan sums it up when he says, "I've been in this industry for thirty years and when I think about all the change that has occurred, it's exciting to visualize what will happen over the next thirty years."

3

Eli Lilly Company Profile

One summer's day, a boy of sixteen was walking around the square of Lafayette, Indiana, seeing the sights of the thriving town. Standing among the neighing horses and buckboard wagons of the frontier town, this young farm boy glanced up at a store sign. It was a coincidental moment that would change history. The sign read THE GOOD SAMARITAN DRUG STORE. It was 1854.

Drugstores a century ago were remarkable places. Much like today, they sold paints, varnishes, glassware, hardware, and groceries. They also specialized in natural medicines such as beeswax, ginseng, and various plant roots, along with alcoholic "treatments" such as sherry, brandy, port, and whiskey. In an otherwise dreary town, the drugstore was a place of terrific excitement.

Young Eli Lilly was instantly smitten with the idea of becoming a druggist's apprentice. Armed with little more than moxie and a handshake, Lilly entered the store and introduced himself. He was immediately accepted as an apprentice and put to work. The strict master gave him the tasks of cleaning, taking care of the fire, washing bottles, running errands, keeping the shelves stocked, and, when things were quiet, tending to the boss's horse.

Above all, he was expected to keep his eyes and ears open. His nights were spent studying, by candlelight, the *United States Pharmacopoeia* (one of the very few books available on mixing drugs) and copies of the *American Journal of Pharmacy*. He was not permitted to touch the pestle and mortar to actually mix drugs during his first year of employment. For his efforts he probably received the customary dollar or two per week, plus room and board. At the end of five years the young lad received a "Certificate of Proficiency."

Thus began a career that would bring about some of the finest achievements in pharmaceutical innovation. A young boy's chance notice of a sign initiated a lifelong love that would birth one the world's great pharmaceutical/biological giants.

But it would be nearly twenty years before Eli would realize any dreams larger than working in a small apothecary. The country had commenced a long descent into Civil War, and young Lilly found himself swept up in "Save the Republic" furor. Having completed his apprenticeship, he joined the Indiana militia.

After a short stint on the East Coast, Lieutenant Lilly resigned his commission and returned to Indiana, where he received permission from Governor Oliver P. Morton to organize an artillery battery of Hoosier soldiers. During 1863, the Eighteenth Indiana Battery of Light Artillery participated in epic battles at Hoovers Gap, Chickamauga, and Mossy Creek. In April 1864, Captain Lilly joined the Ninth Indiana Cavalry. Not long afterward, Major Lilly and his unit were captured by Confederate forces. In January 1865, he was released during a prisoner exchange and returned to duty. He served in Alabama and New Orleans and was stationed in Vicksburg when the war ended. On June 4, 1865, a few weeks before his twenty-seventh birthday, he was promoted to colonel. After garrison duty in Mississippi for several months, he was mustered out on August 25, 1865.

Seeing an opportunity to advance himself and his family, he bought a small cotton plantation near Port Gibson, Mississippi, and brought his wife and young son Josiah to join him. The business went belly-up. Drought ruined the cotton crop, his partner absconded with all the funds of the enterprise, his wife Lilly fell seriously ill and died, and he and his young son Josiah were stricken with malaria. Deeply in debt and completely shattered, Lilly abandoned the operation and returned with his son to Indiana, where Josiah was left temporarily in the care of his grandparents. Lilly settled in Indianapolis, the state capital, and it was there that he would muster his legendary guts and vision and make his final gambit: opening his own pharmaceutical lab. But after several unsatisfying business opportunities, including a failed pharmaceutical manufacturing partnership, Eli Lilly was no closer to his dream than when he was a POW of the Confederacy.

All he had were the tenacity and conviction that come when you know you're on the right path. He was a man who was willing to invest, plan, assume risks, and work. He had faith in his products and faith in his country.

On May 10, 1876, he strode up to a small building, opened the large front doors of a rented, dilapidated structure "so small you couldn't twirl a cat around," and set up shop. The sign outside his building said simply ELI LILLY, CHEMIST. Somehow bolstered by the sorrows and setbacks of his young life, he was clearly determined to make this enterprise permanent.

Lilly began with three employees (a drug compounder, a bottler/finisher, and his fourteen-year-old son Josiah), $1,300, and some leftover plant extract. The workday was ten hours a day, six days a week, a common routine for the era. At five cents an hour, Lilly's workers were considered well paid, and those original three employees spent the rest of their careers with the company.

Things went well almost immediately. An early decision, based solely on his own unshakable belief in doing good work and providing the best products that could possibly be created, was to stay away from the popular "patent" medicines—elixirs, snake oils, and other panaceas—pitched by the traveling hucksters of his day. He chose the less lucrative but ethical path of creating scientifically sound medicines for legitimate physicians.

Lilly's first product catalog was a simple twenty-four-page flyer. It listed the following products:

- 312 fluid extracts
- 189 sugar-coated pills
- 199 gelatin-covered pills
- 50 elixirs
- 15 syrups
- 5 wines
- Liquid Pepsine

First-year sales were $4,470.18.

A commitment to quality and innovation would become the hallmark of Eli Lilly and Company. After just one year, the company offered a revolutionary product, gelatin-coated pills. This was a huge advancement, considering that the standard forms of medication of the day were foul-smelling, putrid liquids and bitter powders eaten off squares of paper. Alcoholic medicines were some of the most popular remedies, and while they might have made the affirmed feel good at the time of consumption, they rarely cured anyone. Lilly's gelatin capsules were a giant leap; they made taking medication convenient, tasteless, sanitary, and more exact than ever before possible.

Lilly's sales efforts were focused in and around the Indianapolis area but spread quickly with the invention of the gel caps. Within five years the operation was running profitably and sales topped $80,000. Eli Lilly and Company was incorporated in 1881 and shares of stock were issued to five people. Following his philosophy that "no business worthwhile can be built on anything but the best in everything," Colonel Lilly positioned his company for long-term success.

The company would never relinquish that position.

Toward the end of the 1800s, a minidepression swept the country. Lilly responded in a way that would make his family as well known for their largesse as for his groundbreaking pharmaceutical advances. Most people who grow rich believe in hard work and thrift. Some also believe in helping the less fortunate and needy. Lilly helped found the Commercial Club of Indianapolis (the precursor to the Chamber of Commerce) to put homeless and unemployed people to work on city projects. They were paid in food so they could feed their families. His contributions were considered an act of great leadership and selflessness, but to Lilly this was simply the right thing to do.

His company was carried through the rough times on the popularity of an old Creek Indian recipe that they sold under the name Succus Alterans. It was derived from a vegetable compound and was one of the first scientifically validated venereal disease treatments. Lilly's star was continuing to rise in the eyes of the medical community, as the company's products consistently aligned themselves to the Lilly mission: "To contribute to the progress of medicine by developing new and superior agents through research."

After a year's illness, Lilly passed away at age sixty in 1898. Just one month after his death, Josiah K. Lilly, his only son, was elected president of Eli Lilly and Company. "J.K.," as he was called by Lilly employees, was only thirty-seven years old but had been well prepared to lead the company. As a young man, he had taken a two-year leave of absence to attend the Philadelphia College of Pharmacy. When he returned, J.K. became superintendent of the laboratory. By 1890, his father had become more interested in civic activities, and J.K. was de facto head of the growing company.

By 1900 the company had adopted a logo—a red script LILLY—and a slogan: If It Bears a Red Lilly, It's Right. The logo was copied directly from the colonel's signature and would someday be known worldwide as a symbol of excellence and high scientific standards. Sales in 1905 hit the $1 million mark, and by 1906 Lilly had a sales force that covered every state and city in the country.

At the turn of the century there was ongoing friction between the academic world and business interests. The pure scientists of academia were concerned that rash commercial exploitation of their discoveries could lead to endangering an overanxious, needy public. This is where Lilly stood tallest. The company's own demanding internal standards attracted the cream of established academic and research centers. Its sterling reputation greatly contributed to the expansion of the scientific nature of the firm's work. Lilly continued to lead in the creation of such products as granular effervescent salts, hypodermic tablets, sugar-coated pills, and even gelatin capsules for veterinary use.

In the early 1900s Lilly established a biological laboratory that was instrumental in creating vaccines and antitoxins to treat or prevent some of the worst scourges of the day: smallpox, rabies, tetanus, diphtheria, and scarlet fever. But few of these wonderful advancements would ever match the propitious and lifesaving collaboration that took place early in 1921.

Canadian physician Dr. Frederick Banting and a team of researchers at the University of Toronto had discovered a treatment for one of mankind's most lethal diseases: diabetes. Banting and his colleagues found that diabetes could be controlled through the administration of insulin (the natural chemical in the body—absent in people with diabetes—that renders sugars capable of being absorbed into the bloodstream). Banting's dilemma was how to create insulin in mass quantities.

A partnership was formed with a daunting task: quickly create a safe, reliable means of mass-producing insulin. Through a combination of visionary corporate backing and the ingenuity of the dedicated research staff at Lilly, the miracle was achieved. In 1923, the first full-scale mass production of insulin was perfected and sold under the registered trade name Iletin.

Within three years of this momentous victory, Lilly had established itself globally. The company had sales in 160 countries, including such places as Hawaii, Shanghai, the Philippines, and throughout much of Europe. This global presence led J. K. Lilly to remark, "The sun never sets on the Red Lilly."

In 1926, Eli Lilly, grandson of the founder and affectionately called "Mr. Eli" by employees, reiterated the ethic of hard work and zealous commitment of his granddad when he commented, "Never be satisfied with anything. Everything can be done better than it is now being done." He identified the Eli Lilly and Company formula for success as:

1. A high purpose
2. A program of progress
3. Unselfish personnel of the highest type
4. And plenty of resources to back it up

Mr. Eli is also credited with instituting straight-line manufacturing at Lilly and inventing a patented syringe for delivering insulin.

J.K.'s commitment to leading the industry in scientifically sound pharmaceuticals gave rise to the creation of the nation's first industrial clinical research unit designed specifically to test the efficacy and safety of the company's entire line of products. This advancement was critical in the development of many new and powerful products, including Amytal, the first American sedative of its type; merthiolate, a popular and effective antiseptic and germicide; ephedrine, a vasoconstrictor developed from an extract of the Chinese Ma huang plant; and a lifesaving drug for the treatment of pernicious anemia.

By 1928 Lilly was marketing more than 2,800 items in more than 60 countries worldwide.

The great stock market crash of 1929 devastated the world. Still, not a single Lilly employee was discharged during these trying times. Instead when it became necessary to eliminate a position, an employee would be placed in another position—even if it meant painting fences. Everyone at the company remained on the job, unless, of course, leaving was a matter of choice. (As a tribute to how well Lilly employees have been treated over the years, none of its workforce at any of its manufacturing facilities in the United States has been unionized.) With better management and conservative financials, Lilly was able to expand when others had to retrench. The Lilly family also continued its philanthropic work by providing relief to thousands of needy individuals worldwide, and both a family trust and a company foundation were established to provide medical relief and to support educational programs and civic and cultural growth.

World War II created major problems that Lilly responded to with swiftness and generosity. Before the war, many of the world's leading pharmaceuticals had come from laboratories in Germany. At the outbreak of hostilities, those resources were cut off, and once again Lilly rose to the challenge. It contributed heavily to the war effort in the form of blood plasma (at one point supplying over 20 percent of the nation's supply—at no profit to the company); vaccines for encephalitis, typhoid, and influenza; merthiolate; and gas gangrene antitoxin.

But it was also during the war that Lilly made another one of its legendary contributions. As one of nine companies that supplied penicillin to the armed forces, Lilly scientists devised a revolutionary procedure to mass-produce penicillin for distribution in containers ranging from milk-bottle-size to eight-thousand-gallon tanks. Within a few years, the company would create over thirty different preparations of penicillin.

Between 1945 and 1948, sales at Eli Lilly and Company soared from $71.5 million to $115 million, further adding to the corporate stability and financial wherewithal necessary to promote research. It couldn't have come at a better time. Within several years Nobel Prize–winning scientist Jonas Salk had developed a "safe, potent and effective" vaccination to cure another dreaded disease, polio. Perhaps harkening back to the glory days of the early '20s and the development of mass-produced insulin, Lilly took up the challenge of mass producing the Salk polio vaccine. It was a dangerous and complicated job, requiring skilled workers. But systems were established to handle this difficult chore, and the first commercial shipment was dispatched in 1955. At full production, more than half the polio vaccines used in the late '50s and early '60s bore the Lilly label. By the early '60s the annual number of polio cases had dropped from 18,308 to just a few dozen.

Fueled by added profits and enjoying the rewards of hard work and vision, Lilly continued to produce life-changing products. With the purchase of Corn States Laboratories in 1955, Lilly began offering a line of veterinary products. Several years later, a new $5 million center for agricultural and veterinary research was dedicated. From this endeavor emerged a new agricultural division: Elanco Products.

In 1955, Lilly released V-Cillin, a new oral form of penicillin that was more stable and effective than any previous version. Vancocin (vancomycin), a powerful antibiotic for patients with serious hospital infections, was introduced in 1958. To this day vancomycin is considered a last line of defense for certain drug-resistant strains of bacteria.

The company continued to reap the rewards of heavy investment in R&D well into the 1960s. It launched Keflin, the first of more than twenty new antibiotics belonging to the cephalosporin family developed from a species of fungi of the genus *Cephalosporium.* These antibiotics were useful for anyone allergic to penicillin, and were used to treat a wide range of bacterial infections, from gonorrhea to meningitis and staph infections. By 1970 Lilly operations included manufacturing plants in fifteen countries, international commerce contributed 26 percent to total sales, and one-third of the workforce was located outside the continental United States.

The 1970s were difficult times for the pharmaceutical industry. Patent protections expired for many well-known medications and generic equivalents flooded the market. Yet while most of the drug industry was depressed during this time, Eli Lilly and Company doubled in size and began to diversify. In 1971 Lilly acquired the cosmetic company Elizabeth Arden. By applying tried and true management methods honed over three generations of conservative Lilly family philosophy, it transformed the small cosmetic producer into a giant. Sales improved 90 percent over just four years, doubling in profits to $30 million. Arden was later acquired by Fabergé and continues to be a significant player in the cosmetics industry.

Lilly entered the field of medical instruments with the acquisition of IVAC Inc., a company that manufactures systems to monitor vital signs and intravenous drug administration in hospital settings. Building on this success, Lilly brought other companies into its fold, including: Cardiac Pacemaker Inc., Physio-Control Corporation, Advanced Cardiovascular Systems, Hybritech Inc., Devices for Vascular Intervention Inc., Pacific Biotech, and Heart Rhythm Technologies Inc. These companies formed the core of Lilly's Medical Devices and Diagnostics Division. Despite its diversification, however, Eli Lilly and Company has never drifted far from its core strength: pharmaceutical R&D.

More notable contributions in this area include such medications as Ceclor, a second-generation cephalosporin that became the world's bestselling oral antibiotic from 1988 to 1991; Humulin, human insulin and the first human-health-care product created by biotechnology; Prozac, the first product in a new class of drugs to treat clinical depression; Humalog, insulin that closely mimics the body's natural rapid insulin output after meals; Zyprexa, an antipsychotic agent for the treatment of schizophrenia; Evista, first of a new class of drugs to treat osteoporosis in postmenopausal women; Xigris, a first-in-class product to treat severe sepsis in adult patients with a high risk of death; Strattera, a nonstimulant, noncontrolled medication to treat attention deficit hyperactivity disorder; Cialis, a new treatment for erectile dysfunction; Symbyax, the first FDA-approved medication to treat bipolar depression; Alimta, a treatment for malignant pleural mesothelioma in patients who are not candidates for surgery and for second-line non-small-cell lung cancer; and Cymbalta, a treatment for major depressive disorder and diabetic peripheral neuropathic pain.

The company has remained steadfast to maintaining its vision of creating medicines "as if people's lives depended on it."

Today Lilly employs over 44,000 people worldwide. More than 8,000 of those are directly involved with research and development. Over 20 percent of the annual operating budget is committed to ongoing research efforts. For six years in a row, Lilly was voted as one of the 100 Best Companies to Work for in America by *Forbes* magazine, and one of the 100 Best Companies for Working Mothers by *Working Mothers* magazine (in the top ten for five out of nine years).

Despite the increasingly difficult climate of worldwide health-care concerns, Lilly is keeping its eye on the vision set out by its founder and his progeny. In the words of Eli Lilly's son J.K.:

> As to the future of this business, it was founded and built on quality and integrity. Don't ever do anything to distract from its integrity. If we continue to work and follow those same principles, there are no limits to where we can go.

The Better-Than-Nature Insulin

ELI LILLY'S HUMALOG REINVENTS
DIABETES TREATMENT

D IABETES. It's been a menace for a long time. A sixteenth-century-B.C.
papyrus scroll, found in an Egyptian tomb at Thebes in 1862, refers
to a symptom called polyuria, or excessive urination. Seventeen centuries
later, in 164 A.D., the renowned Greek physician Arataeus of Cappodocia
described the disease as "a melting down of flesh and limbs into urine."
He noted that this illness took a long time to establish itself, but after
that, "the melting down is rapid, the death speedy," which was merciful
since "life is disgusting and painful," and victims suffer "nausea, restlessness, and burning thirst" before expiring.

Later, in 752 A.D., *The Yellow Emperor's Inner Classic*, the ancient Chinese medical book penned by the legendary ancient emperors Shen
Nong and Huang Di, cited diabetes in a reference to *Xia-Ke*, which trans-
lates as "wasting and thirsting," and diabetes was listed among the 1,100
diseases known to Chinese medicine. This document suggests an interesting method of detecting sugar in the urine: the patient was instructed
to urinate on a wide, flat brick and observe whether it attracted ants.

Arab physicians over one thousand years ago are credited as the first
to competently treat diabetes. In the classical text *The Canon of Medicine*, Islamic philosopher Ibn Sina (980–1037) recorded detailed symptoms, causes, and holistic treatment for diabetes. He recommended
exercise, dietary changes, and herbal medicines.

The illness that all of these early medical sources were describing is
still very much present today. Diabetes has impaired and shortened the

lives of countless people throughout history. Today more than 18 million Americans have diabetes. We now know that the cause of their suffering is an absence of or inability to use the hormone insulin, which is normally secreted by a glandular organ called the pancreas and which allows the body's cells to convert carbohydrates into the energy needed to survive. In the absence of insulin, the body turns to its fats as an energy source. This modifies its delicate chemical balance, resulting in kidney failure, heart disease, loss of limbs, blindness, and, eventually, coma and death.

Although both the disease and the pancreas have been known to doctors for thousands of years, a definitive connection between them was not discovered until the beginning of the twentieth century. Herophilus, a Greek anatomist born in 336 B.C., may have first discovered the pancreas in one of his public dissections of human bodies. Four hundred years later, it was named *pancreas* (Greek for "all flesh") by another Greek scientist.

A soft, fleshy organ positioned on the back wall of the abdomen behind the stomach, taking hold of the horseshoe curve of the duodenum, the first part of the small intestine, the pancreas consists of groups of cells that produce various digestive juices that pass through a system of ducts into the duodenum. There, these juices take part in the digestive processes, breaking down the carbohydrate, protein, and fatty foods passed on from the stomach.

Considerable mystery and misinformation about the functions of the pancreas prevailed until the late nineteenth century. Paul Langerhans, a twenty-three-year-old student, observed in 1869 that the pancreas was a gland consisting of one million tiny islands (like the taste buds on a tongue). The first evidence connecting it with diabetes appeared in 1889, when two medical professors at the University of Strasbourg, Oskar Minkowski and Joseph von Mering, made an astonishing discovery. Disagreeing on whether the pancreatic enzymes were vital to the digestion of fat, they settled the issue by surgically removing a dog's pancreas and observing the results. Twenty-four hours later they found that the dog had severe diabetes, with 5 percent sugar in its urine.

Minkowski and von Mering had discovered that, somehow, the absence of the pancreas had caused diabetes, upsetting the metabolism of sugar. The next problem was to discover why. Was it the absence of the pancreatic juice in the intestine that brought on the disease? Apparently not, for Minkowski confirmed the observations of other experimenters who had tied off and/or cut the ducts leading from the pancreas to the duodenum. Stopping the flow of pancreatic juice in this way caused minor digestive problems, but it did not cause diabetes. Only total pancreatectomy did. Minkowski had traced the origin of diabetes to the pancreas, but he did not know that the answer lay in the tiny islands discovered by Paul Langerhans and later named after him. That was for later researchers to discover.

In 1901, Eugene Lindsay Opie, a pathologist at Johns Hopkins University, observed tiny globules of tissue embedded in the pancreas of recently deceased diabetic patients. Opie noted that these tissues had shrunk, and the cells themselves, once chemical stains were applied, appeared glazed, as if their contents had hardened. His discovery was the "missing link" that led to British physiologist Sir Edward Sharpey-Schafer's breakthrough observation that diabetes is caused by the lack of internal secretion produced in these islets. The word "insulin" is from the Latin word *insula*, for "island."

Along with discovering the sugar-storing function of the liver, scientists found that the cells of an organ could pass their material directly into the blood via the capillaries that coursed around them. The pancreas, it seemed, produced two kinds of secretions—the digestive juices that passed through its duct to the intestine, or its *external* secretion, and, as yet hypothetical, an *internal* secretion that was poured directly into the blood. This meant that the pancreas could be viewed as a double organ. Its two parts possessed only a geographical relationship, with the tiny islets hidden away, scattered, in the bulk of the main glandular tissue.

As soon as it was realized that the pancreas controls diabetes, attempts began to use the pancreas to treat the disease—just as diseases of the thyroid were being treated with thyroid hormone. Minkowski was the first of many researchers to try to restore the pancreatic function to diabetic animals (others experimented on human diabetics) by preparing and administering extracts of pancreas. The results of these early experiments were mixed, tending toward the negative. Some extracts had no effect and some had decidedly harmful effects, throwing an animal into shock or worse. Others had temporary sugar-reducing effects that were more than canceled out by harmful side effects. There was no way of knowing what had caused the reduction in blood sugar (glycosuria), the extract or its toxic effect on the system.

Having determined that the diabetic's body was having trouble with carbohydrate metabolism as well as with proteins and fats, physicians began treating patients with diets. Dr. Frederick Madison Allen, a Harvard Medical School–educated physician, was perhaps the most prominent researcher in the field and had published *Studies Concerning Glycosuria and Diabetes* in 1913. The following year, Allen was hired by the Rockefeller Institute in New York and named head of a small ward of diabetic patients. His methods were tried on all sorts of diabetics, mild to severe, recently diagnosed and terminally comatose, old and young, educated and ignorant, well-to-do and desperately poor. The therapy was almost always the same: when a diabetic was admitted to the hospital, he or she was put on a fast (liquids only) until the glycosuria and, in the severe cases, the acidosis (acidic compounds called ketone bodies) disappeared. Then there would be a gradual building up of diet, measuring by carbohydrate tolerance but with strict weighing of all foods to see how much the patient could take until sugar appeared in the urine. A day of fasting would clear the urine again and the diet would be fixed at a total calorie intake just under this tested tolerance.

At the time Allen introduced what came to be called the "starvation diet" of diabetes, America was a country where being well-fed was still a sign of good health. More ironically, he was advocating serious dieting to patients suffering with symptoms of excessive hunger accompanied by rapid weight loss. It was tantamount to putting a man whose weight had dropped from 200 to 100 pounds on a diet to lose weight. Those who complained that they were getting weak were told by Allen that the fasting would build up their strength. And when they complained about hunger, Allen would tell patients that they must be hungry more often and lose still more weight. To many, it seemed as though they had a choice of death by diabetes or by starvation. While Allen's starvation diet is believed to have prolonged a diabetic's life by an average of two years, the suffering imposed was perhaps as cruel as the disease itself. But in spite of the obvious horrors, Allen's diet was the best therapy available at the time. Other diets used then ranged from the "oat cure," a milk diet, a rice cure, and potato therapy, to the use of opium.

THE DISCOVERY OF INSULIN

By far the most important breakthrough in the treatment of diabetes was the discovery of insulin by Frederick Banting in 1921–22 at the University of Toronto. Banting's discovery has in fact since been hailed as one of the biggest medical breakthroughs in the twentieth century, ranking in importance with that of penicillin and the polio vaccine. Prior to his discovery, Banting was an improbable candidate to make such a major contribution to science. Having grown up on a farm in Ontario, Fred Banting was at best an average medical student at the university, and upon finishing his education he served as a field surgeon during World War I. After the war, he opened a medical practice in his house in London, Ontario. He earned just $4 during his first month in practice.

To supplement his meager income, Banting worked as an assistant professor at nearby Western University. One night, too poor to dine out or frequent local taverns, Banting stayed home to prepare a lecture for his students. He read a magazine article titled, "The Relation of the Islets of Langerhans to Diabetes with Special Reference to Cases of Pancreatic Lithiasis." Since it was a technical publication, he purposely read it just prior to retiring to assure a sound night's sleep.

As Banting's memoir reads, "It was one of those nights when I was disturbed and could not sleep. I thought about the lecture and about the article and I thought about my miseries and how I would get out of debt and away from worry. Finally [at] about two in the morning, after the lecture and the article had been chasing each other through my mind for some time, the idea occurred to me that by the experimental ligation of the duct and the subsequent degeneration of a portion of the pancreas, one might obtain the internal secretion free from the external secretion. I got up and wrote down the idea and spent most of the night thinking about it."

Unable to find any more reading material on the subject at Western's medical library, he talked to some fellow doctors and expressed his interest in pursuing a research project that would isolate the internal secretion to relieve glycosuria. Although these are not their exact words, they told him, "Don't give up your day job."

Banting went to the University of Toronto to visit J. J. R. Macleod, professor of physiology and an internationally known expert on carbohydrate metabolism. Since Banting was a graduate of the university's medical school, Macleod agreed to see him. After a brief conversation, a skeptical Macleod consented to Banting's request to allow him to use a lab and to have some dogs to experiment on for a few weeks. Macleod assigned a young science student, Charles Best, to work as Banting's assistant in performing the chemical tests.

Beginning their work in May 1921, Banting and Best succeeded after trial and error in securing an active extract from the endocrine portion of the pancreatic glands of laboratory dogs. On November 19, they gave the first injection of the extract to diabetic dogs. The result was a diminution of sugar in the urine. The next step was to obtain the extract in a sufficiently pure state to test its effect on human diabetes. They were joined by J. B. Collip, a fellow Canadian and a biochemist, who further developed the method of preparing the extracts with suitable solvents and precipitants so that they could be used therapeutically. Starting with fresh whole beef pancreas ground up in alcohol, he tested each batch of extract for potency, perhaps several times at different stages, on rabbits.

By the winter of 1921–22, Banting and Best were presenting their first papers on the internal secretion of the pancreas. George Henry Alexander Clowes, director of biochemical research at Eli Lilly and Company, attended a meeting of the American Physiological Society where he heard Macleod, Banting, and Best present a paper called "The Beneficial Influences of Certain Pancreatic Extracts on Pancreatic Diabetes." In it, the three scientists reported on their research and discussed their extract. By this time they were officially calling it insulin. They explained how it had reduced blood sugar and kept two diabetic dogs alive. Most of their audience was unimpressed but Clowes was captivated. After the lecture, he suggested to the three presenters a possible collaboration with his company in the commercial preparation of insulin. Not wanting to make a commitment to a single profit-driven company, the Toronto men politely declined.

By this time, they were ready to test their extract on humans. At Toronto General Hospital, an extremely ill young boy, Leonard Thompson, became the first diabetic to receive insulin. His condition began to improve immediately.

THE WORLD'S FIRST MANUFACTURER OF INSULIN

On May 22, 1922, Clowes and his company's chairman, Eli Lilly, went to Toronto to meet with the discoverers. Several days later, the University of Toronto agreed to give Eli Lilly and Company an exclusive license to produce and sell insulin in the United States for one year. The Canadians and Americans promised to share techniques and knowledge throughout this experimental period. Though the university scientists were still wary of collaborating with a profit-oriented pharmaceutical manufacturer, they were influenced by Clowes's high standing in the scientific community and the company's support of his work. They were also impressed with Lilly's capacity to produce a complex drug in high volume.

Eight days later, the agreement was signed and the company began its attempt to produce large quantities of insulin at consistent standards. Charles Best loaned his expertise, making nine trips to Indianapolis to work side by side with the Lilly team. The first factory-scale lot was made on June 26 and the second on July 5. They had required 75 pounds of fresh hog pancreas and produced 30 units of insulin with a potency of one unit per cc. By the end of July, production was averaging 1,200 units a week.

Meanwhile, word of this miracle medicine was out. By this time, the young Leonard Thompson had risen from his deathbed and was living a normal life. The demand for insulin surged. By April 1923, Lilly's production of insulin was up to 180,000 units per week and potency had risen to 20 units or more per cc. At this point it was made available to physicians to treat the general public.

From the first meeting in Toronto, the company had demanded the right to distribute its insulin, under the trade name of Iletin, to selected physicians until January 1923, in the hope of bonding their loyalties to Iletin. This was years before the FDA was formed and there was no regulatory agency to approve or disapprove the introduction of new drugs. In exchange for providing free insulin to physicians, Lilly was able to collect valuable information on how it was being used and what side effects it caused. After the year of monopoly production and sales, other pharmaceutical companies could enter the insulin market, but none could call its product Iletin.

In 1923, the Nobel Prize committee awarded Banting and Macleod the prize in medicine. Best, who had worked with Banting right from the start, received no prize, nor did Collip, who had completed the development of a clinically safe and usable substance. The vagaries of the prize committee were partially remedied when Banting insisted on sharing his prize with Best, and Macleod did the same with Collip. The Nobel Prize was well deserved. Prior to their discovery of a way to produce insulin, diabetes had been a fatal disease.

By the end of 1923, it was estimated that 7,500 physicians were treating 25,000 diabetes patients with Iletin. Lilly had sold almost 60 million units during the year. The company had prepared extensive guidelines for practicing physicians on dosage determination, suitable potencies, dietary measures, and urine and blood analyses. It had also developed a variety of accessories for patient self-care. By 1925, Lilly had distributed nearly 218 million units; 13 million were shipped abroad. As production volume increased, the cost of insulin decreased. The price stayed the same for nearly 60 years. Due to the cost of pork and beef pancreases, there was a price increase in 1973. The price in the United States today is still relatively low at around a few dollars a day. By 1932, unit sales had reached 792 million and sold for only 10 percent of its January 1923 price. Other companies were also manufacturing this lifesaving medication, and insulin made from beef or pig pancreases was simply called "regular." Regular insulin had to be injected several times a day.

In its early stages, insulin was rough and unrefined; it had a dirty brown appearance. Due to its impurity and large needles, the injections were painful and had to be taken several times every day. In the 1930s, protamine, a substance from salmon sperm, was added to insulin to lengthen insulin action time. Protamine is a histone and insulin is acidic. The two came together to form an insoluble material that gave the insulin longer action. Zinc was often added to form crystals in varying sizes, which also enhanced the length of the insulin's action. The larger the crystal, the longer it took to dissolve from the injection site. At first there was hope that a single shot of insulin could last for the entire day, thereby freeing people with diabetes from having to take multiple injections. Later it was realized that this one-shot dosage would be akin to taking a time bomb in the morning because later on in the day blood glucose levels dropped sharply. Only when home blood-glucose testing was available in the 1980s did it become apparent that the longer-acting insulins could not maintain satisfactory glucose control. Short-acting insulins were needed to control postmeal glucose rises.

An insulin-requiring diabetic's blood sugar level can also get too low if he exercises more than usual, he doesn't eat enough, doesn't eat on time, or takes too much insulin. The likely symptoms of the hypoglycemic reaction that can occur as a result include headache, nervousness, shakiness, heavy sweating, rapid heartbeat, hunger, confusion, dizziness, and even unconsciousness.

EARLY IMPROVEMENTS IN INSULIN

Steady advances in the field of diabetes were made during the twentieth century. In the 1940s, scientists found the link between diabetes and long-term complications such as kidney and eye disease. In 1944, a standard insulin syringe was developed that contributed to making diabetes management more uniform. In 1955, oral drugs to help lower blood glucose levels were introduced.

Another major breakthrough of the 1950s resulted in a second Nobel Prize awarded to a biochemist in the field of diabetes. Frederick Sanger from the United Kingdom was awarded the coveted prize in 1958 for determining the exact order of the insulin molecule's amino acids. Starting his work in 1943, Sanger came up with the exact mode in which the fifty-one amino acids of the insulin molecule are linked together. Sanger demonstrated that the molecule contains two different chains with different end-groups, and he managed to isolate them after breaking the molecule by oxidation. Thus the problem was simplified. Instead of one molecule with fifty-one amino acids, Sanger now had two molecules with thirty and twenty-one amino acids. Remarkably he was able to determine the exact sequence of the thirty amino acids in one chain and the twenty-one in the other. Earlier he had shown that the two chains were held together to form an insulin molecule with the aid of bridges of sulphur atoms. The structure of insulin had thus been established—an extraordinary achievement. Sanger's discovery marked the first time that anyone had determined the molecular structure of a protein.

In 1959 it was confirmed that there were two major types of diabetes; type 1, which is insulin dependent, and type 2, which is non–insulin dependent. Children are more likely to have type 1 diabetes, which is also known as juvenile diabetes. Type 1 occurs when the pancreas fails to produce enough insulin; in advanced stages, it does not produce any insulin. A type 2 diabetes patient's pancreas simply does not produce sufficient insulin, but it does not shut down completely. The Centers for Disease Control and Prevention states that 95 percent of all diabetes cases are type 2 adult-onset diabetes, largely brought on by lifestyle issues such as obesity. An obese person develops diabetes because his pancreas is unable to produce enough insulin as a result of excessive fat.

When only one type of diabetes was known, everyone took four shots a day of "regular" insulin. Later improvements in the purity of insulin, blood glucose meters, and insulin pumps contributed to the treatment of diabetes.

Ever since 1923, when it became the world's first manufacturer of insulin, Eli Lilly and Company has maintained a leadership role in the field of diabetes treatment, having introduced more than 40 products that have helped improve the lifestyles and saved the lives of diabetics. In 1946, to commemorate the twenty-fifth anniversary of the discovery of insulin, Lilly sponsored an international diabetes clinic at Indiana University Medical Center. In the 1950s, they introduced animal-source insulin with 500 units per cc (U-500). During the same decade, Lilly scientists succeeded in purifying and crystallizing another substance found in pancreas glands—glucagon—that was later used in terminating hypoglycemic shock resulting from low blood sugar in diabetics. By 1960, Lilly was marketing glucagon for the treatment of insulin-induced hypoglycemia. In the 1970s, Lilly began producing "single-peak" insulin.

A MAJOR BREAKTHROUGH: RECOMBINANT DNA TECHNOLOGY

In 1976, leading scientists from around the world attended an international meeting held in the Lilly Center in Indianapolis. The focus of the meeting was a new technology involving gene synthesis and how it could be applied to the production of insulin. One year later, in 1977, a small startup company, Genentech, became one of the early pioneers to synthesize genes. Prior to this, scientists had to isolate genes, and only through a complicated series of procedures could they obtain the gene they wanted. Now scientists could tailor the genes to order. In 1979, Lilly scientists were able to demonstrate the full biological potential of rDNA human insulin and make zinc crystals, the first crystals of an rDNA protein. Lilly's Jim Hoffmann, Fred Mertz, and Ronald Chance are the three scientists credited with proving that recombinant DNA technology was going to be a viable source of human insulin. To this day these three Lilly scientists still remember the exact date, December 7, 1979, when this monumental event occurred. (Coincidentally, Fred Mertz's grandfather was the first chemist hired by Eli Lilly and Company back in the 1880s.)

Thus, sixty years after Eli Lilly and Company became the world's first manufacturer of insulin, they achieved one of the biggest breakthroughs since Banting's and Sanger's discoveries. In 1983 the FDA approved the world's first recombinant human insulin, called Humulin. The approval came after years of clinical research led by Dr. John Galloway, Lilly's primary diabetologist.

This diabetes medicine was also the first human drug produced through recombinant DNA technology. In brief, recombinant technology enables scientists to harness bacteria to make certain drugs or hormones. Essentially, one takes the gene of interest, which codes for the sequence of amino acids that form the protein of interest, and inserts this gene into bacteria. The bacteria cells can be grown and will produce insulin protein. The bacteria makes 1 percent of its total weight as the protein, and there can be no margin of error in separating that 1 percent from the other 99 percent. One thing is for certain: there can be no bacteria anywhere near the manufacturer's product. Using this technology, the protein insulin is isolated, purified, and formulated. While Lilly was the first to make a medicine with recombinant technology, hundreds of other medicines have since been made with it.

THE DISCOVERY TEAM

Dr. Ronald Chance, a Lilly protein biochemist who joined Lilly in the 1960s, devoted his career to the field of diabetes. A major contributor to the development of Humulin, he explains the reason the company made the decision to make it: "Insulin is a hormone from the pancreas that is vital for carbohydrate protein lipid metabolism. Without it, the body cannot survive. Dr. Banting's insulin was extracted from a mixture of beef and pork pancreases, and in 1929 Lilly introduced a special beef animal source insulin. They took the pancreas of pigs and cattle and it took something like seventy pig pancreases to provide one diabetic person with enough insulin for a year. Since the pancreas of cattle is larger, fewer were required. In the 1970s World Health Organization [WHO] studies showed that a high percentage of the packing plants throughout the world were not equipped with appropriate sanitary and refrigeration systems, and were therefore unable to avoid infection by immediately freezing pancreases. So obtaining high-quality pancreases was a definite problem. We began to look at alternative ways to produce animal insulin because our data back then showed that the population of diabetes patients was growing at an alarming rate and that meant risking encountering a shortage of pancreas glands of swine and cattle. The possibility of not having enough insulin for patients was a frightening thought. We believed that if we could find another source for insulin and not have to depend on bovine and porcine, we could eliminate the risk of exhausting the supply of insulin."

After a successful career in the U.S. army medical corps, James Anderson M.D. joined Lilly in 1985. Anderson says that what attracted him to the company was its strong leadership role in the making of insulin. "Lilly was the primary manufacturer of insulin the United States," he points out, "and at the time, the diabetes community was concerned about the rising number of people requiring insulin. The number of cases was increasing, and concurrently, there was anxiety about the available supply of animal pancreases with the islets of Langerhans [these islets have the beta cells to make insulin]. Up until this time, the company's supply was dependent on animal pancreases obtained from meat-processing plants where animals were slaughtered. In the 1970s people became more health conscious and started to cut back on meat consumption; at the same time, the cost of meat was rising. This caused concern that a time might come when there wouldn't be enough animal pancreases to provide the demand for insulin.

"There was always the option to chemically synthesize insulin as a chemical compound is synthesized," Anderson explains. "This was being done in other labs, but it involved as many as two hundred different chemical steps, so it wasn't feasible. We could also take beta cells from the pancreas in animals to make insulin. There are specific cells in the pancreas that are devoted to synthesizing insulin. If these could be grown in large amounts you could produce insulin. The problem is that the beta cells in animals are like ours and cannot be grown in large quantities. Consequently this approach to producing insulin is not currently an option. It wasn't economically feasible, considering the market price of insulin. Keep in mind that since 1923 the pharmaceutical industry has strived to keep the price of insulin affordable. This assured that people with diabetes would always have access to this vital medicine."

Another key player in our story is Dr. Bruce Frank, who joined Lilly in 1966 as a young twenty-eight-year-old chemistry Ph.D. Frank also was attracted to the company's strong position in the field of diabetes. "When I came to Lilly, I had the opportunity to hear Charles Best speak at our insulin symposium. The company would bring in scientists from around the world and we'd hear about the latest developments in diabetes and insulin chemistry. The company would invite leading experts to speak on all aspects, ranging from a physicist who was doing X-ray crystallography to get the structure of insulin to a scientist who was doing the research that demonstrated how insulin is actually made in the cell. Having these people in one place created a wonderful synergy that resulted from their creative thinking and vast knowledge. It was a wonderful opportunity to be able to sit down with these brilliant people and pick their brains."

In the 1970s, an alarming long-term trend came to light: Americans as well as citizens of other prosperous nations were consuming more calories, which led to increases in obesity. As already mentioned, obesity is a cause of diabetes because most of the food we eat is turned into glucose for our bodies to use for energy. In the early stages of obesity, an obese person actually produces or has a higher level of insulin in his blood than a normal person. That insulin is used less effectively to take the sugar out of the blood and put it into the cells. Due to this constant demand for more and more insulin to get sugar under control, the pancreas eventually wears out and at some point is no longer able to make enough insulin to control the blood sugar. It is estimated that 80 percent of those who develop type 2 diabetes are obese.

It was in this environment that the need to make Humulin existed. Far-sighted scientists and business executives were thinking ahead to a day when there might be people with diabetes who were unable to obtain their daily insulin medication. The consequences of such an event were frightening. The race that began in the 1970s to get this new form of insulin to the market became a reality in 1983 when Humulin was approved by the FDA. It was a major victory in the field of medicine: it made a shortage of insulin unlikely. Lilly could eventually manufacture Humulin by culturing molecules in huge 10,000-liter tanks, thus producing this precious drug on an industrial scale.

HUMALOG: THE IMPROVED INSULIN

Humulin is only a prelude to the story of Humalog, the next generation of insulin introduced by Lilly. Like its predecessor, Humalog is a product of recombinant DNA technology; however, it has specific benefits for diabetics that are not provided by Humulin. And like Humulin, Humalog also took years of research, development, and clinical testing, beginning back in the mid-1980s.

It should be noted that, due to the complexity of many processes required to make insulin's biological ingredients, the cost of manufacturing the drug is very high. Moreover, to assure that insulin remains available to diabetics, its price continues to be kept affordable. The cost of insulin made by other pharmaceutical companies has also remained affordable, and as a consequence, it is difficult for a generic competitor to sell a generic brand of insulin following a patent expiration.

So what incentive did Lilly have to develop an improved version of insulin, especially when its current drug was enjoying strong sales? Why should the company come out with a new insulin that could potentially cannibalize the sales of Humulin? The fact is, had Lilly been driven strictly by its bottom line, Humalog would never have happened, not when the revenues generated by Humulin were rolling in and likely to continue for the foreseeable future. The initial impetus came from the scientists, men and women who wanted to make a medicine that they believed would improve the lives of people with diabetes. Without these dedicated individuals, Humalog would not exist today.

During the initial R&D stages of Humalog, Dr. Richard DiMarchi headed the research department. A modest man, he is reluctant to take credit as the team leader. But according to others, Richard DiMarchi did indeed lead the team. A protein chemist, DiMarchi did his postdoctoral work in peptide synthesis at Rockefeller University prior to joining Lilly in 1981. At Rockefeller, he had the good fortune to work under Bruce Merrifield, the future 1984 Nobel Laureate in chemistry. "What attracted me to Lilly," DiMarchi says, "was the opportunity to use the biosynthesis, recombinant DNA technology to make better medicines. I wanted to use the technology to make better hormones—ones that didn't exist in nature. This was controversial, since it was generally believed that one could not improve on the sequence found in nature."

Initially, DiMarchi cut his eyeteeth at Lilly working on Humulin.

"When we started our work on LY275585, the molecule that is now called Humalog," explains DiMarchi, "my colleagues and I were driven by the belief that we could build a better molecule because nature had optimized the sequence for physiology. I emphasize that the way the hormone is delivered in a normal individual differs from the way it is used by a patient with diabetes, which is pharmacology. We had finished the biosynthesis and the registration of native human insulin, Humulin, and we set our sights on making something that was superior to what exists in nature. Our ambition was to develop rapid-acting insulin. Of course we had some hints from previous discoveries. We knew about the two chains of insulin referred to as A Chain and B Chain. We also understood that, on the end of the B Chain, one insulin molecule comes up against another and together dimers, a complex of molecules, form inside cells. Then when dimers aggregate around zinc, they form a so-called hexameter."

Ronald Chance explains further that when Humulin was injected after a meal, it worked much like the pancreatic insulin. But since Humulin's action was prolonged, it could do more than was desired. Diagramming on a blackboard, the chemist explained: "When these two units of insulin come together to form a dimer, and when this solution is added, it takes the form of a hexameter. Once it's injected, it has to dissociate back to a dimer to a monomer. As a hexameter and having become a higher molecule form, it interfered with the speed of action. This happened because, being six times as large, it takes more time to diffuse from the site where it was administered (i.e., an injection in the thigh or stomach). Previously we were restricted, but now we can make the gene we want and we can modify that molecule to do what we want it to do. This is when we started thinking about ways to improve on nature."

In 1985, Richard DiMarchi, Ronald Chance, and a handful of other Lilly people attended a conference in Monaco held by the Juvenile Diabetes Federation International, an organization dedicated to finding ways to improve the lives of juvenile diabetics, and perhaps thinking ahead to the day when there would be a cure. By this time, Humulin had already been approved for three years. The conference had a major impact on Chance's life. As he explains, "What really got my attention was a statement I heard from a study group at the conference. It made such an impression on me that I quote it verbatim: 'The need for a physiologic mimic improved absorption of insulins or new insulins are required to mimic more accurately the physiologic insulin profile. Modern Americans want an insulin derivative to be tested.' That was the main recommendation of the study group.

"Based on the findings of that study, some of us at Lilly believed we should be making an insulin to be taken at mealtime—something that works right now. When a diabetic eats, he or she gets results. Normally, a diabetic would have to take insulin about an hour ahead of eating. It had to be coordinated with meals. In the real world, it's difficult for people to do that. Many times they don't even know how much they are going to eat, or for that matter, when. Things happen. A meeting runs overtime, there's a delay at a railroad crossing, and so on. So the ideal would be for a diabetic to administer insulin just before a meal. Or for that matter, just after a meal. There's a need not only for quick-acting insulin, but for long-lasting insulin, so one need not wake up in the middle of the night with cold sweats and a hypoglycemic reaction because his or her insulin was peaking. One might not have a chance to eat during the night to knock it down. Of course their spouse would know what was happening because they'd be all wet and clammy."

Ron Chance was chairman of the company's insulin research committee, which also included Richard DiMarchi, Bruce Frank, and Jim Shields. There were other members too, all of whom had previously worked on the development of Humulin. The committee recommended that management pursue production on an improved insulin that would also be an improvement over nature's insulin. The challenge for the scientists was to change only what they wanted changed—the time of action and its potency.

The DNA makeup of Humulin was known to the Lilly research team. They discovered that by slightly altering the sequence of insulin, they would have an insulin that worked in a different manner than the original insulin. The amino acid sequence is what makes all proteins unique. The new molecule resembled insulin growth factor (IGF-1), a protein that is produced naturally in the body. This difficult, complicated process took two years to accomplish. Once the new insulin was in the bloodstream it would break down more quickly, allowing for improved efficiency of the insulin. This insulin could be given safely within minutes of mealtime for optimal control of the diabetic's sugar level.

Sometime in 1986, Lilly scientists Chance, DiMarchi, Frank, and Shields were having one of their many informal get-togethers in a conference room at Lilly in Indianapolis. Each man in the room had his own specialty; their combined knowledge on diabetes was vast. Chance was a biochemist with years of experience in insulin chemistry. DiMarchi was an expert in the area of synthetic chemistry, experienced in physical chemistry. Frank had worked for years at Lilly studying insulin aggregation. And Shields was a peptide chemist with a long history of working on insulins. Shields would do the physical modeling of insulin, which meant he would draw pictures of what molecules might constitute a better insulin. That would enable the others to make the desired molecules and to test hypotheses. Frank would recall later, "There we were, putting pieces of information on the table. Ron knew how to take a chunk of peptide and put it back on insulin after a portion of the molecule had been removed from the insulin. Jim could diagram models. And I could do the physical characterization to determine if a molecule made by Ron was different from insulin itself. We were looking at data that told us that a particular molecule made in Ron's lab was monomeric when we compared it to insulin. However, it wasn't aggregating the way insulin does. So we said, 'Okay, we got one molecule, and what else can we put in there? How can we change that structure in that area? Do we really have the optimum molecule, and is it optimal in the sense of chemistry, biology, and toxicology?' Our assignment was to bring these factors together as quickly as possible."

"Insulin that the body produces is a miraculous substance but an imperfect drug," DiMarchi explains. "Nature designed this molecule to be produced and released from the pancreas when it's needed. Insulin is a molecule that binds to another molecule and this way it is stored in the pancreas. The pancreas keeps the molecule in an inactive form until it is needed. IGF-1 is a very similar protein that exists in nature. We made the observation that it doesn't self-associate. It doesn't stick to itself. So we concluded that this was our challenge—to make insulin in the lab that didn't self-associate. That's because when insulin is used as a drug, it's used under very different conditions. Nature did not design insulin to be carried around in a vial or sucked up in a syringe and injected into the arm, thigh, or stomach. Those were not the conditions under which nature designed it to work. We, as scientists, set out to make something that would do just that. Our challenge was to make something that changed its physical properties without changing its biological properties.

"I hypothesized that we could do the same thing by inverting the order in insulin. In the case of IFG-1, there is another protein that binds to it and carries it in an inactive form. And since IFG-1 has to bind to this carrier protein, you would never want it binding to itself. That would interfere with binding to the carrier protein. So while the proteins are very similar, by sequence and by structure, how they work in the body is completely different. We took the time action of one molecule and married it closer to the biological activity of another."

Working with DiMarchi's hypothesis, Jim Shields, the team's expert in computer graphics, began the laborious task of translating physical interpretations of analogs and model insulin into images on the screen. Supercomputer technology was used to make calculations that Ron Chance would use in the lab. After months of work, Chance conceived of a way to invert the natural sequence in human insulin. Chemically, he took two amino acids that occur naturally in the molecule and inverted their sequence. Now, instead of having ABCD, as the last four amino acids, the order was ACBD. This changes the properties of the molecule so that it is absorbed more rapidly.

Insulin lispro is the generic name of this short-acting insulin. Compared with regular human insulin, the objective of this insulin analog was to have faster subcutaneous absorption, an earlier and greater insulin peak, and a shorter duration of action. "We actually removed a part of a molecule from human insulin," Chance explains, "and replaced it with part of a synthetic molecule that had the sequence we sought. Using chemical procedures, we were able to make a synthetic peptide. In January 1988, when we condensed it with this other molecule, my lab had actually made a grand total of three milligrams. At this stage, we were just experimenting to see if we could get the right biology because we knew it would take some time to perfect it. By March, we had made forty-one milligrams of the new insulin—that's not very much material. Next we did chain combinations. We had an A chain (a human chain) and we made a whole B chain. We synthesized a whole B chain containing the lispro and condensed both chains to form the molecule. The result wasn't good enough, but it was good enough to get some material to work with."

By October 1988, Chance's lab had made 796 milligrams of the new insulin. That was enough for testing purposes, allowing the team to determine how it would behave biologically. Now it was Bruce Frank's turn to do his thing. "In basic research, concepts are created," Frank points out. "As I would always say to my guys in discovery research, 'You haven't found a drug, you've found a chemical.' The people in development are the ones who are going to turn it into a drug." Frank would test the lispro from Chance's laboratory in order to demonstrate that it was not aggregating and therefore would be quick acting. Toxicology tests would be made using small animals such as rats and guinea pigs. These were the first of many tests to be made over a period of time to assure the safety of a new medicine.

On a wall in Chance's office is a photograph that he points to with obvious pride. "The guy on the end is Andy Anderson, and standing next to him [are] Richard DiMarchi, me, and Bruce Frank," he says enthusiastically. "The company designated the four of us [to] receive the American Chemical Society Teamwork Innovation Award on Lilly's behalf. You know, we started as a small team, but at the end, when you take into account all the people involved in the clinical tests, there were more than five thousand people involved." Chance pauses for a moment and grins at a photo that shows a turtle sitting on a fence. He smiles when he says, "I appreciate this one because I grew up on a farm. You see that turtle there? Well, you know he didn't get there by himself."

PRESENTING TO THE LILLY REVIEW BOARD

January 25, 1989 was a big day for the Lilly scientists who had been working on the new insulin, lispro. The time had come for them to make a formal presentation to a review board to seek approval for the resources they would need to do large-scale work on the discovery that they believed would someday serve diabetics as an improved insulin. If approved, Lilly's stakes would be significantly increased, running into the hundreds of millions of dollars it would take to get a new drug to the marketplace. So far lispro was in the research stage, where the costs pale in comparison to the huge amounts of money spent in development. In research, a relatively small number of employees, perhaps a handful, are at work in a laboratory. In development, the expenses skyrocket, because now large sums of money are spent on running extensive clinical tests, filing FDA applications, setting up manufacturing facilities, and purchasing large quantities of chemical supplies and other miscellaneous costly endeavors. Thousands of people will now become involved. Management must carefully evaluate all of the relevant facts about a potential drug before granting its approval to move forward.

Prior to the meeting, a briefing book had been distributed to the review members. They would do their homework in advance and come prepared to ask questions—and to challenge the research team on why the company should invest hundreds of millions of dollars on a new insulin.

As committee chairman, Ron Chance was the key speaker. He would address an audience of thirty Lilly people from various levels of management, including senior executives, scientists, the head of the clinical group, and so on. With two years of their blood and sweat invested in this project, the members of the research team had diligently done their homework. "I spent my Christmas vacation assembling data and drafting a lengthy document that I circulated to the other members of the team," Chance recalls. "We wanted to be well prepared, to make sure we came with all our facts and had anticipated all questions that might be thrown at us."

The team members had no way of knowing how they would fare. They were all aware that other well-prepared teams made presentations only to be turned down by a board review. Some of the team members had personally experienced rejection at previous review boards. A source of additional anxiety was the fact that Richard DiMarchi would not present. He was with his wife, who was about to give birth to a baby girl. DiMarchi was an articulate, persuasive speaker, viewed by management as someone who really understood diabetes. DiMarchi also knew how to communicate his research knowledge up the corporate ladder. He would be an ideal spokesman for any group of scientists. Chance, of course, was a brilliant scientist, but did not have DiMarchi's charisma or speaking ability. Without the presence of their team leader, there was indeed cause for apprehension.

There were many reasons why the lispro project might be canned by the review board. From a strictly business standpoint, Humulin was a hugely successful insulin and already in Lilly's portfolio of drugs. In addition, it is expensive to make insulin, and it must be kept affordable. Would it be a good business decision to make a sizable investment in another insulin when the current one was enjoying brisk sales? Another consideration was what other competitors were doing. Did another drug company have a similar product that would make it to market before Lilly's? The marketing executives present would certainly want facts about how a new drug would fare against the competition.

The biggest obstacle that the team faced was human nature's resistance to change. The discoverers of the new drug were claiming to have made a molecule that was an improvement on nature. To some, this was heresy. How dare scientists suggest that they can make something better than what existed in nature! As DiMarchi would later say, "I assure you that what we did was quite controversial at the start, because most people begin with an assumption that nature knows best. To those in this school of thought, trying to change the sequence was dangerous. And it was this very change of sequence that made lispro work."

Another major hurdle facing the team was convincing management that the newly invented molecule could be produced in large quantities. After all, it is one thing to make 796 milligrams in the laboratory, but quite another to mass produce it in vast quantities.

The presentation was a question-and-answer session. What ultimately sold the review board was the promise of what the proposed drug would do for diabetics. The cold fact was presented that an insulin lispro molecule is absorbed four hundred times more rapidly; when injected it behaves like natural insulin. It reaches peak activity in twenty to thirty minutes, meaning that it matches the absorption that is eaten at a meal. The patient could inject this insulin just before he ate. "This is a tremendously convenient feature," the board was told. "It means that the patient can be much more compliant. It's also safer because if you were a typical patient who didn't want to take your insulin injection in your office before you left for lunch, worried that you might get tied up in traffic, or have another delay due to poor service at the restaurant, then this was the insulin for you. As you know, when you take insulin and there is a delay before eating, you have a risk of hypoglycemia. What we are proposing is an insulin that you can take just before the food arrives, with good results. This drug is designed to heighten the quality of life of the patient, which will result in better treatment."

The tone of the meeting was later described as sober, with one brief moment of levity. Bruce Frank had just delivered a twenty-minute dissertation when Bill Lacefield, a review board member and highly respected organic chemist, raised his hand to speak. A former coworker and close friend of Frank, Lacefield said, "Well, this has been a very interesting presentation. And I think it would be fun to see whether Bruce's physical chemistry is worth a damn, so to find out, I am going to vote in favor of it." His words would later appear verbatim in the minutes of the meeting.

"That was Bill's way of letting me know that he was supporting the project, and it also served as an icebreaker in a tense meeting," Frank says.

The meeting lasted for two hours. When it was over, there was no doubt that the proposed drug was a better product than any existing insulin. In a nutshell, its main features were that it gave the diabetic better control, making it safer and more convenient. These advantages prompted the review board to give its consent for lispro to move forward to development.

TRANSITIONING FROM RESEARCH TO DEVELOPMENT

For most of his career at Lilly, Bruce Frank had worked in research, so it came as a surprise to him when he was asked by management to work as research adviser in lispro's development. The promotion was necessary to fill a void; a scientist with a strong background in the biotechnology-protein area was needed to head a group in the development and formulation of existing as well as new protein products. Frank was a perfect candidate for the job. From time to time he had served as a troubleshooter around the world, visiting Lilly plants when there was a technical problem that could not be solved internally. Brilliant and experienced, Bruce Frank was considered the man to whom other scientists and plant managers turned when something went wrong and needed fixing. "I like it when someone says to me, 'Something here is wrong, and I don't have any idea how to fix it.' " Frank explains. "I thrive on such a challenge. I feel that I have enough basic knowledge about the behavior of this insulin molecule that if you tell me you're seeing a problem, I know the kinds of insults [things that are mishandled] that will make that happen. So, I was sent to solve problems."

As research adviser, one of Frank's responsibilities would be to serve as coordinator between the research and the development staffs. "In the laboratory, you can get from A to B by taking X path. In a manufacturing environment, however, X path may be impractical. For instance, it could be too expensive or it could be that the time frame is wrong. You're going to run a reaction at 4 degrees centigrade. Well, that requires cooling that is expensive and difficult to achieve on a uniform basis. It may be easy to do in a 50-milliliter beaker, but if you have to run processes in entire cold rooms, you're talking about an expensive facility. So the development scientist is faced with taking the initial finding and turning it into something practical."

Frank would know how to make things happen when lispro moved into development, so when the position was offered he didn't hesitate to accept. "I was thrilled," he says, "because this was my child and I could go right along with it. When I moved over in the development side, I started with a small group consisting of five Ph.D.s and a handful of their associates. Once in development, we're now saying, 'Okay, we have a chemical entity here. We need to get it ready for the clinical tests.' This also includes filing the investigational drug application [IDA] and the new drug application [NDA]. Once we assembled all of our data, the first step was to apply for permission with the FDA to use the drug on humans."

A project management team was formed consisting of clinicians, toxicologists, biologists, chemists, an expert who would work on producing a bulk drug, marketing people, and still others. "It was a little business within the company," Frank states. "Our first job was to get the compound out to the clinic."

Prior to testing lispro on humans, animal studies were made, primarily on pigs. "To get into the clinic," Frank explains, "you first have to do toxicology studies. You've got to do formulation studies. You've got to do stability studies. You've got to do metabolism studies. The results of all these studies must be included in the package that goes to the FDA that in effect says, 'We believe that you ought to allow us to do these safety studies in humans.' "

THE CLINICAL TRIALS

In 1990 the first Phase I clinical trial was conducted at the Lilly Clinic in Indianapolis by Daniel Howey M.D. Eight nondiabetic patients received injections of lispro. This served as a demonstration of principle to show the effects of rapid-onset lispro taken by humans. The rate of absorption, peak level, and efficacy of the new insulin received high marks. The study showed that the compound had the potential to do everything that the researchers expected of lispro, the better-than-nature insulin. Based on these results, the decision was made to develop the Phase II and Phase III clinical trials.

"Once management gave its approval to develop a clinical plan and the funding to do it," Jim Anderson explains, "we moved swiftly. The key players—everyone from medical people to regulatory people—convened at a downtown Indianapolis hotel away from Lilly's Corporate Center. There they would establish a game plan. We accomplished a great deal at this one-day meeting, including putting together a timeline stating when we would have our clinical trial material and how long the actual trials would take. We designed the entire Phase II and Phase III clinical trials, and even earmarked a plan that took us all the way to registration with a predicted date when we'd file the new drug application with the FDA. And for the first time ever, we were going to conduct clinical tests simultaneously in all markets where we'd sell the insulin, versus the traditional way, one country at a time. As far as I know this was a first in the industry.

"There were several good reasons why we did this. First, given the different cultures of countries around the world, eating habits vary. Consequently, insulin injections vary from country to country. Americans generally eat three daily meals, but that is not practiced universally. The Italians and the French don't eat breakfast, and in Germany they have an early breakfast and a midmorning breakfast. Then there is the issue in countries where Ramadan is observed and requires Muslims to fast during the daytime and eat at night for thirty consecutive days. And in some countries, notably Japan and India, diabetics didn't inject themselves with insulin; they got shots at doctors' offices each morning and each evening."

"We invited all of our people outside the U.S. who would be involved with the clinical trials to participate in the initial stages," Anderson continues, "so they'd take ownership. We let it be known that we welcomed their feedback. We informed them that there would be an eight-week enrollment for patients to sign up for the studies during the months of July and August. There were some protests from Italy and France because those are the two months of the year when they take their vacations. Since we gave them months of advance notice to line up physicians and patients, we actually ended up with 103 percent enrollment. Jeff Baker, the man with the job of making the insulin in large volumes, also attended the meeting. 'Yes,' Jeff committed, 'we can get the product made and put into vials by that time.' " As it would later turn out, this was a very big commitment.

Another reason Lilly conducted clinical trials in and outside the United States simultaneously was the fact that insulin was a drug that was used around the world, so lispro would be sold everywhere. It was also a matter of getting a jump on the competition. Two Danish companies, Novo and Nordisk, were in the race to come out with a fast-acting insulin. (Novo and Nordisk merged in 1989 to become Novo Nordisk.) Novo had started production of human insulin using genetic engineering in 1987, and it was generally believed that its product was likely to get FDA approval before Lilly's.

The project management team was off to a good start. To keep the momentum going, they decided to move off Lilly's sprawling world headquarters campus to a nearby office building in downtown Indianapolis. "Our main campus has seventy-plus buildings and the thirty of us were scattered all over," Anderson says, "so we relocated to where we could work more efficiently, all under one roof. This promoted open communication. It was a slight problem having our people abroad in different time zones; just the same, we made a concentrated effort to be in constant communication with them. For instance, if somebody was running clinical tests and solved a common problem, it would be passed on to the others. As an extra bonus, we discovered that we were able to accomplish a lot more away from the corporate environment."

To coordinate the clinical tests, Dr. Milton Perelman, who at the time was president of Lilly Research Laboratories, made periodic visits to the company's affiliates around the world, addressing questions and keeping everyone abreast of the latest developments. This served as a strong morale booster.

Jim Anderson was in charge of running the Phase II and Phase III clinicals, a monumental undertaking considering that it would be coordinated with clinical tests conducted around the world. He had prior experience working on large-scale operations during his military career, when he was stationed at Fort Dietrich, an infectious disease center. While in the service, he was responsible for thirty-five vaccines developed specifically for the armed forces, each under FDA rules and guidelines.

In comparison to Humulin, which received rapid approval due to the potential shortage of insulin in 1982, lispro would require more clinical tests. Generally drugs that are improvements over existing ones are slower in getting FDA approval, mainly because there is not an emergency to rush them through. Conversely, breakthrough drugs that promise to cure terminal illnesses are more likely to be put on the fast track. This meant that the clinical tests for lispro would have to unequivocally demonstrate its safety and efficacy. While Humulin had been tested on an estimated four hundred diabetics, Humalog was ultimately tested on more than four thousand diabetics.

The highest costs for a pharmaceutical company occur when a drug moves into a full-scale clinical trial. This was particularly true for a drug like lispro because it would be taken by a large population of people for a very long time. Being tested on more than four thousand diabetics was indeed a full-scale clinical trial.

While today studies are done under the authority of the European Inspection Union (Europe's version of the FDA), clinical tests for lispro were conducted in several European countries as well as Canada, Africa, Australia, and, of course, the United States. Participating physicians here and abroad had little trouble signing up their patients with diabetes. After all, lispro was so convenient to take. "You can take it just before the meal," patients were instructed, "and you don't have to figure out how much time you need *before* you eat like you do with your current insulin."

With other drugs administered in clinical trials, it often takes a while before a patient realizes any benefit. Within two hours it was clear that lispro worked better than the patient's current insulin. In a lispro clinical study in South Africa, patients were treated by their primary physicians on Saturday mornings. The patients were randomized; some were on placebos and others on lispro. On the second Saturday, when the patients were seated in the doctor's office, they began to talk among themselves. When the ones on lispro told about how convenient it had been for them, the patients on placebos also wanted it. When they were told they couldn't have it, they actually started to talk about suing Lilly so that they also could take the drug. "This was comforting to hear," Anderson grins, "because it was the first time I had ever heard about a lawsuit to *take* a drug rather than to protest its side effects. Fortunately we worked it out with the FDA and the South African regulatory agency to provide Humalog to these patients."

HARD TO MAKE IN LARGE QUANTITIES

A senior development scientist for lispro, Dr. Jeff Baker loved his job so much that he sometimes had to pinch himself to see if it wasn't just a dream. "Back in the 1970s when I was in undergraduate school at Northwestern," he tells, "I remember lying on the floor in my dormitory reading an article in *Time* about how Eli Lilly and Genentech were collaborating on this cloned insulin. I recall how all the undergraduate scientists were saying, 'Wow, that is so cool!' It seems like yesterday when I said to some of my fellow students, 'Yeah, this is cool, but the day will someday come when scientists can design proteins that have certain properties.' Then ten years later there I was. I would be working on it."

When asked to describe his job, he explains: "When the company identifies a promising drug candidate, a discovery scientist says, 'Here's something that will help you run faster, jump higher, live longer, and increase the quality of life for you and your heirs.' Next the company makes an important decision on whether to take it forward to the clinical trials. Due to the high costs and the low success rate, a company can make the wrong decision now and then, but not too often. Like I said, it's an important decision.

"As a development scientist, it was my job to look at the discovery science that had a very good way to make small amounts of lispro. But now the question becomes, 'How are we going to make this in a commercial setting, both in terms of quantity and quality? We also have a slew of engineering considerations and economic issues. Our process development group must determine how we are going to make the drug in a commercial setting. Ron Chance had been working with a test tube in his lab, but in manufacturing we can't have a factory that has ten million test tubes. Our job is to produce lispro in three thousand-liter tanks. Obviously it is not a direct translation."

To illustrate his point, Baker uses an analogy of a woman cooking Thanksgiving dinner for her family of five. "Now if you ever cooked for five, you know that if you had to prepare a Thanksgiving meal for thirty people, the dynamics are quite different. And imagine if you had to prepare a wedding meal for three hundred guests. Now expand that to a stadium filled with one hundred thousand people. Obviously, you'd have to do things quite differently than if you were cooking for your family of five. This is what we face when we have to make a medicine for large numbers of people versus what the chemists make in the lab. It's a whole new ball game.

"We start making our materials in a pilot plant, where, using our lab process, we make it on a small scale—say, one tenth or less of the commercial scale. We start making grams of materials, whereas milligrams are made in the laboratory. Then we make hundreds of grams, and eventually kilos.

"We were trying to move very quickly, trying to get Humalog on the market. Now and then there was an unplanned equipment failure. Some errors that set us back days or weeks, and other times we were able to concoct a plan B on the fly. It's as if we were trying to build a ship while sailing on it.

"Something that looked like a really good idea in the lab failed when it was hundreds and thousands of times bigger. There are so many things that can go wrong. Remember that this had never been done before and our staff was learning while we were making it. Our plant's staff consisted of a diverse workforce ranging from scientists with technical degrees to operational people with high school diplomas. But if you want to know who I think the real heroes are—these guys on the floor get my vote. They are valued partners in the development of a truly manufacturable process. They are the eyes, ears, and hands of the development program on the floor.

"We were working 24/7," Baker continues, "and one morning I walked in and one of the operators was waiting outside my office. I was surprised to see him because he should have gone home, and seeing how upset he was, I knew something was wrong.

" 'I was adding acid to a solution,' he said in a barely audible voice, 'and I put in too much and we lost the lot. I couldn't go home without telling you in person, Jeff. I'm so sorry.'

"It was human error and that happens. Sure, I was upset about it, but I wasn't angry at him. I just gave him a tap on the arm and said, 'Look bud, don't worry about it. We'll pick it up next time.' We lost four weeks because of it, and with a hundred or so people working in the pilot plant, a setback of this nature costs a lot of money. While we try to prevent mistakes, mistakes happen, and some can be quite costly."

Frank adds: "In the manufacturing process during development, there are various steps along the way. Certain chemicals are added into the system that may require using new solvents, and specific types of chemical derivatives are formed due to reactions of the protein with added reagents. As a result, we had to develop tests to show removal of those reagents or that there was no reaction or only a minimal one that we could control. Later, as we got to our final product, there was a list of specifications to check off. For instance, we must identify what the amino acid composition is and show that we verified that it has biological activity. This and many more tests must be run and filed with the FDA. And every test must be approved. It can take months, and be very costly, to demonstrate that the material we make is fully representative of the final commercial product. We need to be able to say, 'Oh, I got the same results in my animal testing. And these are the results in my clinical reports.' When I make the actual material over here at the plant site, the data has to be valid. Everything has to be uniform so it's predictive."

Baker also emphasizes that there were special challenges in making Humalog because it is a nonnatural sequence protein. "It is made up of amino acids," he points out, "like beads on a string, and the beads are in different colors and come in different shapes. Insulin is always the same beads in the same order, and this is what gives it its properties. With lispro, we switched the order of two of those beads. This was a small, subtle change that gave very significant pharmacological results and, not surprisingly, a different set of issues in its preparation and purification than what we had seen before with insulin. Looking beyond diabetes, what's important here is that it was one of the first, if not the first, example of a protein engineered to have specific properties. Today there is a tendency to take biotechnology for granted, but at the time it was a real breakthrough. Our challenge was to make lispro for clinical testing as well as develop a process to make it commercially, meeting the needs of the business and the regulatory environment. This required an understanding of how these 'beads on a string' behaved in a number of situations, the expectations of the business and the regulators, and a fair amount of risk management.

"Humalog is made by a special non-disease-producing laboratory strain of Escherichia coli (E. coli) bacteria that has been genetically engineered. So instead of grinding tons and tons of pork and beef pancreases, which we did at Lilly for many years to make glandular insulin, we grow thousands of liters of bacteria in enormous tanks to make this protein.

"This is different from penicillin, which is a natural product. A bacterium makes penicillin, but no bacteria ever made insulin. The bacteria have very complex machinery for making complex molecules using their DNA as a blueprint. By engineering the DNA we give it different instructions on what to make. It's as if I'm putting a call to the bacteria factory floor and saying, 'Hey, instead of making widgets, we are going to make wudgets.' The bacteria are good at taking orders, so they reply, 'Okay boss, instead of making widgets we'll make wudgets.' Next the bacteria [are] off and running, and we can gleefully rub our hands together because we are able to take advantage of the incredibly sophisticated biomolecular machinery that nature has put into that bacteria. Assembling the lispro precursors is a synthesis that none of us could do in a test tube, yet a single bacteria cell can do it quite handily. All biochemists learn early in the game, 'Science is good, nature is better.' "

"After making bunches and bunches of this strange little molecule that they have no use for whatsoever, the bacteria 'take out the garbage' by putting the lispro precursors into little clots of protein called inclusion bodies," Baker continues. "We then isolate the inclusion bodies and proceed with the chemistries that convert the precursors that are in the inclusion bodies into the actual lispro molecule. This produces highly purified lispro crystals."

While the Chemical Manufacturing and Control Team geared up to manufacture Humalog, the clinical testing was in full swing. A supply of the new insulin was needed to run the Phase I and Phase II tests and would be taken daily by 4,000+ diabetics. Large quantities of Humalog were required. Baker recalls how his team received a request to make a substantial amount, and how he doubted it could be done in time. In particular, he was concerned that the installation of the necessary equipment would be a huge additional cost that typically wasn't spent during a pilot plan:

"I did my homework and had all my facts well organized," Baker tells, "and I marched into David Frankham's office. Frankham was a wonderful boss, and as usual, he was extremely patient and listened carefully to what I had to say. I gave him all the reasons why we couldn't possibly fulfill the request.

" 'You know, Jeff,' he said calmly, 'I'm not really interested in what you can't do. It doesn't interest me at all. I want to know what it's going to take to do this, and then I'll tell you if it's too expensive.'

"What a terrific lesson I learned, one that I've applied ever since throughout my career. After my meeting with Frankham, I told my group, 'Don't say what you can't do. I'm not interested in what you can't do. In fact, it's terribly uninteresting. What's it going to take to get it done? We can do anything. I know prices vary, and we will make smart choices on prices.' Then we reconfigured our pilot plan, and we did install new equipment, and indeed it turned out to be the largest investment in equipment that Lilly ever made during a pilot plan. Remember now, this was several years before FDA approval and actual paying customers."

Later on during the Phase II and Phase III clinical tests, the company made the decision to use the existing plant that manufactured Humulin to make Humalog. "We were on an aggressive timeline to get the product to the market," Baker explains. "As it turned out, it was a double-edged sword. It was a building that we knew, but it was also old and designed to run a different process, so we had to make compromises."

"Being a process development scientist requires the sort of person who loves seeing how all the puzzle pieces fit together. It's not a job for a specialist. For me, there is no greater joy than watching all the puzzle pieces fit together at the end," Baker asserts.

When working on a long-term project that takes years from start to finish, a good leader keeps his people focused on the big picture. Bruce Frank recalls an anecdote that illustrates this point. "A friend's son had gotten married in Buffalo, New York," Frank tells, "and something happened at the reception that I related to my group that Monday morning when I was back at work. I told them about a gentleman sitting at our table. Other tables had been served, but not ours. He seemed quite anxious and asked the waitress how soon our table would be served.

" 'I estimate in about fifteen minutes,' she told him.

"He took out a little insulin pen and injected himself, knowing that thirty minutes from now, his food would be in front of him. Well, thirty minutes comes and goes, and still no food. I could see the sweat on his face."

" 'Is there anything I can do for you?' I asked.

" 'See if you can get me some orange juice or something.'

"At that point they brought some food to the table and he quickly ate something, and we got him a glass of orange juice so he could get some sugar in his system quickly.

"[This] was an illustration of what happens when there is a time delay between the injection of insulin and the arrival of food. Do you see what diabetics face? It was right there at my table. You want to know why you are working on this drug? What we've seen in the clinic so far is that when they get their food, they can inject themselves right then. And it works perfectly. So this is why we're working on this, guys. This is what we're after. This is the real world. This is why you should feel good about what we're doing."

ASSURANCES

"What it boils down to," Jeff Baker emphasizes, "is not only a matter of satisfying the FDA; we have a responsibility to society that demands we do three things. One, the drug has to be safe. Two, it has to work. And three, we have to be able to make it the same way, over and over and over. This means we must generate data in our clinical trials that it is safe and it works. It's all about assurances."

He continues: "Right around the same time when we came out with the Humalog clinical trial results, I attended the International Diabetes Federation Congress in Japan. I was sitting at a bar drinking Japanese beer when a physician asked me, 'Do you know how to make Humalog?'

" 'You bet I do,' I told him.

" 'I bet you don't,' he said, 'and I will tell you. I pull out a pad of paper, and I write a prescription. I send it to a pharmacist. The patient gets Humalog. *The pad of paper makes Humalog!*'

"He wasn't being disrespectful—he was teaching me a very valuable lesson. I thought about what he said, and I realized that I can accept my role of being behind the scenes. To the consumer, it's that pad of paper that makes Humalog. The patient may be thinking that we've got this Humalog tree and we pluck medicine bottles from it. This is the beauty of the pharmaceutical system in the United States. The average Joe knows that if the FDA approved a drug, the doctor recommended it, and the local pharmacist hands it to him over the counter, then there is no reason to give the manufacturing process much thought. The consumer never thinks about the years of laboratory work that go into making a molecule, the clinical tests, the manufacturing processes. And the best part about it is that he doesn't have to."

After years of hard work coupled with ingenuity, a sophisticated plant equipped with state-of-the-art equipment was up and running. The total cost was hundreds of millions of dollars, a risky investment considering that Humalog had not yet been approved by the FDA, so not a drop of the new insulin had been sold. (Sometime in the future this Indianapolis plant would operate 24 hours a day, 365 days a year.)

Jeff Baker figured that he would finally be able to catch up with some well-deserved sleep. "We finally got it done," he tells, "and a few nights went by, and then the phone rang at midnight and woke me up out of a sound sleep.

" 'Dr. Baker?'

"I recognized the voice because I had received so many previous middle-of-the-night calls from the same lead operator at the plant. 'Yes, Nate, what's up?' I asked.

" 'Oh, nothing really. We've just called you every other night for the last few years, and we thought we'd call you tonight.'

" 'That's really thoughtful of you, Nate, but do you mind if I go back to sleep?'

"I laughed about it after I hung up the phone, because it always seemed that every time something went wrong, it was in the middle of the night or on a weekend. I'd ask myself, 'Why don't these things happen during the day? Would that be too much to ask from the gods?' I was so used to getting up at one and two in the morning, getting dressed, and going down to the plant that I had a hard time adjusting to a normal routine."

SEEKING WORLDWIDE APPROVALS

The Phase II and Phase III tests were nearing completion, and concurrently applications for approval were being submitted to the FDA and other governing agencies in other countries around the globe. Like the other pieces of the puzzle that had to be finalized, this too was a complex undertaking that had to be executed with professionalism and precision. Cathy Lawrence, the company's medical writer, was responsible for coordinating writing the application submissions. She also worked with the other members of her team to communicate information to physicians who would ultimately prescribe Humalog for their patients. Lawrence was a pharmacist, and after completing various internships in pharmacy school, she had worked for three years at Merck prior to joining Lilly in 1992. The first of many filings began in 1993: "When I came aboard, I became one of six medical writers for the company," she says. "I was the only one who didn't have a writing background. Nobody knew better than the scientists and physicians what they wanted to write, so my job was to articulate their thoughts on paper. I had to make sure their facts and figures were accurate; misinformation and inconsistencies were unacceptable.

"While I wrote everything in English, translators were hired in the European Union and in Russia. Because we were running global trials, we had to factor in different diets and eating habits in different countries. We also had to give specific instructions within the trial at different religious observance times. Here I am mainly referring to Muslims who fast daytimes for thirty days during Ramadan."

In 1996 approval was granted in all countries where Lilly applied to sell Humalog, and the marketing campaign for the new drug was launched.

THE IMPORTANCE OF BEING AN INFORMED PATIENT

During the early stages of diabetes, there are often few symptoms or warning signs. In this respect diabetes is similar to a handful of other chronic asymptomatic conditions such as hypertension and high cholesterol. Unfortunately, when a diabetic develops blindness, kidney disease, or other related conditions, the damage has already occurred. So there are good reasons why people must be informed about diabetes before it's too late.

It is mandatory for a person with diabetes to be an active participant in his or her treatment. One can't go to a physician and say, "Here's my body. You fix it." There are too many judgment calls that a diabetic must make. Certain decisions can fluctuate on a daily basis depending upon one's activities, and then it is necessary to determine how much insulin to take and when. The amount will vary based on diet and exercise. A person with a normal functioning pancreas utilizes 35 to 50 units of insulin a day. A type 1 diabetic whose pancreas doesn't produce any insulin may require an injection of 35 to 50 units. An obese person with type 2 diabetes may require 60 or more units a day. Staying well depends on taking injections at the right time and doing premeal and postmeal blood testing.

There are no definitive answers for what's required because there are different levels of diabetes. While Lilly made Humalog to provide diabetics with a more convenient lifestyle, all diabetics must be knowledgeable about the disease. With or without Humalog, an informed diabetic knows that nibbling on candy or eating some bread or having a drink with sugar can get him through the timing of his peak. He knows that thirty to forty-five minutes after his injection his system requires carbohydrates. He also knows his body takes less time for sugar to digest a candy bar (five to ten minutes) than a loaf of bread (thirty minutes) or a steak (forty-five minutes to an hour). Since the introduction of blood glucose monitoring, a diabetic can measure his sugar level.

The proper treatment of diabetes requires a diabetic be properly educated and be an active participant in his treatment. Good health care goes beyond simply injecting insulin. A diabetic must be aware that if one's blood glucose drops too low, it stimulates the release of sugar reserves in one's fat cells or liver. This condition, known as hypoglycemia, causes many symptoms and can be life-threatening.

Larry Ellingson was a young pharmacist back in 1971 when he joined Eli Lilly as a sales representative. "Having the right education was a requirement in those days," Ellingson says, "and about 95 percent of the drug salespeople graduated from pharmacy school. I had worked for a brief time at a hospital, and when I started here, I was given a sales territory in Fargo, South Dakota. Two years later, I was transferred back to Indianapolis as a marketing associate."

Ellingson, who had spent his entire career at Lilly in marketing, made a major move in 1986. "This is when Wally Lang, vice president of marketing and my mentor, asked me to run the diabetes business for Lilly. To do it right, I knew, meant a lot more than bringing a molecule to the marketplace. 'I'll do it Wally,' I said, 'but I want to stay in it. I don't ever want to leave the job.' When he asked me why, I answered, 'Customers don't like it when we change people. When customers want to talk to someone, they'll know they can talk to Larry Ellingson because I'm managing diabetes at Lilly. So if you want me in this position, Wally, don't ever promote me. By staying here I feel I can make a difference.' Starting on my first day at my new position, I took all calls from everyone— doctors, nurses, dieticians, and, yes, patients. And I returned calls to every patient who called me.

"This is what builds trust in a company. It's about building relationships with people, and it's especially critical with a chronic disease. The disease doesn't go away in six weeks or six months, and I wanted them to know that I wouldn't either."

To Larry Ellingson, being in the diabetes field isn't just about manufacturing a drug, it's a way of life. Like other company employees, he takes very seriously what Eli Lilly, grandson of the company's founder, once said: "Insulin is the elixir of life." "We're not just treating people with medication," Ellingson stresses. "We're also helping them to change their behavior by learning better ways to take care of themselves. We're creating a way of health care and monitoring, not just for the patient but the entire family. As they say in Africa, 'It takes a village to raise a child.' It takes a village to raise a patient with diabetes."

In his new role, Ellingson immediately established a relationship with the American Association of Diabetes Educators (AADE), an organization founded in 1975. "When I was first introduced to this group in 1986, there were 21 chapters and 1,200 members. What really caught my interest was that the organization was developing a national certification examination. Doctors, pharmacists, nurses, dieticians, and physiologists would receive appropriate training in order to become certified diabetes educators. Doctors, mainly family practice physicians, would then refer patients to these qualified individuals. A certified diabetes educator teaches patients such things as nutrition, exercise, insulin, how and when to take injections, and how to use devices to monitor sugar. It's generally one-on-one training, and there are group sessions for family members. Lilly worked with the AADE to train these educators to be effective in their communities; this helped their network grow. Today these diabetes educators number about 14,000 across the country."

The role of the certified diabetes educator is crucial in the treatment of diabetes. Studies have shown that when people are first diagnosed, they have little or no understanding of the disease. Interviews conducted with diabetics have confirmed that no matter what they have heard in the doctor's office or a pharmacy, patients rarely got the facts right. Often they would be unclear on the correct dosage, or when and how they should inject themselves. As head of the company's diabetes program, Ellingson clearly understood how the welfare of the patient and the success of Humalog depended on teaching diabetics what they needed to know.

"When Humalog was introduced," he explains, "our sales reps had the names of the certified diabetes educators in their areas. Typically, an educator works one-on-one with a diabetic for forty-five minutes to an hour, giving six to ten lessons over a period of four to six weeks. For the record, with all its merits, Humalog was not an overnight success. People had to learn how it worked and how to use it. Back in 1996, 75 percent of the insulin used in the world was what we considered long-acting or mixture insulin. Diabetics would take regular insulin, NPH insulin, or a mixture of the two. With the mixture, the patient could get himself down to taking two good doses during the day rather than taking only the regular that would peak within one to two hours. Remember now, NPH peaked in six to eight hours. This meant that the patient gave himself a shot of a mixture of regular and NPH thirty-five to forty minutes before meals, and that dose would cover him for his mealtime and most of the entire afternoon, and if necessary, he'd eat a snack to avoid hypoglycemia. Then before going to bed at night he'd take a shot of NPH.

"[Adjusting to Humalog took] some getting used to. If they took Humalog that way, they would have hypoglycemic reactions because the drug would have acted long before food was ingested. So we changed the paradigm. The drug would be taken after a meal. The FDA said, however, that we couldn't promote it this way until we did studies showing that it worked safely when taken after meals. We did studies and were able to demonstrate that the results were the same before and after a meal. There was an added convenience about taking it after the meal, because then people would know what and how much they ate, and about how much sugar there was. And they could adjust their insulin dose accordingly."

There is a story about two clinical investigators in Germany who wondered how Humalog would work after a severe meal challenge. They concocted a special diet consisting of pizza, tiramisu, and regular Coca-Cola that was served to two groups of patients, one on regular insulin and the other on Humalog. The regular insulin took a long time to have an effect; the Humalog took care of the glucose immediately. The story of these results has become legendary and is repeated to groups of diabetics again and again to illustrate how Humalog works.

Communicating these kinds of results to diabetics helps to convince them to change how they take insulin, especially those who have been longtime users of a particular insulin. Ellingson tells a story about identical twin sisters from Goshen, Indiana, who had taken Lilly's regular insulin for more than fifty years. "I had lunch with them," he says, "and each sister said she had taken four shots a day for all those years and never had any complications. They were doing very well. I had to convince them that they could now take Humalog so it would be easier for them to have their tea and Cola-Cola and then take their shot and adjust the insulin dosage accordingly. They were elated and they made the change. This is what it took to get people to change—it was a matter of sitting around tables with patients and having everyone talk about their experiences. Then after a meal, they'd take out their insulin pens and they'd all give themselves an injection. It was something they had never done before."

It was only a matter of time before Lilly was marketing a combination product of Humalog that also contained protamine. This mix allows a diabetic to have quick-acting insulin coverage at mealtime as well as long-acting insulin coverage between meals and throughout the night. "Diabetics who are loyal to a particular kind of insulin," Ellingson points out, "that started on Humalog are going to work with Humalog and Humalog 75/25 mix rather than getting involved with mixing Humalog with a longer-acting insulin of some other brand."

In addition to his long association with AADE, Ellingson served as a board member of the local American Diabetes Association in Indianapolis for many years. Later he became a member of the ADA's national board of directors and served for three years as its fund-raising committee's board chairman. In 2002, he was elected chairman of ADA, and, to fulfill this time-consuming position, took an early retirement from Lilly. Why does Ellingson have so much passion for his work in the field of diabetes?

"Having diabetes used to be an automatic death sentence," he explains, "but today, it's not about death. The real message is that it's about hope. If you have diabetes, and you pay attention to what your doctor and your health-care team are saying, you can live a full, rich life."

Nicole Johnson Baker is living proof that a person with diabetes can live a full, rich life. Crowned Miss America 1999, today Baker continues to travel across the United States and around the globe encouraging other diabetics to dare to reach for the stars. Her message is direct and inspiring: "Don't limit yourself," she tells her audiences. "If I can do it, you can too."

Baker didn't always think this way. In 1993, while attending the University of South Florida, the vivacious sophomore was the picture of good health when she fell ill during one of the preliminaries of a Miss Florida contest conducted in Sarasota. Rushed to a local hospital, a series of tests were conducted. Her initial diagnosis ranged from anemia to Beijing flu. It was even suggested that she had appendicitis. Following more extensive blood work, it was determined that she had type 1 diabetes. Her blood glucose levels were over 500.

"Nobody in my family ever had diabetes," the attractive brunette says, "and at the time, I knew nothing about the disease. The only thing I knew was that I shouldn't eat sugar or dessert." Baker quickly learned the serious nature of diabetes when her doctor informed her in no uncertain terms of her dismal future.

"You can no longer compete in pageants," she says he insisted. "Furthermore, you will never be able to have children. Nor should you continue to pursue a career in journalism. As a diabetic, it would be too strenuous. In fact, I recommend that you discontinue college altogether. In your condition, it will be too difficult."

"Suddenly my entire future had been taken away from me," Baker says. "Ever since I could remember, I wanted to be a journalist and raise a family. Just like all little girls have dreams, those were mine. Besides, I competed in beauty pageants so I could earn the scholarship money necessary for my college education. Now my doctor was telling me that all of the above were no longer options. I was devastated."

On the doctor's recommendation, Baker dropped out of school and moved in with her parents in Seminole, Florida, a small town of ten thousand residents west of St. Petersburg. Five months later, she reluctantly entered the Miss Seminole Pageant, competing against twenty contestants. The scoring of the contest was based on talent (30 percent), and how well a contestant did during an extensive interview with a panel of judges (30 percent)—simply being beautiful wasn't enough. Baker was crowned Miss Seminole, making her eligible to compete in the Miss Florida competition. It was her first-ever pageant crown, and it did wonders for her self-confidence. "I realized that I *could* do something that the medical people said I could never achieve," she explains. "It made me think that perhaps I could do the other things that I was told were also off-limits."

Shortly afterward, Baker went back to college. She didn't win the Miss Florida contest, but she did continue to participate in pageants while attending the Universty of South Florida. Following her graduation, she enrolled in Regent University in Virginia Beach, Virginia, where she went on to earn a master's degree in journalism, still competing in pageants. In 1997, on an early Saturday morning of the finals of a pageant, Baker collapsed in her hotel bedroom, nearly slipping into a diabetic coma. Her mother, who had accompanied her, called 911. When paramedics carried her through the lobby on a stretcher, the cat was let out of the bag! "Until this episode, I never let people know about my diabetes," she explains, "I was afraid that people would have prejudices and it would ruin my chances of winning. And, in fact, that night I was told by one of the officials that I should no longer compete because I had diabetes.

"Humalog had just become available. A few weeks later I went off regular insulin and started taking Humalog. At this time, I decided that I was no longer going to hide the fact that I had diabetes and I would use an insulin pump. It's been incredible for me and [I now have] what I consider the closest thing to a normal working pancreas."

The pump is about the size of a pager and has a little rubber tube that is attached to a canaula, which is a needle about a half-inch long and put at an insertion site, which in Baker's case is her abdomen or hip. It is secured by medical tape. Every three days she rotates its location. The pump releases insulin like an IV drip, but it's not in the vein.

The pump is small enough to attach to an article of clothing such as a belt or a boot, or can be placed in a pocket. Depending on the outfit she wears, Baker sometimes straps it on her bra. "I've had the pump for nearly ten years," she says, "and I prefer it to insulin injections. I adjust the amount of Humalog I take depending on my activities and food intake. I feel it's more predictable, because now instead of combining insulins, I only use one form. It has different rates that automatically drip into my system at various times of the day. I count the carbohydrates I eat in order to determine the amount of insulin I take. I no longer have to eat lunch at a specific time, say for example at 12:00 sharp regardless what I am doing, no matter if I am hungry or not. Previously, if I didn't take my shot, my blood sugar was going to be high, and if I didn't eat, the insulin from the shot was going to drop me. In addition, that insulin would stay in my system for four to five hours, and by the time 6:00 P.M. rolled around, I had to test my blood sugar and had to eat no matter what was going on. Humalog has been a godsend to me. I realized, 'Yes, I can be a journalist. I can cover a story, do my research, write it, and then at 2:00 I can have my lunch.' Likewise, I can have dinner at 8, if that's what works in my schedule."

Once Baker made the decision that she would "come out" and reveal her diabetes, she openly talked about it during interviews with pageant judges. She candidly revealed how she overcame adversity, and as the record books show, pageant judges didn't view it as a detriment. On the contrary, they admired her frankness. In June 1998, a month after receiving her master's degree in journalism at Regent, Baker was crowned Miss

Virginia. That September, she was crowned Miss America 1999 in Atlantic City. During her twelve-month reign, Baker traveled across the country educating the public about diabetes. Since then, she has lobbied the U.S. Congress and has also addressed numerous state legislatures. Her platform ranges from medical insurance reforms to assure adequate coverage for diabetics, to the allocation of funds for diabetes research. Today, Baker serves as a consultant to diabetes-related organizations including Eli Lilly, the American Diabetes Association, and Animas Corporation, a manufacturer of insulin pumps.

Baker has dedicated her career to helping others with diabetes. She has authored three books on the subject, ranging from her autobiography to a diabetic's cookbook. She is also a cohost of the CNBC weekly television show *d-Life*, a program that addresses diabetes issues.

In 2003, she married Scott Baker, a popular television personality in Pittsburgh, where they currently reside with his three children from a previous marriage. In January 2006, she gave birth to a healthy eight-pound-four-ounce daughter, Ava. Only weeks afterward, she was back on the road giving talks to diabetics, taking her baby with her. "Sure I was showing off with Ava," she says, "but when speaking to crowds about how they mustn't limit themselves, I wanted them to know that it is possible to have diabetes and give birth to a healthy child. Like other expectant mothers, I worried during my pregnancy about my baby, knowing that high blood sugar counts increase the risk of spinal bifida and other kinds of birth defects. The mom is also at risk that she may encounter health problems. Following a speech in New York City, a young expectant mother with diabetes e-mailed me to explain that she was six weeks pregnant and was unable to be there when I spoke. Her message said, 'I have two questions. One, did your baby have any birth defects, and question two, how high did your blood sugars go, and how often were they high during your pregnancy?' "

"What I read into her e-mail," Baker continues, "was that this young woman was thinking as I did when I found out that I was pregnant. Like I, she was desperate and scared. She knew that in the last couple of days she had had high blood sugar, and yes, I told her, mine was high at certain times during my pregnancy. I understood the internal anguish and turmoil she was experiencing. I knew the anxiety she was having from not knowing. I told her what I often tell other diabetics: 'Don't be captured by this. Instead, capture the possibilities.' "

Baker adds, "A diabetic faces obstacles every day, and it's something I've learned to live with. Humalog gave me more options because it provided more freedom to do things, and in turn, I had more strength and confidence. I felt more in control, and most important, I believed I could give birth to a healthy child."

Baker acknowledges that a diabetic must be well informed on how to manage his or her diabetes concerning the physical aspects—knowing how to inject a shot, testing one's blood sugar count, taking the right amount of insulin, and so on—but: "I am of the opinion that there is so much emphasis on the 'numbers' of the disease (i.e., what's a patient's three-month average or percent of glucose in the blood), and while I don't underestimate its importance, not enough attention is being paid to one's emotional makeup. Sure, the numbers are important, but the truly difficult part of the disease is dealing with your psyche. A diabetic is on a continual emotional roller-coaster ride. There are the highs and the lows that result when you are unable to control your disease. As a consequence, you become moody and irritable and this can lead to periods of depression. I discuss these aspects of diabetes when I speak, letting other diabetics know that they are not alone when these periods occur. It's the nature of the disease. While you try to stay on top of it, you sometimes are unable to."

The former Miss America summarizes by saying, "I know it may sound bizarre, but I've come to accept my having diabetes as a blessing. In fact, I wouldn't trade having it for anything. Unless you have adversity, you are not forced to reach down into the inner depths of your soul to discover who you really are. My diabetes challenges me to do my life's mission. It is my purpose that permits me to serve others."

There are countless stories about people like the twins from Goshen and Nicole Johnson Baker that illustrate the miracle of insulin, and, in this case, of Humalog, Lilly's miracle drug. One brief story to end this chapter is told by Jeff Baker about a Lilly coworker. "My friend participated in a clinical trial," Baker says, "and one day, as we passed each other in the hall, he said to me, 'Boy, my wife and I really love Humalog.'

" 'I didn't realize that your wife was diabetic,' I replied.

" 'Oh, she's not. But now she worries about me a lot less.'

"He had really said a lot, I thought. Because she's a primary caregiver.

She's part of his life, as are their children. You see, he is what's known as a brittle diabetic, which means he had control issues, and with Humalog, his problems were greatly relieved. But what an interesting response. 'My wife and I love it. She now worries about me a lot less.' You see, it's not just the patient, it's the family too."

4

GLAXOSMITHKLINE COMPANY PROFILE

GlaxoSmithKline (GSK) is recognized today as the United Kingdom's most successful and most prestigious company. But unlike the stories of so many other international conglomerates, GSK's story is much more than just market share, cash flow, and net earnings. Rather, it is five stories of no less than eight men, all working in far-flung corners of the globe to create entrepreneurial ventures reflecting the grit, innovation, and risk taking that propelled each to world-class success.

This is a people story. It is a testimony to the vision and relentless effort of a handful of determined entrepreneurs, each of whom began his career under modest circumstances. The eight players are Joseph Nathan (Glaxo), Silas Burroughs, and Henry Wellcome (Burroughs Wellcome & Co.); Thomas Beecham (Beecham); and John Smith, George Smith, Mahlon Kline, and Harry French (Smith, Kline, French and Co.). The late-twentieth-century convergence of their spirited work is the story of GlaxoSmithKline.

GLAXO

The Glaxo story began in the impoverished, run-down East Side of London. Joseph E. Nathan, the son of a poor Jewish tailor, would grow to become the central drive to an enormous global force. His father, Edward, was said to be a "charming old man with very little [sic] brains," and his mother, Rachael "a highly intelligent woman . . . with very little education." Devoutly orthodox, the family was forced to endure the privations and ugly stereotypes common in anti-Semitic environments.

Joseph, born in 1835, was an asthmatic child, and he suffered greatly in London's dampness. His poor health fueled his desire to escape England, where class and religious discrimination was considered a life sentence. Though in poor health and undereducated, he showed promise of having exceptional business acumen when at the age of twelve he encouraged his father to "don a tail coat and silk hat and travel by horse and gig to boost sales." At that age he saw export potential, but his father was not persuaded, and young Joseph's dreams languished.

Gold was discovered in Australia in 1851. Upon the death of his mother in 1852, Joseph Nathan decided to leave London and find his fortune down under. He was the ripe age of seventeen.

Australia was a very tough place, and competition in the gold fields was fierce and dangerous. Spying opportunities in the trading business, Nathan moved on two years later to New Zealand. To his surprise, New Zealand was worse. In comparison to Australia it was quite primitive; immigrant ships had begun arriving only ten years earlier. The country lacked transport and was quite isolated. Each year only a few merchant ships made the three-to-five-month trip.

Along with his brother-in-law, Jacob Joseph (Nathan had married while in New Zealand), he formed a trading company in Wellington, a garrison town of 3,500 rough and tumble frontiersmen. The partnership dissolved in 1873, and days later, operating under the name of Joseph Nathan and Co., Nathan started out as an importer and exporter of goods ranging from whalebones to patent medicines. Slowly, he expanded his product line and dealt in simple stock items such as colonial produce, fancy goods, clocks, jewelry, ironworks. He also sold the general tonics and cure-alls of the day, including such items as the exotic "Wolfe's Romantic Schiedan Schnapps," a popular European concoction. His patent medicines were the forerunners of many vitamins and drugs.

Nathan established a reputation as a pious man—a fair, honest, and exceedingly bright businessman. (In his obituary, it was said of him, "Mr. Nathan joined to his integrity a cool brain, untiring energy, and wide and profound knowledge of business. He was a man of great resource and judgment . . . [having a] firm belief in the virtues of straight shooting, a cheerful confidence in the years ahead and an invincible determination to attain by honest means, honest ends.") His most ambitious enterprise was the marketing of dried milk. Utilizing this recently discovered technology, Nathan built a factory in 1904 to produce dry milk. In the beginning, his business floundered, but when sanitary milk came to be viewed favorably by doctors, baby food products were soon in great demand. To expand the company into new markets, Nathan's youngest son, Alex, moved to London, which today is the home of the company's world headquarters. The company sold its milk under the brand name Lacto, but because other companies were selling dried milk products with similar-sounding names, the company was forced to rename its product. While Nathan was playing with the letters of the word Lacto, the name Glaxo was born.

Alex decided to take the marketing one step further: he spearheaded the 1908 publication of *The Glaxo Baby Book*. It was the first parenting and baby care book of its kind, and it not only took off but made Glaxo a household word. (The book sold over a million copies in just a few short years and was published for over sixty years.) The company changed its name to Glaxo.

In 1908, there were more than three hundred brands of dried milk being sold in the United Kingdom. To increase market share, a full-page ad was placed in the *London Daily Mail* that featured the slogan, "The food that builds bonny babies." The catchy slogan caught on and was used for many years. But it was the baby book that won the hearts of British mothers and eventually made Glaxo a household name throughout Britain.

This enormously successful foray into the world of health products significantly affected the growth and ultimate direction of the company. In 1919 it hired pharmacist Harry Jephcott, who immediately raised the quality standards and was a guiding hand in taking Glaxo more deeply into pharmaceuticals. Its first pharmaceutical product was called Ostelin, vitamin D extracted from fish liver. During World War II, the company played a role in the development of penicillin (and was the major supplier to the British for some time). Energy drinks, veterinary vaccines and products, corticosteroid preparations for arthritis, and vaccines were also part of the company's product line. Decades later, Glaxo scientists would create the popular anti-ulcer treatment Zantac.

While eminently successful, Glaxo never lost its vision to serve people and provide the most effective and research-based products available. It is a corporate priority that has stood the test of time.

BURROUGHS WELLCOME & CO.

Silas Burroughs and Henry Wellcome were two Americans who relocated to London to establish their pharmaceutical empire. Burroughs was an ambitious young businessman, and after graduating from the Philadelphia College of Pharmacy, he started a small neighborhood apothecary in Philadelphia. From the start, he envisioned a pharmaceutical company that would extend far beyond the walls of his small shop. In short, he recognized the potential of overseas expansion of the American pharmaceutical revolution, patent medicines in particular. By the late-1870s Burroughs was already representing U.S. interests in the United Kingdom and envisioning an operation there based on a personal invention, the compressed pill.

Henry Wellcome was a preacher's son, born in a log cabin in Wisconsin in 1853. The Wellcome family moved to the quiet prairies of Minnesota shortly after Henry's birth, and it was there that he came under the influence of his uncle Jacob, a surgeon, and his teacher and mentor William Mayo (of Mayo Clinic fame). It was under this guidance that young Henry grew to have an appreciation for the scientific aspects of pharmaceutical development. (Mayo once quoted Louis Pasteur as saying, "Men without labs are as soldiers without arms." Wellcome never forgot this quote, which inspired his future work in research.) He traveled extensively throughout South America in his first job as a pharmaceutical salesman.

Like his friend Silas Burroughs, Wellcome also graduated from the Philadelphia College of Pharmacy in 1874 but took a different postgraduate path—he became a drug salesman. He was a big thinker with a gregarious personality, both of which proved to be a big asset when he was assigned the task of opening new markets in South America. Though international traveling was difficult and time consuming, his winning ways helped him to succeed in faraway places. It was in South America where Wellcome studied many of the exotic plants that would be part of his future research endeavors.

The comfort that the two men felt in venturing out to an international arena led to their future successes on a worldwide scale. In 1880, the two met in London and established Burroughs Wellcome & Co. Their first job was to trademark the name they'd devised for the compressed pill, which they called a "tabloid." Unfortunately they couldn't protect it, particularly when the term changed in the common lexicon to refer to a certain kind of newspaper. The friction over this and other factors soured the relationship between the two men. The early death of Burroughs in 1895 (at the age of forty-nine) made Wellcome the sole owner of the company.

Wellcome was an irrepressible showman and entertainer. He could not bridle his enthusiasm and was responsible for creating many memorable advertisements and staging wild events to promote his products. As an avid collector of antiquities, exotic keepsakes, and philanthropic adventures, his attention was frequently diverted away from business.

But Wellcome's energy was boundless, especially for his pet project: Tabloid Medicine Chests. These nifty little boxes stuffed with "tabloid" pills of the most effective pharmaceuticals of the day were wildly popular with men like himself: explorers, pioneers, aviators, seafarers, British royalty, and even a U.S. president, Teddy Roosevelt. He supplied these chests for the African expeditions of Henry Stanley as well as polar and Himalayan expeditions.

Wellcome promoted and paid for great research. He successfully attracted some of the best and brightest pharmacists in the world to study treatments for immune system problems, insulin production, diphtheria vaccines, yellow fever vaccines, digitalis for heart trouble, and curare extracts. One of his most daring ventures was the "Wellcome Tropical Research Laboratories," which floated up and down the Nile to study diseases that existed in inaccessible places. He was generous in spending his own personal fortune to establish first-rate medical research facilities.

The company's research was instrumental in the creation of such products as Actifed, an antihistamine; Septrin, a broad-spectrum antibacterial treatment; and eventually Retrovir for the treatment of AIDS. The credibility of Burroughs Wellcome research has been further validated by several Nobel laureates. In 1936, Sir Henry Dale won the Nobel Prize for his work on the chemical transmission of nerve impulses. In 1982, Sir John Vane (and two fellow researchers) won the prize for "their discoveries concerning prostaglandins and related biologically active substances." In 1988, the Nobel Prize for medicine was awarded to Burroughs Wellcome researchers George Hitchings and Gertrude Elion and to Sir James Black for "their discoveries of important principles for drug treatment." (Black had worked at the Wellcome Foundation as well as for Smith, Kline and French.)

BEECHAM

Thomas Beecham started life as a shepherd. Born in 1820 in Oxfordshire, England, as a young eight-year-old boy, Beecham began noticing something strange about his sheep: they were very picky about the grasses they ate. Curious, he began to experiment with different grasses and herbs, noting their medicinal value. Over the ensuing years he realized that his passion lay in medicinal science, and he deftly put himself in the trade as a medicinal vendor.

By the age of twenty-two, in 1842, Beecham already had his first wildly successful product based on his work with the sheep: "Beecham's Pills" for the treatment of constipation. He marketed his truly remarkable laxative with slogans such as "Worth a guinea a box," "Make life worth living," "Keep running right with good spirits," and "Quite better, thanks."

Unlike many of his contemporaries, Beecham kept the focus on his core business and never swayed from it, even to his death in 1926. At that time the business was thriving, producing one million pills per day. So captivated by the potential he saw swelling within the company, financier Philip Hill acquired the operation. Immediately he set upon a course of expanding the product line. Within months he'd released "Beecham's Powders" for such ailments as headaches, nerve pains, influenza, colds, and rheumatism.

Over the years Hill acquired all sorts of consumer brands to put under the Beecham umbrella, such as Maclean's toothpaste and Lucozade energy drink, two popular products in the United Kingdom. Horlick's malted milk and a popular black currant juice product called Ribena were also big sellers. In 1939, Beecham purchased County Perfumery Co. Ltd., the manufacturer of Brylcreem, a well-known men's hair application.

In 1943, Beecham Research Labs was established to focus solely on basic pharmaceutical research. Its first major discovery was information that would lead to treating the numerous infections that had become resistant to the miracle drug penicillin. Essentially they succeeded in identifying the nucleus of the penicillin cell and, using this as a starting point, created an almost infinite number of new semisynthetic penicillins whose chemical activity could be specifically directed. Over the next several decades Beecham scientists would become world leaders in anti-infective therapies.

One of its most impressive discoveries was amoxicillin in 1972. It was a broad-spectrum penicillin that quickly became the most widely prescribed antibiotic in the world. Amoxil, amoxicillin's brand name, was particularly useful for ear and throat infections in children.

Continuing in the tradition of creating anti-infectives, Beecham released Augmentin in the early 1980s. At the time it was hailed as the gold standard for treating seriously resistant bacterial infections, particularly respiratory infections.

In the mid-1980s Beecham purchased the American firm of Norcliff Thayer, and thus added its two star products, Tums and Oxy (skin cleaner) to its already impressive lineup. In 1989, SmithKline Beckman and the Beecham Group merged to form SmithKline Beecham. The combined company was recognized as one of the largest research and development organizations in the world. The combined product portfolio, pipeline, and geographic networks positioned SmithKline Beecham at the forefront of the global health-care industry.

SMITH, KLINE, AND FRENCH CO.

John Smith began a successful pharmacy and drug wholesaling business with his brother George in Philadelphia, circa 1830. It quickly became a bustling operation by offering a full line of standard pharmaceutical products of the day, including drugs, medicines, chemicals, dyes, paints, oils, glass, and patent medicines. They also became known as friendly and reliable "customer service"–oriented businessmen.

Business flourished, and some years later they hired a nineteen-year-old bookkeeper, Mahlon Kline. This was to prove to be a pivotal choice, for Mahlon was much more than just a bookkeeper. He possessed business acumen, marketing savvy, and salesmanship far beyond his years. Hungry and determined, he asked for additional responsibilities, including sales, and in a short time he added several substantial new accounts. He was rewarded by being given ownership in the company, and at this time the firm changed its name to Smith, Kline and Co.

Business continued to boom. In order to grow and continue to remain focused on the company's primary business, the decision was made to expand its line by acquiring another successful pharmaceutical wholesaler, French, Richards and Co., in 1891. The combination gave the new company, Smith, Kline & French Co., hundreds of new products virtually

overnight, including fine perfumes, liniments, tonics, hair oil, cough medicine, and a host of home remedies.

With the acquisition completed, Mahlon Kline became obsessed with finding a solution to a problem that had long plagued the industry: order fulfillment. Applying his bookkeeping background, Smith, Kline & French became the first company in the industry to establish the policy that all orders received in the morning would be shipped by no later than that afternoon. Such promptness was unheard of in that day, and the company's policy created considerable popular appeal and goodwill. Kline also insisted on only the highest quality in the company's products. He demanded, for instance, that all products that could go bad (e.g., unprocessed drugs, waxes, balsams, and turpentine) be inspected by a laboratory chemist before being stocked. His high standards won solid allegiance throughout the company's customer base.

The company remained focused on consumer products and superior customer service for many decades. But coexisting with this priority was a firm corporate commitment to basic pharmaceutical research, which was heavily funded in the years leading up to World War II.

It was a wise investment that began showing dividends as early as 1945. One of the main challenges facing the industry was how to create a drug that would "time-release" over the course of a day. Smith, Kline & French scientists discovered a solution that involved putting tiny pellets covered in medication inside dissolvable capsules. The pellets were designed to dissolve at different rates, thus allowing a time-release phenomenon. The pellets comprised the capsule that was ingested for pharmacological effect.

This was a major technical breakthrough. In 1952, Spansule, a time-release capsule, was unveiled, and its first use was for Dexedrine, a psychiatric drug for depression. It was so successful that the company began marketing other drugs with the same Spansule time-release capsule, the most famous of which was Contac cold remedy, which could slowly release its medication over a ten-to-twelve-hour time span. (Though today time-release capsules are common, it took seven years and more than 35,000 hours of research to develop this delivery system.)

Developments during the 1950s were ongoing in other areas as well. Of particular note was the release of a new antipsychotic medication called Thorazine. It was in the first generation of "central nervous system" drugs. At first the drug was not accepted because at the time it was

believed that using drugs to treat mental illness was illogical. Not until several clinical trials demonstrated that mental function was improved in clinical patients did the idea of using medication for this purpose catch on. Thorazine eventually gained the stature of "a fundamental drug in medicine," the standard against which all other tranquilizers were measured.

In 1976, Smith, Kline & French unveiled another breakthrough product: Tagamet. This drug revolutionized peptic ulcer treatment. It became one of the company's blockbuster drugs and one of the most prescribed medications in the world. The research of Sir James Black led to the discovery of Tagamet and earned him a Nobel Prize in 1988. Not long after, the firm merged with the Beecham Group to form SmithKline Beecham.

In 1993, SmithKline Beecham entered a multimillion-dollar research collaboration with the company Human Genome Sciences (HGS). The agreement gave the company certain rights to develop medications based on the gene-sequencing information discovered by HGS.

TODAY'S GLAXOSMITHKLINE

The mergers that formed GSK did not happen all at once, but they were executed within a relatively short time frame considering how big they were. It began in 1989 when Smith, Kline & French merged with Beecham to form SmithKline Beecham. In 1995, Glaxo merged with Wellcome to become Glaxo Wellcome. Then in 2000, the megacompany known today as GlaxoSmithKline was formed.

The motivation for the merger of these great companies was to combine assets and pool brains for the purpose of advancing medical research and creating new medications. To that end the merger was a terrific success. GSK has an estimated 7 percent share of the world pharmaceutical market. The company continues to be heavily involved in consumer health-care products, including over-the-counter (OTC) medicines, oral care products, and nutritional drinks, all of which are among the market leaders. Based on 2004 annual results, GSK had sales of $37.2 billion and profit before tax of $11.1 billion. GSK has over 100,000 employees worldwide. Over 40,000 of those employees are in sales and marketing—one of the largest sales forces in the industry. Around 35,000 employees work at 82 manufacturing sites in 37 countries, with more than 15,000 directly involved in R&D. GSK Research and Development

is based at 24 sites spread across 11 countries. Due to its large R&D budget (about $5 billion in 2004), the company has a leading position in
genomics/genetics and new-drug-discovery technologies.

It was long ago that seventeen-year-old Joseph Nathan boarded a
lonely steamer for Australia. His keen insight, along with the vision of
Silas Burroughs, Henry Wellcome, Thomas Beecham, John Smith, George
Smith, Mahlon Kline, and Harry French, made a major impact on the
pharmaceutical industry and has greatly benefited humankind. There's
no doubt that the integrity and passion all these men felt for their purpose and their public will continue to inspire this successful enterprise in
the foreseeable future.

Clearing the Airways

GLAXOSMITHKLINE'S ADVAIR FIGHTS ASTHMA AND CHRONIC OBSTRUCTIVE PULMONARY DISEASE (COPD)

THE TERM *ASTHMA* comes from the Greek word *panos*, which means "to pant or to breathe with an open mouth." The Greeks had a great deal of respect for *panos*, or asthma, as they believed it was a sacred disease that signified a visit from the gods. A description by the Greek physician Aretaeus from the second half of the first century A.D. vividly captures the struggle to breathe characteristic of a severe asthma attack:

> They go into the open air, since no house suffices for their respiration; they breathe standing, as if desiring to draw in all the air they can possibly inhale; and, in their want of air, they also open the mouth as if best to enjoy more of it. Pale in countenance, except the cheeks, which are ruddy; sweat about the forehead and clavicles; cough incessant and laborious; expectoration small, thin, cold, resembling the efflorescence of foam; neck swells with the inflammation of the breath.

More than a century later, another Greek physician, Galen, described asthma as a seizure-like disorder of the lungs. Although he incorrectly surmised that the bronchial tubes were connected to the brain, Galen contended that the probable cause of asthma was an obstruction of the bronchial tubes. He was centuries ahead of his time when he tried to dilute the mucus causing the obstruction. In the twelfth century, Moses Maimonides, a famous Egyptian rabbi, philosopher, and physician, wrote

the first treatise that was specifically about asthma. Among his recommendations were: moderation in food, drink, sleep; avoidance of polluted city environments; general fitness; and eat a lot of chicken soup.

In the 1600s, Johannes Baptista Van Helmont, the renowned Belgium physician referred to as the father of biochemistry, was the first to associate smoke and irritants with asthma. Helmont, an asthmatic himself, recorded that asthma comes from the pipes of the lungs. In the 1700s, Sir John Floyer, a famed physician in his day, was the first to differentiate asthma from other types of breathing disorders. Floyer also recognized that several factors contributed to the state of asthma, including heredity, weather, seasons, and atmospheric pollution, including tobacco, occupational influences, personal idiosyncrasies, and emotions.

SIGNIFICANT PROGRESS

In 1816, French physician Rene Laennec made a major contribution to medicine when he invented the stethoscope. Laennec's invention made it possible to hear and isolate wheezing, the distinctive physical sign of asthma. Most important, with the stethoscope it was possible to examine the thorax. In 1850, German physician Paul Gerhardt identified the means by which chemical odors such as strong perfumes and changes in temperature or humidity can set off an asthma attack, and in 1864, British physician Henry Hyde Salter determined that animal dander could spark off asthma. By the turn of the century, the link between asthma and allergy was established. While early in the twentieth century a school of thought toyed with the notion that asthma was a psychosomatic disorder, scientists later determined that it was definitely a physical illness with multiple causes.

A major breakthrough for treatment of asthma came at the turn of the twentieth century when Solomon Solis-Cohen, a Philadelphia physician, used adrenal extract to treat acute asthma and Jokichi Takamine, a Japanese American scientist, isolated and purified the hormone adrenaline from sheep adrenal glands, a feat that had never been accomplished with a glandular hormone. Takamine filed a patent application in 1900 for "Glandular extractive product" on a blood pressure–raising principle. He named the crystalline substance "Adrenalin." In 1901, he received a U.S. trademark for the word Adrenalin. The hormone was synthesized in 1904; adrenaline was the first bronchodilator with beta-agonist properties.

Shortly thereafter, Parke-Davis, at the time a small pharmaceutical research company in Detroit, began manufacturing the product and selling it under the trade name of Adrenalin, a medicine that became the first major blockbuster drug introduced in the twentieth century. In addition to an effective drug in controlling hemorrhaging in surgery and a stimulant during cardiac arrest, Adrenalin was also used in cardiology, obstetrics, and the treatment of asthma and other allergies. Adrenalin shots were given in doctors' offices and emergency departments for severe bouts of asthma. Adrenalin caused the heart to race, the chest to pound, and a jittery, shaky feeling, perhaps resulting in a headache, plus a rise in blood pressure. It was widely used because it prolonged the action of certain anesthetics. Adrenalin is sold under the chemical name epinephrine in the United States (adrenaline outside of the United States), and is still being used as a bronchodilator and antispasmodic to treat asthma and allergies.

Considerable progress has been made in the development of beta-agonists since epinephrine was first purified and chemically synthesized for medical use in 1904. The first major advance was the modification of epinephrine to eliminate the undesirable effect of constricting blood vessels throughout the body, causing high blood pressure. A derivative of epinephrine called isoproterenol achieved this goal and was introduced in 1948; its brand name was Isuprel. The drug was delivered by an Isuprel Mistometer, a pocket-size multidose metered-dose inhaler that produced a spray of medication that was breathed into the bronchial tubes. Prior inhaled medications were administered in antiquated forms such as bulb nebulizers, cigarettes, and steaming pots of boiling liquid.

By the mid-1960s, isoproterenol (isoprenaline outside of the United States) had become a popular drug to treat asthma. Like Adrenalin, it was a compound not far removed from the body's "fight or flight" hormone adrenaline. Following an asthma attack, all that was required was a quick puff to alleviate shortness of breath, and the airways reopened for a gaseous exchange between the carbon dioxide–enriched air in the lungs and the newly inhaled air. Unlike Adrenalin, isoproterenol did not increase blood pressure. It did, however, cause rapid heart palpitations; it was also short-acting, lasting only twenty minutes or so.

DIFFICULTY IN BREATHING

The airways of people with asthma are abnormal. They are more likely to react to inhaled substances by causing the constriction of the muscles surrounding the bronchioles, thus narrowing the air passages within. The airways of people with asthma are also supercharged with cells and chemicals that initiate the early phase of asthma. When these cells are activated by asthma promoters and triggers, irritation and inflammation occur that block airways.

For most people, difficulty in breathing can be overwhelming but it is by no means the only symptom of asthma. Shortness of breath is often accompanied by a sensation of tightness in the chest that can make one feel as if there was a wide rubber band bound tightly around one's torso. As a condition that causes inflammation and obstruction of the airways, an asthma attack is literally the panting for breath. The muscles surrounding the airways known as bronchial tubes go into spasm, the mucous lining swells, and secretions build up, making breathing difficult. The difficulty is a result of the extra work involved in having to move air through these narrowed tubes. Often a wheezing or whistling sound can be heard, produced by the air rushing through the thin tubes. The irritation of the nerves in the walls of the breathing tubes brings upon excessive coughing or perhaps the spitting up of mucus, which is also referred to as phlegm or sputum. In the case of mild asthma, a chronic dry cough may be the only symptom.

Frequently an allergic condition, asthma causes can vary and range from a reaction of the system to the weather, food, drugs, perfumes, and other irritants. An asthma attack might also be precipitated by a combination of allergic and nonallergic factors, including emotional tension, air pollution, and hereditary factors. Not all asthmatics have allergies, however. People with no allergic sensitivities can have asthma attacks initiated by exercise, respiratory infections, and other nonallergic stimuli.

When discussing asthma, a commonly heard word is "trigger." Doctors tell their patients about triggers or stimuli that induce airway narrowing, causing the symptoms to flare up. Triggers can be a result of a walk on a damp day, cigarette smoke, strong perfume, or allergic occurrences such as dust mites, cat and dog dander, seasonal pollens, and mold. While asthma is a year-round condition, the winter is a particularly hard season. For obvious reasons, the exposure to frigid air is harmful because it causes the bronchial tubes to constrict even more. Cold weather also drives people indoors, where closed windows and poor air ventilation foster the inhalation of house dust, firewood smoke, mold, and other irritants. Certain medications and emotional stress can also trigger an asthma attack.

One of the first cases of the use of environmental controls to reduce asthma attacks can be dated to 1552, when the longtime asthma sufferer the archbishop of Saint Andrews in Scotland summoned the physician Girolamo Cardano to help ease his wheezing. In addition to prescribing a proper diet and exercise program, Cardano removed a leather pillow and feather bed from the archbishop's bedroom. The patient's breathing improved dramatically. Cardano probably succeeded because he reduced the archbishop's exposure to asthma triggers.

Asthma can be inherited, but it does not always follow a predictable line of inheritance. This means that it can skip from one generation to another or surface in cousins, uncles, or aunts. Many asthmatics who lack a family background of asthma probably have a parent or grandparent with a wheezy condition that was incorrectly labeled as chronic bronchitis or pulmonary emphysema. When one parent has asthma, especially the allergic type, the chances are fifty-fifty that a child will develop asthma. When both parents are afflicted, the odds increase to three out of four.

Asthma is commonplace around the world, although it is more prevalent in some places than others. The world's hotbed, Tristan da Cunha, is a small southern Atlantic island where one of every three of its three hundred inhabitants has asthma. The high incidence on this island is undoubtedly due to inbreeding; three of the island's original fifteen settlers had asthma.

Asthma is more common in urban than rural areas. Inner-city blacks have an alarmingly high rate of severe asthma that leads to more hospitalization and a higher death rate than in the white suburban population. The higher incidence among blacks is mainly due to lower earnings that result in inadequate health care. For some unknown reasons, asthma is much less common in Native Americans, Canadian Eskimos, Asians, and people in Third World countries. Scandinavians have a lower incidence of asthma than their Western European neighbors, possibly because their high rate of infant breast-feeding reduces the likelihood of developing asthma, eczema, and other allergic conditions in infancy and early childhood.

While asthma sufferers live in all parts of the United States, a 2005 study by the Allergy and Asthma Foundation of America showed the top ten worst cities as:

1. Knoxville, Tennessee
2. Little Rock, Arkansas
3. St. Louis, Missouri
4. Madison, Wisconsin
5. Louisville, Kentucky
6. Memphis, Tennessee
7. Toledo, Ohio
8. Kansas City, Missouri
9. Nashville, Tennessee
10. Hartford, Connecticut

The list illustrates that asthma is prevalent across the country. Government figures show that twenty million Americans are affected by asthma and it causes five thousand deaths each year. An estimated 50 percent of the asthmatics in the United States are children. Childhood asthma persists into adulthood in 30 percent of cases. In children aged ten or under, the male to female ratio is two to one; however, between the ages eighteen and fifty-four, the ratio is reversed, with double the number of women being affected.

PROGRESS WITH ASTHMA

Asthma medicines had made relatively little progress since the turn of the century; however, in 1969 Glaxo launched Ventolin in the United Kingdom, and twelve years later, in 1981, the product was approved by the FDA in the United States. Ventolin was originally developed in Ware, England, and marketed by Allen & Hanburys, one of the oldest and most prestigious pharmaceutical companies in the United Kingdom. Founded in 1715, Allen & Hanburys was acquired by Glaxo in 1958.

The chemical name for Ventolin in the United States is albuterol, a bronchodilator that was considered a breakthrough drug—a distinction it earned by being the first selective beta II agonist. Beta II agonists are less likely to produce the cardiovascular side effects seen with nonselective agonist medicines that interact with beta I receptors. Ventolin dilates the airways by relaxing the surrounding bronchial muscles.

GlaxoSmithKline and its predecessor companies also have a long history in the field of anti-inflammatory treatments, dating back to the 1960s when Glaxo made topical corticosteroid medications for skin problems. Three years after the launching of Ventolin, Glaxo scientists were working on beclomethasone dipropionate (BDP), a topical anti-inflammatory steroid for respiratory disease. The company's director of research at the time was Sir David Jack, one of the most high-profile British researchers in the pharmaceutical industry. Jack, who retired in 1987 and is now deceased, had graduated from the University of Glasgow with degrees in pharmacy and pharmacology and in 1953 joined Menley and James, a pharmaceutical company that was later acquired by Smith, Kline & French. In 1961 he was named research director of Allen & Hanburys. He served as research and development director of Glaxo from 1978 to 1987.

A creative scientist, Sir David came up with the then-novel idea that if steroids could be applied topically to treat inflammation of the skin, they might also be capable of treating inflammation in the airways. Had a scientist of less stature made such a suggestion, in all likelihood it would have been disregarded. But coming from Sir David Jack, Glaxo scientists agreed that his idea could have merit. A program was then initiated to put steroids in an inhaler device to be delivered into the lungs. Jack's assumption was correct. BDP did work as an inhaled anti-inflammatory drug, specifically in the airways. His brainchild ultimately changed the nature of treating asthma. Prior to this approach, steroids were used systemically but could cause serious side effects. Getting steroids directly into the lung by the use of an inhaler device, however, allowed considerably smaller doses of the medicine to be directed to the desired site of action, thereby reducing side effects. This prompted Glaxo to come out with the first inhaled corticosteroid, in addition to its beta II agonist bronchodilator.

Dr. Tachi Yamada, chairman of R&D at GSK until his retirement in June 2006, explains that in drug development, the full range of applications is not always apparent. "An advantage in being a very large pharmaceutical company," he points out, "is that we have considerable expertise in many therapeutic areas. This means we might develop a compound for a novel target before absolutely knowing its potential application. Later on it becomes known that its application can be very different than what it started out to be. We've got a compound being studied for overactive bladder, diabetes, and irritable bowel syndrome."

The story of topical corticosteroids is similar. Originally they were used to treat skin diseases, but the company came up with an entirely different application and used it to reduce inflammation in the airways. This is not a unique experience in this industry. "We're certainly not the only company to benefit in this manner due to our size and overall expertise," Yamada continues. "For example, Pfizer started out developing Viagra for hypertension. It turned out that Viagra could be used to treat erectile dysfunction. However, had Pfizer not had some understanding of the physiology of erectile dysfunction, Viagra might not have ever happened. So again, it was a matter of a very large pharmaceutical company that was able to apply its expertise that consequently had a different application, and it went on to become a blockbuster drug."

By the early 1980s, Glaxo's Ventolin was enjoying brisk sales in the United States and abroad. Ventolin was helpful in controlling asthma, but it has a short duration of effect, lasting about four to six hours. Again, Sir David Jack envisioned the goal of a next generation of asthma medicine that would be a long-acting beta-agonist medicine used only twice a day. Not only would this be a convenience, it would better serve the nocturnal asthma suffered by many asthmatics—those who have decreasing lung function in the early hours of the morning that interferes with their sleep. A drug that would work for twelve hours at a time would reduce or eliminate nighttime asthma attacks.

Jack, having set the goal, turned to a team of the company's scientists and chemists to invent a new molecule. One member of this group, Larry Lunts, had prior experience in coming up with revolutionary asthma drugs. Back in the 1960s, Lunts, as a Glaxo chemist, synthesized albuterol as a short-acting beta-agonist. To increase its duration, Lunts now had to develop a beta agonist molecule that would interact with the lung's beta receptors for a longer period of time. One theory on how to accomplish this was to increase the lipophilicity of the molecule. Lipophilicity refers to the drug's ability to be absorbed in the fatty domains in the cell membrane around the receptor.

Lunts, working with an experienced team of chemists and other scientists, including biologist Ian Skidmore, made and tested countless compounds in the search for a beta-agonist having a long duration of action. Eventually, with insight provided by a team of chemists working on an entirely different medicine (who had found some beta-agonist activity in their molecules), Lunts combined various structural features from the two groups' molecules to eventually arrive at the structure of an entirely new molecule, called salmeterol. Salmeterol was then passed to the drug development group, including GSK's Malcolm Johnson, to shepherd the molecule through the arduous series of clinical studies required to prove that this new pharmaceutical drug was safe and effective.

James Palmer M.D. a young pulmonologist who joined the company in 1985, played a key role in the development of the company's modern-day respiratory medicines. Two years after joining Glaxo Research Group, Palmer was promoted to director of respiratory clinical research, and by 1992 had risen to the position of senior vice president of medical operations and chief medical officer. When GlaxoSmithKline was formed in 2000, Palmer became senior vice president for new product development, with a staff of more than five thousand worldwide.

Palmer, who is also now deceased, shared Sir David Jack's vision of developing a long-acting drug that would be taken twice daily. It was also his insight that promoted a combination asthma medicine capable of treating patients with salmeterol, the long-acting beta-agonist, and fluticasone propionate, a steroid. The company marketed each drug separately for the treatment of asthma. While these drugs were two entirely different types of molecules with different effects in the lung, Palmer promoted the idea of combining them to treat asthma. Palmer's approach went against a common bias against combining drugs in fixed doses and the thinking that such combinations rarely produce a feasible drug.

Malcolm Johnson, director of respiratory sciences at GSK, commented on the development of the programs resulting in the new Advair product. Johnson has a Ph.D. in pharmacology and had worked for ICI before it became Zeneca. In 1980 Johnson joined GSK as head of cardiovascular pharmacology and the respiratory pharmacology department. In January 2005, Johnson celebrated his twentieth anniversary with the company. Tongue in cheek, he says, "When I came here, I worked for Glaxo Group Research, and that company became GlaxoWellcome, which merged with Smith Kline Beecham in 2000 to become GSK. So in a twenty-year period, I've worked for three different companies in the same place without going anywhere!"

Johnson might have physically stayed in the same place, but his career rose meteorically. He worked closely with Sir David Jack and James Palmer. Johnson and other GSK scientists recall with admiration the commitment to excellence possessed by these two scientists. Reflecting on the development of Advair, Johnson notes that "it was Sir David Jack's genius that moved us in the direction to apply steroids to bronchial inflammation, and later he guided the company toward a long-acting beta-agonist drug that would be good for twelve hours. Then it was James Palmer who promoted the concept of combining the two drugs into a single medicine."

Jack has also been credited with having lessened the time it takes to get a drug to market—an accomplishment that to many at GSK may have been his biggest contribution. Salmeterol, under the brand name Serevent, was launched in 1990 in the United Kingdom only seven years after it had first been synthesized in the laboratory. That's half the fourteen-year period it was taking other companies in the 1980s and early 1990s. Jack's approach cut the time in half by taking an unconventional, potentially riskier approach. Rather than advancing sequentially through the different stages of development, for example, by first doing the genetic toxicology followed by a one-month study in two animal species and then waiting for all the data from each experiment before starting other studies, Jack's approach was to simultaneously do as many studies as was possible. By not having to wait for the results of one study before starting the next procedure, significant time was shaved off the clock.

His approach was not without risk; if something were to go wrong along the way, it could cause the entire program to be shelved, thereby costing considerably more money. The upside in doing it this way was that if everything went smoothly, the company would gain significant time in bringing a new product to market. In the case of a top-selling drug, this would ultimately translate into millions and millions of dollars of additional revenues, especially if the new drug could be released and marketed for several years prior to a competitor's drug. Jack's innovative approach to drug development has since been adopted by other companies.

CHALLENGES FOR A COMBINATION PRODUCT

As Johnson explains, "The medical community expressed a strong resistance to a combination therapy, especially among middle-aged and older physicians. These doctors had been taught in medical school that combination therapy was a bad idea because it took away their flexibility to titrate the doses of two drugs by giving fixed combinations—even if they gave them in different dose strengths, which, at the end of the day, is what we did with Advair. So in their minds, this was simply bad medicine, and this is the barrier we had to overcome.

"Changing the minds of the agnostics required the company to show that there is a rationale in putting molecules together because they bring different things to the table. We also had to demonstrate to our senior management and eventually to regulatory authorities that each of these components is bringing a significant amount of efficacy—a different sort of efficacy—to the total patient. We had to convince them that this combination therapy was a good thing to do.

"Combining drugs also creates challenges for pharmaceutical development—it isn't always easy to mix drugs because they have different properties, different stability profiles, and so on. And when you put two drugs together, you can create huge pharmaceutical development problems in terms of maintaining the stability of the two. You move from the difficulties of conception to challenges in terms of how this product would be received, and the task of convincing a regulatory authority like the FDA that this makes sense to put these two together. And internally, you could create significant problems regarding development timelines. Then there is always the possibility that the combination of drugs can result in one or both drugs losing its effectiveness. Plus there is always the possibility that the combination of two drugs will exert toxicity. There is no predictability that two individually safe and effective drugs, when combined, will remain so. We were sailing on uncharted waters with no assurances whatsoever that we would succeed."

A basic business maxim dictates minimizing risks and maximizing profits. However, in the pharmaceutical business, one must be willing to invest in new drugs early on when the odds are heavily stacked against a particular molecule having potential to become a viable drug. As Yamada emphasizes, "I think that there are some people who pride themselves in knowing how to cut bait quickly. In the pharmaceutical field, those individuals often end up with no pipeline of new medicines. The hard part is to know when to keep fishing when all the odds are against you. Honestly, I don't know of many products in today's marketplace that have not gone through a period when there was some early resistance. Even Lipitor, the world's bestselling drug, faced a lot of internal struggles because it faced such strong competition that it appeared as if its market share would put it in fourth or fifth place. For a while, few people at Pfizer had a lot of faith in it, and consequently there was talk about pulling the plug on Lipitor. Anyone can pull the plug, and everyone can look smart by pulling a drug early. The really smart person knows when to stay with a product when the chips are down. If you're not willing to take risks in this field, you're in the wrong business."

Dr. Kathleen Rickard, a graduate of the Hahnemann School of Medicine in Philadelphia, did her pulmonary medicine training at the University of Nebraska. She served on the university's faculty for several years, and prior to joining Glaxo in 1993, Rickard worked at Procter and Gamble, where she directed early research in asthma and other lung diseases. Today she is respiratory clinical vice president at GSK. When asked why she doesn't practice medicine, Rickard replies, "I believe I can do more good helping millions of people by making contributions to finding new medicines that will treat their disease. I still see a small number of patients at the University of North Carolina; however, I'm primarily involved in research here at GSK in Research Triangle Park."

Rickard recalls that when she started with the company, GSK had only beclomethasone dipropionate (BDP) and albuterol on the market. "BDP is a corticosteroid in the same family as fluticasone," she explains. "Albuterol is a rescue medication, which means it's taken when an asthmatic experiences such symptoms as a severe onset of the tightening of the chest, wheezing, or an inability to breathe. In the medical profession, such an attack is known as a crisis situation. In such instances, the individual must use a rescue inhaler with a rapid onset of action in order to restore normal breathing. A severe asthma attack is not only debilitating, it can possibly be life-threatening. Advair is a maintenance medicine that helps prevent an asthmatic from encountering a crisis situation. The drug's objective is to eliminate or, at the very least, appreciably reduce the number of instances of severe respiratory attacks. It should be noted that once an asthma attack is in progress, maintenance medicines have little or no effect. For this reason, asthmatics on a maintenance medicine must also carry a rescue medication inhaler on his or her person because one's never certain when adverse conditions could set off an attack. So that's the goal—we want to reduce the need to use a rescue drug. But if you're an asthmatic, don't leave home without it. It's better to be safe than sorry."

Rickard points out that an asthma attack can be triggered by a particular allergen such as ragweed in the late summer months. "But with another patient," she explains, "it could be tree allergens in the spring. Still, not all asthmatics have an allergy. There are some who experience inflammation in their airways; however, no allergens are detected, so it's not clear where the reaction comes from. When an attack occurs, the airways in one's lungs constrict. This narrowing makes it difficult to breathe. Salmeterol relaxes the muscles around the airways and opens them to get more air in and out. Asthma is an inflammatory disease akin to what happens when you cut your hand—redness and swelling occur—that's inflammation and the same kind of reaction happens inside an asthmatic's lungs. Fluticasone propionate, a corticosteroid, inhibits the underlying inflammation in the lungs.

"Because an asthma attack isn't always triggered by environmental factors, it's difficult to predict what will cause an attack. For instance, a person can have only minor attacks and not think much of it, and then suddenly have a severe attack that requires hospitalization. That's why carrying a rescue drug like Ventolin is mandatory. A Ventolin rescue inhaler with two hundred doses might be used only once or twice a week or not at all for long periods. Just the same, an asthmatic should carry one at all times for the same reason a person has a fire extinguisher."

A WINNING COMBINATION

In the United States, Serevent is the brand name for salmeterol and Flovent is the name for fluticasone. Back in the mid- and late-1980s, salmeterol, a long-acting beta-agonist, and fluticasone, a steroid, were discovered and marketed as two separate drugs. While the combining of two asthma drugs conceptually sounds plausible, it is complicated and difficult to implement, and more often than not, doesn't work. It took years of research to pick salmeterol from hundreds of compounds, and likewise, fluticasone was also picked from hundreds of other compounds. Why should it be expected that these two different drugs would complement one another as a single medicine?

Simply put, the combination of two drugs may bring about a chemical reaction that eradicates the efficacy of one or both drugs. Or worse, the mixing together of both drugs' chemicals can produce adverse effects. To complicate matters, the company researchers wanted the combined drug to go directly to the airways via an inhaler. Hence the equation involved two separate drugs and an inhaler; getting the three to work as a single product was indeed an ambitious undertaking. As it turned out, having salmeterol relax the muscles around the airways while fluticasone simultaneously reduced the inflammation worked wonderfully. GSK scientists were elated to see that the combined effects of both drugs surpassed all expectations.

"We never anticipated that by putting the two drugs together, the combination would work better than taking the drugs independently," Tachi Yamada explains. "In the beginning, we were more focused on the considerable convenience a combination drug would offer as a single treatment. But by combining two drugs in a single easy-to-use device, we saw evidence during our early trials that asthmatics were doing better with Advair than we expected. Part of the reason was that when a drug enters the lung, you are never sure which cell it will go to. However, with Advair, the two drugs, salmeterol and fluticasone, hit the same cell at the same time. When drugs are given independently, it may be that one drug is better absorbed by one cell, but the other drug won't necessarily go to the same cell. It can't be predicted that this will happen when two drugs are given independently. But with Advair being delivered to the lungs with an inhaled device, the patient receives both medications with a single treatment."

In April 2001 Advair was launched in the United States, making it one of GSK's first products following the 2000 megamerger. Darrell Baker, who was vice president of marketing in the United States at the time, explains what he believes was a major feature of the new drug: "Advair is an inhaled corticosteroid and a long-acting bronchodilator in the same medicine. This means that the patient feels much better from the inhaled bronchodilator at the very beginning, and over time, he continues to feel better and better from the anti-inflammatory steroid. In fact, patients felt so much better, we'd hear them repeatedly say, 'Advair allowed me to forget that I had asthma. It enabled me to live as if I didn't have asthma.' Asthmatics say this because they not only felt good very soon, but by continuing to take Advair, they were able to get the long-term benefits from the steroid. I know personally because I've been on Advair ever since it's been available. With prior asthma drugs, people tended to stop taking their steroid medicines once they were feeling better. However, with a combined medicine, they couldn't take one without the other. Then, of course, there is the convenience factor. Taking one drug is easier than having to take two drugs. Its convenience adds to the drug's clinical benefit."

Yamada concurs. "The most important thing is that the patient gets the most benefit from Advair by taking it every day like his physician pre-scribed him to do. For obvious reasons, a patient who complies with a prescribed medicine will enjoy better health than one who doesn't."

Pharmaceutical companies receive hundreds of thank-you letters, e-mails, and telephone calls from patients who have benefited from a miracle drug. GSK received so many testimonials from patients who raved about Advair that it is not possible to include them in this book. One such correspondence representative of these favorable responses was a letter from a survivor of one of the attacks on September 11. This individual described the ordeal of being forced to escape the area of the attack. Had the writer not been using Advair regularly, survival was ques-tionable, according to the letter. This is just one of numerous stories of people who feel that Advair has given them back their lives. When correspondence of this nature is received, it is shared with everyone, from scientists to manufacturing people, to let them know how patients benefit from their work. To these thousands of men and women who rarely have contact with patients, such feedback is welcomed and deeply appreciated.

GOOD STEROIDS

Malcolm Johnson points out that when Advair was first introduced, some people resisted it because it contained corticosteroids. "People don't like the idea of taking steroids. There are misconceptions about steroids, and the confusion was between inhaled steroids and other forms of steroid therapy. There is a lot of misinformation about steroids. Many lay people confuse the steroids that athletes take to enhance their perfor-mance with steroids taken for asthma. The steroids that athletes abuse for performance enhancing are anabolic steroids that increase their weight, and in particular, build up muscle mass. And they increase their perfor-mance ability. Those are the ones we read about in the newspapers—this baseball player or that track star, and so on. But they are [so] different from corticosteroids like fluticasone that it's like comparing an airplane to an automobile. An airplane and automobile are both means of trans-portation but they are completely different forms of transportation."

Many people don't understand that the human body requires steroids to function properly. Our bodies produce three distinct classes of ster-oids. The first group, mineralocorticoids, regulates the body's salt balance. The second group, anabolic steroids, controls our muscle mass and sexual features. The third group, glucocorticoids, controls the levels of our sugar, fat, and protein in the body. Cortisol, a glucocorticoid, controls inflammation in the body, and it is the group of steroid drugs used to treat asthma. The corticosteroids used in the treatment of asthma have no anabolic effect (they do not increase hair growth or muscle mass), and they have little effect on the body's salt balance.

Says Johnson: "In our field, we call this corticophobia. As a result there are many different research approaches taking place in GSK and I am certain at companies where people are searching for new approaches to control inflammation that don't involve the use of steroids. Actually one of the most successful asthma medicines in the U.S. that is not a steroid is Singulair from Merck. Merck has done an excellent job in marketing it, and Singulair does well in the U.S. market where steroids are a concern. Even today there are many people with corticophobia. For example, they read about athletes on steroids that become sterile and develop heart problems at young ages. They've heard about how steroids were first used to treat asthma that were taken orally and produced terrible side effects that caused such conditions as osteoporosis, skin thinning, and cataracts. And all of this was true with the oral steroids. But when fluticasone is delivered directly to the lung, the patient receives only a small fraction of the dose, say as little as 2 percent as compared to what was being given by mouth. Consequently, taken by inhalation is not just more effective, it's many times safer."

"Then there are parents who have heard about children on inhaled steroids who had reduced growth velocity," Darrell Baker explains. "While a child might not grow as fast, there are data that show he or she will still grow to the same height. My daughter and I each have asthma and we both take Advair. If I had any doubt whatsoever about its safety profile, we wouldn't be taking it. I'm a strong advocator that parents as well as all adult patients should have full access to information concerning their medication. Everyone needs to understand that having a disease—any disease—is never totally free of risk. Taking one's medicine is about making an appropriate risk-benefit decision. I believe we have a responsibility at GSK to make sure patients are well informed and educated."

Baker emphasizes that it was a matter of educating patients that inhaled corticosteroids are very different from other corticosteroids that some people have experienced, and in particular, elders that took it for rheumatoid arthritis. "All steroids have some side effects that you want to avoid," he says, "and the kind of enhancer steroids taken by athletes is not like what's inhaled by someone on Advair. Furthermore, minute amounts of steroid are being inhaled that are going directly into the lining of the lungs—which is where the inflammation is that causes those symptoms we call asthma. Our job was to educate physicians and their patients on how Advair works."

"Inhaled steroids have been proven to be a good idea for quite some time," Johnson explains further: "While there had been some resistance in the United States, the rest of the world had acknowledged it as the recognized asthma therapy. In fact, it was practically a dogma that all you needed to do to treat asthma effectively was to make sure that a patient received enough inhaled steroids. But it was by no means a given that the idea of controlling asthma with a combination therapy was going to be accepted. There had been some resistance regarding combination therapies in the medical community but the company made the commitment to move forward with a drug that combined salmeterol and fluticasone, the medicine that eventually became Advair. It wasn't until 1994 that results were released of a study by Andrew Greening, a respiratory physician, and his colleagues from the University of Edinburgh. They studied a group of asthmatics taking inhaled steroids but [who] had not been well controlled on their medication. Greening then took the traditional route and increased the dose with 50 percent of his patients. He kept the dose constant with his other patients but added in the long-acting beta-agonist. To everyone's surprise, in spite of considerable skepticism, especially in the respiratory community, Greening got a far better clinical effect when he put the two drugs together with the lower dose of the steroid than he did by increasing the dose of the steroid.

"Allen & Hanburys funded Greening's clinical trial, and it was a courageous thing for the company to do," Johnson stresses, "because it was practically flying in the face of the popular belief at the time. Instead of turning out the way it did, the study could have reinforced what the respiratory community was thinking. By going against the grain and ending up with the completely opposite effects, Greening captured everyone's attention. As a physician outside the pharmaceutical industry who was able to find something extraordinary and unpredictable, [he and] his studies received considerable attention, being broadly published in various medical journals and widely read by physicians and members of the pharmaceutical industry.

"Greening's 1994 paper was a mind-changing experience to those respiratory experts who believed that it was better to increase the dose of steroids given to a patient. Ann Woolcock, an Australian professor who had serious doubts about Greening's paper, conducted her own study to determine the accuracy of Greening's conclusions. Woolcock's study focused on a population of more severe asthma patients than Greening's, but upon its completion, she came up with the same findings. I think the fact that the two studies were done so closely within the same time frame and on different severities of the disease . . . made the international respiratory community take notice. Greening's and Woolcock's work changed the entire nature of how asthma was treated. These independent studies provided solid data on the right way to treat asthma, and interestingly, they were conducted years after James Palmer had first conceived the idea."

There is a third element that contributes to the two drugs' capacity to simultaneously treat asthma. For optimal performance, GSK developed the unique Diskus, an inhaler device that delivers Advair in a dry powder form.

For more than a half century it has been known that medicines used to treat asthma have been more effective when they are inhaled directly into the lungs. To accomplish this, asthmatics have used a variety of contraptions over the years. Inhaling substances to relieve asthma goes back a long time. Early civilizations, including some that were primitive, boiled an assortment of herbs and inhaled the steam. An 1859 article in Scotland's *Edinburgh Medical Journal* read, "One of the commonest and best reputed remedies of asthma, and one that in many cases is more effective than others, is strong tea or coffee." Unfortunately, this sage advice was ignored for more than fifty years, until German and American research teams set out to determine why many asthma victims stopped wheezing when they drank strong tea or coffee.

Additional research efforts eventually led to the important discovery of a caffeine-like drug called theophylline, which alleviated acute asthma. Epinephrine was used in the early 1920s, as were asthma cigarettes until the 1950s. Along with the smoke, medication was inhaled into the lungs. The concept of treating asthma by inhaling medications has prevailed over the years and many forms of inhaling devices have since been used.

Upon being introduced in the United States, aerosol inhalers that delivered asthma drugs to the lungs were preferred over oral preparations. That's because the drug goes directly to its target versus a drug that is swallowed and absorbed into the bloodstream, returned to the heart, and then pumped throughout the body. Furthermore, a relatively large dose of the oral drug is often required to deliver a relatively small dose to a selected target, which, in this case, is the lung. For example, oral ephedrine works well in the lung, but the brain reacts to ephedrine, leading to insomnia or tremors. The shortcomings of oral drugs for respiratory conditions prompted researchers to develop drugs that could be delivered directly to the targeted organ. The major advantage of an inhaled asthma medication was that it could be propelled into the lungs, which meant it produced a faster onset of action while minimizing side effects.

Metered-dose inhalers, or MDIs, for delivering drugs to the lungs and nasal passages have been popular since 1955. That's when the thirteen-year-old daughter of Dr. George Maison, president of Riker Laboratories, a wholly owned subsidiary of Rexall Drug Company (now 3M Pharmaceuticals), asked her father why her asthma medicine couldn't be put in a spray can like her hair spray. The idea intrigued Maison, and he passed it along to company researchers; within months the first pressurized metered-dose inhalers (pMDIs) were being tested in clinical trials. With an MDI, it takes only five to fifteen minutes for short-acting bronchodilators to have an effect, compared to oral asthma medicines that can take one to three hours. An MDI requires a patient to have coordinated breathing, which means one must be taught by a health-care provider how to activate the device while simultaneously breathing in. While the MDI is used by millions of asthmatics, it can be difficult for young patients and elderly patients to use, and definitely more taxing than swallowing a pill.

The field of respiratory drugs is extremely competitive, and to come out with a blockbuster drug to treat asthma, GSK needed not only a superior medicine but a superior inhaler as well. While inhalers have been around for more than fifty years, new and improved devices started to be introduced in the 1980s. Predecessors to the Advair Diskus were the Rotahaler and the Diskhaler, both of which were dry powder inhalers. Rotahalers are used with individual capsules that contain the medicine. Diskhalers use a disk-shaped insert that contains multiple doses of the medicine.

THE DISKUS

GSK began to work on what is now known as the Diskus in 1988. Two key players in its development were Andrew Grant, who now serves as GSK's director of worldwide device technology, and Paul Rand, GSK's industrial design manager. Both men are based in the United Kingdom.

Grant joined Allen & Hanburys in 1973 after receiving his pharmacy degree, and left the company to work for a manufacturer of generic aspirin tablets, powders, preparations, and creams and ointments that were sold at retail outlets. Two years later, Grant was hired by Allen & Hanburys to run the GSK manufacturing department for inhalation aerosols. In 1984, he set up the aerosol manufacturing department for Glaxo's factory in Zebulon, North Carolina, and later returned to the United Kingdom, where he worked on the development of inhalation aerosol products and dry powder inhaler formulations.

In 1973, upon receiving a degree in product design, Paul Rand joined a consulting firm based in the United Kingdom that designed a wide range of consumer products, ranging from garden tools to razors. He worked there for nine years; one of the firm's clients was Glaxo. Rand's firm designed the Rotahaler for Glaxo; it was one of the company's first dry powder inhalers. Rand left the consulting firm in 1993 when he moved to Glaxo to work as an appliance designer in what was then known as the company's department of packaging science. One of his first assignments was to work on the Diskhaler dry powder device.

Unlike the Rotahaler and Diskhaler devices, the Diskus has a thirty-day supply of Advair that provides a morning inhalation and an evening inhalation, or a total of sixty doses per month. It has a built-in dose counter, so the patient knows exactly how many doses remain before running out. Its counter starts at number sixty and counts down after an inhalation—it should be discarded at zero or one month after removing the Advair Diskus from its protective foil pouch, whichever comes first. The Diskus is breath-activated, so hand-breath coordination is not necessary. Since it is breath-activated, it contains no aerosols, which makes it environmentally friendly. It's also a low-resistance device. The patient basically breathes at will. This is an important feature for young and elderly patients, as well as patients with severe asthma who may have difficulty drawing in air. It's easy to use; the directions read: "Open, click, and inhale." A health-care provider can teach a patient how to use it in a matter of a few minutes. The Diskus device's shape resembles a hockey puck but is smaller and fits in a shirt pocket.

"One of the strengths of the Diskus," Grant explains, "is that the patient's inhalation takes the drug from the foil blister inside the device and delivers it to the patient's lungs. It doesn't require systems to coordinate delivering the doses in order to get it into the patient. You don't need other mechanical systems to discharge the powder. A major challenge in developing the Diskus was making sure its stability was precise so it could release the powder in exact doses with no variations. What makes it so difficult is that to be effective the particles of the powder must get into the right part of the airways to be absorbed. This means they have to be just right, ranging in size from two to five microns [a micron is one-millionth of a meter]. If the particles are made too small [less than two microns], they will enter the very bottom of the lung and be absorbed into the blood and could cause side effects. If the particles are too large, they will get cleared out of the lung and won't have an effect."

"The Diskus had to be precisely constructed to keep moisture out," Rand says, "because if moisture gets in, the formulation could aggregate and could make the fine particles coarser. We had to make sure each and every individual dose had the best protection, and to do this, each is packed in a double foil aluminum blister. So it was essential that the drug was well protected."

In an age of high technology, the Diskus requires no source of energy other than one's inhalation. Perhaps its simplicity is what makes it so special—and why experts in the pulmonary field rave so much about how it's so user-friendly. But as low-tech as it appears, the Diskus was exceedingly difficult to design. "We designed the Diskus to be small enough for people to comfortably carry around so it could be taken out and used discreetly," Rand explains. "We didn't want it to be large and cumbersome, but making it compact and still able to hold a thirty-day supply was no easy matter. We tried many different ways in search of a solution. Then one day I had one of those eureka moments when I was looking at an assortment of different products that packaged things into compacted spaces, and I started thinking about how film is stored in a camera. This is when the idea originated about having a device to dispense a consistent quantity of powder packaged in individual blisters—with sixty of them on a strip similar to the film in a camera. Having a thirty-day supply of the drug in a single Diskus was a major convenience for the patient. For example, the Diskhaler took either four or eight doses in each pack, which meant the patient had to keep reloading the device."

Rand's ingenuity was brilliant but easier said than done. "The challenge was to get a consistent and reliable delivery even when the patient was only able to put a relatively low flow rate through the device on one occasion," Grant explains, "and on another occasion, the patient was able to muster up a high airflow rate and still get the same delivery of the drug to the lungs. For this reason, the delivery had to be insensitive to changes in airflow. In order to minimize the inflammation in people's asthma to prevent them from having exacerbation, a patient must be stabilized on the right dose for him or her, and for the product to be most effective, it's important to always have the same dose."

To make their device even more user-friendly, during a development study the Diskus team did ergonomic handling studies with patients, comparing their product with those of competitors. The purpose of the study was to come up with a device that was more easily and readily usable for patients, which would in turn reduce possible errors. Studies also showed that patients were enamored with the counter feature displaying the number of doses left in the Diskus. Devices such as the Rotahaler and Diskhaler required the patient to keep track of the doses used. Grant states, "Patients told us: 'With the Diskus, I can see that I have ten doses left so I need to now think about getting another prescription.' There was also positive feedback from parents, who said, 'When I used to send my child to school, I had no way of knowing if she took her medication. Now I can see that the number of doses is down on the counter so I have some assurance that the device is at least being operated.' I was personally surprised to see how important this feature was to parents and how passionately they felt about it."

While the company used cutting-edge technology, including CAD with 3D imagery, the design of the Diskus's mouthpiece came from an unlikely source, one that was definitely not high-tech. "We wanted to create a shape that was easy, convenient, and a nice fit in people's mouths," Grant says, "but we were having difficulty translating the shape we were looking for into a drawing that the toolmaking cutters could work with. We struggled with the design for quite some time and were not making any progress. Then we came across an African woman's neck collar that came from an archaeological site. It was several thousand years old, and it was almost the same shape of the mouthpiece we were designing. With all our efforts that we put into trying to define the complex shape in geometry so we could translate it reliably and consistently into machines and lumps of steel for producing components, people from an ancient civilization were able to do that same shape for a necklace."

"We also spent a lot of time trying to make the Diskus as robust as possible," Rand explains, "particularly for children, where it might get kicked around on the playground, dropped on concrete, or accidentally sat on. Somebody once joked, 'When the Diskus is out of medicine, the kids could use it as a hockey puck,' and in jest I replied, 'Precisely. They can even use it as a puck before it runs out.' Of course no one, young or old, should use the Diskus as a puck!"

The Advair Diskus comes in one color: purple. Why purple? GSK and other companies have inhalers in various colors, and in the 1990s, asthmatics on more than one medication used multiple inhalers. By having a relatively unusual color, it is less likely that a patient might reach into a drawer or purse and take the wrong inhaler.

For his work on the Diskus, along with team members Michael Davies, David Hearne, and Richard Walker, Rand is listed as a coinventor on the patent. There was other recognition. In addition to the several design and packaging awards they received, in 1995 the International Society for Pharmaceutical Engineering presented the team with an award. Then, in 1999, the team received the Queen of England Award for technology. This prestigious award was presented to the company by the lord lieutenant of the county, a representative of the queen, at the company's Diskus development and manufacturing site. Later, Grant, Rand, and their director were invited to Buckingham Palace and presented to the queen in recognition for their achievement.

As GSK's vice president of respiratory regulatory affairs, Elaine Jones was responsible for getting Advair approved by the FDA and other regulatory authorities throughout the world. Jones received a bachelor of pharmacy degree at the University of London's School of Pharmacy and then went on to earn a Ph.D. there. During a 1989 job interview in Glaxo's drug development department, a woman from human resources advised her: "If you want to really do well in development, you should start your work with the company in a commercial environment."

"She told me," Jones says, " 'Start your career as a sales rep because once you're in development, you will never go back.' I took her advice, and for the next year, I was a sales rep selling mainly the inhaled steroid medicine, beclomethasone, to physicians. She gave me excellent advice because I came away with a clear understanding about this business by seeing things from a physician's and pharmacist's perspective. In 1991, I moved into development and straight into regulatory affairs."

THE 3-IN-1 FDA APPROVAL

"I became involved with Advair in 1993 just after the preclinical tests were conducted on animals," Jones explains. "The animal toxicology data was needed so we could find out if it was safe to test on humans. The nature of drug development is that it is unpredictable because one can never be sure about what is going to happen until the clinical results are in. And with Advair, we were dealing with a combination medicine consisting of salmeterol and fluticasone, plus the Diskus, all of which had to be filed and approved by the FDA. This meant that the company was required to do clinical tests on both the drug and the device.

"My work isn't running clinical trials. You'll find me in my office behind big stacks of papers," Jones tells, shugging her shoulders. "When a study is conducted, a pharmaceutical company has to prespecify what it wants to show. My job was to prepare the clinical trial application and state upfront what we planned to do. We had to let the FDA know that this was what we were going to show. This was what we were going to measure. This information is submitted to the FDA in the form of a protocol, which specifies the primary and secondary end points that we intend to measure. All of this [is] completed prior to starting a study, and then we work toward meeting the objectives in these protocols. The FDA lives and dies by these protocols and the specified end points. When a study is run and the clinical results come in, we have to analyze the data according to the protocol and end points that we put in the application. There are three stages of the clinical studies—Phase I, Phase II, and Phase III—and we really can't do the Phase II studies until the results of the Phase I studies are in, and the same for Phase III—you can't really do that until you have the results from the Phase II studies. It's like what you do with building blocks; the lower blocks support the ones on top. Phase III is the last segment of the pre-approval drug development process, and what was so amazing with the Advair was how the data came in so positive. It's extremely unusual to have everything fall in place, and this drug did exactly that, across the board."

"Like I previously said," Jones concludes, "it doesn't matter how many times you've done it [drug development] before, it's never predictable because you don't know what's going to happen in the clinical trials. You can't be sure how patients are going to respond; you really aren't certain until you study the data."

During the clinical studies, compliance records are kept, and generally patients comply, if for no other reason than because they are being closely monitored by physicians. In some studies, they are required to fill out a daily diary card and, in the case of Advair, jot down notes on minute details, including how many times they wheezed and coughed. Since they were so closely scrutinized, compliance rates were high during the clinical trials. It's another story, however, when nobody is monitoring patients.

The convenience of Advair may contribute to better patient compliance. The Diskus receives high marks for convenience. Earlier powder inhalers had to be loaded by the patient, and the devices could not accommodate a preloaded thirty-day supply of medicine. Advair is used twice a day, once in the morning and again at night before getting in bed, just as a toothbrush.

Both the Diskus and Advair had to be approved by the FDA. It was a package deal. The Diskus was not approved separately as a medical device but as part of one complete drug product in conjunction with the medication. "It's considerably harder to make inhalation products," explains Jones, "than to make a medicine in tablet form. The most difficult part is getting the particles to be an exact size so they can get into the part of the airways where they have to be absorbed, and the FDA has demanding specifications that regulate the size of those particles. We also wanted to come out with three different strengths. This meant we had to conduct clinical studies on each strength, and since the amount of medication differs, we had to have three separate Diskus devices. It's all quite complicated, much more so than changing the dosage of a drug taken in pill form. Each strength of Advair had to be approved by the FDA. The FDA has specialist chemists in its pulmonary and allergy drug products division that work with both the device and the medication. They primarily review inhaled products and intranasal products."

During the Phase II studies, Diskus devices were initially made on a small scale in a pilot plant. As Advair moved forward to the Phase III trials, thousands of Diskuses were required to complete the tests. To assure an adequate supply, Andrew Grant and Paul Rand worked overtime with their team to make sure that the company's manufacturing capacity would be able to produce quality Diskuses in large quantities, to be used not only for the completion of the Phase III trials but also to meet future demand for the product.

"We had to invent the manufacturing process," Grant explains, "which meant developing the equipment that would ultimately make the Diskus. We designed and built the first two machines and, using them as models, we approached an equipment manufacturing company to make our production machines for us. All this was necessary in order to demonstrate to the FDA that we'd have everything in place when the time came to have product available to fill all prescriptions following approval."

Toward the end of the clinical trials, the company's manufacturing plants cranked up production. The FDA also requires a pharmaceutical company to provide manufacturing data that demonstrates it not only can make adequate quantities for the trials but has the capacity to produce large quantities following a drug's launch. It must also be validated that there will be no compromise in the drug's quality when it is mass-produced.

A new drug that is "first in class" is usually reviewed by an FDA advisory committee, which makes a recommendation to the FDA on whether the drug should be approved. As a fixed combination of two medicines, Advair was "new enough," which meant that GSK was required to make a presentation to an advisory committee of about a dozen experts in the field. This particular committee included pulmonologists, allergists, and even a nurse practitioner. Following its review, such a group of experts makes a recommendation for approval or nonapproval to the FDA. While the FDA can overrule the committee, it generally goes along with its recommendation. "We prepared for nearly two months for this all-day affair," Jones explains. "So much was riding on it. The committee members riddled us with questions about Advair, and they didn't let up for the entire day. It was truly a nail-biting experience. At the end of the day, the committee took a vote and it unanimously voted in favor of Advair. This is unusual and was a feather in our cap."

Advair received FDA approval for three dose strengths, of 100, 250, and 500 micrograms of fluticasone; the dose of salmeterol remains constant at 50 micrograms. This allows the physician to treat different severities of the disease, with lower or higher amounts of the steroid dose, according to a patient's needs. The doctor can also titrate down or up based on the patient's progress. As with other medicines, it's generally better to control a disease by having a patient take the minimum amount of a drug that suits his or her needs. It is, however, more costly and challenging to seek FDA approval for three strengths because a company must do clinical development programs on each strength.

During the clinical trials of Advair, the company worked on the development of the Diskus and an aerosol device using a propellant that does not harm the ozone. The Diskus progressed quicker and it received approval first. "When Advair was launched, our challenge with the Diskus was to make doctors feel comfortable prescribing it," says Darrell Baker. "There was some initial resistance, and to win doctors over, we had to teach them how to instruct the use of it to their patients. To convince them that it was easy to use, our sales reps provided sample placebo Diskus devices to doctors that they could use themselves during a demonstration with patients. Seeing how easy it was to use, they felt comfortable prescribing the Diskus, and there was no more problem. Their patients willingly accepted it as an easier and more effective way to take their medication."

MAKING IT

To receive FDA approval to manufacture Advair at GSK's plant in Zebulon, North Carolina, a rigorous inspection by regulatory authorities was conducted. GSK started setting up this manufacturing facility in 1999, nearly two years prior to Advair's approval date. This meant the company incurred huge capital expenses in machinery, recruiting, training, and salaries for people on the payroll—all in anticipation of receiving approval of the Zebulon plant as a manufacturing site.

Will Boykin is production manager at GSK's multidose powder inhaler plant in Zebulon. In this position, he can relate firsthand to the role that the FDA plays in the manufacturing of drugs in the United States. "The FDA regulates everything that goes on here, everything—the Diskus and the active ingredients in it," he emphasizes. "The agency does a general inspection of the site every two to three years, and if there is a problem, they'll come back to make sure we take care of it. Meanwhile, we get visits from the FDA both announced and unannounced. We have to be ready for them to come by at all times. We keep the factory sanitized like what you'd expect in a surgery room. Our production area is as clean and fresh as air can be. The air you breathe in there goes through a HEPA filter that removes organisms, dust, and particles down to the smallest, minute size. To get in, you must wear special clothing and shoes and enter through a door to a room with airlocks. Once the first door closes, you go through a second door. This assures that the air inside is crystal clean. Believe me, you've never breathed in such fresh air. In fact, unlike other people who take a break and go outside to get fresh air, in our case we have to come inside to get it."

"Everything we do here must be documented, so when the FDA asks for it, it's available," Boykin tells. "This means keeping accurate records of inventories of all batches of the powder and of course the Diskus and its components. Our computer systems keep records of every unit that goes out of here, so if something goes awry, we can track it down. Because we know what batch its ingredients came from, we can locate all of it. Every unit can be traced back to the day it was made, and with our systems, we can locate where it's been shipped."

Each Diskus consists of fifteen components. The final product is assembled in Zebulon as well as in two plants located in the United Kingdom and France. The raw materials for the powder—fluticasone and salmeterol—are made at the company's Jurong site in Singapore and shipped to GSK's Ware site in the United Kingdom to go through a micronization process; they're then transported to Zebulon to be inserted into foil strips that contain sixty or twenty-eight doses per Diskus. "It's a lot more complicated than putting sixty tablets in a bottle," Boykin asserts.

In 2005, 21 million Advair units were shipped from the Zebulon plant. Another 40 million units were made in the United Kingdom to supply the United States and other countries where Advair is marketed; 35 million units were produced in France for markets other than the United States. The Zebulon plant operates 4 shifts, each working 3 12-hour days a week. While there is not a regular Saturday night or Sunday shift, these times are reserved for overtime production. Boykin explains: "We have two priorities: safety and quality, and these are achieved through repetition. Our people understand that it's crucial to do the same thing each time. There can be no variance because every unit must be made exactly like every other unit. It's a very controlled kind of production. We're after repetition—good repetition.

"Everyone here knows that we work in a competitive industry, and with the American public's concern about the cost of medicine, there is an ongoing effort to come up with ways to produce a good quality product at a low cost. With two sites abroad that make an identical product, our people are aware that we're engaged in a global economy, and if our production costs run too high, it would be poor business for management to continue operating this plant. While we internally engage in friendly competition, we work closely with our sister plants in the U.K. and France. My counterpart in Ware and I are constantly exchanging ideas, and if a problem arises here, I don't hesitate to call him. 'Here's what's happened,' I'll say. 'Have you ever experienced this in your plant? What do you recommend?' We talk constantly on the phone. We work as a team, sharing a goal to efficiently produce a better product."

"A lot of folks living in this part of North Carolina have asthma and they take Advair," Boykin adds. "Our people are constantly being reinforced with comments from patients about how well they're doing since they were prescribed Advair. We are very much aware that we are contributing to the welfare of people and this fills us with pride. We know our work is important. It's not as if we're making T-shirts here."

FDA APPROVAL FOR ANOTHER INDICATION

While Advair was being launched as a medicine to treat asthma in the United States in 2001, the company was conducting still more clinical studies to eventually receive FDA approval for the drug for another indication—the treatment of chronic obstructive pulmonary disease (COPD). "Asthma was relatively easy to test," says Darrell Baker, "because it could be studied in a shorter period of time. It was only a matter of weeks or a few months before we could demonstrate Advair's efficacy for asthma. That's because asthmatics react quickly to the drug. This was not the case with COPD, so longer studies were needed to establish efficacy. Additionally, it's a more difficult disease to treat. As we learned, like asthma, COPD patients also have a form of inflammation in their lungs, although it's not the same form of inflammation. And they too respond to the bronchodilator component in Advair because it opens their airways. Their response, however, is not as quick as an asthmatic's. This meant more time was necessary to get the clinical studies' results."

"Over a period of time, the standard of practice evolved for treating COPD with a combination of steroids and bronchodilators," explains Tachi Yamada. "This practice has been more prevalent in Europe than in the U.S. and is probably why the company received approval for our COPD indication in the European market earlier than in this country. I believe our clinical studies and the drug's track record in Europe played a role in demonstrating to the FDA that Advair should be granted an approval for COPD in the U.S."

"As recently as the 1990s, COPD has been known as 'the neglected disease,'" Malcolm Johnson points out. "It was very much seen as a smoking-related disease and one that was the patient's own fault." Sixty-four percent of smokers are not concerned about developing COPD, even though more than half of them (55 percent) experience at least one of the disease's symptoms a minimum of once a week. Based on a 2004 survey by the American Lung Association, a majority of smokers who could have COPD are ignoring the signs. Although COPD is not as well-known a disease as asthma, according to the American Lung Association it is America's fourth-ranking cause of death, claiming the lives of more than 120,000 Americans annually. It is estimated that COPD will be the third largest cause of death worldwide by 2020.

The term COPD includes chronic bronchitis, chronic obstructive bronchitis, emphysema, or combinations of these conditions. Asthma and COPD are two different diseases, although both have adverse effects on the respiratory system. COPD symptoms can range from chronic cough and sputum production to severe, disabling shortness of breath and chest pains. Like asthma, there is swelling and irritation of the airways. And there is bronchial constriction, in which the actual muscles around the airways constrict and impede the flow of air in and out of the lungs. In the United States, cigarette smoking is by far the biggest risk factor. Other factors include other forms of smoking, such as second-hand smoke. Occupational dusts and chemicals pose another threat. COPD is diagnosed by testing with spirometry and is confirmed when airway obstruction is evident. Once a person has COPD, there is no known cure. However, treatment will relieve symptoms and improve quality of life. But what has been damaged remains damaged.

The FDA approved Advair for a COPD indication in late 2003, and in early 2004, GSK sales reps began calling on pulmonologists and aller-gists. While Advair comes in three strengths, 100/50, 250/50, and 500/50, it is the 250/50 strength that is approved to treat COPD, used twice a day, in the morning and at night.

In contrast with asthma, there was not a strong focus in the past on developing drugs to treat COPD. Part of the reason is, reveals Elaine Jones: "It's quite obvious when you have asthma, because the symptoms are apparent. When an asthmatic runs out of breath, the fear factor takes over and motivates him to see a physician. COPD, however, is a progres-sive disease, and in its early stages has no noticeable symptoms, so unless an individual is tested, he won't even know he has it. The symptoms and the onset of the disease happen concurrently, and only then does the in-dividual become frightened and choose to seek treatment. As one COPD patient described it to me: "It's like breathing in with three-quarters of a breath. Then hold it, and then breathe in again on top of that. Then you'll know what it feels like."

"Since smoking is the main cause of COPD, smokers resist telling their doctor, 'I'm having trouble breathing,' because they don't want to hear, 'You have to give up smoking.' There is also the guilt factor. Patients are embarrassed because the disease is something they brought upon themselves. They are ashamed that they didn't listen to all the warnings on smoking. Rather than see a physician they'll sometimes cut back or even quit smoking. But it's too late. Advair may help prevent their condi-tion from getting worse, but it won't restore their health. The character of the airway obstruction is that it is a fixed obstruction. Even if a person with COPD stops smoking, he or she won't get [back] much of the lung function that has been lost. That's because there's been destruction of the air sacs that are responsible for exchanging oxygen and removing carbon dioxide from the blood—that's what the lungs do. I can only say that, with Advair, there is a good chance the condition won't get worse."

COPD exacerbations can be life-threatening, with a 30 percent mortality rate over a five-year period. The clinical results on Advair for treating COPD were very promising, however, demonstrating that the drug has good efficacy, controls symptoms, and significantly reduces exacerbations.

Due to the number of people in denial who don't seek treatment for COPD, it is difficult to pinpoint just how many people have not been di-agnosed. Many experts estimate approximately twenty million Ameri-cans have COPD, about the same number of people with asthma.

With an indication to treat COPD along with treating asthma, there are millions of people in the United States who might benefit from Advair. An estimated 5.5 million Americans take Advair, and 10 million people take it worldwide. Sales in 2004 were $2.4 billion in the United States and $4.5 billion worldwide, making Advair GSK's all-time top-selling drug, and one of bestselling medicines in the world.

5

JOHNSON & JOHNSON COMPANY PROFILE

It was 1861 and cannon fire was beginning to rumble throughout the Confederate South. Volunteers were being recruited to join the rapidly escalating Civil War and young men from both sides were heeding the call to arms by the thousands.

Sylvester Johnson, a hardworking farmer from the Wyoming Valley of northeast Pennsylvania had a large family, eleven children in all, and several boys were of draft age. His eldest two sons, Charles and William, were sturdy and patriotic young men. Completely unable to resist the challenge and romance of the great conflict, they promptly marched off to join the Union army, Charles becoming a second lieutenant in the Pennsylvania Volunteers and William a private.

Sylvester Johnson was unable to bear the possibility of losing another son to the war. To spare himself and his family an unspeakable tragedy, he sent his next eldest son to apprentice with his cousin James G. Wood in his bustling apothecary business in Poughkeepsie, New York. At the youthful age of sixteen, Robert Wood Johnson began a journey that would eventually culminate in the Johnson & Johnson companies, one of the most revered and ubiquitous companies in the world. It can be said that if corporate America were to seek a model of a company that cares for the public *and* its employees with equal vigor, Johnson & Johnson would be at the top of the list.

Poughkeepsie was a thriving manufacturing hub when young Robert arrived. A constant stream of traveling salesmen, belligerent street hawkers and con men, bawdy nightlife, and the constant vibration of a city created an eye-opening scene for a young boy fresh from the quiet farmlands of Pennsylvania. To keep the boy from experiencing too much of the wrong element, James Wood allowed Robert to stay with his family, and he in turn worked long hours at the store.

As was true with most drugstores of the day, the Wood & Tittamer Apothecary sold not only drugs and medicines but chemicals, paints, perfumes, and window glass. Johnson's early days at the store were spent pushing a broom, running errands, and doing odd jobs, but in time evolved into more important work, especially learning an art that would forever influence his professional life: making medicinal plasters.

From the beginning of time, people have tried to create ways to treat ailments and illnesses. One early technique involved applying various juices, gums, roots, plants, herbs, and even animal substances right on the skin. It was believed that the healing elements of these concoctions would be absorbed by direct application. The Chinese, for example, used opium and elephant fat, the Egyptians used slime from the Nile, the Hindus used arsenic, and the Greeks tried poppy juice and mustard. The problem was in getting the "medicines" to stick on the skin. Various attempts were made to apply the treatments by making "plasters" and affixing them with animal skins, plant leaves, and flexible bark. Primitive as it sounds, these treatments were somewhat effective. By the mid-1860s, the highest form of the art was the creation of a mixture of medicinal products mixed with flexible rubber, commonly known as "skin plaster."

But as Robert Johnson soon discovered, making the skin plaster was backbreaking work. He'd work for hours with a hot iron heated over a lamp trying to mold crude rubber into a pliable lump that could be shaped into a medicated plaster. It failed more often than it succeeded and was widely regarded as the worst job in the pharmaceutical trade.

Toward the end of 1864, Robert Johnson's apprenticeship was completed. With the help of Mr. Wood, the young boy obtained a job with a wholesaling firm in New York City. After several uneventful years, he set himself up as a broker and importer of drugs. It was in that venture that he met up with another ambitious young importer, George J. Seabury. In 1873 the two young entrepreneurs teamed up and formed Seabury & Johnson, Inc.

Medical practice at the time was primitive. The average physician had less than a high school education, and a medical degree was earned by attending the same four- or five-month course of medical lectures for two consecutive years with no written examination required. The "better physicians" typically had a bachelor's degree, the same medical school regimen, and one to three years of study abroad, typically in Germany, which was the hotbed of scientific and medical development at the time. The "patent medicines" available at the time were essentially worthless, consisting primarily of alcohol and peddled by quacks and pseudomedical charlatans off the backs of buckboard wagons. Unfortunately, the "real" medicines offered by the thinly credentialed physicians were not much better. Surgery was nearly a death sentence, and in some hospitals the mortality rate for patients hovered around 90 percent. What was worse was that nobody knew why. The surgeons of the day couldn't accept the fact that they might be contaminating their own patients by operating ungloved with unsterile instruments. While it's hard to believe today, back then, it was not uncommon for a doctor to perform an operation wearing his street clothes.

Transferring curative agents through the skin via plasters was considered the most advanced method of medicating an ailment. The therapeutic value of medical plasters was relatively high, and well received by serious physicians. Thus the business of Seabury & Johnson prospered and grew. Johnson had become fascinated by the teachings of an iconoclastic English surgeon, Joseph P. Lister, who had theoretically identified invisible bacteria as the cause of the infections ravaging patients who underwent surgery. Lister shook the medical establishment when he suggested that the bacteria were airborne. He referred to them as "invisible assassins." Johnson's fascination stemmed from the fact that Lister used "antiseptic bandages" to cover surgical incisions. The twenty-nine-year-old entrepreneur became absolutely convinced of the merits of Lister's radical theories on sterilization when he heard Lister address the International Medical Congress in 1876 at the centennial exhibition held in Philadelphia.

Another major problem addressed by Lister was that of closing incisions of surgery patients. Up to this time, only two options were available: (1) closing the wounds with nonsterile sutures made of sheep intestines (called "catgut" even though no cats were ever used; rather they derived the name from the German *kitgut*, meaning "fiddle," or "fiddle string"), or (2) cauterizing with a red-hot iron pressed to the flesh (more patients died from the shock and pain of this procedure than from the surgery itself).

The ever curious and innovative Johnson became intrigued with the possibility of creating a sterile surgical dressing to combat postoperative infections. He not only succeeded in creating sterile dressings, but he also continued to develop new forms of sterile sutures, antiseptic and medicated gauze, superabsorbent cotton, and revolutionary new plasters made of recently acquired India rubber. The 1879 Seabury & Johnson catalog listed thirty pages of medicated plasters for a wide variety of diseases, and "Lister's antiseptic gauze." In 1880, sales were $381,765.

Johnson's younger brothers James Wood and Edward Mead were the first of many relatives that the company hired. When Seabury protested that his partner had put too many family members on the payroll, it was mutually decided that the partnership should be dissolved. This prompted the Johnson brothers to form a family partnership in 1886, and, along with fourteen employees, the company moved into its new quarters on the fourth floor of a small building that had once housed the Janeway Wallpaper Factory. The following year the company incorporated and became Johnson & Johnson. In 1888, Fred Kilmer joined the company as its first scientific director, a position he held for forty-five years. His son was Joyce Kilmer, the poet-hero of World War I. Evidently there were writing genes in the family—Fred Kilmer was also an excellent writer who penned countless articles in Johnson & Johnson's magazines, *Red Cross Notes* and *The Red Cross Messenger*, two publications that had a major influence on the scientific community.

The first products were improved medicinal plasters containing medical compounds mixed in an adhesive. Then a revolutionary surgical dressing was quickly developed and placed on the market. Recognizing the critical need for improved antiseptic surgical procedures, the company designed a soft, absorbent cotton and gauze dressing that could be mass-produced and shipped in quantity to hospitals and every crossroads physician and druggist. One of the company's most innovative early products was packaged gauze and cotton complete with medications in a bottle. Initially it was distributed to hospitals and doctors' offices—it was a time when most surgery was performed in the doctor's office because people avoided hospitals, and for good reason. Hospitals were not sterilized as they are today. Johnson & Johnson was a leader in making sterilized hospital supplies and has remained so to this day. From the beginning, the company's cotton was wrapped in blue paper, a tradition that continues to this day.

By the late 1880s the medical world had still not fully embraced Lister's ideas about germs. This prompted Robert Johnson to collaborate with Kilmer in 1888 to publish a book entitled *Modern Methods of Antiseptic Wound Treatment.* Not only was the book a rousing success, but it literally changed the medical practices of the entire country, selling nearly four million copies. The book became the standard text on antiseptic practices in the United States. It also served as a powerful promotional piece for Johnson & Johnson, as their product line fit neatly into the "enlightened approach" urged in the book.

Business soared, and in a short time the company's new headquarters in New Brunswick, New Jersey, was the hub of tremendous activity with new employees being added constantly. This was the period when Johnson & Johnson's revolutionary corporate identity began to emerge and it became known as a company that stood for creating products that improved life, cared for workers, and gave back to the community that supported its products.

Robert Wood Johnson was the driving force behind the evolution. As history would prove, he succeeded in passing along this deep care for workers and an uncompromising demand for product quality to everyone at the company.

One of the company's early landslide success stories was Johnson's Baby Powder. Johnson & Johnson got in the baby powder business by accident. One type of medicated plaster sold by Johnson & Johnson created skin irritation. To help alleviate the blisters, the company included a small sample of Italian talc with each order. Soon, they began receiving orders for just the talc as mothers discovered its beneficial effects on infants. Johnson's Baby Powder is known worldwide today, and with its recognizable fragrance, it is one of the company's most enduring legacies.

In 1893 the talc was packaged in a box that was originally distributed to midwives and given to mothers following childbirth. The mothers liked it so much, the company started to sell it in drugstores. Also in the midwife's box were twelve sanitary napkins. Prior to this, there was no such product available to purchase. After the company received hundreds of letters from women wanting to know where they could buy these products, the company started to manufacture them—the first company to make sanitary napkins in the United States. The baby powder and the sanitary napkins were the first products in the company's personal products line—and years later, when sales became so big, Johnson & Johnson formed its personal products company. Incidentally, this is a pattern that the company has followed over the years—when a particular product or line of products enjoys large sales, it was "spun off" to become an entity of its own. Today Johnson & Johnson consists of more than two hundred companies.

The Johnson brothers became known for more and more consumer-oriented products, including sanitary napkins, toothpaste, corn and bunion shields, maternity/obstetric packets, infant nutrition products, bath soap, cola syrup, sterile gauze, sterile sutures, adhesive tapes, first-aid kits, and much more. These were all considered revolutionary contributions and led to the observation that "you can't get well without Johnson & Johnson." They even continued in their publishing tradition, creating *Johnson's First Aid Manual*, the first of its kind and hailed as a major achievement by the medical establishment. The company's help during such crises as hurricane relief in Texas, the Spanish-American War effort, and the Great San Francisco Earthquake of 1906 would only serve to add further proof that Johnson & Johnson placed aiding human misery above corporate profits.

Robert Wood Johnson died in 1910 and was succeeded by his brother James. Earlier Edward had left the company to pursue his interest in nutritional products. James Wood Johnson succeeded his brother and was president until 1932. He maintained the company's continuity from his brother's leadership and further expanded the company's employee benefits, including higher wages, health benefits for the workers and their families, legal and marital counseling, pensions, and even meals on some occasions for workers on the late shifts. Under his leadership morale and employee satisfaction ranked among the highest of all U.S.-based companies. During James Wood Johnson's tenure, the company introduced the Band-Aid Brand Adhesive Bandage, which remains today one of the company's most famous products. And in 1927, the company came out with Modess Sanitary Napkins. (It wasn't until 1970 that Stayfree Napkins were launched. Using new technology, they were the first nonbelted, adhesive-backed sanitary protection product.)

But for all the drive and vision Robert Wood Johnson had brought to the ever-widening Johnson & Johnson world, his namesake—charismatic and philanthropic son Robert Wood Johnson II—would outdo him. This young man's vision, commanding presence, and self-assured attitude ensured that Johnson & Johnson would thrive under his leadership.

Robert Wood Johnson II was just seventeen when his world-renowned father died in 1910. He was attending prep school at the time, but following his father's death he made an abrupt career change: he announced that he would not attend college as planned but instead would work for Johnson & Johnson, starting at the bottom and working his way up. Over the strong criticism and advice from his family, Robert Wood Johnson II took a job in the power plant of the company. He soon began migrating from department to department, staying on just long enough to master the job. He had an easy rapport with the workers, who loved his attitude and quickly adopted him as one of their own.

Johnson was a fast-rising star in the company, a competent and respected businessman who exhibited flash and daring combined with a quick, insightful mind. This combination proved to be an invaluable management asset to his uncle James. It was clear that it was only a matter of time before Robert II would be chosen to head the company.

He assumed the presidency in 1932, at the height of the Great Depression. Just prior to the depression, Johnson & Johnson annual sales were $20 million. Through deft management and a commitment to his employees, Johnson was able to maintain those sales figures throughout the downturn, and never had to lay off a single employee. This was a significant accomplishment in comparison to the mass layoffs that occurred during these hard times.

Young Johnson realized that long-term corporate stability for Johnson & Johnson would require great political savvy welded to a philosophy of taking care of the masses of both his customers and the company's growing employee base. His first act in this regard was sending newly elected president Franklin D. Roosevelt a letter outlining a plan for the financial recovery of the country. Included in this plan was a call for a federal law increasing wages and reducing the hours in the workweek. To set the pace, he gave his own employees a 5 percent raise. Though few companies followed suit, the goodwill created among his employees was vast and would add considerably to his legacy.

But he went a step further. In 1936, Johnson took 12,000 of his own shares of Johnson & Johnson stock and launched a foundation to give grants to help New Brunswick families recover from the depression. The money was used to feed children, provide free dental work, enable people to afford down payments on homes, and more. His largesse became legendary, and the foundation was later named in his honor, the Robert Wood Johnson Foundation.

Johnson's sense of civic duty and patriotism led him to Washington, D.C., in 1942. Shortly after America was bombed at Pearl Harbor, Johnson had volunteered for the army, but because of his stature and business savvy, he was named chairman of the Smaller War Plants Corporation, based in the nation's capital. His job was to champion the cause of small companies in the contract-bidding process. In recognition of his contribution to the war effort, Johnson was given the honorary title of "brigadier general," and thereafter was referred to as General Johnson as well as "the General."

His rebellious streak and acerbic tongue displeased many Washingtonian politicians. His higher pay/lesser hours and more benefits philosophy riled the establishment, although among the working class he received hero status. He strongly supported the practice of funneling war appropriations to smaller companies and away from the large contractors. In the process, he stepped on so many toes that when he left after spending the full year of 1943 in the nation's capital, it is said that a collective sigh of relief could be heard on Capitol Hill. Always the darling of the media for his outspoken and tart portrayals of the realities of Washington politics, he said in parting, "Washington is a magnet for mediocrity."

In 1944 Johnson & Johnson became a publicly held company and was listed on the New York Stock Exchange. That same year, General Johnson wrote a "credo" that codified the company's socially responsible approach to conducting business. The credo states:

> We are responsible to the communities in which we live and work
> and to the world community as well.
> We must be good citizens—support good works and charities
> and bear our fair share of taxes.
> We must encourage civic improvements and better health and education.
> We must maintain in good order
> the property we are privileged to use,
> protecting the environment and natural resources.

Interestingly, the General was way ahead of his time when he stressed protecting the environment and natural resources. Unlike some companies that have a credo, a code of ethics, or a mission statement, Johnson & Johnson created a credo that is not a fancy slogan. Every year the company conducts a survey with its workforce and employees, who are asked:

how do you rate the company against the credo? While the wording has changed over the years, the philosophy has never been altered. Indeed, it is a living document.

Following the war, Johnson & Johnson greatly expanded its operations and began an aggressive program of acquiring other companies. This was the time when many new businesses were added to the "Johnson & Johnson family of businesses." Fast-forwarding to the present, the Johnson & Johnson Consumer Products Company, a division of Johnson & Johnson Consumer Companies, Inc., is a prime example; this group develops and markets baby care, wound care, and skin care products. Neutrogena Corporation develops, manufactures, and markets premium skin and hair care products. Ethicon, Inc., develops and markets products for surgery, wound management, and advanced wound care treatment. These are only a few of more than 220 companies in today's Johnson & Johnson family.

The company's decentralization concept allowed its different entities to be managed independently, giving the men and women who ran them the freedom to exercise their expertise without being smothered by bureaucracy that is commonplace in many large international corporations. This form of management allows the various companies to run efficiently and provides a "lightness of foot" in decision making.

The transition into pharmaceuticals did not come easily. Even the General was opposed to the idea, insisting that the company should stick with what it knows: consumable health products. Initial forays into the field included the acquisition of Ortho Pharmaceuticals, a heavily research-oriented company and home of the world famous Dr. Phillip Levine, discoverer of the Rh factor in blood.

But establishing a strong presence in the pharmaceuticals field languished. In 1959, to energize the company's efforts, it acquired McNeil Laboratories of Philadelphia. McNeil specialized in sedation and muscle relaxants, and later introduced Tylenol, an analgesic that would be deemed both the high and low point in the entire history of the Johnson & Johnson brand.

In the spring of 1963, the General, age seventy, retired as chairman and CEO. His legacy was profound; he was respected by his peers and loved by the rank-and-file. His successor, Philip Hoffman, had big shoes to fill. Hoffman rose to the occasion and smoothly assumed the role of leadership with barely a ripple. Over the next six years corporate profits doubled from $500 million to over a billion dollars.

When Robert Wood Johnson died at the age of seventy-four in 1968, it was disclosed in his will that he left nearly his entire estate ($1.2 billion) to the foundation bearing his name to "improve the healthcare of the nation." So well known were his philanthropy and wide-ranging humanitarian interests that he was praised by the House of Representatives as "a patriot whose love for America was as deep as his love for people."

At the time of his death, he was one of the last family members to work for the company. But Johnson & Johnson continued to grow and diversify under the leadership of other highly qualified leaders with the philosophy of its deceased leader deeply ingrained. They all stuck closely to a corporate credo written by Robert Wood Johnson himself, a credo that prioritized the need to provide the best products possible for the public at large, take care of employees, serve the community, and guard the financial well-being of the stockholders. With this credo serving as the backbone of the company, Robert Wood Johnson and his corporate heirs succeeded in building an organization that became respected and loved worldwide.

That stature was severely tested in 1982 when an unknown person laced capsules of extra-strength Tylenol with cyanide, killing seven people in suburban Chicago. Overnight, Johnson & Johnson was faced with a catastrophic and completely unprecedented public confidence nightmare. The consequences appeared to be overwhelming. Nonetheless, the Johnson & Johnson management team took swift and decisive action. No cover-up, denials, or lame excuses were offered. No Johnson & Johnson employee was instructed to respond to questions posed by the media with a "no comment" answer. Working with the news media and local authorities, management stepped to the plate to inform and protect the public. The company issued an immediate recall of Tylenol and urged all consumers to destroy whatever stock they had at home: thirty-one million bottles in all.

Following this heinous crime and the staggering financial losses incurred by Johnson & Johnson, a rejuvenated company vowed to rebuild the Tylenol product and clear its good name. Within an amazingly short time of six weeks, the company introduced a triple-sealed bottle (which became an industry standard), and began a new, aggressive marketing campaign. Within a year the brand was back to its predisaster sales level.

Yet in 1986, lightning struck again: a repeat of the crime took place in New York and one person died. The company, having learned from its previous experience, initiated a series of actions similar to those in the

1982 incident, and within several months the public responded by making Tylenol the leading seller once again. (The killer was never found in either case.)

The leadership at Johnson & Johnson provided unprecedented access to the media. Chairman James E. Burke went before the cameras to assure the public. What was the public response? Overwhelmingly positive. In the wake of the disaster, the *Washington Post* summarized the company's actions by saying, "Johnson & Johnson has effectively demonstrated how a major business ought to handle a disaster." As a result of his swift and honest action, in years to come, James Burke was hailed as one of America's most influential and admired business leaders.

At the time of the 1986 Tylenol debacle, Johnson & Johnson was the sixth largest pharmaceutical company in the world. Through the company's various subsidiaries it has since been responsible for the creation of thousands of new chemicals useful in such fields as mycology, parasitology, psychiatry, gastroenterology, and blood circulation. Over the next decade the company would also be among the first to venture into biotechnology, the use of "DNA probes" for rapid diagnostics, and infectious disease diagnostics.

With more than 220 operating units around the world, Johnson & Johnson has made decentralization its mantra. Worldwide sales exceeded $47 billion in 2004; the company spends in excess of $5 billion per year in research. It is currently the fourth largest pharmaceutical company in the world and the number-one maker of medical devices. It has over 110,000 employees worldwide.

The Johnson & Johnson product line is extremely diverse. Through a strategic mergers and acquisitions plan, Johnson & Johnson has diversified into many areas beyond health-care and pharmaceutical products. Yes, the company is best known for its consumer brand products such as Johnson's Baby Products, Band-Aid Brand, Neutrogena, Stayfree Napkins, and Tylenol. However, among the orthopedics community, the company is a world leader in technologies for joint replacements such as its revolutionary DePuy Orthopaedics Rotating Platform Knees. And through its Cordis unit, it manufactures stents that are tiny devices inserted into arteries to keep blood flowing freely and prevent the reclogging of arteries, thereby reducing the risk of heart attacks. Other innovative breakthrough products include: Onetouch Horizon blood glucose monitoring systems, Pillcam Eso (a video camera in a swallowable pill that replaces unpleasant endoscopy), Topamax for prevention of migraine headaches, Levaquin for multi-drug-resistant bacteria, Procrit for chemotherapy-related anemia, Duragesic for pain associated with cancer, and Zarnestra, an innovative cancer drug.

There are very few companies that can lay claim to an unblemished, century-long record of putting the customer before any other concern. Johnson & Johnson has carefully and patiently earned this reputation through hard work, a commitment to the values laid down by its founders, and a steady eye for doing what's right. The ultimate benefactor is all of us.

In celebration of the sixtieth anniversary of the company's credo, originally penned by General Johnson, William C. Weldon, chairman and chief executive officer, said in September 2003:

> Sixty years ago we committed to a set of beliefs about the way we do business, and we work hard to foster the values espoused in Our Credo in people around the world. Our ability to live up to this commitment is reflected in the reputation conferred upon us by those who observe the way we behave, and this reputation has become a great source of pride and a most important asset.
>
> Over time, we have recognized that good decision-making requires not only a statement of values like those embodied in Our Credo, but the analytical tools and strategies to make that commitment of values a way of life in our business. Through Credo surveys and other exercises, we assure the relevance of Our Credo in every decision we make.
>
> As we work together to build the future of Johnson & Johnson, it is critical that we remain focused on the importance of every decision, and that we all recognize our responsibility to use Our Credo values and personal good judgment to achieve the best possible outcome.

A Miracle Biotech Medicine

REMICADE: JOHNSON & JOHNSON'S TREATMENT
FOR IMMUNE-MEDIATED DISORDERS

R EMICADE, a miracle medicine made by Centocor Inc., a Johnson & Johnson unit, was first approved for Crohn's disease in 1998. Today, Remicade is indicated for many more diseases (rheumatoid arthritis, psoriasis, ulcerative colitis, and ankylosing spondylitis).

How can a single drug treat so many different kinds of diseases? What is the connection between Crohn's disease and psoriasis? Or for that matter, what do rheumatoid arthritis and ulcerative colitis have in common? To a layperson, none of these diseases seems remotely related, but thanks to biotechnology, it has now been determined that they are. The scientists that developed Remicade have found that the underlying causes of one disease could be a common element among what appear to be seemingly unrelated diseases. Therefore, by developing a "biomedicine" to treat one disease, it could be applied to treat a multitude of diseases that have similar causes. This is where biotechnology plays an important role in medicine. Most drugs are made using synthetic compounds and chemicals. Biomedicines are made from biological ingredients—that is, from living human or animal proteins.

All of the diseases mentioned as well as several others are immune-mediated inflammatory diseases (I.M.I.D.s) that arise from an overactive immune response of the body against substances and tissues normally present in the body. To put it a different way, the body attacks its own cells. A common denominator of this class of diseases is cytokines, which are hormonelike proteins produced in the body that control defenses against infections and tumors. In the case of these diseases, one particular cytokine, tumor necrosis factor-alpha (TNF), plays a role in the body's defense against infections. TNF is a naturally occurring protein involved in normal human inflammatory and immune activities. But when produced in excess, TNF is harmful, especially during chronic inflammatory processes and autoimmune disorders. Preventing the action of TNF prevents the inflammatory responses it causes.

This is fairly sophisticated science that wasn't around until only a few decades ago. All of this has been made possible by the mind-blowing advances in the biotech industry that only a decade or so ago would have been strictly science fiction.

It is true that today's biotechnology has roots in chemistry, physics, and biology, but in recent times, the field has expanded to include genetic engineering, diagnostic techniques, and cell/tissue techniques. Technically speaking, biotechnology applies to nonmedical fields such as agriculture and petrochemicals, but today, biotech companies have become synonymous with drug development, genetics, and genetic screening tests. In recent years, biotechnology has been defined as:

A collection of technologies that capitalize on the attributes of cells, such as their manufacturing capabilities, and put biological molecules, such as DNA and proteins, to work for us; it also refers to the type of manufacturing process of the drug (biological process vs. chemical process).

Biologics, or biomedicines are medical products derived from living sources, such as vaccines, blood and blood derivatives, monoclonal antibodies, other proteins, and products derived from recombinant DNA technology.

During research for this book, scientists spoke about pharmaceutical drugs versus biotech drugs and differentiated the two by making reference to "small-molecule drugs" and "large-molecule drugs." In this context, pharmaceutical companies typically work with small molecules that can be chemically synthesized. Biotech companies work with big molecules that produce drugs that are not made via chemical reactions. In the manufacturing process, traditional pharmaceutical drugs are made by combining various chemicals that are subjected to certain purification techniques; the purified chemical is constantly the same, time after time.

With biological drugs, living organisms are used to produce a medicine, and the molecules are considerably larger than drugs that are chemically synthesized. With Remicade, mouse cells are used to produce a protein; this protein is a cross between a mouse protein and a human protein that is engineered into a gene structure and is introduced into a mouse cell to produce a specific protein. That protein is Remicade.

Today's biotech companies are also referred to as biopharmaceutical companies, in part due to their close relationship with pharmaceutical companies. In fact, with the $500 million to $1 billion and fifteen years it takes for a drug to move through clinical development and the FDA approval process, it has become uncommon for a small company to succeed without teaming up with a large pharmaceutical company with sufficient resources to develop these products and take them to market. The story of Remicade begins with Centocor, a biotech company founded in 1979 that was ultimately acquired by Johnson & Johnson, one of the world's largest and most prestigious diversified health-care companies. Why and how this merger came about is told later in this chapter.

CENTOCOR'S EARLY YEARS

Centocor was founded in 1979 in Philadelphia, Pennsylvania. Its two main principals were Hubert J.P. Schoemaker, a twenty-eight-year-old biochemist, and Michael Wall, a venture capitalist. Born in the Netherlands, Schoemaker came to the United States in his late teens to improve his English. He stayed and became a full-time student at the University of Notre Dame. Upon learning that the classes were full in the university's business school, he went on to earn a bachelor's degree in chemistry. Afterward, he studied at the Massachusetts Institute of Technology, where he received his doctorate in biochemistry. Next, Schoemaker worked for Corning Medical, a division of Corning Glass Works that developed diagnostic tests. During his employment at Corning, Schoemaker headed its immuno assays program. (Immuno assays provide a relatively simple, quick, specific, and reliable method for detecting and quantifying biochemical molecules.) After a short stay at Corning Medical, he started Centocor and served as the company's first chief executive officer.

Wall graduated from the Massachusetts Institute of Technology, where he earned a degree in electrical engineering. Out of college in the 1950s, he worked for several start-up companies in the electronics field.

By the 1960s, he switched to biology and with partners formed Flow Laboratories. In 1969, the company was sold to General Research Group, a biomedical company where Wall worked for ten years. It was at General Research where he became interested in the budding field of biotechnology. Possessing strong entrepreneurial instincts, Wall joined forces with Schoemaker to form Centocor. The diverse skills possessed by the two men made for the basis of a good partnership. Two other cofounders were Hilary Koprowski, who was the director of the Wistar Institute of Anatomy and Biology in Philadelphia, and Vincent Zurawski, another scientist. Not long after the company was founded, Koprowski left Centocor to pursue other interests.

It was an opportune time to start a biotech company. When Centocor was founded, investors on Wall Street had an eye on the biotechnology industry as a potential mother lode for those who invested early. With the discovery of recombinant DNA, the investment analysts had determined that it was only a matter of time before the use of gene splicing and recombinant DNA technology would be used to provide plentiful medical value. Recombinant DNA allows sections of unrelated DNA to be cut and pasted together. The first recombinant organism was created in 1973. For his contributions to recombinant DNA technology, Paul Berg was awarded a Nobel Prize in 1980. These major breakthroughs coincided with the launching of Centocor. Having no revenues and in need of large sums of money for R&D, Centocor was only three years old when it had an initial public (stock) offering in 1982 and raised $21 million. Over the years another $923 million would be raised through a variety of additional public and private stock and debt offerings. In 1982, Centocor also introduced its first product, a diagnostic test used to detect the rabies virus. This same year, the company moved to a larger headquarters in Malvern, Pennsylvania, just west of Philadelphia.

Centocor was founded with the premise that monoclonal antibodies could be used to treat a variety of illnesses in a specific manner. Monoclonal antibodies are laboratory-produced antibodies that can locate and bind to specific substances in the body. They can target, for example, an exact antigen such as a foreign protein, bacteria, virus, or pollen. In 1979 monoclonal antibodies were a relatively new technology. Due to their high degree of specificity to what they targeted, they were often referred to as a magic bullet. Unlike small molecules made from chemicals through chemical synthesis, monoclonal antibodies had fewer side effects and were hailed as the wave of the future. The company's business plan was to enter licensing agreements with outside researchers to isolate an antibody, obtain the rights to it, and then prove its clinical relevance for diagnostic use. With limited financial resources, this business strategy differed from that of other biotech start-ups that typically funded costly in-house research with venture capital.

Centocor used its limited cash reservoir to piggyback off discoveries made in university, government, and even private laboratories. When Centocor found a promising discovery for which it saw a marketable use, it would buy the technology and allow its in-house team of scientists to develop the breakthrough into a marketable diagnostic test. "Early on we recognized that we couldn't do everything on our own," states John Ghrayeb, who was in charge of preclinical research in the 1980s. "We had to reach out to other smart people in academia to work with them. Our job was to make their science into a product—that's something that can't be done at academic institutions."

With the capability to target specific antigens, monoclonal antibodies showed great promise for being used therapeutically and diagnostically. With the enormous cost of developing a new drug from discovery through the costly clinical trials and to market, Schoemaker and Wall put together a business model whereby the company would focus on diagnostic products rather than therapeutic products. They would use biotechnology to develop diagnostic medical tests. The proposition was ambitious because the diagnostic testing market at the time was dominated by health-care giants like Abbott Laboratories and Warner Lambert. Those companies generally developed proprietary tests to run their own analyzers, which they sold to laboratories, blood banks, and hospitals. To compete directly in that market, Centocor might have to invest hundreds of millions of dollars to develop and promote its own analyzers.

The company was able to bypass another cost barrier by designing diagnostic tests that could be processed on other companies' analyzers. Centocor then sold the tests to distributors, which were usually companies that sold their own analyzers. The company's game plan also called for forming alliances with big pharmaceutical companies that had proficient sales organizations and strong customer relationships with the targeted market for Centocor's diagnostic products.

Harlan Weisman M.D. is chief science and technology officer of Medical Devices & Diagnostics at Johnson & Johnson. Prior to joining

Centocor in 1990, Weisman was assistant professor of medicine at Johns Hopkins University. He served as Centocor's head of clinical development during the 1990s and later as head of research and development. Trained in internal medicine and cardiology, Weisman has authored more than ninety journal articles and book chapters in the fields of cardiovascular disease and drug development. In the summer of 1989, Weisman received a call from a headhunter who was working with Centocor. "I had never heard of the company," Weisman says, "and I told him that I was very happy with my job at Johns Hopkins. 'Just go up and meet with these people,' the headhunter urged. I kept putting it off, but in October I finally decided to make the trip to Philadelphia. I met with the company's executives and scientists and I fell in love with the place. I had previously believed that when you're at a leading academic research center with the prestigious reputation of a Johns Hopkins, you're where the real stuff is happening. I was a research physician, and only after retirement did someone in such a position go out to graze. That's because nothing much is happening there and it's all profit motive. Boy, did I ever believe everything I read in the newspapers!

"Upon meeting the Centocor people, I could hardly believe the energy, the excitement, and the passion of what seemed nothing short of a revolution in science. There were two things in particular that caught my attention. One, there were monoclonal antibodies but nobody had been using them therapeutically. At the time, only one had been approved by the FDA and that was Johnson & Johnson's OKT3, a medicine used to block transplant rejection, and it had many side effects. Two, this drug [OKT3] is actually made in mice in what's called 'mice ascites.' They would inject the monoclonal cells that made these antibodies into the mice and then process them. Since antibodies could not be successfully maintained in-vitro, it became necessary to invent a method to synthesize monoclonal antibodies. It was a primitive method of manufacturing by today's standards, and due to the side effects, it was reserved for only a small number of patients. The common belief was that antibodies would go nowhere. There wasn't an easy way to make them since they were made from foreign protein in mice and would be attacked by the human immune system. Therefore it wasn't going to be very useful. Antibodies were considered interesting from a research standpoint, but as a human therapeutic, it was thought to be a dead end. Even so, I was fairly naïve and I was enamored with the company.

"I used monoclonal antibodies to figure out the mechanisms of underlying cardiac disease," Weisman explains. "At Johns Hopkins, when we thought a specific molecule or a specific cell was key to a disease process, we'd take labeled monoclonal antibodies and examine them under a light microscope or an electron microscope and then in a blood test and observe if something was lighting up in tissue or in the blood. Due to the high specificity, these antibodies would only bind to their target. So this enabled us to identify the pathway."

"Let me explain how this works," Weisman continues. "Antibodies are molecules that are naturally occurring proteins. They are made by immune cells that are a line of defense against viruses and bacteria that invade the body. They are also involved in I.M.I.D., in which the antibodies can become directed against what are known as autoantigens. It happens in a highly evolved system of very specific targeting on the same order that a vaccine generates antibody responses. Note now that the purpose of most vaccines is to generate antibody responses. Using a vaccine as an example, the first wave of antibody responses is somewhat nonspecific. But over time, through a selection process with immune cells responding, the antibodies become more and more specific to the target. And that specific molecule target is called an antigen. That antigen may be on the cell wall or a component of a bacterium or part of a virus. It is this specific targeting that allows the antibody to participate in either the killing of the target or the neutralization of the target. What causes it to get highly specific occurs over a period of time [and] is a mini-evolution that takes place in the body; it's a Darwinian process. The cells that make the most specific antibodies form what's called a clone, and the most highly specific one is a single clone, a monoclone. Hence, we get the term 'monoclonal antibodies.'

"When this technology was first developed, scientists learned how to make mouse antibodies against human targets. By injecting an antigen—remember, this is the target—into the mouse, the mouse's immune system would start to make antibodies against it. It then became known how to select the most highly specific antibody as well as the cell that was making it. This enabled scientists to cause that cell to keep reproducing itself. By doing this, scientists identified a cell that produced the most specific antibody against its target for neutralization—or if it was a cell, maybe destruction.

"What I just explained was the technology base where Centocor began. The company began with the premise that we could use these antibodies to diagnostically light up a target—for example, in a lab test—to find the identity of a protein or some other molecule target as a diagnostic blood test. It could also be applied to an imaging agent, a test used in nuclear medicine. While it could be used therapeutically, when the company first started management decided that its niche would be diagnostics."

With a focus on diagnostics, Centocor sold monoclonal products. The company's first product was a hepatitis test. However, in a crowded field, the test had no competitive advantage and enjoyed only marginal success. What put Centocor on the map was the CA 125 test to detect ovarian cancer. Researched by the Dana-Farber Institute and licensed to the company for development, this was the company's first success. In addition to saving money on original research, Centocor was able to reduce the time it took to get its products from the laboratory to the marketplace. To this day, CA 125 is one of the leading diagnostic tests for ovarian cancer. Other early diagnostic products were used to detect pancreatic cancer and breast cancer.

Hubert Schoemaker was a brilliant scientist. He also possessed a dynamic, charismatic personality. While the personable Dutchman had an appearance more fitting of somebody who belonged in academia than in the corner office of a CEO, he was an insightful businessman. He was a man for all seasons. In addition to being an astute scientist, Schoemaker was a lover of classical music and an outstanding athlete—a champion tennis player as well as a scratch golfer. A charming man who could converse with people from all walks of life, Schoemaker attracted talented men and women to his small company. His conviction for the great things that would someday come Centocor's way was contagious. It permeated throughout the organization. His dream became the dream of his colleagues. Employees and visitors alike have often commented on how there was a constant excitement that filled the halls and the laboratories at Centocor's headquarters. It was in this environment that scores of talented men and women joined the ranks of this fledging biotech company that, for years, had little revenue and generated no profits.

Like all start-up biotech companies, it took years for Centocor to develop viable products. And faced with a high overhead and little or no revenues during its early years, the odds of succeeding were stacked against Centocor. Succeeding in this highly competitive arena would depend on them making a series of judicious decisions, choosing the right path to follow, and then implementing their game plan to near perfection. Brilliant implementation was essential, because without it, brilliant ideas are fruitless.

It was a doable game plan. Just the same, it would be years before the red ink would stop flowing and Centocor would realize an annual profit.

WHERE THE MONEY IS

In 1983, Hubert Schoemaker persuaded David Holveck to join Centocor. The two men met when they worked at Corning Medical. Holveck worked in marketing at Corning and had left in 1978 to join GE Medical, just a few months before Schoemaker also left to start Centocor. At GE, Holveck sold CAT scanning equipment—imaging equipment used to diagnose diseases. During his time at Corning, he had worked with Schoemaker, and a friendship blossomed.

Holveck had studied home and physical education at West Chester University, a small liberal arts college in southeastern Pennsylvania. "My aspiration was to be a physical therapist," he says, "but it was during the Vietnam War and I was in the naval reserves. I did my active duty time, got married, and started a family. Then I got into medical sales because it paid more than physical therapy and I had a family to support."

A former college athlete, at six feet three inches, Holveck is still trim. Only his thinning silver hair divulges that he is past age sixty. He is articulate and speaks with a booming voice. His voice rings with enthusiasm. You can tell he loves his work. Holveck is often asked why he was willing to leave GE Medical, an established company, and go to work for a small start-up company. "The company had some very bright scientists," he says, "and I thought there was a lot of potential to do something significant here in both diagnostics and treatment. With a small company, I personally could make a difference. With a large company like GE, the effect I had on the company's success was never clear. At the level I was at, I was unable to determine what value I added. And when I came here, there were only about fifty employees."

Upon joining Centocor, Holveck headed the company's diagnostics division. At the time, the company didn't have a sales force and its products were sold through distributors and other manufacturers. He eventually went on to become president and then CEO of Centocor. Today, as president of Johnson & Johnson Development Corporation, he spends much of his time in search of promising companies to invest in or acquire. Having been in on the ground floor of a start-up biotech company, Holveck has been there and knows what to look for.

It was during Centocor's formative years that Holveck made an astute observation on the direction that the company should take. "Early on, when I was working with bankers, it became obvious that there was considerably more interest in therapeutic medicines than diagnostics," he says. "While it was far more costly to make therapeutic medicines and a more difficult area to get into, the returns on a successful medicine were far greater. Consequently, we made a conscious decision to change our business model and gradually make the transition from diagnostics to therapeutics."

It's like what Willy Sutton, the famous bank robber, said when he was asked why he robbed banks: "Because that's where the money is." On a similar note, the Centocor business plan was changed to go where the money was. And while it might not sound as exciting as robbing banks, in the world of biotechnology, coming up with a successful medicine for warding off disease is about as exciting as it gets.

It was a sensible transition for the small biotech company to go from making diagnostics products to therapeutic medicines. As Harlan Weisman explains, "The interesting thing about antibodies is that because of their degree of specificity, the same molecule that is used to test the hypothesis of the underlying mechanism of the disease can also be used as a therapeutic agent. So it's a diagnostic probe and it's a therapeutic treatment. This was the beauty in developing these early antibodies. It was also the reason those of us who were in research were having so much fun."

"In the early days of Centocor," Holveck adds, "we were run like a small family business and the driving force was science. There wasn't an emphasis on such things as analyzing markets or this-and-that had terrific financial potential. But when the red ink continued to flow, and as more new people from the pharmaceutical industry were hired, our culture started changing. By the late 1980s, the company's business was equally divided between diagnostics and therapeutics, and while it was the diagnostic arm that actually made some money, the fact that we were a biotech company with a revenue stream was a great story for the street, and the price of our stock started going up—keep in mind now, we still had no annual net profit. However, we gave the appearance that we were successful, and so who's to argue? But internally, some of us weren't so comfortable that it was a good fit. It was like having a suit that you didn't quite fit into."

Centocor and the entire biotechnology industry received a big shot in the arm in the early 1980s when a Supreme Court ruling allowed genetically engineered bacteria to be patented, thereby ensuring that the efforts of biotech innovators would be rewarded if they are responsible for a commercially viable treatment or cure. The ruling got the attention of the investment community, and large sums of money were invested in the biotech industry. As a result, the biotech companies were able to burn even more R&D dollars than ever. Yet the fact remained that not a single significant commercial product was yet to hit the marketplace.

By 1985, Centocor had revenues of $20 million, mainly from research contracts and product sales. Sales rose to $27 million in 1986, $55 million in 1987, and hit $72 million in 1988. A successful product developed in the mid-1980s was Myoscint, which diagnosed heart attacks. While the company was showing signs that it could turn a profit, management was no longer satisfied with solely making diagnostic products. Instead, their sights were set on evolving into a full-fledged biotechnology company—one that would develop, manufacture, and market drugs. The game plan had changed. The new game plan was to parlay its profitable base of diagnostic tests into a research and development engine for monoclonal antibody products.

THE CENTOXIN CATASTROPHE

At the start of the 1980s, many "magic bullet" drugs were being touted by biotech companies to treat hitherto incurable diseases. Some were cancer drugs that involved oncogenes—genes that regulate cell division and are permanently active due to the mutation and loss of their normal regulatory sequences. When oncogenes were no longer in favor, Interleukin-2, another member of the cytokine family, was being hailed as a major breakthrough but turned out to be highly toxic during clinical trials. Then TNF became the next magic bullet class of drugs to be placed in the limelight in the ongoing battle against cancer. In 1985, Centocor embarked on a new journey in biotechnology, switching its emphasis on building a successful diagnostics business to therapeutic medicines. Through the aggressive pursuit of licenses for new discoveries from academic institutions, Centocor amassed a rich coffer of potential product candidates, the most promising of which was HA-1A, or Centoxin, a human antibody drug designed to treat gram-negative sepsis, a bacterial infection that was killing an estimated eighty thousand Americans out of the two hundred thousand diagnosed cases in the United States. Symptoms of sepsis include a fever and drop in blood pressure that may be followed by septic shock and cause organ failure and death. The fever can be generated by trauma such as major surgery. Sepsis is the most common cause of death in the intensive care unit.

HA-1A was developed in 1985 by Dr. Henry Kaplan of Stanford University, Dr. Abraham Braude of the University of California at San Diego, and Dr. Nelson Teng of Stanford. They reported that, in their laboratory and animal tests, the drug had bound to exactly the right molecules on the bacterial surfaces and that it had protected animals from septic shock. Dr. Elizabeth J. Ziegler of the University of California at San Diego was also a developer of the antibody and a consultant to Centocor.

With a market of 200,000 cases a year in the United States alone, Centocor's management foresaw an estimated market potential for the drug at $1.5 billion a year by the mid-1990s. With those numbers, Centoxin would be the ticket for Centocor to become a major pharmaceutical company. Nobody ever accused Schoemaker and Wall of thinking small. With the results of the company's in-house development and testing, they firmly believed that Centoxin would succeed. They were entrepreneurs who walked the talk. Not men who shied away from risks, they were willing to make huge investments in Centoxin—amounts that would ultimately be so high that failure was likely to bankrupt the company.

Other companies had thrown their hats into the ring to be the first to launch a drug to treat sepsis. One by one they ran into problems and dropped out of the race. Meanwhile, in-vitro studies demonstrated that Centoxin looked promising. These results created a buzz on Wall Street and the price of Centocor's stock started to rise. Expenditures rose too. "We had faith in our game plan," explains Harlan Weisman, "and it required us to invest a lot of money in people. In 1990 alone, the number of employees at our Malvern headquarters jumped from 340 to over 500.

We invested hundreds of millions of dollars in a manufacturing facility in Leiden in the Netherlands. We knew there was no way to get the product to the market unless we made it ourselves. A biotech product is so much more complicated to manufacture than producing pills. And although we were strapped financially, there were two reasons why we didn't want to outsource manufacturing. One, we didn't want to be put in a position of being dependent upon somebody else. We didn't want to risk having a future supply shortage that would put us at the mercy of a second party for inventory. Two, there simply weren't many companies that manufactured biotech drugs, so our choices were limited. We thought we'd be better off determining our own destiny so we bit the bullet and invested heavily in manufacturing in advance of getting the results of the Phase III clinical trials. And why shouldn't we? We had every reason to believe that Centoxin would receive FDA approval."

"Centoxin looked so good," says David Holveck, "that it changed the direction of the company and moved us from diagnostics to therapeutics. We brought in another management team to focus on building a therapeutics business. And to make sure we had enough medicine for the trials and an available supply when the drug was approved, we made the bold decision to build a plant in Leiden."

In anticipation of the great demand that would follow upon receiving FDA approval, the company recruited and trained a sales force to be in place on the day when Centoxin would be launched. Hiring three hundred sales reps was an expensive and risky venture. In addition to the cost of recruiting and training expenditures, there was the cost of paying salaries to a sales organization that was unable to generate sales revenues until the product was approved. By 1992, the Centocor workforce had grown to 1,500. For the years 1991 and 1992, the company's combined loss exceeded $300 million.

A clinical trial was initiated in 1992 to unequivocally establish the efficacy of Centoxin to treat sepsis. Despite an endorsement by an FDA advisory panel, Centoxin was not approved on the basis of its single clinical trial. The FDA requested a second trial in which the company would have to prove the drug's safety and efficacy in order to be granted approval. Interestingly, Dr. Jay Siegel, who headed the department that reviewed the license application for Centoxin that failed to receive the FDA approval was hired by Centocor a little more than a decade later. Under FDA rules, the designers of a clinical trial must state precisely how the study will be conducted and interpreted and what groups of patients the drug will help. Sometimes, however, by statistical accident, a particular group of patients that had not been identified beforehand may appear to benefit from a drug unexpectedly. The FDA standards thus seek to prevent such a group of patients from being cited, after the fact, as proof that a trial was a success.

With its back against the wall, Michael Wall, then an emeritus member of the board, was brought in to work with investment bankers, and the company negotiated a deal with Eli Lilly whereby Lilly forked out $50 million for a 5 percent stake in the company. The deal called for Centocor to relinquish the worldwide rights to Centoxin in exchange for half of the drug's future profits. It also effectively promised to give Lilly the marketing rights to ReoPro, a second drug that was still in development if Centoxin failed to be approved. Lilly was a strong partner—not only did the Indianapolis-based company have deep pockets—the company had a wealth of know-how. It also had dozens of alliances with other pharmaceutical firms.

On January 18, 1993, the company abruptly halted the second study and withdrew the drug from ten European countries where it had been approved. It did so for good reason: the study indicated a higher death rate among one group of patients with sepsis that had received the drug than those patients who had not.

According to Schoemaker, "Centocor missed an important cue from the medical marketplace: sepsis had become an increasingly complex disease. It was found to result not only from a complex cascade of biochemical events, but also from infection originating from multiple sources—including Gram-negative bacterial, viral, and fungal sources. Further complicating this picture was the fact that new immunosuppressive drugs, which had become a therapeutic mainstay in oncology and transplantation medicine, were a significant factor in multiple infections. Without a highly specific diagnostic test to establish the infectious agent responsible for the sepsis, a single therapy was not predicted to succeed. The difficulty in developing sepsis therapies is illustrated by the fact that twenty clinical trials conducted by other pharmaceutical companies and academic institutions subsequent to Centocor's trial also met with failure."

The roof fell in. Centocor's stock dropped from a previous high of $60 per share in December 1991 to $6 by the following April. The company's market value plunged from $2.3 billion to a meager $250 million. Management refused to concede defeat. The company still had $150 million in cash to get by, and it did have some revenues from its diagnostics products. Still, with a cash burn rate of about $50 million per quarter supporting the corporate infrastructure and its 1,600 employees, the company was on its knees and down for the nine count. That spring Holveck was elected president by the company's board of directors and he was issued a directive by the board to reduce cash burn to the lowest possible level.

Centocor, which had been a high-flying stock and the darling of the biotech stocks, had become a laughing stock. A cartoon that appeared in the *Philadelphia Business Journal* is framed and sits on Holveck's wall at his office at Johnson & Johnson's world headquarters in New Brunswick, New Jersey. The cartoon shows a toilet and the caption reads: *Septic shock.* "We were down and it was hurtful to see that cartoon," Holveck says. "There was an article that referred to the company as 'Centocorpse.' We might have appeared dead, but we didn't feel that way. In fact, seeing that kind of press made us more determined to prove to the world that we knew what we were doing. I put the framed cartoon on my wall as a reminder that we weren't going to allow other people's opinions to influence how we thought about ourselves. We knew we had good science, so we were just going to keep pushing ahead."

"I joined the company in January 1990," Weisman tells, "and at the time the price of the stock was just under $20. Based on the high hopes placed on Centoxin, the stock went to $50 to $55 a share by January 1991. I remember it well because it was my one-year anniversary, and I was awarded stock, which counted as income by the IRS. But when my taxes were due in 1992, the stock had fallen to $5.50 and I had to pay taxes on the price at $55. My taxes due were higher than the value of the shares I owned. I had to borrow money from the company to pay my taxes."

Holveck had been with Centocor since 1983, and as one of the early executives and in his position as the company president, he had accumulated many stock options at even lower prices than Weisman. On paper he had lost a fortune. When asked how he reacted to seeing his potential wealth nosedive, he nonchalantly says, "Honest to truth, I never had it [the money], so I never counted on it. It just wasn't there. Sure, some of the people came onboard for monetary reasons and they were the first to jump ship. But there was a core group that was there because we loved the science and strongly believed in what we were doing. We knew we'd succeed, so we never paid much attention to the price of the stock."

"Our obituary was written in 1993," Weisman points out. "Nobody expected us to survive. But we had two other drugs in our pipeline, such as ReoPro, a drug that would be used in high-risk angioplasty. And then there was Remicade, a drug that looked promising for treating immune-related diseases. Yes, Centoxin was our flagship research project, but it was no longer in the picture, and we were not about to roll over and play dead. We had other things to do. The day after we received the disappointing news, I had been working in cardiovascular research on what was to become ReoPro and I called a meeting with my group. 'Look, yesterday morning, every one of us believed in what we are doing,' I told them. 'We believed in the product and we believed in the company. Nothing has happened in the past twenty-four hours to change those beliefs. So let's continue on.' And they did. We lost only a small number of people. I had a very dedicated and committed group of people working with me. They stuck it out. We refused to allow a temporary setback to defeat us."

The graveyard is filled with biotech and pharmaceutical companies that had set their hopes on a particular drug only to see it fail to receive FDA approval. Then too, even medicines that are approved have no guarantee that they will succeed in the highly competitive marketplace. Such is the risk that comes with the territory. This is not a business for the fainthearted. It takes strong leadership to move a company forward when the sky has fallen in on it. Schoemaker's, Holveck's, and Weisman's strong faith in the future of the company permeated the organization; their conviction let others know that they must not allow a major setback to get to them.

MOVING ON FROM CENTOXIN

After graduating with an M.D. from Stanford University, Jay Siegel trained in internal medicine at the University of California at San Francisco and then in infectious diseases and immunology at Stanford University. Long before his college education, he had decided on pursuing a career in medical research. Immediately following his education and training, Siegel worked at both the NIH and FDA. With his pedigree education and training, he could have earned considerably more money practicing medicine than being employed by the government. However,

the young doctor believed that he could reach more people and contribute more to humankind by working in the public health sector. In
1996, the FDA promoted him to the job as director of the Office of Therapeutics Research and Review. In this position, he was responsible for the
evaluation and approval of all biological therapeutics. Specifically, he was
in charge of the FDA department that had rejected Centoxin. He had
previously worked with biotech products for years, and in this capacity,
was very familiar with Centocor and its problems in failing to receive
FDA approval for Centoxin.

In 2003, after twenty years of employment with the government,
Siegel joined Centocor, and has since been promoted to president,
Biotech, I.M.I.D., and Oncology research and development, for Johnson
& Johnson. With his FDA background, many pharmaceutical companies
sought his services. Having been an FDA insider for so many years, Siegel
knew the people and he knew the ropes on how to work with the agency.
His comments on why he joined Centocor are noteworthy:

"My office regulated all the biotech companies," Siegel says, "so I got a
close-up look at their people and their products. I wanted to be involved
with a company that did solid, careful science and held to the highest
ethical standards. I knew that Centocor was this sort of company. I was
very involved with the Centoxin filing, and there were a lot of people
who thought its lack of approval would be the death knell for the company. I observed how its management team reacted to this tremendous
setback, and I saw how major changes were implemented. The company
was downsized to about one-third of its size. Plus, starting with making
Dave Holveck president, there were some big changes in management.
The new management team did some serious soul searching, looking at
everything they were doing, asking the right questions about what went
wrong and why. It was a major wake-up call. Consequently they came
out a much stronger company. Over the ensuing years, the company developed a very solid reputation for doing meticulous science, for having
smart people, and for being straightforward with the FDA. I also liked
the fact that the company had open-minded people who had scientific curiosity. Over the next ten years following the Centoxin cata-
strophe, Centocor had proved itself to be one of the exemplary biotech
companies."

NO OTHER CHOICE

Having slashed overhead, and with $150 million in reserves, Centocor had some breathing space, but not all that much. In addition to the stake that Eli Lilly bought in the company, in the fall of 1993 Wellcome in the United Kingdom bought a 5 percent piece of Centocor and received full rights for marketing Panorex, a cancer-fighting drug. Wellcome also agreed to invest $16 million in its development. As Holveck said at the time, "We recoiled and refocused. We are using alliances to gain cash and to concentrate on our core strengths of research and development."

With its huge cuts in expenditures and the infusion of cash from Lilly and Wellcome, Centocor was able to buy some time to keep the wolves from its door. But time was running out, and the company badly needed a new drug that would generate some sizable revenues. If not, its name would be added to a long and growing list of biotech companies that had gone down for the ten count.

When it was becoming apparent that Centoxin was a dead issue, ReoPro looked like it was Centocor's best chance to come up with an important drug. It also helped the cause that Lilly had a vested interest in its success; at this point, Centocor was in need of a strong ally.

"The bane of the exploration industry is choices," Holveck stresses. "In a larger company where there are more choices, when a drug faces many major obstacles, a company can afford to push it aside and go with something with more favorable odds. Back in the early 1990s with our small company, we didn't have choices. We had to stick to what we had and make it happen. At the time, we were in a survival mode. Prior to the Phase III clinical trials for Centoxin, it was our most promising medicine. ReoPro was an absolute by-product of Centoxin's failure. We had little else, so there was no alternative but to succeed with ReoPro. This drug is representative of the company's culture. It's a culture that evolved around people [who] were passionate about making something happen. The people that came aboard in the early days had a pioneering spirit. They were involved in this new wave of technology. At the forefront of this new technology, they were united in their vision and passion."

ReoPro was originally discovered by Dr. Barry S. Coller, a faculty member and hematology researcher at the State University of New York (SUNY) in Stony Brook. It had been supported by funding from the NIH. Centocor bought the development rights in 1986. The agreement with Coller and SUNY involved a modest amount of upfront money and Centocor would pay royalties on the drug pending FDA approval and future sales. Obtaining the rights was an incidental cost, in particular in comparison to the estimated $200 million that would be invested in the clinical tests and manufacturing facilities by Centocor and, in part, by Lilly. Two Centocor scientists, Dr. Bob Jordan and Dr. Dave Knight, coinvented the patent covering ReoPro. Jordan, now a senior research fellow with the company's R&D effort, was responsible for elucidating the unique pharmacokinetics, pharmacodynamics, and immune response of ReoPro in-vitro, in primates, and in humans. Knight, now a vice president in biopharmaceutical research with Centocor R&D, is credited for having the foresight to produce the mouse-human chimeric version of the original parent mouse antibody. He then led the efforts to characterize the antibody, produce the cell lines for manufacturing, and, working with Jordan, characterize the immune responses. Producing chimeric antibodies was cutting edge at the time, and Knight was instrumental in taking a bench technology and making it commercially viable.

In addition to providing financing, Lilly had a long history of successful medicines on the market, and with its vast past experience, its management mentored Centocor through the difficult process of getting a new drug approved by the FDA. In this go-around with the FDA, the company was advised to stay focused on furnishing material that was relevant. It was a case of less is more. Too much unnecessary paperwork slows up the process. In its zeal to file its application for Centoxin, the company had actually delayed the process by filing too much information. And because Lilly's sales organization would sell ReoPro, Centocor didn't have to spend time and money in sales and marketing. "Our focus was mainly on manufacturing and clinical development," Weisman says. "We continued to invest heavily in manufacturing because we knew that if we had to depend on a second party to get these drugs to the market, we were likely to encounter serious problems down the road. Meanwhile, we weren't building a pipeline. Like I said, we didn't have many choices. But we were building manufacturing. Many people on Wall Street were shaking their heads. 'What the heck are you doing with your money?' they kept asking."

After spending eight years and in excess of $200 million, the company received FDA approval for ReoPro in late 1994. According to the March 1995 issue of FDA Consumer, the drug was "licensed for use in patients undergoing angioplasty who were at high risk of complications from this procedure to restore blood flow to narrowed coronary arteries." It was the second therapeutic monoclonal antibody licensed. Eight years earlier, in 1986, Ortho Biotech's Orthoclone OKT3 was approved for reversal of acute kidney transplant rejection. ReoPro was the first monoclonal antibody approved for broad use in patients. It was hailed as a groundbreaking medication that inhibits the formation of platelets that aggregate to form life-threatening clots during cardiac intervention processes like angioplasty. When ReoPro was first launched, there was some initial resistance. There were protests that the $1,350 cost per patient per use was too high. But when compared to the amount offset by reduced medical complications and shortened hospital stays, the cost of ReoPro was not objectionable.

Holveck's game plan was to generate revenues from ReoPro so the company could be self-sustaining. The company had budgeted sales of $60 million for 1995. However, ReoPro got off to a slow start, generating revenues of only $23 million in its first full year, which hardly made a dent in recouping the large investment that had been made in it. Later, when physicians saw how well the medicine worked, sales started to rise. In 1997, annual sales hit $196 million. With a net profit of $11 million, Centocor became the first Pennsylvania biotech company to make a profit.

"Centoxin is often referred to as a failed drug," Holveck points out, "but it was really the seed that allowed us to focus on ReoPro. Those of us who stayed on were able to recognize why Centoxin blew up. We understood what went wrong, and we continued to believe that we could learn from it and go on. In retrospect, Centoxin reinforced our belief that TNF was going to be a competitive product. I call it serendipity, but had Centoxin succeeded, we probably wouldn't have done ReoPro, and we certainly wouldn't have done Remicade.

"Back in the early- to mid-1990s, there were many nonbelievers in the industry who didn't think the use of antibodies to inhibit platelets had merit. The platelets are the major element in coagulation, and the skeptics believed that by blocking them from doing their job, it would cause hemorrhaging. Just before we received FDA approval, an editorial in the *New England Journal of Medicine* had recognized ReoPro as an academic endeavor but a drug that would never have commercial application. Up until then, antibodies had not been authenticated as an acute therapy. ReoPro broke the barrier by demonstrating that antibodies do work. It also opened the door for us to develop Remicade. Still, there were many cynics who said that it wasn't possible to use an antibody for chronic therapy because its repeat use would have immune response issues."

Receiving FDA approval on ReoPro was the first major good news to come Centocor's way in many years. Sadly, it was also in 1994 that bad news was received. Schoemaker was diagnosed with medulloblastoma, a fast-growing and almost always fatal cancer that strikes several hundred Americans each year, most of them children. Shortly after he was diagnosed, Schoemaker was told there were only ten adult survivors of this type of brain tumor in the country. "Well, I will be number eleven," he vowed. A courageous man who refused to be defeated, Schoemaker took an aggressive approach to fight his cancer. He had surgery, received chemotherapy, radiation, and a bone-marrow transplant, and he did survive, although the illness sapped him of much of his energy. In 1999 he left the company to start a biopharmaceutical company, Neuronyx, also located in Malvern, Pennyslvania. His brain cancer recurred and he died on January 1, 2006.

Bruce Peacock, a former Centocor executive who is now CEO of the Little Clinic in Louisville, Kentucky, described Schoemaker well when he said, "If you look up optimist in the dictionary, there'd be Hubert's smiling face right next to that definition. When the FDA said 'no,' to Centocor's first major product, his employees were fearful, shareholders were stunned, and the industry saw it as a bad omen. After he received the news, he replied, 'Yeah, well, I will just have to raise another $100 million and we'll bring the next product forward.' Soon enough he did just that. He raised that $100 million. He focused on those next couple of products, and that was the key to success for Centocor."

Although Schoemaker is gone, he leaves behind a never-give-up legacy that is deeply engrained in the company's culture.

AND ALONG CAME REMICADE

One of Centocor's early collaborations with academia was with Jan Vilcek, a Ph.D. at New York University School of Medicine. Vilcek devoted his entire career to the study of cytokines, those hormonelike proteins produced in the body that control defenses against infections and tumors. He was one of the pioneers of interferon, the first-identified immune system protein. Along with his NYU colleague Junming Le, Vilcek generated a monoclonal antibody that inactivates TNF. Impressed with Vilcek's work, Schoemaker arranged to meet him. After discussing how TNF was an excellent target for which to create drugs to treat auto-immune diseases with an inflammatory component, they agreed that Vilcek would do research for Centocor. After injecting mice and identify-ing hundreds of antibodies, Vilcek determined that the CA2 antibody had the most desirable characteristics. The binding region, however, was still mouse. Conventional wisdom at the time was of the opinion that it was not possible to successfully develop a chimeric antibody for a chronic disorder. Still, Centocor and Vilcek persisted and eventually came up with a way to develop infliximab, a TNF-alpha-antagonist. Vilcek's work led to the development of a monoclonal antibody that binds to TNF-alpha receptors and blocks the cytokine's action. This was the start of Remicade.

To curtail current expenditures, Schoemaker offered to pay royalties to Vilcek rather than upfront research fees. The arrangement turned out to be quite lucrative for Vilcek—as well as for NYU. A believer in the phi-losophy that one has a duty to extend a helping hand to those less fortu-nate, in 2006 Vilcek donated his royalties from Centocor to the NYU School of Medicine—totaling $105 million and making it one of the largest single gifts ever given to a college or university in the United States.

To understand Vilcek's philanthropic views, one must know his back-ground. Vilcek is Jewish and was born in Czechoslovakia. For several years while under the Nazi occupation during World War II, his family was hidden by strangers in small villages. The punishment for harbor-ing Jews was execution. With the help of these courageous people, the Vilcek family circumvented being sent to a concentration camp. In 1964 Vilcek and his wife left communist-ruled Czechoslovakia to come to Amer-ica. They arrived with all their earthly possessions packed in two suit-cases. Vilcek succeeded in America beyond his wildest dreams. A humble man, he has never forgotten his roots. In remembrance of those kind and courageous Czech villagers, Vilcek committed his life to helping others.

REMICADE ON ITS WAY

"Our researchers initially thought Remicade would be used to treat sep-sis," says Julie McHugh, a former president of Centocor, who joined the company in 1996 after spending a decade in the pharmaceutical industry holding various marketing positions. "From our experience with Centoxin," she says, "we learned that our target for Remicade was not sepsis. Instead we learned how it could be extraordinarily important in the treatment of other diseases. To paraphrase an old adage, 'From the ashes of that failure came Remicade.' "

When Centocor scientists started concentrating their efforts on indications such as rheumatoid arthritis and Crohn's desease, the company gained an advantage over competitive companies that were focusing on TNF to treat sepsis indications. "We realized early on that Remicade wasn't the mechanism for sepsis," explains John Ghrayeb, who headed the drug's preclinical research. "My group worked closely with Vilcek and Le. The original Remicade that we got from them was a mouse antibody. We engineered it to make it more human. Once we accomplished that, we worked on getting it ready for the clinical trials."

Ghrayeb, who is vice president of licensing and new business development at Centocor, is listed on the Remicade patent as a coinventor along with Vilcek and Le.

"Sepsis is a systemic infection that can cause a systemic release of TNF into the blood," explains Tom Schaible, vice president of medical affairs at Centocor, "and there had been several earlier studies with anti-TNF therapies on septic patients, but none realized positive results. Back in the mid-1980s, Ravinder Maini and Marc Feldmann, two professors at the Kennedy Institute of Rheumatology in London, had been developing a hypothesis that TNF was a significant inflammatory mediator. Maini, a rheumatologist, and Feldmann, an immunologist, made an excellent combination of scientific disciplines. They developed some early animal models that indicated the importance of TNF. Their mice models showed that it was possible to get dramatically positive results by experimentally inducing an inflammatory arthritis that blocked TNF with a monoclonal antibody. These results were preclinical preliminary data that [were] available in the late 1980s. Their findings, coupled with our interest in sepsis, led us to Jan Vilcek at NYU. It was Vilcek who developed the molecule that became Remicade. Remember now, at the time, we had a diagnostic business that was selling monoclonals. Our annual revenues were around $50 million, but all the development work was funded from venture capital money, plus we had many partnerships. We were spending a lot more than we were making in those days."

Schaible, who received a B.S. in biology at Trinity College in 1972 and a Ph.D. in physiology at Rutgers University in 1976, was a former assistant professor of medicine and physiology at Albert Einstein College of Medicine in New York. He had worked as a clinical research scientist at Berlex Laboratories prior to joining Centocor in 1987, when he was hired as a clinical research director. When asked what attracted him to Centocor, a company that was struggling to keep its head above water, his face lights up and he quickly blurts out, "Two words—monoclonal antibodies. It was the promise of the technology. Monoclonals were first described in 1976. Because of their exquisite specificity for identifying a biologic target, their potential as either diagnostic or therapeutic agents was vast. It was a matter of understanding the basic biologic defect that occurred in a disease. If you could do that, then you'd have the ability to create a therapeutic molecule that could basically seek out and bind to its target and correct the defect. The thought of it was mind-boggling. 'This is the most exciting place imaginable to be,' I'd tell everyone. In my area of research it was 'Star Wars.'"

"When Dave [Holveck] took over as Centocor's CEO after Centoxin tanked," explains Joe Scodari, worldwide chairman of Johnson & Johnson's pharmaceutical group, "he was faced with the decision of which programs to keep alive. There were limited choices of products to develop, and he was very much aware of the urgency to get a product to market, because we had to make money. In spite of the Internet craze, like any business, we couldn't go on for much longer without generating sustainable earnings. We looked at our pipeline, discussed what was in development and what resources we could put into moving them forward. The conversations went like this: 'Look, even with our limited resources, we can't place our bet on a single product. We have to apply some portfolio risk management.' With this thinking, we focused on ReoPro, but because we liked what we saw with the Remicade molecule, we concluded that we must budget our funds so we could continue to learn more about it."

Scodari was hired in 1996 as Centocor's executive vice president and president of the pharmaceutical division. The following year he was named president and chief operating officer and a member of the board of directors. Previously he had held executive positions at Rhone-Poulenc Rorer and Sterling Drug. He had been approached by a headhunter who introduced him to Centocor; he had several meetings with Holveck and Weisman prior to being convinced to come aboard. "By the time I came here, the Centoxin debacle was behind us and ReoPro had been launched. Dave could begin to see some light at the end of the tunnel. Having started as a diagnostic company, the company's long-term vision was to use antibodies as therapeutics. Well, it took until 1995 for that vision to become reality. This is when the company wanted to bring in somebody who could help build the pharmaceutical business, and I was Dave's choice for the job."

Making a career transition is never easy. "It is, in particular, difficult for one's family," says Scodari. "Plus it's hard to leave a company that's treated you well, and I was treated very well at Sterling and RPR. My colleagues said, 'Are you crazy, Joe? Centocor is barely keeping its head above water.' Now they're saying what a smart move I made. I remember when Dave and I got on the subject of compensation, the only thing I told him was, 'I don't want to make my family sacrifice. The cash comp has to be competitive with what I am being paid today.' And it was. There were some things I left on the table and some things that I got as well. When I was offered the job, the stock was trading at $9. By the time I joined, it was trading at $35, so I missed a bit on the upside. So what! At the end of the day, I wanted to work for a company where I could make a difference. Dave wanted someone to help him rebuild the company. That's what I like to do. We ended up being an absolutely perfect team. We work together very closely and we complement each other."

A CONSEQUENTIAL TRIP TO LONDON

During the 1980s, James Woody was the company's senior vice president of R&D and chief scientific officer, a position he held for five years before leaving the company to become president of Roche Bioscience in Palo Alto. Woody's educational background included a medical degree from Loma Linda University, residency training at Duke University and Harvard Medical School, and a Ph.D. in immunology at the University of London. He had served as a commanding officer in United States Naval Medical Research, and in this capacity Woody supervised more than 1,200 staff in 11 worldwide research institutes engaged in biomedical research in transplantation, immunotherapy, blood products, and vaccines. Having accumulated many contacts around the world during his illustrious career, Woody recommended that the company contact Ravinder Maini and Marc Feldmann at the Kennedy Institute of Rheumatology in London. Maini and Feldmann were the same duo that had achieved earlier preclinical results with TNF experiments on mice models.

"Since Remicade is specific for human TNF," explains Tom Schaible, a member of Centocor's clinical research team in the early 1990s, "it doesn't work for any other animal with the exception of chimpanzees, which have identical DNA as ours. However, chimpanzees don't get rheumatoid arthritis. At this point, we developed analog antibodies that were specific to either mouse TNF or rat TNF, and the time had now come to treat patients. We contacted Maini and Feldmann to do an early Phase II clinical trial, or what you might call a Phase IIA, because Phase I trials are normally conducted on healthy volunteers. Maini and Feldmann initially treated twenty patients at the Kennedy Institute, and although it was a small number to treat, they produced profoundly favorable results. Remicade was given by infusion, and within seventy-two hours, they were able to see dramatic clinical benefits.

"I recall seeing a video of a young woman who previously could barely walk downstairs. Then, the video showed her walking down the same steps two weeks later and again four weeks later after she had received her first two infusions of Remicade. It was remarkable, and you could hardly believe it was the same woman. She actually pranced down those steps. The corresponding data confirmed that her joints had vastly improved. These initial tests demonstrated that Remicade worked on rheumatoid arthritis and showed an acute benefit. However, since rheumatoid arthritis is a chronic disease, the question was how long would that benefit last?"

The news of the early Phase II clinical trial results was joyfully received at Centocor headquarters in Malvern. Shortly afterward, CEO Dave Holveck and president Joe Scodari flew to London to meet personally with Feldmann and Maini.

"We wanted to hear the results firsthand and have the opportunity to ask questions about their clinical study," says Joe Scodari. "After all, it was the first substantial human work ever done in rheumatoid arthritis patients. Both men elaborated on how remarkable the results were, pointing out that even in a blind setting, it was very plain to tell which patients had received Remicade and those who hadn't. Shortly after receiving one or two infusions, most of them were able to get back to their normal lifestyles."

"At the time, the company was struggling to stay alive," Scodari tells, "so after the meeting Dave and I took the train from the city back to the Hilton at Heathrow, London's airport. Note that we didn't have a limousine take us back; we took the train. After having cut the workforce of 1,600 people down to 350, we were watching our pennies. This was in 1997, and we were in a cost-cutting mode. When Centoxin failed, the board of directors made the decision that we would never be a fully integrated company—that is, a company that would do the whole ten yards. Instead we would basically be a development company. Once we had developed a drug, we'd allow big pharma to commercialize it—to take the commercial risk. However, we would do the manufacturing because that was a competency we had built from the beginning. We realized the importance of being able to have control over this part of the business. Making biotech products is so difficult and we didn't want to be at the mercy of having another company do it for us. So that was the game plan. We'd invent, develop, and make the products."

"On the train back to the hotel," Scodari continues, "I said to Dave, 'Based on what we just heard, we have a breakthrough product, and I think we'd be crazy to give it away. It's in an area of medicine where there is an unmet need, and there are not any drugs that currently provide substantive benefits for these patients.' We both realized that rheumatoid arthritis is very debilitating and patients eventually lose all of their ability to physically function.

"Dave listened intently and nodded his head. I stressed that there was a low commercial risk. 'This is an audience where the number of rheumatologists is very small,' I continued. 'There are only about 2,500 rheumatologists in the United States to treat most of these moderate to severe rheumatoid arthritis patients. With a relatively small commercial effort, I believe this is a relatively low risk and there is low competitive intensity. Dave, I think we would really have to be crazy not to do this on our own. Let me work on a business plan, and we can make the decision on what I come up with.

"Working closely with Dave, I worked on the plan for the next couple of months. We met regularly, and we finally concluded to do it ourselves in the U.S., but due to limited funding, outside the country we'd partner with another pharmaceutical company.

" 'You'll have to run it by the chairman of the board,' Dave said. 'With Hubert's support, I'm certain the board will give its approval.' "

"Hubert was an undying optimist, and even though he was fighting his brain cancer, he maintained an upbeat attitude," Scodari adds. "After I explained how Dave and I thought we should revise our game plan, Hubert said, 'Joe, I will support you on this one thousand percent.' After a brief pause, he added, 'But the board is going to have an anaphylactic reaction!'

"It was an uphill battle. After Centoxin, the company had been struggling to keep its head above water and, through Dave's leadership, the company had redefined itself. While we had a small diagnostics business, which, by itself, was profitable, and ReoPro that looked promising, our business model put an emphasis on a small 'R' and a big 'D' as in research and development. And as I mentioned, our competency was in manufacturing. Dave had also identified a short-list of molecules that the company would focus on, and the plan was to become self-sustaining. The board was sold on this plan, and now, with the early Phase II results on Remicade, we were asking the board members to approve a new strategy that had considerably more risk. However, if it worked, it would be more profitable. It took probably another year to fully convince the board to buy into our plan and keep Remicade in the U.S. We ran into further complications when we engaged in partnering discussions with other companies. Most companies wanted a global transaction. Ultimately we did it with Schering-Plough in all markets outside the U.S. except Japan, China, and some small Asian countries. In Japan, we have an alliance with Tanabe."

MORE GOOD NEWS—FROM AMSTERDAM

Sander van Deventer, a noted gastroenterologist and internist at the Academic Medical Center in Amsterdam, had participated in sepsis trials that Centocor had conducted in the early 1990s. Van Deventer had a particular interest in inflammatory bowel disease and was fascinated with the prospects of how monoclonal antibodies could work against TNF. He was familiar with Centocor's researchers who identified high levels of tumor necrosis factor in animal models in rheumatoid arthritis and Crohn's disease. Centocor scientists had also identified it in tissue specimens from patients with those diseases. Van Deventer himself had observed that TNF was elevated in the tissue of the gastrointestinal tract in the intestines of patients in those areas where Crohn's disease was occurring.

A patient of van Deventer's, a fourteen-year-old girl, had severe

Crohn's disease. "He had heard about the results that Feldmann and Maini got in London when they treated patients with rheumatoid arthritis," John Ghrayeb says, "and he had a theory that although arthritis was a disease of the joints, Crohn's disease that happens to be in the intestines is also involved with TNF."

Crohn's disease, an inflammatory disease of the gastrointestinal tract that often affects the intestine and colon, is a type of chronic inflammatory disease. Its symptoms can include abdominal pain, diarrhea, fever, loss of appetite, and weight loss. Intestinal complications may include bowel obstruction, bowel perforation, formation of pus collections (abscesses), and fistulae. Crohn's disease can also cause intestinal hemorrhage as well as cancer of the bowel and the small and large intestine. Massive dilatation of the colon and rupture of the intestine are potentially life-threatening complications.

The girl was put on various medications including steroids but nothing worked. She underwent surgery and part of her intestine was removed. She continued to have severe symptoms and it appeared that it would be necessary to remove part of her colon. Concerned that her life was in jeopardy, van Deventer contacted the company to request a supply of Remicade. Although the drug had not yet been approved and launched, Centocor was able to grant his request for compassionate use. (Other than for those patients participating in a clinical trial, a pharmaceutical company is not permitted to provide an unapproved drug to treat a patient—except in a case that falls into the category of compassionate use.)

Centocor overnighted a dose of Remicade to van Deventer, and upon receiving infusions, the girl was no longer debilitated and resumed a normal life. "Van Deventer wrote an article about his success with Remicade to treat Crohn's disease that appeared in the influential medical magazine *Lancet*," Schaible says. "We then did our initial ten-patient clinical trial with him in Amsterdam. Again, we had incredibly good results."

TWO INDICATIONS—WHICH ONE FIRST?

Going back to when Dave Holveck was named CEO, the plan for Remicade was for its first indication for an immune-mediated inflammatory disease to be rheumatoid arthritis. In time this became the company's number-one priority. The initial results from the clinical tests by Maini and Feldmann in London supported this plan. It would be a real coup to be the first to come out with a drug for immune-mediated inflammatory diseases, and in particular for a crippling disease like rheumatoid arthritis. However, when the results for van Deventer's patient were known, it opened debate over whether Crohn's disease was a better first indication to pursue. It wasn't as if there was a Plan B to replace a failed Plan A. All the evidence from the clinical tests strongly indicated that Remicade was on track to be an approved drug for treating rheumatoid arthritis. But now, the company had a drug that showed exceptional promise for not one indication but two, and both were significant diseases.

This was by no means a bad position to be in, and in fact it was a very good position. Had the company had deep pockets, undoubtedly it would have moved ahead full steam to develop its miracle drug for both indications. But that was hardly the case. A choice had to be made—Centocor did not have the financial resources to simultaneously develop it for both indications. Certainly it would have been preferable to develop Remicade for both without having to curtail one in favor of the other. The longer the period of delay in getting the drug to the marketplace for an indication, the more risk there was that another company could gain valuable ground or perhaps even get its product out first. Being first in the pharmaceutical industry is undeniably a strong advantage.

Unquestionably there was a strong need to have both indications approved. Each is a terribly debilitating disease. And as different as the two diseases appear, both are caused by a defective immune system. A healthy immune system is the body's best ally—an automated engine of biological warfare that can destroy almost any microbial parasite it encounters. But, like any other agent of destruction, when it spirals out of control, it is as deadly to friend as it is to foe. In rheumatoid arthritis, the immune system attacks the joints and eventually weakens the bones, causing excruciating pain, fatigue, and daily bouts of fever. Most of us have bouts with arthritis in their joints, but rheumatoid arthritis is not the same as having aches and pain in our joints. It is a chronic disease that cripples people, and in its most severe state it can take away their will to live.

Crohn's disease has already been described. There's one thin layer of cells standing between you and a bellyful of misery. That layer lines the intestines, helping to protect against irritating bacteria and bile acid.

Something goes wrong with that layer, as well as with the rest of the intestinal wall, in people with Crohn's disease. In its advanced stages, it can cause unhealing draining fistulae that can go through the skin from one's gut. It is socially disabling and makes employment difficult. It can make sitting extremely difficult, sometimes not even possible. It also can be extremely painful.

Centocor recognized there was a need for both indications. Remicade's availability to those in need would be a godsend.

"We agonized over which to go with first," explains Harlan Weisman, "but in the end, we decided to first develop the drug for Crohn's disease. We chose that path because, quite honestly, we could only afford it. While we did the Phase II clinical tests simultaneously, when it came time to do Phase III trials, we didn't have the money to do both. Although we initially started with rheumatoid arthritis, we recognized that it would be considerably more expensive and take longer to get to market."

Julie McHugh, who was director of marketing at the time, explains, "We were concurrently in Phase II development for both indications but realized we could only afford to come out with one. We concluded, 'Let's get a product to market and then we will be able to expand our development of Remicade more quickly because it will then be a revenue-generating drug.' We wanted to have the first anti-TNF product on the market. We figured our best shot was to focus on Crohn's disease."

"We learned a valuable lesson with Centoxin—that it's more difficult to get a drug approved if the trials are too broadly designed," Scodari states. "With Crohn's disease, there was a clearly defined patient population with an enormous need. This time, we methodically designed it to start with a narrow patient population where its benefits would be very clear. Rather than going for an indication to treat all Crohn's disease patients, we limited our indication to treat patients with moderate-to-severe Crohn's disease who [do] not respond to traditional treatments and may find short-term relief with a new genetically engineered product. While there are more than five hundred thousand Crohn's disease patients in the U.S., by narrowing it to this indication, the patient population was under two hundred thousand. Because we developed it for moderate Crohn's disease, and for a smaller number of patients who failed conventional therapy, the size of that segment of the then-current market was smaller and fell under the orphan drug categorization for the disease. As an orphan drug, it would be entitled to certain tax benefits and be put on the fast track for FDA reviewing."

It was also helpful that Remicade was a monoclonal antibody treatment. Traditional treatments at the time had included corticosteroids and other immune-suppressing drugs and antibiotics. A new Crohn's disease treatment had not been introduced in three decades; hence there was virtually no other competitive drug in the market.

"In the case of a drug like Lipitor for high cholesterol," Schaible says, "a patient doesn't have an active disease. Lipitor is a medicine that prevents getting a disease. But with Remicade, Crohn's disease is an active disease, and in fact, these patients have a rip-roaring disease. Every patient in the clinical trial had rip-roaring disease activity. There were patients with eight bouts of diarrhea daily and severe abdominal pain. Where every patient stands to benefit and benefit clinically, it's a different story in terms of the number of patients needed to show that a favorable benefit-risk relationship was proved in a clinical trial. So although our total Crohn's disease experience at the time we completed our clinical trials was about two hundred patients, it was a sufficient number."

"In 1998, we filed an orphan application for an unmet medical need," Schaible continues. "We received a six-month review from the FDA, which is considerably shorter than normal. However, we had to go before an advisory committee. I was the presenter. Going into it, we understood that getting a recommendation was not going to be a slam dunk. It wasn't our data that would hurt us. We knew Remicade worked effectively, if not profoundly, in these patients. Our concern was that the committee would not think we had enough clinical trial experience."

The meeting was conducted in May 1998 in a Holiday Inn banquet room in Bethesda, Maryland. The members who sat on the advisory committee were not FDA employees. They were mainly scientists and physicians from industry and academia. Because no two advisory boards are alike, it is not possible to predict what they may advise. Schaible and the Centocor team spent weeks preparing in advance for this meeting. A conscientious man, Schaible wasn't sure which direction the dialogue might go in, so he came overprepared. He and the other Centocor participants had good reason to be apprehensive. Failure to get a favorable recommendation could delay Remicade's approval by a minimum of months, and with limited funds, such an outcome would be a grave setback.

A federal regulation states that advisory committee hearings must be

open to the public and that time must be allotted for anyone in attendance to voice an opinion. At some point during the hearing, the committee's chairman will ask, "Does anyone in the audience wish to make a
statement?" Typically there is a small attendance and nobody speaks out,
and the chairman will continue with the proceedings.

"On this particular day," Schaible tells, "there were a handful of
Crohn's disease patients in the audience. They were unsolicited and totally unexpected. I had no idea beforehand they would be there. When
the chairman opened the meeting to the audience, three patients stood
up and described their personal stories about how the disease had affected their lives. They had the floor for nearly three-quarters of an hour,
and what they said put everything in perspective. They described how
terrible the disease is, and how they suffered. Their stories put a face on
the disease. . . . They were not statistical data—they were real people
with faces. Yes, we had our key investigators present who were internationally recognized experts on Crohn's disease, and they supported
us and fielded questions by the committee. But having those patients
there had an immense impact on the hearing. They were saying, 'This is
a terrible disease, and now we have a drug that can really make a difference. Please don't take it away from us. It works and we desperately
need it.' "

The committee advised that the company should go forward with
Remicade. As an orphan drug, it was put on the fast track for a prompt
approval by the FDA. In August 1998, Remicade received its approval by
the FDA.

In March 1997, Schaible started a trial for Remicade for three rheumatoid arthritis indications. The trial was called ATTRACT, an acronym for
Anti-TNF Trial in Rheumatoid Arthritis with Concomitant Therapy. The
two-year ATTRACT trial was one of the largest and longest controlled
clinical trials involving patients with rheumatoid arthritis. The study
compared Remicade in combination with methotrexate to placebo with
methotrexate in 428 patients. At the time, methotrexate was the standard
treatment. The ATTRACT trial was a double-blind, placebo-controlled,
randomized clinical study conducted at 34 centers in North America and
Europe. It evaluated prevention of structural damage by assessing a combination of bone erosion and joint-space narrowing. The patients in the
trial had a level of disease considered very difficult to control, with a me-
dian duration of the disease of 8.4 years, and all were taking methotrex-

ate. About half of the patients had taken methotrexate for three years or more, and over one-third had had prior joint surgery. Half of the trial patients were classified as functional class 3 or 4, indicating progressive, advanced disease. Researchers found that the first dose resulted in significant relief.

"We designed ATTRACT as a rolling trial," explains Schaible, "where we reviewed the data, closed the database after six months, and took it to the FDA. We got the approval for the clinical signs and symptoms and the trial continued. We kept it blinded for one year. We closed the database again, and we filed the structural damage benefit with the FDA and got it approved. The trial continued and it was still kept blinded. At two years, we stopped the trial, unblinded it one last time, and we filed the physical function benefit with the FDA. It was one trial, but we got three separate claims out of it.

"We finished enrollment of the trial in 1998, but the trial continued and we were finished with the last patient in January 2000. We followed the patients for progression and other structural damage throughout the two-year period in that trial. The trial demonstrated that there was a benefit for treating rheumatoid arthritis beyond clinical improvement. Plus, it was more than just joints getting better—the patients' joints weren't swollen. Nor were they as painful, and Remicade actually could stop the erosive process occurring in one's joints. The trial demonstrated to all those with suspicions that Remicade worked great, not only for a short period but for a long period of time."

On November 10, 1999, the FDA approved a second indication for the use of Remicade with methotrexate for the treatment of rheumatoid arthritis in patients who have had an inadequate response to methotrexate alone. At the time, methotrexate was considered the current standard of treatment.

MAKING IT

Remo Colarusso Jr. received a B.S. with highest honors in chemical engineering in 1983 and an M.B.A. with high honors in 1988, both from Rutgers in New Brunswick, also home to Johnson & Johnson world headquarters. From 1988 to 2001, he held various management positions in manufacturing at Johnson & Johnson, then moved to Centocor, where he is vice president of worldwide manufacturing. In this position, Colarusso is in charge of the company's 1,500-plus production plant personnel that make Remicade in Leiden and Malvern.

"What we do here is known as large-molecule manufacturing," Colarusso explains, "which means we make a product that is not made via a chemical reaction. When traditional drugs are made, various chemicals are thrown in that have certain reactions. Then there are specific purification techniques and a purified chemical comes out the same way every time. With biotech drugs, living organisms are typically used. In our case, we use mammalian cells that produce the protein that is Remicade. With chemical synthesis, it's a straightforward process. There is nothing straightforward about what we do here. We are a large-scale manufacturer of monoclonal antibodies—a biological product that is made by living cells. Remember now, those living cells can die. We have to keep them alive. And we have to make sure they are free of viruses and other contaminants. With genetic engineering, a fully humanized cell line will replicate 99-plus percent, and when it enters the body, the body recognizes that it is human. We are reproducing an antibody to match an antigen that is produced in the body. The goal is to have an exact match. Then when it finds the TNF floating around in the bloodstream, which is a mechanism that the body has in its immune response, it binds with that TNF and prevents an inflammatory response in the body."

Taking a walk through the Malvern plant isn't anything like you'd expect. For starters, there is considerably tight security to keep the plant free of germs. Every visitor—and there are relatively few outsiders who ever receive permission to go inside—must first view a seventeen-minute video. This video informs the visitor how to put on the special spacemanlike gear that is required to be worn inside. Street clothes are forbidden. The gear includes a jumpsuit, special shoes, gloves, and so on. You must wash your hands with a special solution three times during the check-in procedure. The details of this check-in are too long to spell out here; suffice it to say that every precaution is made to create a germ-free environment. As a consequence, the plant is so clean it would be envied by an operating room surgeon.

Once inside, you see stainless steel tanks in different sizes. Some are 2,500-liter tanks and others are 1,000-liter tanks, all connected by stainless steel pipes. To an outsider, it looks like a complicated maze, housed in a 120,000 square-foot building, with many rooms containing stainless steel tanks, all with pipes connecting them to other tanks. The cost of building the facility and its equipment is reported to have been hundreds of millions of dollars. To an outsider, it is difficult to understand why it is so expensive.

Shortly after Johnson & Johnson's acquisition, its CEO toured the plant. Having paid a lot of money for Centocor, he wanted to see what his company had purchased. "Wow," he exclaimed. "It looks really complex, but what's happening?"

It does look complex. And unlike other manufacturing facilities, there is no movement, no noise, no odor. It's a serene environment, and without a company official accompanying you through the plant, it's impossible to have any idea of what's happening. But rest assured, a lot is going on inside those tanks. "It's a clean room operation," explains Bob Sheroff, president of Johnson & Johnson's Global Biologics Supply Chain. Sheroff holds a B.S. degree in pharmacy from Rutgers University and an M.B.A. in pharmaceutical marketing from Fairleigh Dickinson Univeristy. Prior to joining Centocor, he spent seven years as a manufacturing vice president at Warner Lambert and also held various biological and chemical manufacturing positions at Ortho-McNeil Pharmaceutical and Ortho Biotech, both units of Johnson & Johnson. His current responsibilities include overall strategy and leadership for manufacturing, quality and compliance, logistics, process sciences, and engineering. "With chemical synthesis, you will always get the same product at the end because it's based on physics and chemistry," explains Sheroff. "Here, because we are dealing with living organisms, they can be affected by a number of things. How healthy are the cells? How well are they feeding? Was there any contamination? And because we are growing cells, anything else will grow in there too. Indeed, we are running the perfect conditions for any other organism to grow. Contamination is a big challenge in the world of biotechnology."

Biotech manufacturing plants are sometimes referred to as farms because they grow cells. In the case of Remicade, mammalian cells are grown to excrete the protein as a by-product, and it is the protein, not the cells, that comprises medicine. Like all living things, these cells require oxygen and food to live. And living cells multiply. It takes six months from start to finish to make Remicade. As Colarusso explains, "Starting with a one-milliliter vial of the cells, we produce a huge amount of it. What we are doing is expansion. We get them from storage in the vapor phase of liquid nitrogen, warm them up to room temperature, and we put them into a liquid called media that consists of carbohydrates and proteins. We purify everything and put it in tanks to feed the cells so they grow and multiply. The cells consume the sugars and carbohydrates and eventually there is nothing left in the media for them to feed on. At this point, which we call a passage, the cells in the solution are transported to another tank with fresh media that has all the nutrients. The cells continue to grow and multiply. We keep repeating this process—the idea is to keep taking those same cells and putting them into a bigger volume. When it uses up that media, we take it and put it into a still bigger volume. Eventually, at stage two, which is continuous perfusion, there is a large-cell culture bioreactor [in which] the cells are living and are given seven hundred liters of fresh media every day. Here we take off seven hundred liters of product. Now [we] are actually producing product at the same time as [it is] growing. We'll go through twenty to thirty generations of cells—they multiply and multiply. There [is] a finite number of uses we can get out of one particular vial of cells that we start with. We make sure there is no genetic alteration during this time."

During the six-month period it takes to make Remicade, the process has ten different stages. The cells never sleep. They eat. And, like we do, they breathe 24/7 and must be tended to. The emphasis is always on avoiding contamination. All workers are on the alert for this because it doesn't take much to contaminate. A valve might fail, and if air gets inside from the environment, the batch is infected. "Depending [on] what stage the batch is in during the process," Colarusso says, "it can be quite costly. For instance, we make seven hundred batches upstream a year, or approximately two a day. But downstream, we make only forty. So if one of those goes, it's a much bigger problem. More important, we're working around the clock throughout the year to supply our patients. So in addition to a monetary loss, we worry about lack of supply. Our goal from day one has been: 'No missed infusions.' There have been times when we came within the skin of our teeth, but today, we've got adequate inventory. This is compared to those times when we had less than a week's inventory. That's a scary thought!"

Prior to joining Centocor in 2000, Bob Sheroff spent thirteen years working for Johnson & Johnson units, holding various biological and chemical manufacturing positions in the United States, England, and Puerto Rico. Additionally, for seven years he was vice president of worldwide quality operations for Warner-Lambert, the maker of Lipitor, the world's biggest selling drug. "When Lipitor was launched," he says, "it soon became obvious that it would be a blockbuster drug. So there were a couple things we were able to do to keep up with demand. We went to a three-shift operation—and we bought faster tablet presses. With higher-speed machines that take the powder and compress it into a tablet, we increased our capacity. In the world of biotechnology, when you're already running 365 days a year, 24 hours a day, what you've got is what you've got! You can't speed up the process of the cells growing or the cells expressing product. This is the challenge of working with a living organism."

As president of Global Biologics Supply Chain, Sheroff works closely with Centocor's president in forecasting how much Remicade must be produced to meet the demand. "When we go to that container and take out our cell line, which is the test tube of the cells, we must know what we'll have to make—from that point to when we have a finished product ready to sell in about six months. With a small molecule, you need two to three months' lead time. Here, the accuracy of the forecast is that much more important. Now that Remicade is an established product, it's easier for the company to project sales, but the launching of a new product is more difficult. Then too, Remicade has a shelf life of about two to three years, which is somewhat less than small molecule drugs."

Back in 1985 when the company had high hopes for Centoxin, the decision was made to build its Leiden manufacturing facility in the Netherlands. Why overseas? "At that particular time," explains Dave Holveck, "the rules were that if a company manufactured in the U.S., it could not ship the product to other countries even though it had been approved in other countries. For instance, if you wanted to sell it in Germany, the FDA prohibited us from selling it there even though Germany approved it. We wanted to open other markets, so we decided to get approved in the international market first, and this meant making [the product] overseas. The rule has since changed, but that's what prompted us to make it outside the U.S. And since there is such a hand in glove relationship between the research bench and the manufacturer, if you're in biologics you've got to make it yourself. With the FDA's strict approval process for biotech medicines, we have always believed it imperative to control our own destiny. Early on we poured hundreds of millions into the plant because we always knew that we'd have to manufacture our medicines rather than job [them] out to another company."

Pharmaceutical companies spend hundreds of millions of dollars in R&D prior to receiving FDA approval or disapproval of a drug. Only about 15 percent of biologics that enter human clinical trials will eventually become marketed products. It is indeed a risky business. As Tom Schaible says, "If you think Las Vegas is a gamble, it doesn't compare to this business. What about putting down a couple hundred million dollars to build a plant when you're not really sure you have a product to begin with!"

When Centoxin failed to receive FDA approval, the company had to reduce the Leiden plant's staff to a skeleton crew, knowing that it would eventually use the plant to make enough Remicade for the clinical trials, and then, once approved, for patients. But the facility's overhead was an ongoing financial burden. Even after seeing Centoxin fail to make it to the marketplace, Centocor's management team was optimistic that Remicade would succeed. So, in anticipation of the demand for the drug following its FDA approval, Holveck and Scodari made the decision to build a second manufacturing facility. The decision to build another plant in Malvern was made in 1997, a full year before Remicade was approved for Crohn's disease. The Malvern plant would require a $200 million investment, and while they were at it, the decision was made to invest another $75 million in the Leiden plant for expansion purposes. "The investment community thought we were nuts," confides Scodari, "but from our perspective, if Remicade was actually going to be commercially available to patients, we had to spend that money. Some asked why we even needed a second plant. We were a bit landlocked in Leiden, but even more important, we didn't want to put ourselves in a position where we put everything in one basket. What if we had a failure in Leiden? A fire or a natural disaster? We thought about building it at a place that would offer us a good tax shelter, but we ended up here in Malvern without one. We chose Malvern so our manufacturing could be next door to where our scientists were. Today, the pharmaceutical development people and manufacturing people have only to walk across the parking lot to see each other. We figured that was worth more than the tax benefits at the time.

"Two years later, in 2000, we were churning out antibody and supplying it to our patients. Meanwhile, Immunex launched Enbrel, also a biotech drug for rheumatoid arthritis, but didn't risk immediately expanding its manufacturing capacity, and instead jobbed it out. Well, it turns out they couldn't supply the product, and it caused the company to limit product availability in the marketplace and delay launching outside the U.S. When the investment community saw what happened to them, suddenly we were looking pretty good. Looking back with 20/20 vision, it now looks like a brilliant decision. But at the time, it wasn't so easy. And today, we take pride in the fact that no patient has ever been denied an infusion of Remicade due to a supply problem."

Meanwhile, in anticipation of the need to manufacture still more Remicade for still more indications, Centocor is building a $600 million plant in Cork, Ireland. "While it's not across the parking lot," Scodari smiles, "it's only a one-hour plane ride away from Leiden."

INFUSIONS

Remicade is taken by intravenous infusion over a two-hour period and administered by a physician or nurse. Prior to the drug's approval for Crohn's disease by the FDA, Centocor had to exhibit to physicians, mainly gastroenterologists, that their patients would benefit by receiving the drug by infusion. Previous medicines for Crohn's disease were taken mostly by pill, and even sometimes by injection. Many issues had to be addressed. Would the infusion be done in a hospital? Would it be done in a doctor's office? Oncologists treated cancer patients with chemotherapy in their offices by outpatient infusion, so there was precedent. But would there be the stigma associated with taking chemotherapy, and in particular, the nasty side effects that are associated with the cancer treatment?

In the beginning, there was resistance. Another problem was that, logistically, extra space was needed in a doctor's office. Then there was a health-care coverage problem; the company had to work with physicians and insurance companies on how outpatient treatment would be reimbursed. This was not a medicine that patients could self-administer. Nor was it one that required an overnight stay in a hospital. It soon became clear that if Remicade was administered in a hospital and on an outpatient basis, the cost would be exorbitantly high. This would be unacceptable to health insurers. However, if it was taken in a doctor's office, this would reduce the cost substantially. It could also be administered by trained nurses and medical technicians.

Today there are an estimated ten thousand infusion sites in the United States, but prior to launching Remicade, there were none for rheumatoid arthritis or Crohn's disease. These are the glitches that had to be solved in order for the drug to succeed. It wasn't easy—being a pioneer never is.

A physician determines the actual dosage by the patient's weight. Starting with the Phase II clinical trials, the company conducted studies to determine the drug's appropriate dosing and what, if any, drugs it should be used with to get the best effect in terms of safety and efficacy for patients.

"Fortunately, Remicade is such a powerful drug," explains Weisman, "that it didn't take a lot of clinical patients to figure what the optimal dosing should be. When a drug is taken in pill form, decisions are made about how many pills should be taken in a twenty-four-hour period. Is it a once-a-day pill? Or is it a twice-a-day, three-times-a-day, or four-times-a-day pill? Because Remicade is long-lasting, we [also] had to determine if it should be taken once a week, once a month, every two months, and so on. We conducted some elaborate studies in which we randomized patients to various combinations of duration and doses to learn what was the optimal dosing for both rheumatoid arthritis and Crohn's disease. One can use doses between three milligrams per kilogram to ten milligrams per kilogram of body weight, and have infusions from once a month to once every two months. Most patients do well on about five to six milligrams per kilogram every eight weeks."

Most patients experience no pain or discomfort while receiving their doses. During the clinical trials, patients read magazines and newspapers; others would engage in conversations with other patients to pass the time. Often, experienced patients told first-timers how much better they felt, sometimes immediately after having received their first dose, and certainly days and weeks later. This rapid response is due in part to having the drug infused into the bloodstream rather than taken in pill form and ingested via the stomach. "In some instances, patients received their first infusion of Remicade," McHugh says, "and they'd realize positive effects immediately. There are stories of adolescent boys with Crohn's disease who spent their days after school lying on the couch, not able to engage in physical activities. Right after getting home from taking their infusion, they'd be playing basketball with their friends and siblings."

"In January 1999, a few months after we launched the product," Scodari recalls, "a man called me. 'Mr. Scodari, I want to thank you for what you did for my younger brother, who's twenty-seven years old. He's had Crohn's since he was eighteen, and he hadn't had a firm bowel movement for nine years. He couldn't control his bowels and always had to be near a bathroom. Anywhere he would go—out with friends in a restaurant, a movie, anywhere—he had to stay close to the bathroom. Until he started with Remicade, it wasn't possible for him to live a normal life. Again I thank you for helping my brother live a normal life.' "

Julie McHugh adds to the testimonials: "It's an amazing medicine that transforms lives. Patients take a two-hour IV infusion every eight weeks and go from having little or no quality of life to a great quality of life. No wonder most people say, 'Okay, bring it on.' And yes, there are some patients who will resist taking medicine by infusion, and like all medicines, there can be side effects. But when people understand the full benefit-risk, and the consequences that it will mean for the rest of their lives, it's not a hard decision to make.

"Basically, a new patient for all of our labeled indications will first receive an infusion during an induction phase that's administered at week zero, week two, and week six. The induction phase is meant to quickly get the disease under control. Then, after that first induction phase, patients are in the maintenance phase and receive an infusion every eight weeks. Their treatment continues as long as they respond to Remicade and don't have side effects.

"One of the nice things about this medicine is that physicians can titrate doses. That's because Remicade is a weight-adjusted dose, so it can be titrated up and down as the dosage interval can be shortened or lengthened, according to what works for a patient. This, however, is not standard practice. Most doctors treat patients at the recommended starting dose and dosing interval."

With the first indication approved by the FDA to treat Crohn's disease, patients received one or two infusions for acute therapy. Their physicians would monitor them and infusions were given on an "as needed" basis. A more recent indication now treats the disease with infusions every eight weeks—the premise based on keeping the disease in remission.

"With rheumatoid arthritis, it is best that patients don't delay taking Remicade," explains Schaible. "The earlier it's treated the better, because you can prevent a lot of its irreversible damage that occurs. We now know this is also true with Crohn's disease. What happens is that a patient's bowels have episodes of inflammation and healing. Then the bowels become inflamed again. It becomes fibrotic. Eventually these episodes cause the stricture or the narrowing of the intestine. If left unchecked, it may become necessary to remove the intestine. However, if this repetitious cycle of inflammation and healing process can be averted and the bowel heals, there is a good probability that surgery can be avoided."

The cost of Remicade is about $15,000 a year, with many variables that can make it more expensive. Although pricey, the drug has a high rate of compliance. First, people with severe Crohn's disease and rheumatoid arthritis can be terribly sick and in grave pain. They can be so critically debilitated that they are unable to carry on with their normal daily activities. So when Remicade succeeds in restoring their health, they want to stay healthy. This gives them a good incentive to stay on their prescription. Second, compliance is high because infusions are given in a doctor's office, which means their condition is constantly being monitored and they are being pushed by a health expert to continue with their treatment.

TAKING IT TO THE MARKETPLACE

The pivotal studies that were done during the clinical trials were subsequently published in medical journals and presented at medical meetings. The impressive results created a buzz in the medical community; gastroenterologists were elated that they could finally offer an alternative to surgery, the standard procedure at the time for severe Crohn's disease patients. And surgery wasn't even necessarily a permanent solution.

Remicade offered a new way to treat a dreaded disease, thereby providing a strong platform on which to build the basis of a vibrant sales organization—because, no matter how good any medicine is, it won't sell by itself. Sales representatives must take a new product to the doctor's office, explain its benefits, its side effects, how to prescribe it, and answer a slew of questions and offer an ongoing service. Only then does a new drug have a chance of succeeding in the marketplace. In the case of Remicade, physicians also had to be educated about infusion.

As McHugh explains, "Crohn's disease was uncharted territory. There wasn't anywhere to go to buy the commercial expertise. We really had to build it. The same was true when Remicade was approved for rheumatoid arthritis. With both diseases, coming out with an anti-TNF medicine was groundbreaking. There were no other branded products being promoted in that space. At the time, all rheumatoid arthritis medicines had gone off patent and were generic. There also weren't any companies with a specialized sales force that were knowledgeable about the disease and capable of speaking with authority to physicians about treatment expectations and anticipated outcomes. Since we couldn't partner with another pharmaceutical company and have its sales reps sell our product, we'd have to do it on our own. Due to limited financial resources, we came up with a hybrid commercialization strategy. We would go it alone in the U.S., and we'd partner with Schering-Plough outside the U.S."

Often pharmaceutical companies recruit experienced sales reps away from another company, but in this case, there weren't any to hire that came with a background in biotech medicines. This meant Centocor had to build a sales organization from scratch. Having learned from its previous mistake, when the company hired five hundred sales reps to sell Centoxin in anticipation of FDA approval, the company was not only more frugal this time around, but also wiser. "Rather than recruiting, training, and paying an idle sales force that's put on hold until this product was approved," explains Scodari, "we waited until we received an approval letter from the FDA, and, estimating it would be ninety days before it was officially approved, we started recruiting and hiring sales reps. Our plan was to start with a small number of reps, and they'd call on a small subset of gastroenterologists with a focus on managing inflammatory bowel disease. Our sales strategy was to hire the best people in this arena. We were amenable to paying very competitively to get the best people—men and women with experience who wanted to make a real difference for these patients. As it turned out, it was actually quite easy to recruit top salespeople. When we told them the Remicade story and showed the data from the studies, the reaction was, 'Wow, this is really an exciting product, and something I'd love to be a part of.'"

"Some of the first reps we hired were nurses, pharmacists, and even medical doctors," McHugh adds, "and we went after seasoned pharmaceutical reps who [had] sold specialty products for eight to ten years. Many good candidates were reps who sold medical devices. We sought out individuals with solid backgrounds that demonstrated they would be capable of talking scientifically to physicians and answering their questions. We had two separate sales departments. The first one was for Crohn's disease, and because patients with rheumatoid arthritis were treated mainly by rheumatologists, not gastroenterologists, we had to set up a separate sales force. Yes, we made our share of mistakes when we got approval for Crohn's disease, but a year later when the drug received approval for rheumatoid arthritis, we were better equipped because we had twelve months of experience under our belt. Still, there were major new challenges because the two diseases are so different and required separate sales reps."

McHugh points out that the sales team learned along the way as they sailed on uncharted water. "When we launched for rheumatoid arthritis," she says, "we only had one area business specialist. This person is a reimbursement specialist whose job is to help set up a doctor's office to give infusions. We kept putting more on to fill the need, and by the end of the first year we had fifty. Today, we have nearly one hundred of them. It just goes to show that you don't know what you don't know until you get out there and start making it happen."

MADE IN HEAVEN

Like a good marriage is made in heaven, the same can be said about mergers and acquisitions. And much like a desirable young woman, a thriving young biotech company will have its share of suitors. In late 1998, with ReoPro starting to come into its own and with the bright future that Remicade promised, Centocor was a prime candidate for a takeover. Following a meeting of the board of directors and senior management, a decision was made to hire Morgan Stanley, the prestigious investment banker, to do an analysis on the probable market value of the company and identify a preferred white knight versus an unfriendly invader. "Once we made the decision, we didn't sit passively waiting to be acquired," explains Holveck. "We were very aggressive. You might say we attacked the process. Our goal was to be acquired by the best company out there."

Meetings were conducted with several investment banking firms. A meeting was set up between Johnson & Johnson's vice chairman, Bob Wilson, and Dave Holveck. "At the time, I wasn't too familiar with J&J," Holveck says, "but like everyone, I was aware of their famous brand products such as Band-Aids and baby powder. Interestingly, when I first got out of the navy reserves in the early 1970s, I applied for a sales rep job with Ortho Diagnostics, one of J&J's mainstay businesses. Ortho was a real class house. I didn't get the job, and now, nearly three decades later, I am a CEO and I'm talking to J&J's vice chairman about an acquisition.

"Right off the bat, before we even sat down to talk, Wilson said to me, 'Dave, this discussion may end in two hours or it may continue, and if so, bigger and broader agreements will be constructed. I want to make it clear right from the beginning that if we get to that latter stage, I want a commitment from you that you can bring your people along. The people are the most important aspect in this field.' "

"When he put an emphasis on the fact that people is what it was all about, I liked him immediately," Holveck emphasizes. "Everyone else was talking about the product or the financials. With Wilson, number one was the people. All along with the talks we were having with different pursuers, my biggest concern was the people. I had to make certain that our people would be able to continue with their mission—they had to be included in the equation. Although Wilson didn't know it, he won me over with his opening statement. After hearing that, I was at ease talking to him and I sensed this was the company that would be right for us."

After meeting with Wilson, Holveck reviewed what had transpired with Scodari. "We identified J&J as our preferred white knight," Scodari says. "Number one, we liked their decentralized operating model. At the time, J&J had more than one hundred separate units that were run autonomously, and with this corporate structure, we could continue to operate independently, as we had all along. Of course, we realized all the problems we faced if we remained a stand-alone company, so this represented an opportunity to have our cake and eat it too. And obviously there were some strong advantages of being under the J&J umbrella. J&J had the financial strength that would help us develop future products, and second, the company had some of the smartest people in our industry who [would be] available when we needed to draw upon their expertise."

Johnson & Johnson acquired Centocor in 1999 for $4.9 billion. As parties on both sides agree, it was a "good fit." What made it work so well was that Johnson & Johnson's corporate structure fosters an entrepreneurial spirit that promotes innovation. Unlike many multibillion-dollar inter-national corporations, in which bureaucracy smothers independence, an atmosphere exists at Johnson & Johnson in which people were encour-aged to think outside the box. Taking risks is supported, not frowned upon. Over the years, Johnson & Johnson has been able to hold on to its entrepreneurial spirit.

The likeness of the two companies' corporate cultures has created a synergy that has benefited both entities. Johnson & Johnson wanted to be a major player in the biotechnology field—and with Remicade, the company has one of the world's best-known biotech medicines. With Johnson & Johnson's support, Remicade has now been approved for four-teen indications and to date has served more than eight hundred thou-sand patients. These achievements would have taken much longer had the company attempted to do it alone. "We wanted to be the 'steak,' not the 'sizzle,' of the biotech industry," Scodari emphasizes. "With Johnson & Johnson, we have that opportunity. With Johnson & Johnson in the pic-ture, we are able to maximize our potential."

"One of the benefits I see that has happened since we became part of J&J is that we're protected from Wall Street," McHugh adds. "We don't have to worry about how the financial community will react about every little thing we do. Consequently, we're able to stay much more focused on building the best possible business as opposed to having to appease Wall Street."

Chris Molineaux, vice president of communications at Centocor, thinks that being able to keep its independence is a key advantage of be-ing a Johnson & Johnson unit. "We've remained a fully integrated com-pany," he emphasizes. "We've got the entire value chain here at Centocor. We've got early discovery, research, development, manufacturing, and sales and marketing. When a small company is acquired by a large phar-maceutical company, the smaller firm generally loses its identity. That hasn't happened in our case."

"The people at Centocor have a lot of pride," Holveck explains. "One of our goals is to be the best acquisition that J&J ever [made]. Just like we set a goal to produce breakthrough drugs—we are very goal oriented."

The number of Centocor executives that have been promoted to se-nior positions at Johnson & Johnson shows how well the two companies complement each other. Following are some Centocor people who have advanced up the Johnson & Johnson ladder:

- David Holveck is now corporate vice president, corporate development for the parent company. Holveck is also president of Johnson & Johnson Development Corporation.
- Joe Scodari is worldwide chairman of Johnson & Johnson's Pharmaceuticals Group, and in this capacity he manages marketing, sales, and manufacturing of $22 billion worth of products.
- Robert Sheroff is now president of Global Biologics Supply Chain.
- Harlan Weisman is the chief science and technology officer, Medical Devices and Diagnostics, Johnson & Johnson.
- Jay Siegel is president of research and development for Johnson & Johnson Biotech, I.M.I.D., and Oncology.
- Dominic Caruso, who had been chief financial officer at Centocor, now holds a senior position that puts him on track to succeed the current chief financial officer at Johnson & Johnson.
- Rick Anderson, who previously ran Centocor's cardiovascular business unit, is now company group chairman of Johnson & Johnson's Cordis Corporation, a medical device company.
- Julie McHugh became president of Centocor Inc. and now is company group chair of Johnson & Johnson's Virology business unit.
- Glenn Mattes is president of Tibotec Therapeutics, a new Johnson & Johnson company that focuses on HIV/AIDS.
- Christopher Molineaux is vice president, communications, for Johnson & Johnson's Biotech, I.M.I.D. and Oncology business unit.

There are more than 220 companies in the Johnson & Johnson corporate family. It is a tribute to Centocor that it has had more than its share of its people promoted to key positions at the parent company. Consider too that Johnson & Johnson has long had the reputation for being one of the best managed companies in the world, and for years it has been acknowledged as one of America's most admired companies. Landing a senior job at Johnson & Johnson involves competing against a field of talented people.

At the time of the merger, with stock ownership and stock options, many members of Centocor's management team acquired substantial wealth, making some financially independent. Yet none of the key people left following the merger, and all continue to work with the same motivation and passion they possessed when Centocor was a budding company trying to find its niche in the world of biotechnology. As a bonus, Johnson & Johnson's headquarters are only an hour or so by automobile from Centocor's headquarters.

When asked about what motivates him today, Holveck explains by asking the question, "Why do I drive an hour and ten minutes to and from work every day if I don't have to economically?" and then he provides the answer: "I do it because I can make a difference. I can make something happen. I think it's the same reason Dom, Harlan, and Joe do it. It's not because of the money. It's like the NFL player who wins a Super Bowl ring. Why does he continue to play? He does it because he wants another championship ring. It's the same with us. In this industry, 90 percent of the people never experience bringing a new drug to market. I've had two experiences—ReoPro and Remicade. That's a rarity in this business, and now I'm looking for that third ring."

REMICADE, A FRANCHISE MEDICINE

As it turned out, Remicade wasn't only a home run, it was a grand slam. When the drug was in the early stages of discovery, there wasn't enough knowledge about I.M.I.D. for Centocor scientists to know that their work would unlock the secrets of the immune system, and that in doing so, they would someday have a medicine that would specifically attack the underlying causes of many unrelated clinical syndromes that share common pathways. While it sometimes happens that a medicine developed to treat a specific disease can also effectively treat another disease, Remicade is unique inasmuch as it can treat multiple diseases—diseases that heretofore were believed unrelated.

After being approved for the treatment of Crohn's disease in 1998, and the following year for rheumatoid arthritis in patients who have had an inadequate response to methotrexate alone, Remicade was granted FDA approval for other indications, initially for treatment of other forms of Crohn's disease and rheumatoid arthritis. By the end of 2006, other approved indications included ankylosing spondylitis, psoriasis, and ulcerative colitis, bringing the total to 14 indications that are being prescribed in 121 countries. Based on the clinical studies currently underway, it is anticipated that the total number of approved indications for Remicade continue to grow and will soon be 16. Worldwide sales for Remicade were around $3 billion in 2005, and this figure could double by 2010.

No wonder Remicade is sometimes referred to as a franchise drug. As John Ghrayeb says, "Most companies would be happy to have an entire line of drugs with so many indications, and here we have a single medicine that treats so many diseases."

In summary, Julie McHugh speaks for many Johnson & Johnson people when she says, "It's a privilege to be part of a company that has become part of medical history with a drug like Remicade. And it's a blessing to come to work every day and be involved with a product that makes such a difference in so many people's lives."

6

NOVARTIS COMPANY PROFILE

In 1996, the then-largest merger in corporate history occurred between Swiss agribusiness and pharmaceutical giants Ciba-Geigy and Sandoz Labs. This enormous conglomerate was renamed Novartis, from the Latin term *novae artes* (meaning "new arts" or "new skills"). The name aptly reflected the mission of the restructured and reengineered international business giant. The new entity proudly proclaimed the title of "World's Leading Life Sciences Company."

There is a sense of pride at Novartis that permeates the organization. It comes from having deep roots with rich traditions in pharmaceutical and agricultural innovation that trace back two centuries. The past is filled with colorful and pedigreed individual histories of the entities that preceded today's Novartis. Their all-Swiss story captures the tumultuous evolution of the world's pharmaceutical industry within one panoramic snapshot.

THE BEGINNINGS

Interestingly, the three predecessor companies to Novartis (Geigy, Ciba, and Sandoz) started in the dye business in Basel, Switzerland, and at one time even united in partnership against the forces of several worldwide manufacturing cartels, political aggression, and war.

In 1758, Johann Rudolph Geigy, an upstart entrepreneur with a wife and four hungry kids, launched a venture: trading in "materials, chemicals, dyes and drugs of all kinds" in his hometown of Basel. Geigy could very well have been the world's first pharmaceutical rep, and his venture marks the earliest beginnings of Geigy the company. His business experienced rapid growth because (a) Switzerland had few raw materials of its own to create chemicals, drugs, and dyes, and thus depended upon savvy entrepreneurs to create the trade, and (b) dyes were experiencing explosive popularity in the clothing industry in Europe at the time.

Little is known about the early days of Geigy's venture, but over the course of the next several decades his family was able to marry into the lucrative silk manufacturing establishment of Switzerland and become firmly entrenched in the dye business.

Nearly a century later in 1858, Geigy's great-great-great grandson Johann Rudolph Geigy-Merian saw that the real money in the dye business was not in dying cloth but in creating dyes. He partnered with Johann Muller-Pack to acquire a local site that would house a dyewood mill and dye extraction plant. Two years later that plant began producing fuchsine (a reddish purple dye).

Creating dyes was a dangerous and filthy job. The chemistry was complex and the research into better and brighter colors was largely trial and error. It involved handling explosive mixtures of hydrochloric and sulphuric acids, mixing caustic alkalis, concocting batches of poisons such as arsenic, boiling and preparing vats of animal fats, and in some unusual cases processing boa constrictor and bat feces (known collectively as guano) for the critical uric acid.

Despite the difficulties, Geigy prospered, and within several decades pioneered synthetic dye manufacturing and became an industry leader.

At about the same time and just across town, the roots of both Ciba and Sandoz were sprouting in the lucrative dye business. In 1859 a French silk weaver named Alexander Clavel moved to Basel, where he opened a factory to make fuchsine. In 1873, Clavel sold his dye factory to Bindschedler & Busch. In 1884, the company was transformed into a joint-stock company named Gesellschaft für Chemische Industrie Basel (the abbreviated "Ciba" became so widespread that the company officially adopted the name in 1945). A few years later, much like his contemporaries, Clavel abandoned the actual process of dying silk, wool, cotton, and leather for dyestuff manufacturing. This shift coincided with the creation of synthetic dye by Geigy, which quickly revolutionized the textile industry by providing an alternative to the extremely unpleasant task of making animal, vegetable, and mineral dyes.

So successful was Clavel that by 1900, Ciba had become the largest chemical company in Switzerland, with a major alkali production works, and the premier manufacturer of inorganic dyes. It was at this time that Ciba (Geigy and Sandoz were soon to follow) began experimenting in the pharmaceutical arena, producing its first drugs, Vioform (an antiseptic) and Salen (an antirheumatic) in 1900.

Sandoz was experiencing similar success. In 1886, Dr. Alfred Kern, a well-known dye chemist, teamed up with entrepreneur Edouard Sandoz to establish a company in Basel manufacturing synthetic dyes. They called their company Kern & Sandoz. Their original plant was built on an 11,000-square-foot tract along the Rhine River and employed ten workmen and a 15-horsepower steam engine. But the upstart had many problems. For example, its original plan to produce violets and blues depended on a patented process Kern had developed years earlier with another chemist. That chemist refused to release his patent on the dye-making process. An alternative process developed by Kern to create the color blue caused a reaction kettle to explode, severely damaging the plant and polluting the Rhine.

Yet despite the setbacks, Kern and Sandoz worked well as a team and their business prospered. While Kern developed new dyes and experimented in pharmaceuticals, Sandoz traveled extensively in search of new customers and new markets for their products. In the short period between 1887 and 1892, their dye production rose from 13,000 kilograms of 6 different dyes to 380,000 kilograms of 28 different dyes. They introduced their first pharmaceutical products in 1895, starting with Antipyrine (for fever reduction), and Saccharin in 1899 (an artificial sweetener).

During this run-up, however, Dr. Kern had a sudden fatal heart attack in 1895. Edouard Sandoz promptly restructured the company, which resulted in worldwide growth and diversification in the pharmaceutical industry.

THE FORCES CONVERGE

Although all three companies were prospering in the dye business and tipping their toes in the pharmaceutical waters, dark economic and po-

However, this didn't stop Geigy and Ciba from talking about merger possibilities. These talks were informal for years but a growing threat from Persian Gulf petrochemical giants during the 1960s stirred interest in a merger. Geigy's strength was clearly in agricultural chemicals and Ciba's strength lay in synthetic resins and petrochemicals. These two giants merged in 1970 to form one of the largest global chemical companies of the day. Geigy immediately benefited from Ciba's research abilities and Ciba benefited from Geigy's superior approach to marketing and management. The new company was called Ciba-Geigy.

Sandoz had prospered after Basel AG was dissolved. The massive size of the company required that it reorganize several times. The company added a nutritional division, expanded the dye division, added a hospital supply division, and eventually added a seed division, substantially increasing the scope and reach of its business (during one eight-year period the number of its employees increased from 6,345 to over 33,000). Later, Sandoz expanded into the construction chemical business as well as the development of low-environmental-impact chemicals. Sandoz, however, also has a strong name in pharmaceuticals. In the 1980s, the company launched breakthrough medicine—Sandimmune—an immunosuppressive agent that transformed and is widely used to help prevent organ rejection by keeping the body's immune system in check. In the mid-1990s, Novartis introduced Neoral—the next generation of immunosuppressants. Sandoz has a long history in the generic business, and today is one of the world's leading generic manufacturers. In 2003, Novartis renamed all of its generic companies under one single, global brand—Sandoz.

Prior to the 1996 merger that formed Novartis, each of the three companies was active in creating newer and more advanced pharmaceutical agents. Geigy was responsible for creating the antirheumatic drug Butazolidin, Tofranil for mental health use, Hygrotone for the treatment of high blood pressure, and the anti-epileptic agent Tegretol.

Ciba meanwhile was creating Coramine, a circulatory drug, and Desferal for the treatment of iron and aluminum overload in connection with certain blood diseases. Sandoz built on its successful experience with calcium therapy products and continued to expand its experimentation into the fascinating and effective properties of ergotamine. This led to further research into psychiatric medications, the most important of which was Melleril, considered at the time to be an important

milestone in psychotropic treatment. Through acquisitions Ciba also became an important player in the fields of antibiotics developed through
biotechnology, and baby food: Ciba acquired Gerber, the famous maker
of baby food.

Through the 1980s and early 1990s, the economic sense and competitive need to team up cartel-style was beginning to appeal to the Swiss giants Ciba-Geigy and Sandoz. Merger talks were arranged when Marc
Moret, chairman at Sandoz, invited the "grand old man" of Swiss pharmacy (and former Ciba-Geigy CEO) Louis von Planta to lunch. Planta
then organized a lunch between Moret and Ciba-Geigy chief Alex
Krauer. In 1996 a deal was made, and the merger of the two, renamed
Novartis, was instantly the second largest drug maker in the world and
twice as large as the next nearest competitor in the agrochemical business. At the time, the new company had a market capitalization of $75
billion. The goal for Novartis was simple and succinct: become the world's
leader in selected therapeutic areas. At age forty-three, Daniel Vasella, a
physician who was the CEO of Sandoz, was named CEO of the newly
merged company, and in 1999 he became chairman as well.

In an industry where it takes years of R&D before a product makes it
to the market, Vasella is an astute businessman and, above all else, he is a
realist. He understands the short-term demands that the investment
community places on a company to produce a healthy bottom line. He is
keenly mindful that a balance must be maintained. A healthy company
must generate profits, and a strong pharmaceutical company must have
a pipeline of new products that require years of R&D. "In our case,
we need both kinds of people," Vasella explains, "those who concentrate
on the short term, like current sales, and others who are totally focused
on new discoveries and the long-term results. These are individuals
who really care about the impact they have on people's health. I believe
that if you can have people in science and discovery with this deep
motivation and it's paired with scientific excellence, it makes for a powerful mix."

The company succeeded, in perhaps greater ways than could have
been predicted. Through various acquisitions and a firm commitment to
expanding its research and development, Novartis has become a world
leader in biotechnology, functional genomics (understanding the functional attributes of the entire DNA sequence and how these attributes
contribute to the disease process), generic manufacture of drugs, and

genuinely revolutionary approaches to medical intervention. In the mid-1990s, the Sandoz chemicals division demerged from Sandoz and became Clariant Ltd Muttenz. Then, in 1997, the specialty chemicals operation of Ciba-Geigy became independent and known as Ciba SC. In 2000 Novartis merged its massive seed business with AstraZeneca to form Syngenta, the world's first global agrichemical business, thus allowing the company to focus on pharmaceutical products.

Novartis's prescription drugs include treatments for respiratory disease such as asthma, nervous-system and eye disorders, cardiovascular diseases, and cancer. Over the last few years through acquisitions, it has a significant presence in the vaccines area. Its Sandoz subsidiary produces finished brand-name pharmaceuticals as well as active chemical ingredients for other generics companies. Novartis's consumer medicines division produces such brands as Excedrin, Ex-Lax, Maalox, and Theraflu. Ciba Vision makes eye drops, contact lenses, and contact lens solutions. Its Gerber baby products are well-known worldwide. Its animal health division offers parasite control products (Sentinel) and pharmaceuticals for pets and farm animals.

The success of the company has enabled it to enhance access to medicines and to discovery. Beyond the GIPAP program, Novartis provides Coartem—its medicine to fight malaria—to millions in Africa through a public-private partnership with the WHO. The company has also supplied multidrug therapy to leprosy patients in another WHO collaboration. Through another agreement, Novartis is providing medicine to treat tuberculosis patients in the world's poorest countries. And, in a novel approach, Novartis opened a discovery research institute in Singapore. A result of a public-private partnership and the Singapore Economic Development Board, The Novartis Institute for Tropical Diseases is dedicated to finding new drugs for the treatment of tropical diseases. The institute's director is the same Alex Matter who started the company's research efforts that resulted in Gleevec.

In 2005, Novartis had more than ninety thousand employees in campuses worldwide. Global sales were over $32 billion, with 15 percent of sales being reinvested in R&D. Its R&D is paying off: Novartis currently leads the industry with fourteen approvals in the tough U.S. market since 2000. It also maintains its position of the industry's leading pipeline with more than seventy-five new drugs in clinical trials, fifty of which are in Phase II trials and beyond.

From its humble beginnings in the mind of a poor Swiss dreamer to the global pharmaceutical behemoth of today, Novartis has become a world leader. It has a close working relationship with twenty of the world's most renowned research and biotechnology centers, forming a solid foundation upon which to develop its pharmaceutical lines. Its well-stocked pipeline and state-of-the-art Swiss-based research campus serves as the fulcrum upon which Novartis works its magic.

A Designer Medicine that
Targets Cancer Cells

NOVARTIS'S GLEEVEC TREATS
CHRONIC MYELOID LEUKEMIA (CML)

IN HIS STATE OF THE UNION MESSAGE on September 22, 1962, President John F. Kennedy articulated:

> I believe that this nation should commit itself to achieving the goal, before this decade is out, of landing a man on the moon and returning him safely to earth. No single space project in this period will be more impressive to mankind or more important for the long-range exploration of space; and none will be so difficult to accomplish.

At the time, the United States was lagging behind the Soviet Union in the space race; Kennedy's speech provided the nation's space program with direction and a clear specific goal. On July 20, 1969, Apollo II landed, and its commander, Neil Armstrong, became the first man to walk on the surface of the moon. It was indeed a giant step for mankind. Had an identical challenge been made a decade sooner by President Truman, all the money in the world would not have landed a man on the moon. That's because advances in science and technology depend on existing knowledge. It also explains why President Richard Nixon's signing of the National Cancer Act on December 23, 1971, committing the United States to a war on cancer, did not achieve the same results as Kennedy's moon landing declaration.

A CHROMOSOMAL DEFECT

Likewise, the making of Gleevec could not have happened without previous discoveries. In this respect, major medical breakthroughs depend on the accumulated knowledge of their predecessors as well as collaborative efforts by coworkers. While it was in 1845 that Scottish and German researchers described a disease that became known as chronic myeloid leukemia (CML), the modern-day story of Gleevec begins in 1960, two years before Kennedy's historic speech. This is when Dr. Peter Nowell at the University of Pennsylvania and Dr. David Hungerford at the Institute for Cancer Research observed that one chromosome, later identified as chromosome 22, in the blood cells of many CML patients was shorter than normal; a big segment of its DNA was missing. Nowell and Hungerford linked it to CML because they could not discover this minute chromosome in the other body cells of those patients. Only the leukemia cells had this minute chromosome. They appropriately named it "the Philadelphia Chromosome."

This discovery marked the first time that a cancer-related genetic abnormality—to be more specific, a chromosomal defect—had been identified. This genetic mutation existed in 95 percent of all patients with CML. What was of particular interest was the fact that this cancer is a result of chromosomal abnormalities, ones that are generated during a person's lifetime. Hematopoietic stem cells divide in the bone marrow to finally make white blood cells—erythrocytes and thrombocytes—and when this occurs errors can happen that can cause one piece of a chromosome to translocate onto another chromosome.

With knowledge of the Philadelphia Chromosome, scientists had a tantalizing clue, but they didn't yet have the tools needed to solve the mystery of CML. Another clue was revealed thirteen years later, when Dr. Jane Rowley, a researcher at the University of Chicago, in 1973 observed that CML patients had an extra clump of DNA on chromosome 9. When Rowley put chromosome 9 and 22 together, she discovered that the missing piece of chromosome 22 had shifted to chromosome 9 and a missing section from chromosome 9 had shifted as well to chromosome 22. Those shifts are known as "translocation" in genetics parlance, a process in which a bit of genetic material from one chromosome swaps places with a bit from another chromosome. In CML, the "tail" of the gene (called "Abl") from chromosome 9 is translocated onto the "head" of another gene (called "Bcr") on chromosome 22, creating the Bcr-Abl oncogene.

The Bcr gene and the Abl gene get in the direct neighborhood of each other and make a new protein formed with pieces of Bcr and pieces of Abl. In contrast to the normal protein, when Abl is in its normal context, the new protein is very active. It is not known why this occurs, but what happens within a white blood cell can have very harmful effects. Because the white blood cell is told to rapidly divide and proliferate, it does not differentiate into a normal white blood cell (a granulocyte). While normal white blood cells divide, replicate, and die off millions of times during a person's lifetime, small mistakes occur during that process that are built into the genome. Those mistakes can sit dormant for decades before the genes release a spurt of growth signals that order the cell to begin dividing and spreading very quickly.

In the beginning this increase in a person's white blood cell count goes unnoticed because there are few if any symptoms, and those that do appear are generally limited to fatigue and anorexia. Hence many people who have CML are unaware of it during the early stages. CML is generally discovered with a routine blood test in the doctor's office. The disease has three stages. First is the chronic phase, with few symptoms. Second is the accelerated stage, which can occur three to five years after the onset of the chronic phase. Here the patient is likely to feel fatigued and experience weight loss and some bleeding. In the last stage, the blast phase, the blood cells divide explosively, and finally death occurs.

THE CATALYST

The story of Gleevec is about teamwork, because without the hard work and talents of many dedicated people, this medicine would not exist today. If, however, one person deserves to be called the catalyst, it is Alex Matter M.D., a brilliant scientist whose innovation and persistence were crucial from start to finish in the making of Gleevec. Matter grew up in Basel, Switzerland, and at an early age determined he would someday participate in the discovery of a new medicine: "I read nearly every book about scientists in my high school library," he recalls, "and these individuals were my constant source of inspiration. My role models were Louis Pasteur and Marie Curie. Pasteur had this incredible scientific mind and yet he was also a practical man. He could do great science but he did it for the people.

"I received medical degrees from the Universities of Basel and Geneva. As a young resident in the early 1970s, I concluded that oncology was a field where simply nothing seemed to work. I found everyone upbeat in the medical profession, but the oncologist was the exception. This was the one guy who was always depressed. I'd hear them say, 'Yes, they will all die. We can't help them.' Not only did I find this depressing, I felt it was an outrageous situation. I later learned that at the time it was a backwater of medical science, and looking back I don't think it was really much of a science. It was just shooting compounds into mice and hoping for the best—maybe the lump would decrease in size. That was about it."

"Also in the early 1970s, along came the era of immunology," Matter continues, "and there was the fantastic discovery of cytotoxic T cells that could eradicate tumors in mice. You could cure mice in twenty-four hours and some immunologists were predicting that the cure for cancer was just around the corner. I bought into this theory and spent five years of my life married to this idea. Obviously it turned out to be wrong. Then there was the notion that we could teach cancer cells to be normal again with so-called differentiation drugs. I worked at Roche, where we experimented with retinoids, which are related to vitamin A. We'd use them to teach infected cells how to be normal again. Retinoids had some effect with so-called hyperplastic cells, i.e., cells that divide abnormally but are not yet fully developed cancer cells. Unfortunately, retinoids didn't work on real cancer cells." With one important exception—they did work on aplastic promyelocytic leukemia.

"Then there was the big euphoria with alpha-interferon. I was just leaving Roche when the company entered a collaboration agreement in this area with Genentech. In the early 1980s, I went on to become the director of an immunology lab for an American company [Schering-Plough] in Paris and Lyon while working on interferon. At the time it was believed the drug could do useful things, possibly in a large variety of cancers. It turned out that interferon had only limited impact in a small number of cancers. Then, in 1983, I joined Ciba-Geigy in Basel, prompted by my old friend and colleague Dr. Peter Dukor, who gave me the task to establish a new effort in cancer research. Frustrated by all the failures of the past, but excited by the groundbreaking discovery of human oncogenes in 1982, I decided to approach cancer in the same way as a scientist working in inflammation or heart disease would approach his or her work. I decided to approach the newly found oncogenes with the tool of pharmacology. Here I could take a close look at some of the new targets that had just been discovered because I could work with identified genes and tangible gene products. Of prime interest were enzymes, and most important, pharmacologists knew how to work with enzymes. It was a rather simple hypothesis that if you could fashion enzyme inhibitors, some of which are called kinases, you could make inhibitors that would work against cancer."

Kinases play an important part in the story of Gleevec, so it is important to understand what they are. Kinases are enzymes that play a major role in each and every cell in the body. They have different functions and they use adenosine triphosphate (ATP) as a source to transfer phosphates to other proteins by what's known as phosphorylation. The phosporylation of proteins changes their activity, which can lead to enhanced proliferation of the cell, and finally result in tumor growth. But the thought of inhibiting protein kinases seemed like an unattainable task. After all, there were so many protein kinases in the body, and most were needed for survival.

Ciba-Geigy, the large pharmaceutical company in Matter's native Basel, had shut down its cancer research unit in 1980. Management had decided that the investment was not worth the paltry returns. Also, drug discovery–based cancer research at the time was a backwater of science and focused on cytotoxic agents with which—at that time—the company did not want to work because of concerns over unwanted and uncontrollable side effects. Then, in 1983, Peter Dukor, a mentor of Alex Matter, took on the task of reestablishing the company's cancer research. One of the first things that Dukor did was to recruit Matter to head what he hoped would become a rejuvenated cancer research unit. But the cancer research program was marginalized and was not a high priority, which meant other research fields received more attention and financial support.

Matter enjoyed the freedom of being able to work independently, left virtually unsupervised. This gave him the opportunity to work in the area of molecular biology research, where he could pursue a concept he believed would lead to a viable treatment for certain forms of cancer. His concept was to fashion an enzyme inhibitor targeted to stop a specific cancer-causing protein in its tracks. It was a highly ambitious objective and one that had never been attempted before. In spite of all the roadblocks that would have discouraged most people, Alex Matter's temperament made him an excellent candidate for such a challenging undertaking. Novartis's CEO Daniel Vasella says that Matter's colleagues referred to him as "a real intellectual bulldozer." This description was meant as a compliment, because as senior people inside the pharmaceutical industry well know, it takes a strong-willed individual to champion a new drug still in its conceptual stage.

"He genuinely believed that, based on the work of incredibly talented scientists in molecular biology," Vasella comments, "he could stand on their shoulders, and see a specific compound that could keep cancer genes in check."

Matter had studied the work of Chinese physicians and had discussions with medical colleagues in Basel about how certain kinases might be involved in the regulation of cell growth. He was intrigued with these findings and felt in his gut that unregulated cell proliferation was a basic indicator of cancer. He observed how tyrosine kinases played some kind of role in normal cells as well as cancer cells. Few pharmacologists shared his views, and, in fact, most rejected his hypothesis that kinases were worthy targets for compounds. The traditional view was that a compound should be aimed at extracellular targets—the receptors at the surface of cells or something floating in the bloodstream. Nonetheless, Matter stuck by his conviction that by aiming at its mark, a compound could be made that would arrive at and hit its specific target.

In his studies, Matter learned that Japanese researchers had determined that staurosporine, a natural compound found in mushrooms, was potent in inhibiting a wide variety of kinases. The doctor considered this an important finding. It intrigued him to know that nature had found a trick to inhibit kinases and thereby solved a medical problem with a natural compound. This information also reinforced his belief that he was on the right track.

"Based on this concept," Matter explains, "starting in 1985, I put together a small team of people to see if we could design such a molecule. In the beginning, because we were a small, independent group, we worked on our own and weren't too specific in telling management what we were doing. Instead we talked in generalities, only mentioning that we were focusing on curing major cancers. We tried this and that, but in the beginning everything we touched failed."

One of the first people Matter recruited was Nick Lydon, a young

Ph.D. biochemist at Schering-Plough until 1985. They had worked together at Schering and were close friends. Matter put Lydon in charge of the team's laboratory effort to study tyrosine kinases.

ESTABLISHING A TARGET

An important discovery was made in 1986 and 1987, when Dr. David Baltimore and Dr. Owen N. White, two researchers writing in *Science,* identified a protein as tyrosine kinase, a kind of enzyme that, among other things, helps regulate cell growth and division. Bcr-Abl, the scientists revealed, changes the cell's normal genetic instructions, jamming the signal that tells the body to stop producing white blood cells. As a result, a cubic millimeter of blood from a healthy person contains four thousand to ten thousand white blood cells in comparison to the same volume of a CML patient's blood, which contains ten to twenty-five times as many. The proliferating white blood cells cause pain, debilitating illness, and, all too often, death. Only three out of ten CML patients survived for even five years. The treatment options were either high-risk bone marrow transplants, or daily injections of interferon, with side effects that have been described as "like having a bad case of the flu every day of your life."

With the groundbreaking discovery that a single enzyme could cause CML, Alex Matter had a well-defined target. Now they would make a molecule that could block the tyrosine kinase known as Bcr-Abl. While the Baltimore-White findings that appeared in *Science* were available to the entire scientific community, the article had not initiated a race to find a better way to treat CML. With the number of new cases in the United States at less than five thousand, and with prevalence worldwide at less than one hundred thousand, it was too small a market to go after. With huge upfront costs to produce a new medicine, plus the high odds of actually making such a molecule, there was little incentive in the pharmaceutical industry to pursue it.

"There are twenty different amino acids, one of which is a tyrosine, and they form proteins," Matter explains. "We figured that in order to affect the pharmacology of a cancer cell, we'd have to get into the inside of the cell. In the beginning, many people said, 'What you propose is quite daunting and there have not been many precedents where that has been done.' But we knew there are compounds that enter the brain by means of getting into brain cells. To do so, those compounds must cross the blood–brain barrier. So as overwhelming as our task seemed, there was a clear precedent that it could be done."

Matter continues, "For instance, these enzymes have to bind in order to be active, and they bind on ATP, a high-energy compound. Note that all living things—plants and animals—require a continual supply of energy in order to function. Well, people said, 'It isn't possible to make selective drugs that inhibit binding of ATP.' They said that without knowing the facts, and they even published articles stating it couldn't be done. The truth was they were biased. Their bias made it clear that what we believed could be done, they thought was impossible. We paid no attention to them. What's more, nature *can* distinguish ATP—and very well. These enzymes have what's known as ATP binding pockets."

In the beginning, says Matter, there was only a small group of people within the company that believed in Matter's theory: "Most other people just smiled and inwardly thought, 'You just don't understand anything about cancer.' At the time, all anticancer compounds were basically cell poisons and worked on the principle that by killing the cancer cell slightly more quickly than the normal body cells, a cancer patient might survive. That was the basic idea of cancer therapy. People even thought that if it is not toxic, it can't be effective and therefore is worthless. This was the bias we were up against. They were convinced that our concept would never work," Matter explains.

"During this period, our team had other drugs in our project portfolio. In this particular case, our kinases research was our 'high-risk approach' while we worked on 'bread-and-butter' projects that were more likely to become drugs. One such drug was an aromatase inhibitor (also an enzyme inhibitor) that we knew from old existing evidence was almost certainly going to work. And it did. It's Femara, an effective breast-cancer drug. By having several medicines at a time on the back burner, we were able to justify our time and effort spent on this crazy project to management."

THE DANA-FARBER HOSPITAL CONNECTION

On the other side of the Atlantic Ocean in Boston, a young physician named Brian Druker M.D. was also determined to make a significant contribution to the treatment of cancer: "From the time I was a medical student at UC San Diego Medical School, I dreamed about the future when cancer therapy would be designed to avoid the terrible side effects of chemotherapy," Druker says. "After completing an internship in internal medicine at Barnes Hospital at Washington School of Medicine in St. Louis, I trained in oncology at Harvard's Dana-Farber Cancer Institute. There I worked in Dr. Tom Roberts's laboratory, where I began studying a family of enzymes called tyrosine kinases. I wanted this research training to gain expertise in understanding how cells regulate their growth, and with this experience I could someday bring better therapies into the clinic. I made a personal commitment that I was not going to do any clinical trials until I had something that made sense. I wasn't going to run a clinical trial on yet another chemotherapy drug. I wanted to know why it would work and on whom it would work. My plan was to someday run a clinical trial. But until then, I would work in the lab. I'd work on understanding cancer at its molecular basis and if that ultimately led to the development of a clinical drug—great! If it didn't, and if my entire career was doing lab work, as long as it helped move forward to the molecular understanding of cancer, I'd be perfectly happy."

It was Druker's reputation in the tyrosine kinases field that attracted Nick Lydon to Boston to seek his counsel in 1988.

Interestingly, when he first began studying tyrosine kinases, Druker had recognized that the most promising cancer for research was CML because it was the only cancer where the genetic cause was known. Still, he was doubtful that it would ever be possible to create a compound that could target a tyrosine kinase selectively. Earlier in 1988, prior to meeting with Lydon, Druker changed his thinking because he had read in *Science* how an Israeli group headed by Professor Alexander Levitzki had been able to selectively inhibit an epidermal growth factor (EGF) receptor. Growth factors are molecules that play a number of roles in the stimulation of new cell growth and cell maintenance. They bind to receptors on the cell surface. Specific growth factors, such as the EGF, can cause new cell proliferation.

Levitzki's article cast kinase inhibitors in a whole new light for Brian Druker. If it was possible to get some specificity (as Levitzki's group did with the EGF), that meant one could now think seriously about creating an effective compound that would inhibit a specific tyrosine kinase.

Sometime in 1988, shortly after having read about Levitzki's work, Druker suggested to Lydon that CML would be the ideal target for his research. "I predict that CML would be the first disease to validate this approach," Druker said with confidence.

Until their conversation, Lydon had made little effort to focus on the Bcr-Abl oncogenes; it was not even on his list of compound candidates because inhibiting the Bcr-Abl oncogene, even if it could be done, meant creating a compound against a disease with very few victims. With this thinking, Lydon and other Ciba-Geigy scientists were focused on creating inhibitors to block tyrosine kinases for other diseases. But talking to Druker, Lydon realized the logic behind his colleague's advice, and it became an influencing factor in Ciba-Geigy's decision to ultimately focus on a tyrosine kinases inhibitor. The meeting marked the beginning of a long relationship that Druker would have with Ciba-Geigy and ultimately with Novartis. As Druker notes:

"By this time, it was becoming clear that the Philadelphia Chromosome [Bcr-Abl] was an activated tyrosine kinase that caused CML," Druker tells. "For the next five years I devoted myself to these studies in an animal model of cancer. While working on a rodent tumor model, I developed a reagent to detect tyrosine kinase activity, which was basically an antibody that would make it possible to look for evidence of the kinases themselves. Between 1990 and 1993 I had moved all of my lab work to CML because by then I felt I could apply my expertise in tyrosine kinases to a human disease. I wanted to establish my independence from Dr. Roberts and decided this was the area where I could contribute the most. In particular my interests were in leukemia, and I worked in collaboration with Dr. Jim Griffin at Dana-Farber, an expert in the field of leukemia. At the time I was setting up test systems, but I had no access to inhibitors. My research focused on how the Bcr-Abl tyrosine kinase works to regulate cell growth. Again, I was just developing reagents and model systems to study the molecule biology of CML."

In 1990 Dana-Farber signed an exclusive agreement with Sandoz to work on signal transduction compounds. Sandoz was a rival company, and it meant that Brian Druker would no longer be permitted to continue his work with Ciba-Geigy.

THE MEDICINAL CHEMIST

Meanwhile, Juerg Zimmermann, a thirty-two-year-old medicinal chemist, joined Matter's research team in 1990. Its youngest member, Zimmermann came with impressive credentials. He had studied chemical engineering at the Engineering School in Burgdorf, Switzerland, and then at the Swiss Federal Institute of Technology (ETH) in Zurich, where he received his Ph.D. in organic chemistry. Zimmermann did postdoctoral work at the Australian National University on the study of radicals and then at the University of Alberta in Edmonton on the design of synthesis of DNA-binding ligands: "When I came here," Zimmermann tells, "Alex Matter challenged me to design a molecule that blocks the enzyme that triggers CML without harming other members of the same family. At the time, it was believed that this kind of enzyme class is not really a good one because Bcr-Abl belongs to the class of protein kinases. The kinase is just the name of this family. It causes a chemical reaction in the body. Of course there are many, many different kinases in our body, but at the time Alex wanted to have a molecule that inhibits the action of just one kinase. But while blocking this one kinase, all the others in the body should continue to function. I remember thinking that he was really asking a lot."

"Even within the company there were many people who thought it would never be possible," Zimmermann says. "I remember colleagues laughing during coffee breaks and calling us 'crazy kinase guys.' Meanwhile I had come out of academia and had never worked for a pharmaceutical company, so I'm thinking that in industry there evidently are stretch calls and obviously this was a prime example of one. I was young then, and if the boss said, 'You have to do it,' I didn't ask questions."

Zimmermann's assignment was to make a molecule that would be able to get inside the cancer cell and, once inside, inhibit (or block) the action of one kinase, all the while not interfering with the activities of other kinases. It is important to note that those other kinases in a healthy cell have important housekeeping functions such as metabolism and cell growth, so the compound had to be made in a way that wouldn't harm the good kinases. The general consensus in the early 1990s was very clear—it wasn't possible. Not with all of those kinases. (There are literally hundreds of different types of kinases in the body, and as more is learned about human pharmacology and physiology, scientists are finding even more kinds. The number today exceeds five hundred. The molecule ATP binds to all kinases.)

"It was comparable to having one key to open many, many nearly identical locks, all of which have nearly identical keys," Zimmermann explains. "Then it was having my boss tell me, 'Find a key that fits into the one lock.' At first it seemed like an endless task. Then we started to work, and the more we learned, the more we realized that these keyholes really looked different when we compared one kinase to another. In the beginning, in an indirect way we learned that when we made a key for one keyhole, it didn't really fit into another keyhole. And from this finding, we deduced that these keyholes were obviously different. Later when we had X-ray structures of these enzymes, we learned that, yes indeed, they do look different. Initially, however, it was one of those hopeless programs that nobody really likes to work on."

Like the other original members on the team, Juerg Zimmermann quickly became aware that he was working for a man who strongly believed in the team's mission. Matter's conviction that the team would eventually succeed was contagious. As the group's leader, he continually challenged the others to find solutions to problems that seemed insoluble. "Look, Juerg, the other guys have been making molecules that bind to DNA," Matter repeatedly told Zimmermann. "Those kinds of drugs have been on the market for a couple of decades. They have terrible side effects causing the patient to suffer because DNA is not only present in cancer cells but is also present in all other cells. We want to do it differently. We want to do a better job."

"Now there I was, thirty-two years old and a very ambitious scientist," Zimmermann readily admits, "so what Alex was saying was exactly what I wanted to hear. He's telling me, 'I've got something for you. It's very difficult. Nobody has ever been able to do it. But we will try and we will succeed.' Between Alex's high hopes and an occasional small success in the lab here and there, I soon found myself sharing his conviction, and eventually thinking that we had a good shot at making an important discovery."

In his early research work, Zimmermann did not have the luxury of being able to use computer-assisted molecular modeling (CAMM), and consequently he worked with pen and paper without the use of chemistry slides: "It's a little embarrassing to talk about the archaic way we operated when the project was first under way. But we were a low-budget operation and didn't have the luxury of being able to project X-ray structures on a computer screen. We didn't actually know the structure of an enzyme, so when I drew them, I'd create an image of what I thought it should look like. Then I'd draw it again, trying to envision on paper what it might be shaped like. Not knowing what the shape of the next key might be, I'd draw a molecule to see if it would fit in the lock. I must confess I used a lot of paper.

"In-vitro, we'd isolate the enzyme in the test tube to find out what it inhibited, and we'd test it against other enzymes that we didn't want to be inhibited," Zimmermann continues. "Then Nick had an assay that allowed him to measure whatever molecule I submitted to him. He did tests to see if [it] really did inhibit this enzyme, Bcr-Abl, or if it didn't. This process was repeated again and again. I'd synthesize the molecule, hand it to Nick, and two or three days later he'd give me the results. Then I'd repeat the same process, looking to find the right molecule. Once I found a molecule that seemed to work, he'd tell me, 'Now you have this wonderful key that allows you to open one door. Now it must be tested to make sure it doesn't open all the other doors that we don't want opened.'

"Nick and his colleagues in biology checked out my lab findings when I worked on finding inhibitors for the molecule to target. The issue at this point was selectivity—coming up with a molecule to fit one key and no others. For a second opinion, Nick would frequently send our work to Brian Druker at Dana-Farber."

THE CELL BIOLOGIST

Once he and Lydon had identified compounds, Zimmermann would then work with Dr. Elisabeth Buchdunger, a cell biologist, the member of the team that would test the molecules on cells. Buchdunger had received her Ph.D. in biology from the University of Freiburg, Germany, and following her postdoctoral positions at the Friedrich-Miescher Institute in Basel and the University of Basel, she joined the oncology research group at Ciba-Geigy in 1990. She started working in the signal transduction field, and in this capacity studied inhibitors that would block tyrosine kinases. "There was a lot of evidence that certain protein kinases had a role in causing various types of cancer," she explains, "and we were running a program aiming at the identification of selective kinase inhibitors that might be useful for the treatment of cancer. In this program, we thought that it would be great if we could design an inhibitor that blocks the Bcr-Abl kinase, which had been shown to be the cause of CML. So the concept was very clear that such an inhibitor would be very useful in treating the disease."

In a team effort, Zimmermann and his colleagues were given the responsibility to design and synthesize compounds. Buchdunger and her colleagues would test the molecule against the cancer-causing enzyme. The biology work involves testing the compounds coming from the chemist's bench and then attempting to identify which compound(s) are worthy of further consideration. Then the biologist must determine how to optimize the compounds that come out of the program and profile them in an orderly fashion.

Zimmermann and the biology team worked in tandem. Following testing of the compounds against isolated enzymes, those inhibitors looking most promising were passed on to Buchdunger to evaluate their activity on cells. This meant testing the compound to determine if it penetrated the cell membrane and actually inhibited the targeted enzyme in a living cell. While a compound might work in the chemist's lab, the biologist zeroes in on its toxicity. If it killed the cell, irrespective of whether its target was inhibited, it was almost always rejected. There was the rare occasion, however, when Buchdunger would send a compound back to Zimmermann with an explanation that it worked in some respects but needed to be improved. For example, it might have entered the cell, but was hitting other kinases, and therefore was toxic. Or perhaps it specifically inhibited the targeted enzyme and wasn't toxic, but its potency was not sufficient. In these incidences, Buchdunger would recommend to Zimmermann that he change the profile of the drug so he might achieve those things that were missing.

Again and again, Zimmermann would send compounds from his lab to Buchdunger to be tested, and again and again, they would be rejected, sometimes perhaps with a note offering a trace of encouragement that suggested he might think about changing a condition in a compound's profile. Zimmermann would then regroup, make changes, or go to work on still other compounds in his search to come up with the right one that would solve the mystery. This is the life of a researcher: a lot of rejection with only an occasional reward. Sometimes Zimmermann would modify a compound in a matter of days, and other times it took weeks before he resubmitted it to Buchdunger, only to have it rejected again.

"She would tell me, 'It's good, it's mediocre, or it's bad,' " Zimmermann says. "I appreciated her comments. It was like shooting on a rifle range and having somebody tell you that you missed the target by ten centimeters or so. Elisabeth was telling me how close I was getting to the target—as well as how far away I was."

ZIMMERMAN'S TENACITY

When asked about his tenacity, Zimmermann, a soft-spoken man, tells a story about his boyhood growing up in Switzerland: "My father was a farmer and we lived in the mountains, and as a small boy I always had farm chores. Every winter there would be avalanches, but come spring, my father could always be found working very hard removing all the rocks and debris he found on his land. Every spring I'd say to him, 'Why are you doing this? Next winter there will be another avalanche. What you are doing really doesn't make much sense year after year.'

" 'I do it because this is what I do,' my father would answer."

"I learned a valuable lesson from my father, and I've applied his advice to my work as a chemist," Zimmermann tells. "You should expect work to be hard, and at times, it will test your will, but you don't quit. You just keep on trying. Sure there are occasions when my work in the lab faces obstacles that seem insurmountable. Then I think about my father and I become determined to find a solution. And I do it because the life of a chemist is what I chose for my career. This is what I do."

While progress was being made in Zimmermann's lab, failures far outnumbered successes. Meanwhile, the research team would meet every so often with management to present an update on its findings. "We'd keep telling them, 'We are getting very close,' " Zimmermann says, "but we said that so often and still had nothing definite to show for our work that we probably didn't always sound that convincing."

"Throughout this period," Buchdunger points out, "the scientific journals were saying that it will never be possible to find a selective compound. And even if we did, the compound would still have to pass the toxicity tests in animals, and then we'd have to demonstrate that it was safe enough that we could give it to humans. Perhaps the best thing we had going for us was that all of us believed we would eventually succeed, and we refused to give up. I am sure our strong determination made a difference and bought us some time."

HITTING PAY DIRT

Dr. Buchdunger explains her area of expertise in relation to Zimmer-mann's: "Juerg and his group make the compounds and these different compounds come out of his laboratory for us to figure out what they do. Do they really inhibit the enzyme we are interested in? That is one thing. But this is not enough, because we want to avoid toxicity. There are many, many kinases in a cell, so if the compound is not selective, it also kills normal cells. So the key question is: does it selectively inhibit the enzyme we are interested in and does this result in killing of the tumor cells only?

"Our mission was to come up with a compound that goes after the cancer cells that cause CML and leave the other cells alone. But we couldn't isolate and purify all these different enzymes. We didn't even know how many existed, and there is always the possibility that we might miss something. For this reason we took the approach of looking at the nor-mal cells to make sure the compound didn't negatively affect the kinases that allowed it to survive and grow. And if we didn't inhibit these normal cells, it lets us know that the compound must be selective. In other words, we'd make sure it was not a dirty one that inhibited all of these good guys. That was my job!"

Buchdunger expresses that it was also her job to determine how ac-tive a compound is. Putting it another way, how potent was it and what dosage was needed to inhibit its target and kill only the cancer cell? "It must be something that is reasonably potent," she emphasizes, "because if the drug ever reaches its target in the cells of the body, its job is to kill the bad guys. Remember, however, that back in the early 1990s there was great focus on putting the most powerful compound in the body to kill the cancer. Sometimes there was a risk of further hurting the body and risking the patient at the same time."

"We knew from the beginning that the reason patients have CML is directly linked to this Bcr-Abl," Zimmermann volunteers. "With most other cancers, the molecular pathogenesis is not known. It was also known that two or more genes unite to form other types of cancer, but only one gene causes CML. Knowing this simplified our job. It gave us a unique target. It was just very difficult in the lab to find a molecule that would inhibit only that kinase and not the others."

When Juerg Zimmermann arrived at work on August 26, 1992, he thought he was getting close to synthesizing the compound. A series of compounds had passed muster in the biologists' labs on all the requisite tests save one: they were active against Bcr-Abl oncogene; they were selective. They had even shown activity in vivo (animal testing).

The one thing keeping the compounds from getting a 100 percent stamp of approval was the issue of solubility. When animals were given the compounds, they were excreted rather than showing up in the blood. To make changes that would make a compound soluble could mean reducing its ability to bind to the "pocket." Zimmermann had had his share of disappointments in the past—there had been other times when he thought he was so close to accomplishing his goal only to see a promising candidate compound fail to get passing marks. So when he nonchalantly turned over this particular compound to Elisabeth Buchdunger like he had done countless times before, he curbed his enthusiasm, not wanting to build up his or her hopes for naught.

When Buchdunger studied the promising compound on a cellular level, she also sensed it was something special. She too had learned to contain her exhilaration. A seasoned professional, she had viewed many previous compounds that looked good at first blush but later proved to be unacceptable. When she had her technicians look at this compound, she observed that they took a longer peek than usual; still, they too were noncommittal. After everyone had expressed his or her opinion, it was agreed they would spend more time looking at the compound. At the end of the day, they felt comfortable that they had made an important discovery. Still, there were more tests to perform on cancerous cells extracted from patients, on animals, and on healthy human beings during clinical trials. The researchers knew that many hurdles would lie ahead.

They also knew that a compound had been found that did indeed inhibit the activity of the cancer-producing Bcr-Abl oncogene. Buchdunger visited Zimmermann to report the good news. It was a moment of celebration.

The compound was called CGP 57148 (after Ciba-Geigy and Sandoz Labs merged in 1996 to become Novartis, it became ST1571). Like all drugs, it would later be given a generic name. ST1571 was named imatinib. In the spring of 1993, the compound that Zimmermann had synthesized and Buchdunger had tested had attained "drug candidate status," meaning that it was ready to go to the next level—the development phase.

Every compound that shows great promise when tested by a team of cell biologists does not automatically move to patient trials. Finding a qualified physician in a hospital to test the drug on patients is a major challenge. Nick Lydon met with many hematologists over the next few months and was turned down by all. Excuses ran the gamut, but the real reason for the lack of interest was that there was little to gain by running patient trials on Gleevec because CML had such a small patient population.

There was also internal strife at Ciba-Geigy. Contrary to public opinion, even with their deep pockets, pharmaceutical companies do not have unlimited financial resources. This caused some company executives to voice opinions that the company should drop its efforts to pursue a drug that would be used by such a small population of patients. They felt that, strictly from a business point of view, it was a poor business decision because it offered little or no return. These individuals insisted that there were better places to invest the company's money. "When a high-risk project that's completely new is proposed to top management," Zimmermann says, "it can be an uphill battle to convince them that it's a good place to spend money."

AN OLD FRIEND REJOINS THE TEAM

For the previous three years Brian Druker had been studying how the Bcr-Abl tyrosine kinase works to regulate cell growth, but since 1990, when Dana-Farber signed a contract with Sandoz, he had not been in contact with Ciba-Geigy. Call it serendipity, but in 1993 the Oregon Cancer Center at Oregon Health and Science University (OHSU) offered a position to Druker that included money and space to set up his own research program. Anxious to head up his own department, it was an offer he couldn't refuse. Druker moved to Portland, and now, for the first time in three years, he was not restricted from doing business with Ciba-Geigy. Upon hearing that Druker had left Dana-Farber, Lydon and Zimmermann sent him a half dozen of the best inhibitors they had developed, including Gleevec.

"The timing couldn't have been better," Druker says. "I was looking for a compound that would inhibit CML cells, and these compounds from Ciba-Geigy arrived."

Shortly afterward, Druker went to Basel to meet with Nick Lydon, who presented the data on Gleevec, touting it as the inhibitor that blocks CML cells. Juerg Zimmermann also attended the meeting; he and Lydon answered all questions their visitor asked, and then it was their turn to ask Druker a question: "Would you work with us on further studies, including on humans?"

Druker's plan at OHSU was to find a pharmaceutical company that made a molecule that inhibited CML cells. So when they posed the question, he eagerly expressed his desire to work with them. "We must do something with the compound," he told the group in an excited voice. Druker believed that Gleevec was clearly the best at killing CML.

Juerg Zimmermann sat across the table from Brian Druker and was filled with joy at the validation that the visitor had given to his work in the laboratory.

By August 1993, Druker had conducted protein and cell studies on the company's top four compounds. Gleevec was clearly the best. It had killed a CML cell without harming normal ones. In February 1994, Druker presented his data for the first time to the Swiss-based scientists. His results showed that the compound killed 90 percent of the leukemia cells in-vitro. This was an important milestone for the drug. Although it was still not proven that Gleevec would help CML patients, nor what long-term effects could be, it was a major step forward.

Based on these results, the company made the decision to proceed with further tests, all leading to patient trials. Of course, if there was poor reaction when the animals were tested, it was probable that the compound would be deemed a failure, and the research team would be back to square one. The thought of this was cause for anxiety. They knew that if this were to happen, the entire program could be scrapped and resources would be used in other projects. Fortunately the animal tests did not initially show any significant issues. Now the scientists could determine the correct dosages to give human beings.

THE BIG MERGER AND A NEW CEO

In March 1996, Sandoz and Ciba-Geigy merged and became Novartis. It was one of the biggest mergers in corporate history and Novartis became the world's second largest pharmaceutical company. Daniel Vasella, Sandoz's chief executive officer, became the newly formed Novartis's CEO.

In today's business world, it is a rarity for a physician to be the head of a large international corporation. At the time, he was forty-three years old. Born in Fribourg, a small town between the French- and German-speaking parts of Switzerland, he was one of four children. At age eight, Vasella was stricken with meningitis and tuberculosis, and following his recovery he experienced another tragedy when his nineteen-year-old sister Ursula succumbed to cancer. He was ten years old at the time, and her death left a lasting impression on the young boy. On her deathbed, she said to him, "Daniel, do well in school."

Vasella listened to his dying sister's final words; he excelled in school and studied premedicine at the University of Fribourg. He then graduated from medical school at the University of Bern in 1979. From 1980 to 1982 he worked in pathology at the university and went into internal medicine. He spent four years as a chief resident at the University of Bern. Intrigued by business, Vasella met with his wife's uncle, Marc Moret, who was the head of Sandoz. Although Moret discouraged him from leaving the medical profession, in 1988 Vasella accepted a marketing and sales position with Sandoz and worked at its American headquarters in East Hanover, New Jersey. In 1989, the doctor-turned-sales-manager took a three-month course in management development at the Harvard Business School. Upon returning to Sandoz, he was named product manager for Sandostatin, a drug that was approved the previous year by the FDA to treat a type of chronic and severe diarrhea caused by slow-growing intestinal cancers. The diarrhea and associated weight loss for patients with malignant carcinoid tumors and vasoactive intestinal peptide-secreting tumors weakened its victims, rendering them incapable of performing even the smallest tasks. Sandostatin had a small indication for about 2,500 patients in the United States. It also treats acromegaly, a chronically disfiguring, debilitating, and life-threatening hormonal disorder that generally results from a pituitary tumor. Sandostatin also treats a small population of this disorder—affecting perhaps 20,000 to 25,000 Americans.

"Basically they gave the job to me," Vasella says, "because nobody else was interested in it. Expectations were low for Sandostatin, but as it turned out, the drug was not only useful in a cancer, but also could be applied to stop severe bleeding. We worked with physicians who tried it on several conditions, and Sandostatin turned out to be a winner, with sales today in the $750 million range. The experience taught me a valuable lesson—that we don't know everything in the beginning. It shows that we should always be open-minded when listening to our customers. Just knowing that a drug works for the patient in one application is enough to get behind it. And with that in mind, let's have confidence that we can make it work both for the patient and the company."

Vasella's success with Sandostatin put him on the company's fast track; he had a meteoric rise up the corporate ladder. After spending four years in the United States, Vasella returned to Basel, where he held several key positions before being named CEO of Sandoz Pharma Ltd. shortly before the merger in 1996. In 1999, he was given the additional title of chairman of the board of Novartis. Vasella has served the company well, as witnessed by a 2004 readership survey by the *Financial Times* that selected him as the most influential European businessman of the past quarter century.

A merger of two companies is certain to cause anxiety among employees. There are corporate cultures to contend with, and in the case of Sandoz and Ciba-Geigy, the two Basel-based companies were longtime rivals. David Epstein, who currently holds two titles at Novartis—president and CEO of the oncology business unit—was involved in the managing of the merger in North America. He had also been on the Sandoz side. "These were two large, very proud corporations," Epstein says, "and with different personalities in the way each did business. Like any merger, employees on both sides worried about if the new company was going to be the kind of place where they'd like to work. People were thinking, 'What's my role in it going to be?' 'Am I going to like the new people I'll be working with?' There are always uncertainties."

As the merger relates to this story, there was the worry that the new management team might discontinue the Bcr-Abl inhibitor program because it showed little promise of being a moneymaker. And even though it showed promise in the lab, it was still not a sure thing. Another concern was the fact that Daniel Vasella, the CEO of the new company, was formerly with the "other" company, Sandoz. Thus he was an unknown factor to the research team at Ciba-Geigy, whose members had been working on coming up with the drug now known as Gleevec for nearly a decade.

Until the merger, Matter and Vasella had never met. Vasella considered meeting the research teams a top priority and had made sure it was on his list of the first things he would do in his role of CEO at Novartis. So, very soon after the merger was a done deal, the two men met: "As the

CEO, I knew that there would be some people that were under a lot of stress and they would react with aggression," Vasella tells. "There were others who would just retract and close the door of their office, turn off the lights, and be under the impression that nobody would pay any attention to them. Some would just leave the company. And many people would be very positive and only want to contribute. There was a whole mix of reactions I observed. I was prepared to meet all sorts of people. Having said this, my first impression of Alex is still clearly fixed in my mind. He was among the most difficult people I have ever met. He wasn't shy about expressing his discontent, and in particular he complained about the merger-related changes, and elaborated about the bureaucracy and inefficiencies it would cause."

"I realized where he was coming from," Vasella continues, "and he was rightly concerned. He had been in the business long enough to have seen good programs get canceled, and even before the merger, he felt threatened and pressured. So the fact that Alex was confrontational came as no surprise. After meeting him, however, I interpreted his behavior as a sign of how passionate he and his people were about their wonderful compound. I was pleased to learn that Alex and his team were individuals with considerable competence and credibility. I also recognized that they had energy and optimism, qualities that are essential to succeed with a new drug. So when I find myself around people like this, the best thing I can do is encourage them and give them the freedom to act and make their own decisions. Then I do my best to remove obstacles that get in their way."

The merger was the best thing that could have happened, as far as Alex Matter was concerned. He was promoted to head of the combined oncology research unit of the two companies, giving him broader responsibilities. Now he had muscle that allowed him to do things that he could never have dreamed of before. The research team had more clout within the company, and since Sandoz and Ciba-Geigy were now one and the same, there was again an opportunity to work with Dana-Farber Cancer Institute.

At their first encounter, Matter expressed his views to the new CEO about how the marketing people were failing to see the big picture. "This is a reoccurring treatment compared to previous treatments," he emphasized, "and because we will have an absolute major patient benefit, the drug may be used by the same people for several years. So even with a smaller patient population, the company can realize a return on its investment." What Matter failed to realize was that he was preaching to the choir. Vasella was an astute businessman and above all else he was a compassionate physician.

It wouldn't be until later when Matter would say to the new CEO, "All of my concerns are gone, and the merger was the best thing that ever happened to us."

"The more I got to know Alex Matter, the more I trusted his competence and judgment," Vasella says. "And so I made it clear to Alex that if he felt so strongly in favor of pursuing studies on this compound, I would lend my support. It was not a matter of my turning over more financial resources to him. It was more as if I was saying to him, 'Go for it,' and that apparently meant a great deal. Alex will tell people that it was my personal interest and enthusiasm for the compound in the post-merger days that got the project really moving."

"But what mattered most," Vasella emphasizes, "is that we had a product that if it worked, it would save lives, regardless of the small patient population."

"The way things turned out, the Gleevec team greatly benefited from the merger," Epstein says. "At the time, they were still doing discovery, trying to find an active drug. Research takes patience, perseverance, and money. There is an accumulation of knowledge that occurs. Eventually you get to where you have a molecule that actually turns the switch on or off. You test for safety and then you make the decision about entering clinic trials. This is when the costs start to escalate. The Phase I trial is typically not very expensive, but when you start going into larger numbers of patients, the goal for the company is to have a fairly good idea about the likelihood of clinical success and of the potential of the product. For those large clinical trials, the company can commit hundreds of millions of dollars. So the way I see research and development in this business, both are important, as they must interact—but these are two very different processes that have different decision-making criteria along the way.

"But getting back to when we on the Sandoz side first got involved, Gleevec was still in research, and at that stage there is no way of telling whether it was going to be a big or small product. At Sandoz we tried to avoid using strict financial criteria in discovery. Those criteria, if employed at all, would tend to be later down the road. With the merger Sandoz added another culture to the table that was heavily steeped in doing the right thing for the patient. We had a culture that always believed if something was going to improve someone's life, then we had an ethical obligation to move it forward. Then we would keep our fingers crossed that it would ultimately make some money. Sometimes you are pleasantly surprised when you find out that a market is bigger or more attractive than you originally thought. So as I said, we also had a company culture that was very nourishing for Gleevec. Without the merger happening and the two cultures coming together, I'm not so sure that the drug's predecessor company would have continued with it."

SETBACK IN THE ANIMAL STUDIES

In April 1996, Brian Druker began planning for patient trials at the intravenous stages for the end of the year—on the premise that the animal studies went well. That May, to generate publicity that would be useful in attracting participants for the human trials, Druker published an article on Gleevec in the *Journal of Nature Medicine*, the first paper ever written on the compound. It was followed by another article that appeared in the *Oregonian*, and the story was picked up by the Associated Press. Although there was much skepticism, there were inquiries about Gleevec from CML patients who were desperately seeking a treatment that offered some hope. From those who contacted Novartis, Druker collected data and began to compile a list of potential patients for the trials.

Then a major setback occurred. Some of the dogs used in the studies had developed blood clots where the catheter tips were placed. It wasn't known if it was a mechanical problem with the catheter or if something went wrong with the compound. Whatever caused the problem, there would be no patient trials until the problem was fixed. This bad news hurt morale, because it meant there would be an obvious delay. The choices were to repeat the studies or wait for the toxicology studies on the oral formulation of the compound, and those studies were six months behind.

It seemed as if everything was going from bad to worse. In November 1996 the compound began to show high toxicity in the trial where the dogs had received doses intravenously. It meant the animal trials would cease immediately. This caused a buzz among the marketing people, who were already of the opinion that the small CML patient population made the compound a losing proposition for the company. Vasella stepped up to the plate and announced that if the compound did work and was medically significant, the company should not terminate the research due to weak commercial projections. "We can always find a commercial solution," he stressed. "What we cannot do is let ourselves be imprisoned by myopic marketing considerations."

Matter showed no visible signs of dismay. Instead he insisted that Gleevec represented a proof of concept, and for this reason alone, they must continue to the end. He was on a crusade and refused to allow anything to get in the way. Of course, he had been in the business long enough to know that no matter how determined he was to see the project get to the patient trials, there were things beyond his control that could kill it. When the negative results of the animal studies put everything in a state of limbo in late 1996, the entire team, including Matter, was shaken up.

Druker came forward and expressed his strong opinion on how the compound deserved a patient trial. "It doesn't matter that there was a liver toxicity problem," he insisted, "because if a patient ever developed a liver problem during patient trials, he would have been so carefully monitored that we'd simply have him stop using the drug. And we wouldn't find out if there is or isn't toxicity in human beings until they've been tested. Isn't this the point of patient trials? Let's not forget, what we have here is a promising, potentially life-saving cancer drug."

While Druker was one of the strongest advocators of Gleevec, he was also a realistic man. He clearly understood the risk that Novartis took to make such a drug with an infinitesimally small patient population. "What would you do if it was your money," he asks rhetorically, "and you had to put a billion dollars into developing a drug that had only one chance in ten of working? And by the way, there were some animal tests that show there might be some fairly significant toxicity. Are you going to put *your* money into it?"

While the project had looked as if it had come to a grinding halt in early 1997, there was enough support within the company to start patient trials. The prevailing argument that persuaded the company to move forward was the potential risk-benefit ratio that highly favored the CML patient. It was also helpful to have Daniel Vasella, the CEO, as an ardent fan of Alex Matter.

Meanwhile there was a discussion on how to give the eventual drug to a patient. At the time, the drug could only be administered intravenously.

Brian Druker opposed this delivery, saying, "Inhibiting a tyrosine kinase will require constant treatment. It isn't practical to have a patient visit a medical facility to receive infusions."

Based on this thinking, other Novartis scientists went to work on developing an oral formulation for Gleevec. These were individuals who were not on the research team. While there were doubting Thomases who said making a pill wouldn't be possible because it wouldn't dissolve properly, they did in fact make one. And when tested on dogs and rats, it worked well. More important, Gleevec taken in pill form would prove to be highly bioavailable, meaning nearly 100 percent of it could be utilized in the body.

The stage was set to move forward and test the drug on human beings. The researchers were exhilarated to see that what they had conceived and pushed through the preclinical tests was now going to the clinical trials.

Vasella supported having the drug tested, but, unlike the researchers, he was not as emotionally involved. "The best scientific progress doesn't mean much," he asserts, "if it doesn't touch human life."

With the dispute over toxicity put to rest and the making of a Gleevec pill, the company could now focus on preparing for the clinical tests. In the pharmaceutical business, this is known as the moment of truth. It's put-up-or-shut-up time. This is when the cost of doing business skyrockets. And it's when you find out if a drug does what it's supposed to do. More often than not, a medicine works well in the laboratory and on animals but fails to work on humans. Going into the clinical trials, the odds rarely favor the drug.

THE FIRST HUMAN TRIAL

In early 1998, Novartis was gearing up to begin the clinical trials for Gleevec. Human trials have to be very exacting. Only certain patients can be permitted into the trials. Because the drug in question is by definition new and experimental, the patients have to be protected against adverse effects. The drug must be administered with extreme care. Every aspect of the trials must be monitored and proper records kept.

The standard procedure for cancer patient trials is to give the drug to the most severely ill with the worst prognosis. It would endanger the life of a newly diagnosed patient to be treated with an unproven medicine when an approved treatment was available. It makes sense; nobody wants to be a human guinea pig. The average survival rate of a CML patient treated by chemotherapy had been four years to six years for patients on interferon. While a four-to-six-year life expectancy doesn't seem long to a young or middle-aged person, the survival rate would be less for a CML patient not receiving treatment. And with a new cancer medicine, it isn't known if it will enhance the patient's survival rate until it has had successful results on humans. For this reason, the patients that participate in Phase I cancer trials are those who have failed first-line therapy, and in the case of CML, had poor results taking interferon.

Newly diagnosed CML patients were excluded from participating in Novartis's Phase I trial. This meant the trial would include only those CML patients where interferon had poor results—and with these patients the prognosis was bleak.

Being designated lead investigator of the Phase I trials was the realization of a longtime ambition for Brian Druker. He had wanted such a job back in his days at Dana-Farber, and for the five years since moving to Oregon Druker had been doing consulting work for Novartis. He recruited Charles Sawyers of UCLA and Moshe Talpaz of the University of Texas M.D. Anderson Center as his second and third investigators. Both were superb physicians who were highly experienced in the leukemia field. Sawyers, an oncologist, had previously collaborated with Druker on scientific work. Talpaz had pioneered the study of interferon with CML patients. It was considered a real coup that he was with M.D. Anderson, which had one of the largest CML patient populations in the world. A fourth member of this exclusive team was Dr. John Ford, Novartis's international clinical leader.

"I was the principal investigator," Druker explains, "but to be accurate about who was in charge of the clinical trial, it was Novartis. Clearly Novartis had no expertise in this disease with patients, so they had to rely on experts to determine what patients should be targeted. How were those patients going to be monitored? What should be expected? What should our end points be? What would a reasonable response be? How often should patients be monitored? So basically here's how it worked: it would be a team of clinical investigators working with Novartis clinicians that would design the clinical trial. Novartis would write up the clinical trial based on our advice and then we would review it. We would make modifications and changes in protocol. Novartis would decide on three clinical sites (Oregon, where I was based; M.D. Anderson in Houston, Texas; and at UCLA in Los Angeles).

"The next step was to enroll patients at the three sites. Of course, Novartis was the sponsor and would pay for everything. Like Sawyers and Talpaz, my staff and I would see all patients at each of our sites, giving them the drug, continually evaluating them, and reporting our results to Novartis—daily, weekly, and monthly. It was Novartis's job to monitor the overall progress of the trial. The company put the information in its database, analyzed the data, and organized their reports that would later be filed with the FDA."

By the spring of 1998, it was determined that the Phase I trial would start during the beginning of summer. Druker had put a lot of time and energy into getting Gleevec to patient trials. He was acutely aware of the large investment that the company had put into this drug. And certainly in the back of his mind was the worry that the drug might fail in the clinical tests after the company had invested hundreds of millions of dollars. If so, he wondered how would he ever be able to face his friends at Novartis who had so much faith in him.

Druker was well aware of what could go wrong. All sorts of things could happen. That nagging problem of the liver toxicity could show up in patients. Or there could be some other new toxicity. The compound might not penetrate into the patients' cells. Or there could be a new, unexpected problem.

The Phase I trial for Gleevec ended up with an enrollment of 149 CML patients, a larger-than-normal number, considering that Phase I cancer trials generally have 30 to 50 patients. The three criteria for a patient to participate were: (1) The patient had to have CML in the chronic phase that was positive for the Philadelphia Chromosome; (2) The patient had to have failed interferon therapy; (3) The patient had to have a white cell count of at least twenty thousand per cubic millimeter.

In the end there were eighty-four CML patients in the chronic phase, fifty-nine blast crisis patients, and six children, all of whom had been resistant to interferon. The children were either in the chronic stage or in blast crisis.

"We ended up having about forty to fifty patients in Oregon," Druker says, "and they came in from near and far. The first patient was a state resident, and then one came from California and another from neighboring Washington. Then we started to expand. One came from

Indiana, more from Oregon and Washington, and one from Italy. For the first three to six months we would monitor them very closely, so we recommended that they stay in Portland for the first month. They were told that it would be even better to stay for three months, and most did. Remember, these were patients who had been put on notice by their referring physicians that they had run out of options. In other words, this was their last chance to live. They were well motivated. We started the trial in the summer and Oregon is quite beautiful that time of year. So if they had to be away from home, it was a nice place to be. Later they had to return every three months for continuing follow-up. When they went home, they were treated by their local oncologist who, in turn, worked with us, sending in blood counts and status reports."

"The immediate response from Gleevec was incredible," Matter exclaims, "absolutely unheard of. Such an effect had never before been seen. Then you hold your breath because you worry about the many different things that can go wrong, such as major toxicity after a few months. You never know—all hell can break loose."

"The first feedback showed that the drug was very well tolerated," Zimmermann says, "and because it was so immediate, it disappointed a lot of people. That's because other cancer agents were very toxic and cause a lot of side effects. Patients and doctors are conditioned to think, 'For it to work, it must kill the other cells as well as the cancer cells.' But when this was not the case with Gleevec, some people actually seemed disappointed because it was not what they expected since they *didn't* get sick. It made them skeptical."

"It took about four to six months before we started to see benefits that were beginning to look so obviously and absolutely positive," Druker tells. "In a Phase I clinical trial, you typically start with low doses that you believe are likely to be safe. But you are not so sure about the effectiveness. Safety is the primary concern. About four to six months later, we started to increase the dosage, and we were reaching doses where we were seeing truly remarkable results. And once we got to effective doses, patients' blood counts were coming back to normal, quite rapidly. The patients were feeling well, and it was absolutely amazing to see these results.

"By January 1999, everyone was responding. The issue then was, 'How long is this going to last?' If it lasted one month, who would care? If it lasted a long time, everyone would care. But between January and June 1998, we didn't know if this was going to continue or not. Interestingly, the patients were quick to point out that they didn't care. They were feeling so well I was hearing patients say, 'I had never expected to even have these extra few months so I consider it a gift.' They were extraordinarily happy with their treatment. They might have been ecstatic, but I was nervous because I didn't know if these results would last. Only time would tell."

The original group of 149 patients was still doing well by January 1999. It had become obvious that Gleevec was the best treatment ever administered to CML patients. "A full year later it didn't cause side effects and it was still working," Druker emphasizes, "plus it was treating the worst of the worst CML cases, meaning those patients that had previously failed to benefit from any other therapy."

The data were astonishing. Of thirty-one patients who had participated in the Phase I trial at 300-milligram doses, all had a complete hematologic response and one-third had a complete cytogenetic response (i.e., the disappearance of the Philadelphia Chromosome). As patients began to have larger doses that produced better results with little noticeable side effects increases or additional risks, it was quite clear that Gleevec was a huge success. (It would later be determined that patients in the early stages of CML who took daily doses of 300 to 800 milligrams did even better than this group of Phase I patients.)

VASELLA'S BOLD DECISION

With the results in from the Phase I trial, the time had come to move full steam ahead, which meant the company would do everything possible to expedite its efforts to get the drug approved and into the marketplace. Meanwhile, to conduct clinical tests, the company would have to produce more quantities of Gleevec. So far, making an adequate supply for the patients in the first clinical tests only took a small amount, and small quantities could be made in the laboratory. However, the company had no quick way to mass-produce the drug. While they had the know-how to do it, there were governmental procedures to adhere to, and rushing the manufacturing process would mean additional expenditures. Vasella made the decision to take whatever steps were necessary to get the job done. It was not based on bottom-line management. His only consideration was: "How could we gear up our resources to produce commercial quantities of the new drug quickly enough to save as many lives as possible? We would have to find a way around the constraints. The quality of the drug was simply too overwhelming. A moment like this comes perhaps once in a lifetime. It made no sense to miss out by being overly conservative."

The CEO explained: "Routinely, our strategy at Novartis is to develop systems that tend to minimize the risk throughout the drug development process. For instance, we typically spread the costs of developing and producing the drug over time so that we can monitor the progress of the drug every step of the way and only produce the needed quantities. We conduct small patient trials before we engage in large ones. I did not think this was the right strategy for Gleevec. I sensed that the risk was high. Though my goal would be to get the drug to the people before they died, if the drug was stillborn, critics would hardly give me credit for trying. They would simply say, 'He should have known better. He wasted the company's resources. He wasted his employees' energy. He wasted time and has forgone better opportunities.' "

Vasella was taking a huge risk because even a slight miscalculation could very well have put his job as CEO in jeopardy. His strong style of leadership is exemplified when he justified his actions by saying, "I deeply believe that if you want a climate in a company where people take calculated but not unreasonable risks, you have to demonstrate that you are not afraid of taking risks yourself—and, most important, you are not afraid of failing."

Following a meeting Vasella had with Joerg Reinhardt, then global head of development, Andreas Rummelt, then global head of technical research and development, and Greg Burke, then global head of clinical development in oncology, a decision was made to move to industrial-scale production of Gleevec. Reinhardt, Rummelt, and Burke accepted the challenge with the same vim and vigor as the members of the research team. This was a highly unusual move that entailed huge risks. There was always the possibility that the Phase I results would fizzle over time and what new side effects might develop was anyone's guess—both of which could kill the drug before it ever made a nickel.

PHASE II CLINICAL TRIALS

In 1999, plans began to start the Phase II clinical trials in May. The purpose of these trials was to validate the results of the Phase I experience. There was no shortage of CML patients to enroll. The word about the new miracle drug to treat CML patients had spread throughout the scientific and medical communities as well as among the CML community. With a rare disease like CML, the patients formed a network among themselves, and with the advent of the Internet, they had the ability to instantly communicate to others around the globe. While support groups for the infirm have been around for decades, the Internet took networking to a new level by providing a constant stream of current information. Chat rooms not only offered moral support via pep talks for the depressed, they imparted the amazing success stories of those blessed CML patients who were enrolled in the clinical tests at the three cancer centers in Houston, Los Angeles, and Portland.

With the number of CML patients in the United States roughly 15,000, it's a diminutive segment of America's population of 300 million people. The small numbers served to the advantage of CML patients. Like a chain letter, one member of a support group communicated to another that she was being treated with a new medicine in a clinical trial being conducted by Novartis. She described being on interferon and how it was a slow death sentence. But after taking Gleevec capsules, her weight had increased, her strength was back to normal, her white cell counts were lower, she had experienced few or little side effects, and, best of all, her bone marrow tests showed a major decrease in the percentage of cancer cells.

The Internet has no geographical boundaries. Before long, the word about the new CML medicine had spread around the world. One such patient was Suzan McNamara, a thirty-one-year-old woman from Montreal who had been diagnosed with CML in March 1998. Her physician told her that she could live three to five years on hydroxyurea, a drug that controlled the white cell count but did not kill cancer cells. Her medication made her so sick that she quit her job as an officer manager:

"I had found a support group on the Internet," McNamara tells, "and I'd go online every day. It was basically my life. One day in March 1999 I heard about a woman who was enrolled in a clinical trial for this new drug for CML. I was so excited. Nobody paid much attention to this disease because there were so few people that had it. 'Wow, they're actually doing something new for CML,' I remember saying. The woman said that after taking the drug, she was starting to feel much better and had no side effects. I couldn't imagine a drug that didn't make you sick all the time. I was on a drug that wasn't curing me, so even if this new one wasn't a cure, at least I could start living a normal life if I felt better. Then when I started hearing how people on this drug were actually having their cancer cells go down, I was determined to have this drug.

"I heard about patients enrolled in a Phase I clinical trial in Portland, Oregon, and nothing else had helped. They were in the blast stages of the disease and now they were doing well. The problem was that to get in the trial, you had to be in that stage of the disease. It was a weird situation. I didn't want to be in the advanced stage, but at the same time I wanted that drug."

"Meanwhile, I was no longer in remission and was starting to get really sick," McNamara says. "I lost forty pounds, my hair was falling out, I was weak, and had an awful rash on my face. I'd spend one week in bed, coming in and out of being comatose. Even so, my boyfriend, Derek, kept on telling me how beautiful I looked—and he meant it. Boy, was I lucky to have his support. My doctor told me, 'Your counts are going up, and I am unable to stabilize it.'

" 'Well, can I get on this new drug?'

" 'I can't get you in it,' he told me, 'and you don't want to go on a clinical Phase I. All drugs get to Phase I clinical trials and they're not important.'

"Yet I kept hearing about the patients in the Novartis clinical trials that were doing well. I said to Derek, 'This isn't living. There is no way I'm going to die on this planet earth when I know there is a drug available in North America. I'll do whatever it takes to get this drug.'

"I learned that Dr. Brian Druker was the primary investigator so I e-mailed him to tell him my story. 'I'm thirty-two years old, and I don't want to die. Please help me.' To my surprise, I received an e-mail from him and he suggested that I call him. I did and I gave him my sob story. 'How could I take the new drug?' I pleaded.

" 'We're doing everything we can but in the clinical trials there is a process we must follow.' He then added, 'Suzan, why don't you write to the company, and by telling your story from a patient's point of view, you might be able to do something that I can't to speed things up." He also forewarned her that there was a limited supply of the medicine.

"After hanging up the phone," McNamara continues, "I felt a surge of energy and decided I had to do something. Plan A would be to get a petition signed by my support group, and while it seemed like a lame plan, it would have to do until I came up with a Plan B. So I e-mailed my online friends in my support group and asked them to get everyone they knew to sign the petition. With 600 of them out there, I thought I'd get about 300 responses. To my surprise, names kept on coming. On some days, there'd be hundreds. Boy, was I excited. As it turned out, within a few weeks later there were 3,030 names. I put a cover letter with the names in a FedEx envelope, paid $53, and sent it to the president of Novartis in Switzerland." The letter stated McNamara's belief that the longer it took to get the medicine to CML patients, the more people were likely to die.

"On November 2, my birthday, Dr. Druker called. 'Suzan, your petition has done a world of good. The company is sending you a letter. I can't give you the details and you can't tell anyone until you get it. Just keep checking your mail.'

"I had to keep this news from my group and that was not an easy thing to do. But a week later a letter arrived. I was so nervous that I was shaking when I opened it. The letter explained that the company was increasing its manufacturing of the drug so there would be an ample supply as well as additional clinical trials. The best news was that I could be enrolled in one that would begin in Portland after the first of the year. I was so elated that tears streamed down my cheeks."

The letter also stated that the company was moving the manufacturing of Gleevec to a facility that would accommodate commercial scale production in order to have a sufficient supply of the drug for the expanded clinical trial program. Shortly afterward, Druker called to congratulate McNamara on her letter. He told her that there would be enough supply of the drug to start three trials in Portland in December, January, and February. "You are welcome to join any one of them," he assured her.

McNamara and Derek flew from Montreal to Portland in time for her to be there for the enrollment that started on January 2, 2000. The couple stayed for five weeks, sightseeing and enjoying a well-deserved vacation in between visiting Druker's clinic. During the next eighteen months, McNamara made six trips to Portland for periodic checkups.

Her letter is living proof that one person—with determination—can get the attention of a multibillion-dollar international corporation. As Daniel Vasella articulated, "We will not drag our feet in meeting her request. And while Novartis will make every effort to act as quickly as possible to make the drug available to the thousands of needful patients, the company must adhere to certain established criteria to assure that the trials would be conducted according to the highest standards."

EARLY RESULTS ON GLEEVEC

A month before McNamara's enrollment, Druker presented the Phase I clinical trial results at the American Society of Hematology (ASH) meeting in New Orleans. It was the first presentation about Glivec (which Gleevec is called in other countries) to be given to the general public and the event was attended by many media people. At the plenary session Druker simply presented the results of the clinical trials and let the facts speak for themselves. His twenty-minute presentation turned out to be the highlight of the entire conference.

"When the ASH attendees heard about the hematologic responses," says Laurie Letvak M.D., who serves as global head of the Glivec Phase IV program, "they knew that this drug was something different. The responses were unheard of—just unbelievable. Suddenly we were deluged with people wanting to know about the drug and how they could get it."

"Literally within an hour after Dr. Druker's presentation at the ASH meeting," says Novartis's Barbara Kennedy, vice president of access and advocacy, "the phone calls started pouring in. Previously our call center would typically receive fifteen calls a month, but suddenly, like an avalanche, we were getting up to two thousand calls a day. We had to staff our call center to handle this huge unprecedented response and train them how to answer questions from callers. In the beginning, the onslaught of calls was a result of the media coverage. As more CML patients and their family members communicated among themselves, the calls kept coming in. A month after the conference, we were still getting up to six hundred calls a day."

A warm, caring woman, Kennedy understood that to CML patients and their loved ones, their calls were of the utmost urgency: "Some of them were literally on death's door," she says, "and they had no other options. Not every one of them, however, was a candidate for Gleevec, and it was very difficult to turn anyone down. For some callers, this drug wouldn't work on the kind of cancer they had. For the majority I could explain this to them in a few minutes. With others, I'd talk to them for an hour or more. At the end of the conversation, they would say that they understood why they were not good candidates. Invariably they'd thank me for spending so much time with them. Whenever appropriate, we tried to provide them with other avenues to explore, and if there would be suitable clinical studies in progress for them to consider, we'd let them know."

"Early on, for the initial studies, I'd have to turn down someone because he or she had recently been diagnosed with CML and had not been on any other therapy," Kennedy continues. "I'd explain why and also mention that there was a limited supply of the drug. 'Thank you for being so open with me,' the patient would say, 'and I understand why you have to give it first to the patients that tried other therapies and their options are limited.' It was heartbreaking, but until we had more supplies, that's what we had to say."

Kennedy conversed with as many patients as she possibly could. She returned all calls that were made specifically requesting to speak to her, and this meant calling people in the evenings and on weekends—during her own time. "It was a very emotional time," she says, "and yes, I did get to know many of them and I did become personally involved. There were many times when I had to close my door after one of those calls and I'd sit behind my desk and tears would stream down my cheeks.

"I'm not the only one around here that feels for the patients. We all do, and that goes for everyone in research, clinical development, manufacturing, marketing, the CEO—everyone. This is why I get so upset when I hear somebody say, 'The pharmaceutical companies can cure this or that disease but they'd rather have their customers take their drugs for the rest of their life, so they don't make medicines for permanent cures.' I think that's such a ridiculous statement. The holy grail in this industry is to find a cure."

Novartis's apparent success with this lifesaving breakthrough medicine was praised throughout the pharmaceutical industry. Even the company's staunchest competitors hailed the Novartis scientists for a job well done. Gleevec was a win-win for everyone—humankind and the industry itself. As Elisabeth Buchdunger explains, "While we are in competition with other pharmaceutical companies, we are on the same team in the scientific world. We want to find cures and save people's lives. When it comes to curing cancer, it's important that we work together and have an exchange of information."

The Internet served CML patents well, much as it previously did for HIV/AIDS patients in the 1990s. It continues to serve CML patients. Today, Web sites such as www.Gleevec.com (a Novartis Web site) and www.CML.com (not a Novartis Web site) are available to anyone seeking information.

The Internet also helped spread the word about the Phase II trials. By now there were few in the entire universe of people with an interest in CML that were unfamiliar with the new miracle drug. There would be no problem finding patients for the upcoming trials. Usually Phase II trials have only fifty to one hundred patients, a large enough number so investigators can learn more about efficacy levels. However, in the case of Gleevec, the CML patient community had united. There was also the vast media coverage, plus Suzan McNamara's petition and a large network of CML patients.

With so many people desperately wanting the new drug—a drug that, at the time, was only available to those who were participating in the clinical trials—it had become quite evident that Gleevec was not your garden-variety drug. Nevertheless, Novartis only had to treat the number required to get FDA approval. Limiting the number of CML patients would cost far less money and it would certainly be less complicated.

DOING THE RIGHT THING

Novartis instead made the decision to attempt to accommodate as many patients as possible. By June 2000, the company launched an expanded access program that allowed more patients to receive the drug than the number of patients normally enrolled in a clinical trial. It would require close monitoring to assure an adequate level of safety. And it would follow a simplified version of the same protocols used for the concurrent Phase II studies. To assure the safety of the patients, cancer centers that were well equipped to monitor patients appropriately for this kind of drug would participate.

Some seven thousand patients were enrolled in the expanded access effort. As the drug became more available, Novartis expanded the program from six to thirty-two countries. The company would absorb the entire cost of all medicine used during the program. To implement the program within an accelerated time frame, the company committed large resources of money and manpower in excess of the norm.

Patients in the Phase III trials were those who had been recently diagnosed with the disease and had never been treated by interferon. This would provide information that was not revealed during the Phase I trials that involved the most severe cases and patients who had done poorly with interferon. The question was: how would these patients fare? While it had been established that patients with the most severe cases of CML did significantly better with Gleevec, would the same be true of the newer cases that had received no prior treatment? The study was opened in June 2000 and enrollment closed in January 2001. Gleevec and interferon were randomly given to participating CML patients. Some 177 hospitals in 17 countries participated. Prior to Gleevec, CML Phase III trials usually included only 500 to 700 patients. While newly diagnosed patients are expected to have a better response than long-term patients who have responded poorly to other treatments, the data from the Phase III study demonstrated that Gleevec was three to four times more effective in achieving a favorable cell reduction response.

The results from the follow-up data of the Phase II trials were equally impressive. As Dr. Laurie Letvak emphasizes, "You can see how Gleevec changed the natural history of the disease. With the accelerated phase patients, they used to live only three to nine months with interferon. Once you went into accelerated and then blast phase, the game was over. In three to six months, the CML patient died. But here, after fifty-four months, overall survival is 90 percent. [Of] the patients on our drug, only 6 percent of them have gone to accelerated and blast crisis in forty-two months. This absolutely changed the disease for most patients to a more chronic disease, and today, they can expect to live many years. These results have impacted consideration of bone marrow transplant treatment for the new upfront patients."

David Epstein and his development team, then led by Greg Burke, played an active role in the Phase III study, in which 1,100 newly diagnosed patients from around the world participated. "We enrolled these patients in record time," he points out, "and this time, we compared

Gleevec to the standard of care, which was interferon. This trial ended up with the most meaningful data because it demonstrated that when the drug was used early on, it was very effective in preventing the disease from progressing. And unlike many chemotherapies, the side-effect profile was so modest that it could be used during the early stages of CML. Later on, that same modest side-effect profile would allow us to start Gleevec at higher doses and get even better results."

A FULL-COURT PRESS

Based on Phase II data, Novartis was now shooting for an FDA approval sometime in the summer, only two and a half years after the first trials began. To have product by then meant it would take an all-out effort to make sure the medicine would be available for shipping within hours after approval had been granted. Earlier, Vasella had risked making large quantities of the drug for the trials. His gamble paid off because it gave the company a head start in gearing up its manufacturing plant to avoid delays in getting the lifesaving medicine to CML patients within hours following approval. His gamble also saved many lives.

"There are examples in our industry, with breakthrough medicines, when there wasn't an ample supply on hand and companies had to ration a new product," explains Epstein. "Some companies even had to resort to a lottery to determine who received a new drug. With a lifesaving drug like this one, we didn't want anyone who needed it to be put on a waiting list."

On February 27, 2001, the company was ready to file its New Drug Application with the FDA. It's important to understand the size of the "application." In the case of Gleevec, the submission consisted of 73 volumes, each volume approximately 400 pages. That's a total of more than 29,000 pages. In March, the FDA granted the application priority review.

Thanks to Vasella's gamble, the Novartis factory in Ringaskiddy, Ireland, had been working in twelve-hour shifts around the clock, seven days a week, making a plain-looking white powder substance that was exceptionally difficult to synthesize. To make it in projected quantities that were needed to serve thirty thousand patients a year, the process required thirty tons of raw materials and five hundred tons of solvent. With a dozen separate chemical steps necessary, it would typically require a two-year lead time.

With a full-court press to get Gleevec out by the summer, employees throughout the entire organization were working overtime. Now, literally thousands of people were involved and working frantically to meet a deadline. Interestingly, sixteen years earlier, Alex Matter, along with a handful of people, started working on a compound, and although extremely complicated and difficult, there were only a few people involved. The ST1571 project had expanded from a small lab to a much larger arena—a worldwide arena. Trials were being conducted in North America, Europe, and Asia. As president of Novartis Oncology, David Epstein was responsible for coordinating this global undertaking, explains, "We made the decision to launch this medicine on a global scale, not one country at a time. Looking back at its complexity and the difficulty of coordinating people from around the world to get everyone on the same page, [this] was a tremendous undertaking. We had to get a consensus on everything, from the design of the packaging and name of the product [to] how we would price the product. Then we had to put a marketing plan in place, and this encompassed everything from creating collateral materials to conducting press conferences. Of course we also had to file and complete the global registrations with various government agencies worldwide. And there were the language barriers we had to contend with, not only for filing the product, but internally, between our manufacturing people in Switzerland and Ireland. For a while, working twenty-hour days seemed to be the norm around here. What drove everyone to work so hard was the wonderful feeling that came from knowing we were doing something so important."

A modest man, Epstein says, "My role predominantly was to make sure that all the pieces and all the different people were moving in the same direction in a coordinated way. In some ways, I served as a cheerleader. I got to resolve conflicts. I became one of the people who helped others feel proud for all the great things that they had done and accomplished. Huge amounts of energy were created that some recycled for the next breakthrough."

GETTING READY FOR THE MARKET

Hugh O'Dowd, who now heads the oncology business in the U.K., headed global marketing for the medicine then. He cut his eyeteeth at IBM in sales and marketing prior to joining Novartis. He shared the same passion that consumed the drug's researchers—the original team in the lab like Alex Matter, Juerg Zimmermann, Nick Lydon, Elisabeth Buchdunger, and Brian Druker. He too has taken ownership in Gleevec. "I loved working at IBM," O'Dowd says, "but I never had a passion for selling a mainframe computer. But here, I go to bed every night and sleep well knowing that there are tens of thousands of patients who are alive and enjoying a quality life because of what we do. There's a higher calling here."

Deborah Dunsire M.D., previously a general practitioner, joined the company in 1988 in a clinical research capacity. She then went into specialty sales for the company and later was named vice president of North American oncology. As a physician, Dunsire has excellent communication skills with other physicians, and her former background has enabled her to contribute to building the company's U.S. oncology sales force, now consisting of 377 representatives, approximately 150 of which sell Gleevec to oncologists. She has been instrumental in training Novartis's specialized sales force that sells Gleevec: "This kind of selling is really about helping physicians to make informed decisions and choices about therapy. So, prior to launching Gleevec, we had to prepare our sales reps to be knowledgeable on the product as well as the whole area of leukemia and the business of oncology. Every time one of our reps makes a sales call, she has to make it worth the doctor's time to see her. By conveying information that's new and necessary, she provides an added value, and I believe this is essential in our field.

"To prepare our sales reps for when the day came that they would present Gleevec to our customers, we invited fifty CML patients to attend our sales meetings. These patients were currently being treated by Gleevec, so when the reps would later call on physicians, they could say, 'I spoke to a patient who has been on this medication, and this is how he felt and this is what he experienced.'"

Dunsire was also instrumental in helping the company's IT department set up a call center to field queries coming in. "One day our head of IT came to me saying, 'We put up a Web site, but we're getting so many calls, I'm afraid it's going to crash.' [I asked him,] 'Greg, how much volume can it handle?' When Greg told me, we had to make some quick changes to handle the incoming calls. We trained over two hundred call center representatives so they could answer questions because we didn't want to fail in our mission, which was to connect patients and caregivers to the right information, right from day one. The whole company was really engaged in making sure that all these various different pieces were in place, so that when one of our physicians or patients [contacted] us, they got a correct answer—they got it quickly and they got it effectively."

In July 2005, Dunsire left Novartis to join Millennium Pharmaceuticals, where she now serves as president and CEO.

"In addition to the other formal training that our sales representatives received," Hugh O'Dowd reveals, "we brought in physicians who would be interested in Gleevec considering their patient population and their needs. Then each representative was required to make individual presentations on the drug data to six physicians. 'You have to make the benefits of the drug clear,' representatives were told, 'and they are going to grade you on whether you convinced them or failed to convince them.' Afterward, the sales representative and his management reviewed his performance. It was unacceptable to be mediocre—particularly with a medicine that was so important. Our people needed to be absolutely clear on how the medicine worked."

The sales organization's mantra became "Leave no patient behind," meaning that every sales representative would be thoroughly trained and equipped to present Gleevec to physicians as soon as the product was launched. "Everyone thought it would border on being irresponsible to be unprepared to sell Gleevec, [with the result that] a CML patient would not be treated with it," O'Dowd says. "We were on a mission and it wasn't about making production quotas or receiving sales awards. We had an obligation to the patient to do a superior job in communicating about Gleevec."

The company had one more challenge to deal with. In late April 2001, with only a month or so to go, the new drug was still technically known as Glivec. The name Glivec had been submitted to the FDA's nomenclature committee. "We had picked this name from our files of a drug that had failed in Phase III studies and was being studied to treat glioblastoma multiforme, which is a type of brain tumor," O'Dowd explains. "While the European regulatory agencies accepted this name, it was rejected by the FDA. There were already two drugs on the American market to treat diabetes that sounded too similar—Glynase and Glyset. So there we were, with literally weeks to go and no name for Glivec in the U.S. Normally it takes two years to get a name approved, but with our drug on priority review for approval, we were forced to very quickly change its name. Meanwhile, we had been calling it Glivec during the trials and it had already gained name recognition. [So] we changed the spelling to Gleevec, a name with the same pronunciation, and the FDA approved it. Once approved, we were able to send our sales literature to the printer, so it was really a close call."

"At a press conference," Epstein recalls, "a reporter said, 'You changed the name to Gleevec so it could be a seven-letter name for calling 1-888-GLEEVEC.'

" 'The thought had never occurred to us,' I told him. 'We're just not that smart.' "

FDA APPROVAL IN RECORD TIME

The entire inspection and approval process took approximately eleven weeks. The usual approval process with such inspections ranges from one year to eighteen months. It was becoming evident that the FDA was ready to approve the drug.

The FDA announced that it would have a news conference on May 10, 2001, an unusual event for giving approval to a drug. Even more un-common, the Health and Human Services secretary, Tommy Thompson, would announce the marketing approval of Gleevec, recognizing it as a breakthrough cancer medication. CEO Daniel Vasella arrived at two in the morning from Switzerland to be present. David Epstein had the op-portunity to join him onstage and later on to answer the many calls from the press.

Secretary Thompson noted that the drug was based on the principle of molecular targeting—killing leukemia cells while leaving normal white cells alone. "We believe such targeting is the wave of the future," he said.

It was, according to Secretary Thompson, record approval time for a cancer drug. "By reviewing Gleevec in just two and a half months, that is an all-time record for a cancer drug and for the evaluation of a highly complex novel drug."

In his remarks, the secretary also told how he had lost three close family members to cancer. "So anytime you have a breakthrough, it is really a red-letter day."

WHAT'S A LIFESAVING MEDICINE WORTH?

When Novartis ventured to make Gleevec, it was with sizable eco-nomic risk. From a risk-reward standpoint, it was an audacious move, considering the high odds against designing a compound to attack a single target—cancer cells only—without disturbing healthy cells. Still another factor to consider: was it worth investing large sums of money to make a drug for such a small patient population? (Gleevec is considered an "orphan product," defined by the Orphan Drug Act as a drug used to treat diseases or conditions affecting fewer than two hundred thousand persons in the United States.)

Novartis's choice to make Gleevec was not based on financial returns—had the company been driven by profit, there certainly were better places it could put its money and get more "bang for the buck." However, now that Gleevec is available in the marketplace, it is entirely reasonable for a publicly traded company such as Novartis to make a profit in exchange for the blood, sweat, and money that it has poured into this drug. So the question that Novartis had to address was: how to price this product so it is accessible to those who need it while making a reasonable profit for the company?

If a product—any product—is priced to sell for an amount of its value, what is it worth to a person who is suffering on his or her deathbed to have his or her health restored? Is it worth the cost of a car? A five-carat diamond? While it is an unfair question, comparable to asking what a glass of water is worth to a man in the desert dying of thirst, it is food for thought. Let it be said that value is in the eye of the beholder. With the huge investment put into Gleevec, the company had many ways to price it. To the good fortune of CML patients, it chose a moderate price point.

"Consider what the alternatives were at the time Gleevec entered the marketplace, and that was primarily interferon with a very challenging profile," explains O'Dowd. "Plus interferon, when combined with another agent—Ara-C—had a survival average of approximately five and a half years. After a lot of deliberation, the price of Gleevec was set at approximately the price of interferon, but with a far superior projected survival curve and safety profile."

With the price of Gleevec approximating the price of interferon, it's a great value—much like buying a Rolls Royce for the price of a Chevrolet. Consider too that a CML patient's bone marrow transplant surgery costs in the $200,000 range. After lengthy discussions on what to annually charge for Gleevec, and having given consideration to affordability based on economic differences between the haves and the have-nots around the globe, it was decided that a worldwide price would be set at $2,200 a month. Knowing that this price would be unfeasible for the world's poor, the company organized a global patient assistance program (GIPAP), which had never before been done for a therapy like Gleevec on such a large-scale basis. In the United States, a patient assistance program (PAP) was also established to provide the drug free to patients with an annual income below a multiple of the poverty level and to cover a portion of the costs for people with incomes below $100,000—never exceeding 20 percent of the person's income. There were exceptions to the program to reflect individual circumstances, including assets, family size, number of children, assets, etc. The company was sincere in its effort to make the drug available to all in need, and while the formula for pricing Gleevec certainly had its critics, it was a plan made with much thought and consideration for CML patients. In the vast majority of cases, however, patients were pleased with the price plan.

"PAP was set up here in the U.S.," O'Dowd explains. "Through the global program—GIPAP—we provide [Gleevec] to the poor for little or no charge based on certain medical and financial criteria. As I said previously, 'Leave no patient behind.' Approximately 15 percent of all CML patients receive Gleevec for free. I don't know of too many companies that can make that claim about their product. I'm very proud of what we have done here."

LOOKING TO THE FUTURE

Suzan McNamara is living a full, healthy life today. She takes one 400-milligram pill a day, and her CML does not interfere with her lifestyle. Like all CML patients, she will continue to take Gleevec for the rest of her life. It shouldn't affect her way of life any more than individuals with a chronic illness such as diabetes or high cholesterol are affected by taking their medication. Fortunately for McNamara, as a citizen of Canada—a nation with a national health plan that pays for all health-care treatment—she is not burdened with the cost of her medication.

Like all survivors of a life-threatening illness, McNamara says that being sick with CML has changed her life. "Since I came back from Portland, this has been the happiest I have ever been in my entire life," she says. "And today I look at every day as a gift. I know it may sound unusual, but I look forward to growing old. When I see a gray hair or a wrinkle, it doesn't upset me in the least. To me it's a blessing."

Today, McNamara is living in Montreal with Derek, and is now working on her Ph.D. in cell molecular biology at McGill University. She plans to devote her career to research in leukemia. While she says, "This is my way of paying back my dues," she has already indirectly saved the lives of the many people who enrolled in the clinical trials as a result of her petition.

With CML, Gleevec has reduced a fatal form of cancer to a chronic illness in some cases. As Brian Druker notes, "As it turns out, we probably can't kill every last leukemia cell. With most patients we can get a spectacular response; however, we probably won't eradicate the leukemia. If the patient stops taking the drug, the leukemia comes back, so patients will continue to take their Gleevec pill every day of their lives. Like one of my patients said to me, 'I have leukemia but it's no big deal.' "

The making of Gleevec has been recognized as one of the biggest breakthroughs in the annals of cancer research. It not only serves as a treatment to inhibit CML, but it has opened the door to treating other cancers with designer molecules. However, Gleevec actually "failed" in one aspect of its job. Alex Matter's goal was to design a molecule that would attack the cancer cell and not interfere with other cells. "The reality is, we're not as good as we thought," David Epstein smiles. "Gleevec actually hit three kinases that we later found out were responsible for other diseases."

In the case of CML, the protein with Bcr-Abl was the target, but as it was learned, Gleevec also attacks two other members of a family of enzymes, or kinases: platelet-derived growth factor (PDGF-R) and c-Kit. The company knew about PDGF-R and Bcr-Abl while it was making Gleevec. But it wasn't until later, as Brian Druker was working in his lab in Portland, that he ascertained that the drug also affects c-Kit, the kinase that causes gastrointestinal stromal tumors (GIST), a rare tumor that affects about five thousand people in the United States. It is a tumor that generally forms in the stomach or intestinal tract and metastasizes to the abdomen or the pelvis. The tumor can be treated only by surgery and, unless it is eliminated, is usually fatal. The FDA later approved Gleevec to treat GIST, on February 1, 2002. It has since received approval for five other rare conditions.

The company is currently developing a new drug, tentatively known as Tasigna or AMN107, that shows promise for treating Gleevec-resistant leukemia. This drug retains half the chemical makeup of Gleevec, while the other half has been engineered to assure a tighter link to Bcr-Abl, thus increasing potency and potentially overcoming resistance due to mutations in Bcr-Abl.

As Novartis's CEO Daniel Vasella points out, "The fight against cancer continues; however, each time we come up with a new, effective drug like Gleevec, it's a small victory in a much larger, ongoing war."

7

PFIZER COMPANY PROFILE

In 1848, Charles Pfizer, age twenty-four, and his cousin Charles Erhart Pfizer, age twenty-eight, emigrated from Ludwigburg, Germany, to the United States. Though they came from well-to-do families, the cousins yearned for adventure and saw America as a land of opportunity. Charles had learned chemistry as an apothecary's apprentice, and Erhart was a confectioner, a trade he learned from his uncle. In 1849, their first year in America, they founded a chemical firm, Charles Pfizer & Company, headquartered in Brooklyn, New York. They borrowed $2,500 from Charles's father and, with a $1,000 mortgage, they purchased a small building in the Williamsburg section of Brooklyn, a predominately German neighborhood.

It was a time when life was not only more primitive, it was also filled with many medical dangers. For example, the lack of refrigeration meant that a diet of meat and potatoes carried the constant risk of intestinal worms. These pests caused some of the most common digestive disorders in America. Unfortunately, the taste of the remedy used to treat this condition—santonin, an extract of the Middle Eastern plant Levant wormseed—was so bitter that few people would even swallow it. Wanting to manufacture specialty chemicals that were unavailable in America, and seeking a competitive advantage over expensive imported products, the Pfizers' first product was santonin. Unlike the terrible-tasting antidote that had been used for centuries to treat patients with parasitic worms, the cousins' innovation was what made their product far more acceptable than previously sold santonin. Unlike their competitors' product, Pfizer's santonin, having been blended with almond-toffee flavoring and shaped into a candy cone, was palatable. Their product was an immediate success, and interestingly, it represented the combined talents of the two partners, one a chemist and the other a confectioner. They delivered their product on foot in wicker baskets and later by horse and wagon.

The two founders made frequent trips across the Atlantic to meet with suppliers. On one trip, Charles Erhart proposed marriage to Charles's sister, Fanny; the couple was married in 1856. Thus the two Pfizers were partners, cousins, and brothers-in-law.

By 1860, the Pfizer line had expanded to include iodine preparations, mercurials, borax, boric acid, and camphor. With the outbreak of the Civil War, the demand for these products soared. Disease proved to be far more deadly than the battlefield, claiming a greater share of the 630,000 American lives lost during the war.

During the 1860s, the Pfizers opened an office in downtown Manhattan on Beekman Street, later moving to Maiden Lane. Soon they were importing argols, the encrustation reside left in casks from winemaking, and turning them into tartar and tartaric acid used by bakers, beverage manufacturers, and housewives. By 1871, the company's annual sales were $1.4 million.

In 1880, using imported concentrates of lemon and lime, the company began manufacturing citric acid, which became the company's main product and served as its launching pad for the rapid growth that soon followed. Pfizer grew and diversified in the latter half of the nineteenth century, but citric acid remained its biggest seller.

Charles Erhart died in 1891 and left his interest in the partnership, worth nearly $250,000, to his son William. However, the agreement stipulated that his cousin Charles could buy it for half its inventory value, an option that Pfizer quickly exercised. In 1892, Charles Pfizer's thirty-two-year-old son, Charles Jr., joined the company as a partner and owner. When the company incorporated in 1900 it had a capitalization of $2 million, with 20,000 shares valued at $100 each. Its first board members included Charles Jr., his brother Emile, and William Erhart. Charles Sr. retired shortly after the company incorporated and Charles Jr., who was being groomed to run the company, was elected president in 1910. Between 1900 and 1912, the young president made a series of disastrous real estate transactions and incurred losses in excess of $2 million. This resulted in a power struggle with John Anderson, who at the time was the company's general manager. Anderson had joined the company as a sixteen-year-old office boy and had advanced to become the highest ranked employee who was not a Pfizer family member. In December 1905, the board of directors sided with Anderson and Charles Jr. was forced to resign.

The forty-eight-year-old Anderson reorganized the company, assuming the titles of senior director, treasurer, and chairman of the executive committee. Emile replaced his brother as president and held that office until 1941; Erhart remained senior vice president.

Charles Sr. had suffered heartbreak by seeing his oldest son driven from the business and dishonored by debt. In 1906, while vacationing at his Newport, Rhode Island, estate, he fell down a flight of stairs and incurred severe internal injuries; complications led to pneumonia, and he died at age eighty-two. In 1914, the board of directors created the post of chairman and elected John Anderson to the office, a position he held until 1929.

With the outbreak of World War I, naval blockades and a cartel of Italian citrus growers put a stranglehold on Pfizer's most important raw materials. Prices of chemicals and medicinals rose sharply. Delivery of supplies was further blocked, and Pfizer's future was threatened. These problems were compounded when many of Pfizer's best men were drafted into the army. Those who served in the military left with John Anderson's personal assurance that they could reclaim their jobs when they returned and that their families would continue to receive paychecks for the duration of the war. Anderson's reassurance demonstrated Pfizer's long-standing tradition of commitment to its people and their welfare.

In addition to the problems with Italian imports caused by World War I, political instability and unpredictable weather in Italy also caused extreme price fluctuations, leaving the company with no choice but to find other supply sources. This prompted a search to find an alternative method for producing a citric acid—from sugar alone using fermentation. In 1917 the company hired thirty-four-year-old James Currie, a brilliant scientist and former chemist with the Department of Agriculture. His assignment was to produce citric acids without using citrus. Currie came with excellent credentials. He had studied fermentation in making cheese and had discovered that one of the by-products was citric acid. This led him to conduct a series of experiments that succeeded in using sugar and bread mold to produce small amounts of crude citric acid. By 1924, Pfizer scientists had perfected the mass production of citric acid from sugar through fermentation. This was propitious timing, since prohibition in the 1920s substantially increased the demand for soft drinks made with citric acid.

Demand was so great that Pfizer constructed a seven-story building to house the operation. A workforce was employed around the clock, 365 days a year. In 1934, the company came up with a method of using molasses instead of the higher-priced white sugar, thereby saving millions of dollars in raw material and production costs.

The knowledge acquired from the production of citric acid was applied to the development of fermentation processes for vitamins C and B-12, as well as antibiotics like streptomycin, penicillin, and Terramycin. As late as 1941, citric acid accounted for 46 percent of Pfizer's sales, but as the company evolved to become a source for synthetic drugs, citric acid products became less significant to the company's bottom line. The citric acid business, which had been the foundation of the company's prosperity, was sold in 1990.

An article appearing in *Chemistry Week* asserted that the chemical business was Depression-proof; however, like most industries, Pfizer and other chemical companies had their share of hard times. Pfizer's revenues plunged during the early years of the war and the company was forced to make cost reductions. In 1932, Emile Pfizer personally donated $250,000 to keep Pfizer workers employed at least three days a week, even if they were paid to only paint and clean. While salaries were cut by 10 percent, nobody was laid off. Emile's donation was a fortune during the Depression, but over the years, it was money well spent in terms of developing employee loyalty.

In 1934 Pfizer produced 5.9 million pounds of citric acid, of which 5.8 million pounds came from molasses. The savings amounted to millions of dollars and the new technique greatly simplified production. The same expertise made the company a leader in vitamin research and production. Company scientists were able to isolate vitamin C, or ascorbic acid, from cabbage, and in 1935 the company started production in ascorbic acid. With the technology to produce its man-made vitamin in vast vats, by 1936, Pfizer was the world's leading producer of vitamin C.

Soon the company was making vitamin B-2, or riboflavin, and later, vitamin B-12 and vitamin A; by the late 1940s, it was the established leader in the manufacture of vitamins.

In 1942, the company had an initial public offering of 240,000 shares of common stock.

In 1928, when bacteriologist Alexander Fleming discovered the germ-killing properties of the "mold juice" secreted by *penicillium*, he knew that it could have profound medical value. But Fleming could not make enough penicillin to be useful in practice, and his discovery was dismissed as a mere laboratory curiosity. A decade later, a team of scientists at Oxford University rediscovered Fleming's work. Armed with increasing evidence of the remarkable powers of penicillin, but under bombardment from Nazi Germany, the British scientists sought help in America.

Derived from the fungus *penicillium*, penicillin inhibits bacterial growth and kills bacteria. It can destroy a wide range of bacteria, including pneumococci, streptococci, gonococci, meningococci, the clostridium that causes tetanus, and the syphilis spirochete. As World War II progressed, it became known that the loss of military lives due to exposure to unsanitary conditions was as big a threat as the enemy's bullets and bombs. Dr. Howard Florey, a colleague of Dr. Fleming, recognized the importance of using penicillin as a weapon to ward off disease and that by maintaining healthy armed forces, the miracle drug would substantially aid the war effort. Florey came to the United States to solicit aid from the U.S. government, and in turn, American pharmaceutical companies enthusiastically volunteered to pitch in. Beginning in June 1943, Merck, Pfizer, Squibb, Abbott, Hoffmann-LaRoche, Parke-Davis, and Upjohn were among the twenty-two companies that participated in a program to produce large quantities of penicillin to help the war effort. When these firms were selected, their prior experience with penicillin, knowledge of fermentation methods for the production of chemicals, and experience with biological products were taken into account. None had adequate expertise in all three areas, but each had expertise in at least one.

By getting involved in the production of penicillin, Pfizer would ironically attempt to turn a former foe into an ally. For years, the company had been plagued by mold, and now it would attempt to cultivate what had formerly been an exasperating pest. In what seemed like a strange twist of fate, the company would actually grow mold in its giant vats.

Using its existing fermentation facilities to make penicillin was a bold decision—the risk was that the notoriously mobile *penicillium* spores might contaminate its production plant. Furthermore, the company would have to curtail its citric acid activities. Still, the company invested millions of dollars in deep-tank fermentation equipment that would be housed in a nearby, recently purchased vacant ice plant. Converting the ice plant into a facility designed to mass-produce penicillin cost $3 million, a sizable amount and a risky venture for a company with $7 million in annual revenues. Once Pfizer had proven it could efficiently do the job, the government authorized nineteen other companies to produce the antibiotic using the company's deep-tank fermentation techniques. Pfizer willingly agreed to share with its competitors. While these other companies made major contributions, Pfizer's quality and production levels of penicillin were unmatched. Using 10,000-gallon fermentation tanks, Pfizer produced 90 percent of the penicillin that went ashore with Allied forces at Normandy on D-Day in 1944, and the company produced more than half of all the penicillin used by the Allies for the rest of the war, helping to save countless lives.

For nearly one hundred years, Pfizer sold its products in bulk through other companies that packaged them under their own brand names. But when Pfizer began producing penicillin in the late 1940s, the company knew the time was right to step out on its own. In those days, the pharmaceutical industry was comprised of two different types of companies: research and manufacturing companies, and marketing and distribution companies. Rarely did one company combine these different aspects of the business. The relative ease of producing large quantities of penicillin changed this scenario. Some of Pfizer's largest customers began to build their own fermentation plants and cancel their standing orders, leaving the company with many idle employees, heavy investment in manufacturing plants, and large inventories of penicillin. Now it was a new ball game. Pfizer would put its own label on the penicillin that it sold to hospitals and its overseas customers.

Other than its vitamin business, Pfizer had never done research to discover new products. It was an expensive and risky business, but the time was now ripe for Pfizer to change its business strategy. A decision was made to forge ahead with a program to screen soil samples for undiscovered antibiotics. This effort led to the eventual testing of 135,000 samples from around the world. The company did it by enlisting the aid of volunteers: travelers, missionaries, explorers, airline pilots, students, housewives, and Pfizer sales reps. They were asked to pick up a teaspoon of earth, seal it in a packet, and mail it to the Brooklyn facility; in turn, they received a modest compensation. Soil came from the jungles of Brazil, the tops of mountains, and the bottoms of mine shafts, from cemeteries, from deserts, from the ocean, everywhere. Samples were labeled, diluted with sterile water, and examined in a petri dish with a nutrient medium to see if a colony of mold would grow. With the 135,000 soil samples that were received, the company conducted more than 20 million tests. What had promise in the lab was then tested with animals.

In 1949, a full century after the Pfizer cousins started their enterprise, a yellow powder with strong antibiotic properties was isolated and labeled PA-76, meaning "Pfizer Antibiotic." It was produced by a new soil organism, which Pfizer named *Streptomyces rimosus.* Generically, the compound, now known as oxytetracycline, proved to be both safe and effective against a range of bacteria that caused more than one hundred infectious diseases. The product was named Terramycin because it had been found in the earth, or *terra* in Latin. Clinical tests were proved successful for treatment of pneumonia and the FDA gave its approval. It was in the market by March 1950. Pfizer Research had discovered and developed its first successful product. At the time, the company had $60 million in annual sales and 3,351 employees.

John Smith, who had presided over the company during the war years, gave this advice to successor John E. McKeen: "Let's sell it ourselves." With this counsel, the company made the decision that it would not rely on other drug companies to sell its important new product. The new direction was a smart move. By 1952, the sales of Terramycin reached $45 million a year, a drug of blockbuster proportions at the time. It accounted for 42 percent of the company's revenues. Shortly thereafter, the company's manufacturing site in Groton, Connecticut, a former naval submarine shipyard, had become the world's largest fermentation plant. The sales force increased from 25 reps in 1949 to 1,300 reps in 1953. Pfizer had made the leap—it had become a full-fledged, re-

search-based drug company specializing in antibiotics derived from fermentation.

With its Terramycin success, and not wanting to be a one-product company in a highly competitive industry, Pfizer recruited top scientists from other companies and universities. One of them was a researcher from the University of Rochester, Lloyd Conover, who joined the company in 1950. With a team of chemists, Conover's goal was to modify a fermentation-derived ("natural") antibiotic without destroying or impairing its therapeutic activity—a feat that most scientists believed was not possible. In June 1952, Conover had achieved his goal; it was hailed a breakthrough process that opened up a new world for the pharmaceutical industry and it marked the beginning of the era of semisynthetic antibiotics. The new medicine, Tetracycline, went on to become the most widely prescribed broad-spectrum antibiotic in the United States. Forty years later, Conover was inducted into the National Inventors Hall of Fame for his discovery. It was an honor that had been extended to only ninety-eight inventors at the time, including Thomas Edison, Eli Whitney, the Wright brothers, and Alexander Graham Bell.

The worldwide demand for Terramycin prompted Pfizer to expand internationally, and during the early 1950s, offices were opened in Puerto Rico, Panama, Mexico, Brazil, Cuba, Canada, the United Kingdom, Belgium, Japan, Spain, Colombia, Venezuela, and the Netherlands. There was a time during the 1950s when Pfizer's annual revenues were the highest of all pharmaceutical companies in the U.K. By 1957, the company's international revenues were $60 million, more than any of its U.S. competitors. In 1960, Pfizer opened its Medical Research Laboratories in Groton, Connecticut, and the following year, the company moved from Brooklyn into its new world headquarters, a skyscraper located at 235 East 42nd Street in midtown Manhattan. Also in 1961, the company was the first to receive FDA approval to market the Sabin oral vaccine against polio. In the 1960s and 1970s, under the leadership of then-chairman John Powers, the company's long-term investment in research was put in place, a business strategy that would pay off handsomely in the future. During this period, the company began to build a strong marketing and sales organization, one that is acknowledged today as the best in the business.

The company officially changed its name from Charles Pfizer & Company Inc. to Pfizer Inc. in 1970. In 1972, the same year that Powers

retired, the company's annual revenues exceeded the $1 billion mark for the first time. In 1982, Feldene, an anti-inflammatory medication, became Pfizer's first product to sell $1 billion in the United States. During the 1980s, under the guidance of its new CEO, Edmund Pratt Jr., the company entered the age when researchers began to replace primitive equipment with technologies such as computer simulations of drug molecules, robotics, and 3-D chromatography to design and test new drug candidates at remarkable speeds. Rather than depending on trial and error to find the right chemicals, researchers were now able to vastly speed up the process, shaving off weeks, months, and years in their efforts to discover new medicines. This technology enabled Pfizer to take decades of research and compile a vast library of chemical compounds; with the use of computers, its scientists would be able to draw upon this wealth of accumulated knowledge for scientific research. Pfizer was one of the pharmaceutical industry's early leaders in this important area.

William Steere became CEO following Pratt's retirement in 1991, and throughout the 1990s, Pfizer experienced rapid growth and matured into one of the world's largest and most respected companies. When Steere took over, the company's annual revenues were $4 billion. By the end of the decade, Pfizer's annual revenues exceeded $15 billion. In 1997 and again in 1998 Pfizer was ranked the world's most admired pharmaceutical company by *Fortune* magazine. With Steere at the helm, the company made its largest-ever acquisition when it acquired Warner-Lambert for $114 billion in 2000. At the time, Warner-Lambert's annual sales were $12.9 billion, and the combined revenues in 2000 were $29.6 billion. Warner-Lambert has a history of growth through acquisition. In 1962, it had acquired American Chicle Company, one of the world's largest producers of gums and mints, including Dentyne, Chiclets, and Trident gums, as well as Certs and Clorets. In 1970, Warner-Lambert had acquired the Schick wet-shave product line from Eversharp, and in 1976, the company had purchased Parke-Davis, a firm founded in 1866 and once the world's largest drug maker. Having launched its new cholesterol drug, Lipitor, in 1998, Warner-Lambert looked particularly interesting. The story about how Lipitor went on to become the bestselling drug in the world is in the chapter that follows.

Under Steere's leadership Pfizer experienced extraordinary growth. He retired in January 2000 and was succeeded by Henry McKinnell Jr. In addition to Lipitor, the company's top medicines include Celebrex for

arthritis, Norvasc for lowering blood pressure, Viagra for erectile dis-function, and Zoloft for depression. With McKinnell at the helm, Pfizer continued to grow; annual sales in 2004 were $52.5 billion, making it the world's largest pharmaceutical company. In 2003 Pfizer acquired Phar-macia for $56 billion. One of its promising products was Xalatan, which was the first ophthalmology medicine to top $1 billion a year in sales. In early 2004, the FDA approved Caduet, a single-pill therapy that com-bines Lipitor with Norvasc.

After a record-breaking earthquake rocked Sumatra, and the tsunamis rolled ashore on lands bordering the Indian Ocean on December 26, 2004, more than 260,000 people were killed and millions were left home-less. Within a day after the disaster, Pfizer pledged $10 million in cash and $25 million in medicines to six global relief agencies. Shipments reached the devastated areas within days. This pledge of cash and medi-cines rose to more than $60 million once medical needs were more accu-rately accessed. Pfizer colleagues went on to raise more than $700,000, much of which was by the company. In addition, Pfizer sent volunteers skilled in logistics, medicine, water purification, and public health to Asia to work alongside relief agencies.

Pfizer now has 115,000 employees worldwide, including more than 13,000 scientists. In 2004, Pfizer was named to the group of 30 U.S.-based companies whose performance determines the Dow Jones Indus-trial Average. Having R&D expenditures of $7.1 billion in 2003 followed by $7.7 billion in 2004, the company is poised for long-term growth.

How the World's Bestselling Drug Nearly Didn't Happen

LIPITOR: PFIZER'S CHOLESTEROL-LOWERING MEDICINE

MILLIONS OF PEOPLE take blood cholesterol–lowering drugs known as "statins," a once-a-day-pill that reduces the risk of heart disease. Most of them have never had any physical signs that their health is in jeopardy—no symptoms such as pain or fatigue. Had their doctor not done the blood work, there would be no way to know their blood cholesterol was at an undesirable level.

Unlike other diseases featured in this book, people with high cholesterol are unaware that they have a potentially harmful condition at the time they are advised to take medication. Cholesterol is a normal component in the blood. However, too much cholesterol can lead to potentially life-threatening diseases. Even if patients neglect their doctor's orders, it's not likely that they will become ill soon or, for that matter, ever. In the case of the other diseases in this book—AIDS, diabetes, rheumatoid arthritis, schizophrenia—failure to comply with one's prescription will assuredly bring upon severe health consequences.

It can also happen that even when people with high cholesterol do comply with their prescription, and their low-density lipoprotein (LDL) (the so-called bad cholesterol) drops to an acceptable level, they still may suffer heart disease. That's because LDL is one of several risk factors for heart disease. Other causes can be such things as high blood pressure, obesity, diabetes, emotional stress, cigarette smoking, and blood clots. Having a low level of LDL does not eliminate the risk of heart failure; it does, however, improve one's odds. This means that if somebody on a

prescribed statin does have a heart attack, it should not be inferred that his cholesterol medicine failed to do its job.

Compliance for patients taking prescriptions for cholesterol-lowering medicines runs around 50 percent. While there is a small percentage of people that neither benefit from these drugs nor experience intolerable side effects, the majority of those who stop taking their medication do so because they (1) are unwilling to pay the cost of their medication; (2) lack the discipline to abide by their prescription; or (3) do not realize the danger of abnormal cholesterol levels.

It is my belief that most people understand very little about high cholesterol. In an informal survey I conducted, which was by no means a scientific study, I ascertained that people in general—including those taking statins—know very little about cholesterol. While they do know that high levels are less healthy than low levels of cholesterol, they know little else. For instance, they can't define what statins are. Nor do they know what level of LDL is considered unhealthy, or what level of high-density lipoprotein (HDL) is desirable. Furthermore, they have no knowledge of why high cholesterol causes heart disease. The majority have only a vague idea and typically reply, "Eating fatty food may cause globs of fat that will clog arteries and reduce or stop blood from entering the heart."

THE BASICS

Since many people are unfamiliar with or misinformed about exactly what cholesterol means, the following is some basic information that may be helpful in reading this chapter.

The word *cholesterol* was derived from the Greek words *chole* and *stear,* which mean "bile" and "hard fat" respectively. Evidently the Greeks observed that cholesterol from the liver in the form of excretion known as bile had the tendency to crystallize to form gallstones. So in Greek, cholesterol means gallstones.

While high levels of cholesterol are associated with health problems, this often-misunderstood substance is vital to human life. This steroid is a fatty waxy matter that occurs in all animal tissues. It is primarily produced naturally in the liver, but it is also created by cells lining the small intestine and by individual cells in the body. It's also a raw material from which cell membranes and some hormones are made. Cholesterol helps

with several important body functions: it facilitates cells to resist temperature changes; it protects and insulates nerve fibers; it contributes to the formation of sex hormones and the production of bile salts that help digest food; and when the skin is exposed to sunlight, cholesterol helps convert it into vitamin D. Plainly, cholesterol by itself isn't bad for your body, and in fact your body requires cholesterol. It's only when the level of LDL is too high or the level of HDL is too low that a risk is imposed to one's health.

For transport to and from the cells, cholesterol relies on two types of proteins: LDL, which is the "bad" agent because it transports too much cholesterol from the liver to the body's cells (when you eat a fatty diet). Conversely, HDL is the "good" agent and has an opposite role because it carries cholesterol in the opposite direction. It acts as a molecular dump truck that carries cholesterol away from the arteries and to the liver to dispose of cholesterol, thereby preventing buildup of plaque. The carrier molecules are known as apoproteins and they are necessary because cholesterol and other fats do not dissolve in water (nor do they dissolve in blood). When these apoproteins are joined with cholesterol, they form a compound called lipoproteins. The density of these lipoproteins is determined by the amount of protein in the molecule.

The "bad" cholesterol (or LDL) is the major cholesterol carrier in the blood. The "good" cholesterol provides some protection against artery blockage much as a drain cleanser that is poured into a sink. Apoprotein (APO1) is the primary protein in the HDL particles that are secreted mostly by the liver. LDL takes the cholesterol to the peripheral tissues through the arteries to enable the production of hormones and other important biological compounds. In contrast, HDL removes cholesterol from the arteries and carries it back to the liver for removal by producing bile acids that are excreted as waste products every day.

A high level of LDL in the blood could mean that cell membranes in the liver have reduced the number of LDL receptors due to increased amounts of cholesterol inside the cell. After a cell has used the cholesterol for its chemical needs and doesn't need it anymore, it reduces its number of LDL receptors. This is what enables LDL levels to accumulate in the blood and causes LDL to deposit cholesterol on artery walls, forming thick plaques.

The levels of one's cholesterol are indicators of risks for atherosclerosis and the risk of a heart attack. Atherosclerosis is a chronic disease char-

acterized by abnormal thickening and hardening of the arterial walls with a resultant loss of elasticity. It is also known as hardening of the arteries. People with high total cholesterol levels are at risk for a heart attack, even if their HDL levels are favorable. In another scenario, a person with lower total cholesterol levels but also with low HDL levels also has an increased risk of heart disease. LDL levels are determined by family history as well as body chemistry. It can be caused by a diet high in saturated fats and/or a lack of exercise. People with high cholesterol that are more influenced by what their liver manufactures are less likely to reduce their cholesterol by following a strict diet.

One class of cholesterol-lowering drugs are the statins, which are also referred to as HMG-CoA reductase inhibitors in the world of science. HMG-CoA reductase is the first enzyme of cholesterol synthesis, the metabolic pathway that produces cholesterol as well as other biomolecules. So the job of statins is to slow down the body's production of cholesterol.

There are different kinds of inhibitors in the world of medicine that are designed to block physiciologic, chemical, or enzymatic action. For instance, protease inhibitors block the pathway that causes the HIV virus, and cox-2 inhibitors are used to prevent the cascade of events that lead to inflammation and pain in arthritis. Statins are a class of drugs that inhibit the HMG-CoA reductase and, as a result, reduce cholesterol levels by enhancing the out-take of LDL particles by the liver and other tissues.

Statins available on the market today are: atorvastatin (Lipitor), fluvastatin (Lescol), lovastatin (Altocor and Mevacor), pravastatin (Pravachol), rosuvastatin (Crestor), and simvastatin (Zocor). There are subtle differences in the statins made by several companies—these subtleties determine the side effects as well as the positive results that a patient experiences. Lipitor is one brand of several statins available by prescription; it is by far the bestselling of the statins. How it differs from other statins will be explained in detail in this chapter.

There are several variables that will affect cholesterol levels that are beyond one's control. As one grows older, cholesterol levels will rise, and although women generally have lower levels than men before menopause, afterward their levels tend to rise. Heredity is also a factor. High blood levels of LDL occur more frequently in some families, so genes will in part determine how high one's cholesterol is. It's important to remember that we are all genetically different. This is why Winston Churchill and George Burns were able to smoke several cigars every day and live to ripe old ages (Churchill lived to be ninety-one and Burns to one hundred). Everything from our dispositions to the numbers of LDL receptors on our livers differs. Different people absorb cholesterol differently. While there are major cultural differences—for example, the American diet versus the Japanese diet—there are variances within the same genetic groups. A Japanese residing in Hawaii, for example, will have a different diet than one living in Tokyo. When it comes to cholesterol levels, the same genetic groups are not necessarily alike. Two siblings can have the same diet in a shared household, work side by side (on a farm, in a factory), and their cholesterol levels can differ substantially.

EARLY PIONEERS

Two individuals, A. I. Ignatowski and Nikolai Anichkov, are credited as being the first to induce atherosclerosis in experimental animals. Their work acknowledged that cholesterol was diet induced. Ignatowski demonstrated this in 1908 when he fed large quantities of eggs and milk to rabbits. His work confirmed earlier claims by surgeons who performed autopsies in the 1700s that obstruction of coronary arteries led to chest pain and death.

Nikolai Anichkov, a twenty-seven-year-old medical school student at the Imperial Medical School in Leningrad, wasn't convinced that Ignatowski's claims were true. This led Anichkov to repeat Ignatowski's experiments in 1912, feeding rabbits with three different diets: one with a muscle fluid supplement, one with an egg white supplement, and one with only egg yolks. He discovered that only the egg yolk diet brought on heart disease in rabbits. Anichkov observed that the yolks caused plaques that appeared to be lipid droplets. He also observed that the rabbits' livers were overloaded with the same lipid droplets. Aware that cholesterol had the same physical qualities, Anichkov put the rabbits on a pure cholesterol supplement diet and, after performing autopsies, it was revealed that their high-cholesterol diet was the primary factor contributing to atherosclerosis of the arteries. With humans, he found hypertension and inflammation of the inner lining of the arteries are contributing factors to the atherosclerotic process. Today's cardiologists concur that Anichkov was correct in his conclusion that cholesterol is one of the prime factors for inducing atherosclerosis.

The works of earlier scientists contribute to the collective knowledge that makes present and future advances possible. In the world of scientific achievement, no person is an island. This has certainly been the case with the team of scientists who are credited with discovering Lipitor. Anichkov and Ignatowski were two such pioneers among many. For example, Adolf Windaus and Heinrich Wieland were two noteworthy German chemists known for their work on the structure of cholesterol and the closely related bile acids. For their achievements in the 1910s and 1920s, they received Nobel Prizes in chemistry, and although their work was later proven incorrect, it should not detract from the contributions they made. The true structure of cholesterol was actually established in the 1930s based on X-ray diffraction data.

There were others who conceptualized the biological synthesis of cholesterol but proving it was not even an option until the introduction of radioactive carbon in the 1940s. Only then was it possible for the brilliant work of scientists Konrad Bloch, George Popjak, and John Cornforth to establish the biosynthetic scheme that showed cholesterol could be synthesized in mammals and ergosterol in yeast from small organic molecules. Eventually it was shown that all twenty-seven carbon atoms of cholesterol were derived from the two carbon atoms of acetate. Bloch, a German-born U.S. biochemist, shared the 1964 Nobel Prize for physiology or medicine with Feodor Lynen. They were honored for their discoveries concerning the natural synthesis of cholesterol and fatty acids. Their efforts led to significant medical research, including studies on the relation of blood cholesterol levels to heart disease.

For a period of more than two decades, Bloch, working out of Harvard University; Lynen at the Max Planck Institute in Munich; Cornforth at the National Institute for Medical Research in London; and Popjak at UCLA were the main players who toiled for countless hours on the biosynthesis of cholesterol. These scientists conducted costly series of extensive experiments with no assurances that a reduction in cholesterol levels would be therapeutically important.

In 1948 the landmark Framingham Heart Study began, a long-term observational study of the inhabitants of Framingham, Massachusetts.

Its purpose was to determine the contribution of risk factors to coronary heart disease occurrence in the general population of the United States. The study focused on cigarette smoking, hypertension, cholesterol levels, diabetes, and aging. In 1961, the study announced that cholesterol level, blood pressure, and electrocardiogram abnormalities increase the risk of heart disease. By the 1980s, the general public had become educated on the dangers of high cholesterol in the blood. People were becoming aware of the fact that they could lessen the risk of heart disease by reducing the amount of saturated fat and maintaining a diet of high-fiber foods like oat bran. Americans were also becoming educated on such details as "bad" cholesterol and "good" cholesterol. Food marketers peddled brands touting the benefits of their products being low-fat and cholesterol-free. In 1988, the Framingham study reported that high levels of HDL cholesterol reduce the risk of heart disease.

In the 1960s and 1970s, there were several drugs available to reduce the levels of cholesterol. Triparanol was launched by G.S. Searle & Company in 1961 as a drug that inhibited the liver's ability to make cholesterol. Two years later it was withdrawn because it produced serious side effects, and in particular, it caused cataracts in the patients' eyes. Another drug was cholestyramine, marketed under the brand name of Questran by Bristol-Myers. It reduced cholesterol by interfering with the absorption of cholesterol in the gut. The gallbladder manufactures bile acid from cholesterol, which is used in the small intestine to digest fats. The drug was indigestible, so when binding with the bile acid in the gut, it was excreted and consequently caused the gallbladder to make more by drawing cholesterol from the bloodstream.

In 1973, after spending two years and studying thousands of broths from fungi and other molds, Dr. Akira Endo, a forty-year-old chemist at Tokyo-based Sankyo Co., discovered mevastatin, the world's first statin. Endo was born on a farm in the snowy north of Japan and recalls being taught by his grandfather about the fungi that grew there. He was fascinated by one poisonous mushroom that kills flies but not people, marveling that a natural substance could have such a subtle effect.

Dr. Endo joined Sankyo after college, researching food ingredients. He says he searched through 250 kinds of fungi to find one that produced an enzyme to make fruit juice less pulpy. The product was a hit, and in 1966, the company let him go to Albert Einstein College of Medicine in New York to pursue his interest in cholesterol research. At the time, cholesterol was a hot area for ambitious scientists and the U.S. press was reporting evidence that it played a role in heart disease. Dr. Endo says he was surprised to see the attention Americans paid to diet. "I thought it was really strange to see that people would cut off the fat before eating their steak. This was a culture shock, something inconceivable in Japan."

Using his past experience, Dr. Endo hit upon an idea: search for something in fungi that would block the HMG-CoA reductase. In college he had devoured a Japanese translation of a biography about Alexander Fleming, the discoverer of penicillin, and he knew that bacteria, like humans, need cholesterol to keep their cell walls together. He reasoned that some fungus probably had evolved a substance that would knock out the enzyme as a way of depriving enemy bacteria of cholesterol and killing them. It was then a matter of finding the right fungus. Beginning in 1971 and working with Masao Kuroda, a chemist who had just joined Sankyo, and two lab assistants, he brewed fungal broths and tested each for its ability to block the enzyme, a supply of which they got from pulverized rat livers. "It was a bet, just like the lottery," says Endo.

For more than two years, he and his team worked into the night at their lab. "We were doing grunt work every day until we got sick of it," he recalls. Some chemicals blocked the enzyme well but were rejected because they were toxic. After testing six thousand fungal broths, they found the right one in August 1973. A substance made by a mold called *penicillium citrinum*, similar to the mold that grows on old oranges, produced a potent inhibitor of the enzyme that helps the body make cholesterol. It was the first statin.

Dr. Endo almost immediately ran into a problem: the substance, soon to be dubbed "compactin," barely worked in rats. Later research would reveal that rats differ in how they make cholesterol. Still, Dr. Endo was stymied until a colleague, whom he met over a casual drink, suggested that he do his tests on some hens that he had and were scheduled to be destroyed. The substance worked in hens.

Sankyo's management was unenthusiastic about his discovery because there was no precedent for it. They preferred to develop refinements of then-existing cholesterol drugs. Dr. Endo conducted what were his own clinical experiments at Osaka University on patients with very high levels of cholesterol. The very first patient to be treated by a statin became so weak from muscle pain she was unable to walk and had to be taken off the drug. Other patients who were put on compactin did realize significant reduction in their cholesterol. When Sankyo reviewed the results, the company put the drug in formal clinical testing.

Michael Brown and Joseph Goldstein, who shared the 1985 Nobel Prize for medicine for their work on the LDL receptor and LDL pathway in the 1970s, wrote in 2004: "The millions of people whose lives will be extended through statin therapy owe it all to Akira Endo."

THREE KEY PLAYERS

The Lipitor story has three key players—Bruce Roth, Roger Newton, and David Canter. Of course, if you were to ask Roth, Newton, or Canter to single out three individuals, they would invariably reply that it was a team effort. That's because each of them is a team player, and it was truly the work of many that is responsible for the success of this miracle medicine. The actual making of Lipitor involved a cast of thousands, but in its beginning stages, like all drugs, there was only a small number of people involved. Only later, when the drug moved from discovery into development and then into clinical studies, did large numbers of people participate. While not wanting to diminish the teamwork aspect that it took to make Lipitor—and it was an enormous team effort—Roth, Newton, and Canter stand out among many that played crucial roles. For this reason, I cite them as deserving of special recognition. Bruce Roth is recognized as "the inventor" of Lipitor. Roger Newton is acknowledged as "the drug's codiscoverer in pharmacology," and, as the one who shepherded Lipitor's move into development, he is also hailed as "the product champion." David Canter headed the crucial clinical trials, and while he was not given a title as catchy as inventor, codiscoverer, or champion, in his capacity as head of the cardiovascular clinical research group, he is the vital third member of this three-legged stool.

After receiving his B.S. in chemistry from St. Joseph's College (Pennsylvania) in 1976 and his Ph.D. from Iowa State University in 1981, Bruce Roth spent a year as a postdoctoral fellow at the University of Rochester. While at Rochester, he worked in an academic laboratory on an insect antifeedant, a chemical that prevents insects from eating leaves. "We didn't make it because we had an interest in insecticides," Roth explains. "We were interested in its unusual structure that could lead to the development of new chemistry. As it turned out, its structure had similarities to compactin.

"Parke-Davis, a division of Warner-Lambert in Ann Arbor, was interested in starting a statin project, so the company invited me to come for an interview. The company wanted to make HMG-CoA reductase inhibitors, and with my background, they thought I might be able to help. While there were other products on the market that lowered cholesterol, there was also concern about the safety of drugs that would do that. The concern was in part because what happened with Triparanol. So when Akira Endo at Sankyo and Roy Vagelos, a research scientist at Merck (who later became the company's CEO) began looking at inhibitors of HMG-CoA reductase, it was considered a courageous step on their part.

"While the insecticides were actually not closely related to statins, they were close enough. Consequently, the chemistry that the company anticipated would be required to develop to make HMG-CoA was more sophisticated. It's more difficult than the kinds of chemistry that the Parke-Davis scientists had historically worked on. At the time, Parke-Davis was making Lopid, a cholesterol-lowering drug that by comparison, is not nearly as complicated as statins."

While one might anticipate meeting a person who is "bigger than life" upon being introduced to Roth, one discovers that he is quite ordinary in appearance, somewhat on the quiet side, but when he starts talking about his work, his face lights up with enthusiasm. You can tell immediately how much he enjoys his work. A stocky man in his early fifties, Roth has a full mustache that goes well with his wide grin. He is a warm, likable, and humble man, and an obviously brilliant chemist, who makes a visitor feel comfortable—even when asking him questions that, to him, are undoubtedly elementary.

While Roger Newton was majoring in biology at Lafayette College in Easton, Pennsylvania, he considered pursuing a medical career. When he witnessed how his great aunt suffered during the final stages of cancer, he had second thoughts. Her death caused the young student to reflect on whether he had the emotional constitution to be a physician. Following his graduation, Newton entered the University of Connecticut to study nutritional biochemistry and took particular interest in his laboratory work with lipids. One summer night while working overtime in his lab, Roger had an epiphany. "I had been reading a book on atherosclerosis and cholesterol," he says, "and I was learning about the link between the two. I thought to myself: 'Why don't I see if I can find some way of treating or curing this disease?' That became my mantra. I wanted to take basic science and use its therapeutic application to treat human disease. Wow. I *can* make a difference!"

With his epiphany came focus. After receiving a master's degree in nutritional biochemistry, he went to the University of California at Davis to study nutrition. "I really fine-tuned my understanding about the role that the liver plays in this whole process and I was particularly interested in liver cells," explains the tall, athletic Newton. "Later I switched over from the nutrition department to physiological chemistry. I became engrossed in metabolism, and after taking a course in pharmacology, I realized that you could actually make compounds that could beneficially alter metabolism with those people who had abnormal metabolism. I focused mainly on cholesterol and lipogenesis, which is the conversion of carbohydrates and organic acids to fat. Then I did my postdoctorate work at the University of California at San Diego, which has a specialized center in atherosclerosis research. I spent two and a half years honing my skills and then figured it was time to look at opportunities in either academia or industry. I started at Parke-Davis in 1981 as a senior research scientist. My charge was to establish the biological screens that could identify compounds that would inhibit cholesterol synthesis overall and specifically the enzyme HMG-CoA reductase. Back then that's what statin drugs were called."

A man in his mid-fifties, Roger Newton is youthful and energetic. His premature gray hair on his temples goes well with his sun-tanned face. He is authoritative and articulate. He looks and speaks like a television news commentator; his outgoing personality doesn't seem to fit a scientist who has spent many years working in a lab. After all, spending long hours in solitary confinement in a lab is usually done by an individual who doesn't mind working alone, and Newton is clearly an extrovert. The twinkle in his eye and his broad grin suggest how much he enjoys his work. Yet, contrary to his demure appearance, one senses that Newton is highly focused and driven to succeed. His passion for his work unveils that he is driven, not by personal gain, but by a desire to benefit others.

David Canter, a native of the United Kingdom, studied natural sciences at Cambridge University and then attended medical school at the University of Liverpool. Following his graduation in 1978, he was a surgical resident at the university. In 1984 he joined Parke-Davis and did clinical trial research in northern Europe. In 1986 he was transferred to Ann Arbor to work in the company's cardiovascular clinical research group. Three years later, he was promoted to senior director of cardiovascular clinical development, and in 1992, he became vice president of drug development. When asked to describe what this work entailed, Canter modestly replies, "I was a project leader. I had eight different projects working on compounds that were in the beginning of an early phase. Lipitor was one of my key projects. I supervised the clinicians who were doing all of the early trials in the cardiovascular group."

An avid biker, David Canter is tall and slender, built like a long-distance runner. With a slightly noticeable British accent, he speaks with authority. A laid-back man, his passion for his work comes through when he talks about his job. Canter is a caring, giving man. While talking about his work, his compassion and desire to do good for others is apparent.

In 1997, following the approval of Lipitor, Canter became director of the Institut de Recherche et Development, Jouveinal, in Paris, France. After the merger of Pfizer and Warner-Lambert in 2000, he was promoted to the position of site director of Ann Arbor Laboratories, where he is now senior vice president, Pfizer Global Research and Development.

When Canter first joined Parke-Davis in the early 1980s, he supervised the trials conducted in Europe for Lopid, a cholesterol-lowering drug in a class of drugs known as fibrates. "Lopid is not a statin, but a good drug for lowering triglycerides and, to some extent, increasing HDL. Its claim to fame was that it was used during the Helsinki Heart Study in the 1980s, the first major intervention trial sponsored by a pharmaceutical company. Lopid is a class of drugs that binds to a protein— one that is in the nucleus of the cell—the nuclear receptor. Statins have a completely different structure that bind to an enzyme that is on the pathway for making a large number of compounds of which cholesterol is one. So don't think of it as a single stream. It's more like a pyramid that has a few smaller molecules at the top that soon become many tens of different steroidal molecules, a family of molecules. So we must stop thinking of it as being a one-to-one relationship. The statins inhibit a pathway that has multiple effects, which explains why there are so many different effects of these drugs."

GETTING THE PROGRAM STARTED

Two years after Akira Endo's 1973 breakthrough discovery with mevastatin, Roy Vagelos, Merck's chief scientist, became interested in his work and started shuttling back and forth to Tokyo to learn more about it. Vagelos, a persuasive and insightful businessman who later became Merck's CEO, eventually came home with a one-page agreement in 1976. Sankyo granted Merck access to its data and methods connected with Dr. Endo's statin. Companies often release such information to potential business partners, but this agreement left a gaping hole: Merck didn't owe Sankyo anything if it found the same anticholesterol properties in another fungal by-product. Sure enough, in 1978 Merck discovered in a different fungus a substance that was virtually identical to Dr. Endo's, this one called lovastatin. Nine years later, the medicine was launched under the name Mevacor, the first drug in its class. Meanwhile, serious toxic problems encountered by compactin during its clinical tests caused Sankyo to abruptly cancel its statin program.

Granted, Sankyo and Merck had a running head start, but just the same, Parke-Davis wanted to enter the statin race. Based on Bruce Roth's past work when employed by the University of Rochester in its chemistry department, Parke-Davis management believed that its newly hired twenty-eight-year-old postdoctoral fellow was the right chemist to lead the way for the company to enter what was certain to someday be a highly important and lucrative market.

Roth was invited to Ann Arbor by Warner-Lambert, Parke-Davis's parent company. At the time, Roth had never heard of Warner-Lambert. The company was better known for its consumer brand products such as Schick, Visine, and Listerine. Roth was impressed with the company's cutting-edge computerized molecular modeling technology—a valuable resource that was capable of testing thousands of possible molecules quickly and efficiently, thereby speeding up the discovery process. Roth relished being able to work with technology and skilled engineers. He was equally impressed with the brilliant scientists that he met at Warner-Lambert. Although it was a Fortune 500 company, the people in the Ann Arbor laboratories were very much like the chemists and Ph.D.s he worked with while doing his postdoctoral work. When an offer was made to work in the company's Atherosclerosis Chemistry Section, Roth eagerly accepted the position.

In 1982, when Roth first started his lab work to find a statin, two other chemists, Robert Sliskovic and Alex Chucholowski, worked alongside him. Not long afterward, Tim Hurley, Don Butler, and Tom Nanninga joined the team. "The first thing we did," Roth explains, "was to study the published data on Sankyo's compactin. By this time, Merck had already filed its patent on Mevacor, so we were able to take a close look at it too. Of course with any FDA-approved drug, we simply buy, grind up a few tablets, and then we isolate out the active molecule. We carefully studied all of that information, and then we set off to see if we could come up something that would be different but would have similar kinds of activity in the body. To achieve this, we worked with several different classes of molecules."

The three chemists toiled side-by-side at separate stainless steel benches in the same lab. They wore white lab coats and protective eyewear. The walls of the lab were lined with benches and shelves stacked with jars. There were also tables with computer equipment in the room. Each of the chemists had a private office adjoining the lab. Their daily lab work involved the tedious task of making one molecule after another, studying each finding, and if something useful was learned from a particular molecule, it was applied toward the next molecule that was made. All of this work was done in search of a compound that looked promising enough to pass on to a biologist who, in turn, would test it to determine if it had merit. The process of coming up with the right compound is mundane because it involves being confined to a laboratory and being hunched over a petri dish for indefinite periods of time. "What we did was extremely iterative," Roth states, "but we were learning from each molecule. To do this work, you have to be the eternal optimist. You can talk to any chemist in this building and he will tell you that the next compound he makes is going to be a drug. You must have that attitude, because if you don't—forget it. Then you take a look at how many drugs they put on the market each year. So there are tens of thousands of chemists in the industry, and only a handful that have ever put a drug on the market."

To many people, the lab work of a medicinal chemist like Bruce Roth would seem tedious and boring. Certainly it takes a special aptitude to enjoy work of this nature, and the fact that we all have different aptitudes makes for a more interesting world. What would be boring is if everybody was like everybody else. And, thankfully, because individuals have an aptitude to be medicinal chemists, miracle medicines are discovered.

What is so interesting is how animated Roth becomes when he speaks about his work. Work that others would find repetitive and dreary, Roth thrives on. "To be a medicinal chemists requires years of training," Roth tells, "in order to learn how to do chemistry, put molecules together, recognize patterns in molecules—and this is just the chemistry side. Then you must learn about biochemistry and enzymatic reactions and physiological plots. You must also know the principles of medicinal chemistry. All of this knowledge is necessary just to come to the table. That's kind of your starting point. Then there's a piece [of] imagination, where you need to look at a molecule and be able to see the possibilities in it and in your mind be able to create other molecules that look like it that may do the same thing. You need a lot of imagination to do that. It takes a spark of imagination—it's like an artist who creates a work in his mind and then puts it on a canvas. In my work with statins, I looked at compactin and I saw a different molecule from what somebody at Sankyo saw, or what a Merck chemist saw with Mevacor."

When asked to describe what visions appeared in his mind, Roth says, "You never really see them except in your mind's eye so you can draw them on a whiteboard. You can model them. It's really shorthand notation for what the molecule looks like. I don't know how you describe it. It's just really a bunch of electrons and neutrons and protons. But you know what it means and you can use this to communicate it to other chemists. And today, some of it can be done with computer graphics and computer modeling. I took the Merck compound and compared it with the Sankyo compound to see how they were alike and how they differed. This way I could identify different parts of the molecule that I thought would be in the same region of space. This enabled me to build a different molecule that held those pieces in the same region of space. My mind says that if I put these pieces together, it will hold what I think are the important parts and the right region of space. In my mind, I was able to think about how these things fit into the enzyme.

"I didn't know what the enzyme looked like, but I did guess what it might look like, so based on this knowledge, I would make a molecule that I thought might fit things together. Then I would find that it was close to what I expected, and I'd go back and rework the model again, make a small change or two in the molecule, and then give it to the biologist to test. The biologist would sometimes then say, 'I think you're going in the right direction,' and if so, you systematically change different parts of the molecule, and you give it back to the biologist. This process repeats itself again and again."

In August 1981, Roger Newton was hired to establish the screening program in-vitro pharmacological screens to identify HMG-CoA reductase inhibitors. "As a research biologist," Roger Newton tells, "my job was to test their chemical compounds. In late 1981, I hired Cathy Sekerke to work with me on the HMG-CoA reductase screen. Shortly afterward, I hired Erica Sandford [later Ferguson] to run the overall cholesterol synthesis inhibitor screen. To complement their screens and to measure the effects of chronic dosing in animal models, Brian Krause joined the team in the fall of 1982 and was put in charge of establishing and running the in vivo screens to measure LDL lowering due to chronic inhibition of cholesterol synthesis. Other important members of the pharmacological team were Dick Stanfield, Paul Uhlendorf, and Tom Bocan. Around 1984 or so, my boss Dick Maxwell retired and I became chairman of the atherosclerosis discovery team. About a year or so later, Bruce Roth's boss, Neil Hoefle, also retired and Bruce became my cochair. He and I continued to build our respective teams, and at its peak, there were about a dozen or so people who reported to each of us. Over a period of six years, we worked on twenty different chemical series. With each series we looked at many different compounds and molecule structures. We continued to learn from our failures to discover the best compound that we could put forward as a lead compound for further development."

"It was comparable to making a patchwork quilt," Newton continues. "We made changes, and ended up with a different look, but everything looked well together. Or you might say it's similar to putting a recipe together. You sometimes add too much salt or too much paprika or another ingredient. Of course with today's available advanced technology, the methods used today are more refined and the turnaround time is so much faster."

In the early 1980s, Roth and Newton were involved hands-on with the project but as they added more people to their teams and had others reporting to them, their responsibilities as supervisors increased. This sped up their output, as did the addition of technical people who were hired. Soon Roth and his team of chemists were turning out one compound after another. All of these compounds were then tested by

Newton and his team of biologists. When a particular compound looked promising, it was reviewed and discussed by the biologists and then sent back to the chemists with recommendation on what modifications were necessary.

"It was the highest performing team I've ever been on," Roth exclaims. "Everyone knew his or role in this and everyone knew where we had to go. I attribute this to the fact that we assembled a group of people with different expertises and that's what allowed everyone to stay focused on his own thing without having to be concerned about what others were doing."

"Roger and Bruce were a great combination," David Canter asserts, "and what made them so effective was their different personalities. Roger was a very passionate person, and he absolutely loved science. He was capable of going in multiple directions. Bruce was very focused. Together there was a synergy that you could feel. They were on a mission, and they were convinced that they were right. While each is very talented, I'm not sure either could have enjoyed the same degree of success on his own."

Another team member who worked with both the chemists and the biologists was Daniel Ortwine, who heads Warner-Lambert's computer-assisted drug discovery group. Ortwine received a master's degree in medicinal chemistry at the University of Wisconsin in 1975 and joined Warner-Lambert straight out of college. While today there is an abundance of courses that teach computer-assisted technology at major universities, as well as formal training programs available, Ortwine, a synthetic organic medicinal chemist, developed his skills the old-fashioned way— with on-the-job training when the field was just in its infancy. He has also taken courses to supplement knowledge gained from years of experience. His contributions in the development of drugs are across the board. With a database today of over two million compounds to which he has access, Ortwine is an invaluable resource for the company's chemists. And equipped with the capacity to make computer presentations in 3D format, he provided invaluable virtual screening to the company's biologists.

Sitting in a room filled with computers and other technical equipment, Ortwine says, "Before computers, the chemists did far more trial-and-error work. They tested thousands of possible molecules, looking at results. It's a lot more efficient and faster today," he adds, pointing to his equipment.

"Do we miss a lot?" Ortwine asks rhetorically. "Of course we do," he answers his own question. "Do we understand scientifically everything that's going on? Of course we don't. But can we enrich the hits? You bet we can. And we are capable of coming up with all sorts of candidates (drugs) considerably more quickly than the old trial-and-error way of testing everything. So now you get a hit, and you can study it in more detail on how it fits in this, and then you can start to say, 'Well, it looks like I have space to modify it out there, and in fact, it looks like I want to put greasy things out here or I want to add things like more water more or more oil because my protein or my enzyme has a site there that doesn't look right.' So we will get teams of chemists together to review synthetic organic chemistry and make suggestions such as, 'Well, I know you can make that easily but it doesn't fit. But what about here?' And they will reply, 'Okay, I can think of a way to do that.' This dialogue will go back and forth and we'll brainstorm."

VIA THE PATHWAY

"When we started our statin project," Roth says, "it had been established that cholesterol was made in the liver, and there are twenty biochemical steps to make it. Cholesterol is a molecule that starts as an acetic acid on a biosynthetic pathway in the liver. It's known as acetyl-CoA. There are ultimately twenty enzymes that acetyl-CoA encounters at the twenty different steps during its journey through its biosynthetic pathway in the liver. When cholesterol comes across an enzyme, the two are catalyzed, and attached, becoming a bigger molecule. This step is repeated twenty times by the time cholesterol goes through the biosynthetic pathway. At the end of the pathway, cholesterol has had twenty enzymatic reactions, and like a rolling snowball, it increases in size and becomes a big molecule.

"From the start, we understood that it was not possible to inhibit each of these enzymatic reactions with a drug. In fact drugs like Triparanol had caused concern in the medical community about whether you could safely block the biosynthesis of cholesterol. We knew that agents of Triparanol inhibited cholesterol at the end of the pathway—at step twenty. We determined that if we could do it safely early in the pathway as opposed to doing it late, based on what happened with Triparanol, cholesterol could be inhibited prior to being absorbed in the bloodstream and causing unwanted side effects. The side effect attributed to that drug working at the end of the pathway was that it created fatty substances that collected in a person's lens that caused cataracts. When Merck made its statin, Mevacor, they understood that if cholesterol synthesis was blocked early, it wouldn't cause the formation of cataracts. The company examined people's corneas for a long time to demonstrate that their drug didn't, and it was established that Mevacor did not cause cataracts. It became obvious that cholesterol could be blocked at different steps in the biosynthetic pathway and by doing it early on, it's safe—if you do it late in the pathway, it's not safe. When we first started, we didn't know this."

David Canter explains that in the early years of developing a statin, a concentrated effort was exerted to come up with ideas on how to make a better drug than the competition. "We'd study what the other companies did," he tells, "and then we'd search for ways to prove they were wrong. And if so, we'd go in a different direction. Then there were other times when we'd attempt to prove them wrong and by going in another direction, we'd end up realizing that they were right but for the wrong reasons. It was with this approach that we came up with the idea that we could make a statin that was tissue selective, meaning that in some way the compound was taken up by the liver but rejected by other tissue. We worked very hard on this premise. And it turned out to be a false idea. But that approach led us to realize, 'This is the wrong way to think.' That's because the way the blood circulates from the guts, it first goes to the liver. Then we considered, 'What happens if the liver was incredibly effective at taking up the compound and very little of the drug actually got into circulation?' We concluded that would be the equivalent of tissue selectivity. It was this thought that led us to choosing atorvastatin, which is the generic name for Lipitor. This was the concept behind making an effective statin, one, that in humans, controls the pathway in the liver—the key to inhibiting the HMG-CoA reductase."

GOING WITH PLAN B

In the preliminary stages of the Warner-Lambert statin program in the early 1980s, it was not known if it was possible to make a cholesterol medicine that was truly safe. By this time, Sankyo had run into toxicology problems with compactin and the company had discontinued its statin program. "After our program was underway," Roth explains, "we heard that Merck had put its development of lovastatin [Mevacor] on hold. They were concerned that their molecule was so much like Sankyo's compactin that they would end up with similar results. Both companies had used the fermentation process to make their inhibitors—the technique used to make penicillin and other antibiotics, and they did the same for inhibitors in cholesterol biosynthesis. People in the industry were thinking: 'Did the potential side effects of lovastatin result from something caused by fermentation or was it something that happened in the biosynthesis pathway?' Not knowing the answer, Merck called off its clinical trials so they could conduct more toxicology studies in order to find out. We took the approach that there were two ways we could look at what was going on with Sankyo and Merck. The glass was either half empty or it was half full. The half empty view was to say, 'Boy, there are some big problems here, and we will never come up with a compound that will safely inhibit cholesterol synthesis.' The half full way to look at it was, 'Here's an opportunity because there is nothing currently on the market. We know that if we can block this pathway we can lower cholesterol.' The question therefore was: if there was indeed toxicity with the HMG-CoA reductase statin that was derived from fermentation, was it related to their structure as opposed to the mechanism that inhibited cholesterol biosynthesis?"

Taking the position that the glass was half full, Roth and his small team of chemists worked feverishly in their laboratories making compounds that were then sent to Newton's team of biologists for examination only to be returned time after time. Their compounds were mostly rejected altogether, but on occasion, one would show enough promise that it was worthy of comment. "Why don't you try this?" or "What would happen if you did such and such?" There are many times more failures than an occasional success. Of course, there are little successes that happen now and then—and these are enough to inspire a spark of hope to a chemist—"this time I might be on to something worthwhile!" But no sooner than he gets his hopes up, does something go awry and what had promise turns out to be yet another disappointment. Such is the life of a scientist. If you can't deal with it, find another job.

Within two years after the statin program began, working with Sliskovic and Chucholowski, Roth had developed a chemical structure that was known as the pyrrole series. It contained the first compound that was the structural motif followed by all of the other statin compounds.

While the pyrrole series showed promise when some of its earlier compounds had shown some toxicity problems, it was put "on hold," where it was certain to remain forever. With so many compounds being produced in the labs of a large pharmaceutical company such as Warner-Lambert, once a compound is put on the back burner and researchers begin to focus on alternative compounds, it is a well-known fact in the industry that "what is put on the shelf stays on the shelf." Almost never do such products ever surface again see the light of day. One compound of the pyrrole series had a code name CI-981. "It came so close to winding up in the compound library," Roth says with a sigh, "and had that happened, nobody would have ever known about it. It would have never gone into development."

Every compound that was a candidate for clinical tests at Warner-Lambert was given a CI number (CI stands for clinical investigation). Having a CI number marked an important milestone for a compound, meaning it had cleared the initial safety hurdles because it had tested well in an assay that determined it had desired activity. If, having passed this test, it then advanced into animal disease models to see if it worked there. The countless compounds that get failing grades receive no name and are identified only by a number—a numbered compound is put in a jar that is tightly sealed and destined to spend an eternity on an out-of-the-way shelf.

It was Bob Sliskovic who is credited for making another promising compound—this one was numbered 123-588; it was not in the pyrrole series. It took months of hard work for Sliskovic to make the compound, and it had passed the screening tests by the biologists. It was definitely the team's leading statin candidate to become a drug that would find its way to the market. It took another six months of hard work to find a way to make it on a large scale, because if a drug can only be made in a lab, it would have no value. "We were quite excited about 123-588," Roth says, "but low and behold, Jim Beck, a chemist at Sandoz, came up with the same idea, and just as we figured out how to make large quantities of it, their patent was published. We were too late. While things like this happen in this business, needless to say, we were devastated.

"Consequently we had to terminate our plans to develop 123-588 and regroup. There were three compounds in the pyrrole series that we had put on hold," Roth continues. "Two of them had tested toxic. As a point of information, nearly all chemical molecules work by binding with a protein somewhere in the body. The art of making a drug is to make the structure of that molecule so specific that it only attaches to very few proteins. A perfect one would attach to the exact one that is targeted. A compound that attaches to many proteins is a poison. Obviously all drugs are poison in overdose—this happens because they usually interfere with a vital process.

"The final of the three compounds was CI-981. Had one of the other two not tested toxic, CI-981 would not have been a consideration. But now it represented our last hope. If it was also toxic, we'd be back to square one. We'd have to start from scratch, and because our competitors were so far ahead of us, it probably would have been the end of our statin program. By this time, it was 1988—more than five years had passed since our statin venture started."

CI-981 was Plan B. Plan A was 123-588, a compound that was too similar to Sandoz's patented cholesterol medicine. CI-981 would have never been reconsidered had Plan A succeeded. It would have been forever buried in the company's compound library. CI-981 was finally given a genetic name, atorvastatin, and has since become known by its famous brand name, Lipitor.

THE MIRACLE DRUG THAT ALMOST NEVER WAS

Going with Plan B, atorvastatin was taken from the compound library. From obscurity it had been elevated to the statin program's lead compound. Admittedly, it was reprieved because the company had no other statin available. Given the green light to be tested on small animals, atorvastatin was placed in the limelight. If the animal testing had favorable results, atorvastatin would be on its way to the clinical trials. While it was good news for the scientists who worked on developing the drug, it was not a time to celebrate. They understood very well that the odds were still against the drug's ultimate success. They were also cognizant that if atorvastatin were to receive a failing grade, it would be placed back on the same shelf in the compound library where it would remain forever.

It was now 1988, nearly five years after Bruce Roth and his team had discovered the pyrrole series from which came CI-981, and one year after Merck's Mevacor had been approved. Furthermore, it was just a matter of time before Bristol-Myers Squibb's Pravachol would soon receive FDA approval (which it did in 1991). When Warner-Lambert's animal test results were compared to compactin and Mevacor, atorvastatin did look a little better—but not a lot better. And a little better wasn't good enough. It would still be several years before the company would have results from the drug's clinical tests, and by then Mevacor would have such a lead over atorvastatin, it was believed that there would be little chance of catching up. It was a sure bet that Merck wasn't resting on its laurels. Who knew what new medicine Merck had in its pipeline? Certainly the people at Warner-Lambert didn't know. Like all leading pharmaceutical companies, Merck was in constant search of ways to improve its products and to gain a competitive edge. And indeed the company did have another statin—Merck's Zocor went on sale in 1992.

"There was a lot of concern that this compound wouldn't look any different than anything else," Roth says. "It would have been wonderful if the animal models had shown our compound was twice as effective at lowering LDL, but that wasn't the case. The tests showed it was only a little better. The fact is, it had just a bit better effect on triglyceride in some animal models, but by the time atorvastatin was launched, it would have been eight years after lovastatin. People around here were asking, 'What's the point?' The thinking here was, 'If we're going to be late to market with a compound, we can't have it be just about the same as what's already available.' If so, doctors wouldn't prescribe it. We would have been the fourth or fifth statin on the market. 'Why do we want to come late and put us under such a handicap?' people kept asking me."

"Parke-Davis had just launched Quinapril, an ACE inhibitor for hypertension," Newton points out, "and the company had high hopes that that drug was going to really take off, but it didn't. Quinapril did only so-so because it had a lot of competition. Well, the company didn't want atorvastatin to mimic it. Our people were expressing a lot of skepticism as to whether atorvastatin even had an advantage, and with the concern about its safety, why even develop it? And of course, there are always questions being raised about where the company should put its money. We had to be selective because the company didn't have the financial resources to do the costly clinical development on every compound. Remember now, this was before the merger with Pfizer and we were operating on a much smaller budget."

Newton pauses briefly and then continues, "On the other hand, we had put so much time and effort into our statin program. And everyone knew that the animal models are not conclusive because humans' systems are different enough from animals that it was possible that tests on humans might get better results. With this thought in mind and having come this far, it made perfectly good sense to take it to the next level and do a Phase I clinical test."

Newton's thinking was logical. A Phase I clinical test on a small number of humans would answer a lot of questions, and unlike a full-blown clinical test, it wasn't outrageously expensive. Newton was determined that he must convince senior management to invest still more money by conducting tests on humans. He estimated the cost would be about a million dollars, but considering the fact that the program had grown to employ about thirty people and had already cost a few million dollars, he believed that the company should step up to the plate to find out how the drug worked on humans.

The company's naysayers argued, "Too little. Too late." They were adamant that additional spending on the program would be "throwing good money after bad." The marketing people, an influential power internally, were in particular vocal. "Without a competitive advantage, we won't be able to sell it," they insisted. In their view, the product's commercial viability looked dismal.

Without the support of marketing, it appeared as though there was not much hope for the statin program. In a last-ditch attempt to gain support, Newton made an appeal to Ronald Cresswell, chairman and chief scientific officer of Parke-Davis. "We have a few million dollars invested," Newton told his boss. "Let's spend another one million dollars to see how it works on humans. We've put all this energy in it. Bruce and I are convinced that it will work. Please, Ron, go along with us on this one."

Cresswell listened intently. As chief scientific officer in Ann Arbor, it was ultimately his decision if a potential drug was to move forward into clinical development. He questioned Roth on how the company would make the compound, because with his extensive background as a development chemist, he knew that even if a drug did well in the clinical studies, its ultimate success rested on having the manufacturing capability to make it at a competitively priced cost.

"I wanted to make sure there would be large quantities of the drug to do the tests," Cresswell explains, a native of Scotland who still speaks with a trace of a Scottish accent. "I recognized how important the human tests would be because while the animal studies can tell a lot about a drug, the real tests on safety and tolerability come from testing in people. Although Roger was very enthusiastic, nobody could say, 'This is really going to be a blockbuster drug.' "

Cresswell heard Newton out, and afterward he consented to take it to the review board, a committee that consisted of twelve senior managers, including the company's new president, Ludwig DeVink, who later became chairman of Warner-Lambert. "I wanted them to examine our statin program's basic science," he emphasizes. "My motto was, 'The science always leads.' I made my decisions on whether a new drug goes forward on what its science tells us."

"I knew how strongly Roger felt about this compound," Cresswell continues. "All scientists that came to present their drug know that the survival of their baby depended on what the review board rules. We were willing to listen to everyone with an open mind but we would only approve a medicine when we were convinced that the science being presented was sufficiently predictive of what the product might eventually look like. We needed to have a certain comfort level with a new drug or we would veto it."

Cresswell also knew that a consensus was needed so that if atorvastatin did well when tested on humans, it would have the support of everyone afterward. Newton thanked his boss and said that he looked forward to the opportunity to present his case on behalf of the statin team.

As the statin program's cochairman, Roth accompanied Newton to the meeting that was held in a meeting room in the company's R&D building. There was nothing fancy about the room. It was a windowless room and had an old oak table surrounded with imitation-leather chairs on medal casters. The room's atmosphere did nothing to make the two scientists feel at ease. Knowing that all their years of hard work on the statin program rested on the outcome of Newton's presentation, they were understandably nervous. But as Roth would later tell it, Newton seemed calm and confident. Of course he knew that was Newton's nature. Newton was a dynamic, charismatic man, and even more important for the purpose of the day's mission, he was bright and articulate. Roth was content in knowing that Newton was speaking on the behalf of the statin program. He could think of no better person for the job.

It was a formal meeting. The members on the review committee knew they were there to prudently make an important decision. They took their responsibility seriously, as evidenced by their stern faces. "It was a somber atmosphere," Roth recalls, "and from Roger's and my perspective, a lot was riding on what would be decided. All those years we put into the statin program were on the line. It was our life."

Just before Newton got up to make his presentation, he said to Roth in a hushed whisper, "Don't worry, Bruce—I'm not going to let management kill this for no good reason."

Newton began by addressing his audience and thanking them for their attendance and consideration of an important decision that he believed could very well define the future of the company. He also reminded them about how much hard work had been put into the statin program by many highly committed and dedicated employees. He then talked about the animal tests and reiterated how the results were not toxic. "That is a good thing," he emphasized. "And as each of us in this room well knows, we don't know how well atorvastatin will be with humans until we test it with humans. We really don't know from the animal models in the preclinical data. There is no direct relationship to how it's going got work in a human."

At this point in the presentation, there wasn't much of a reaction, and sensing this, Newton did something that was so unexpected he even surprised himself. The six-foot-three-inch scientist got down on his knees and pleaded, "You've got to let us do the human tests. I know it's the right thing to do, and I'm begging you to do it."

Recalling his performance, Newton says, "Getting down on my one knee as if I were doing an Al Jolson imitation was spontaneous—something in my gut told me that I had to do something to loosen those guys up so they could think clearly. There had been a lot of tension in the air—it was so thick you could cut it. They were faced with a big decision. My hamming it up caught them off guard. At first, it made them fidget and nobody said a word. Then a smile appeared on someone's face, and then another, and another. The smiles were followed by laughter. At that point I knew they were now willing to hear my story."

He continues: "I laughed to let them know I wasn't actually on my knees begging. But they did know that I possessed so much passion and conviction that I was even willing to risk making a fool of myself to make my point. When the room quieted down, I told them in earnest, 'We showed that we can lower LDL in animal models. We know that it inhibited cholesterol synthesis and it affected the enzyme in the way we wanted it to. Now let's find out exactly how good it is with humans. We've come this far and this is not the time to throw in the towel.' "

The committee consented to grant its approval for atorvastatin to go forward and be tested on humans.

THE MOMENT OF TRUTH

After the meeting, Cresswell said to Newton and Roth: "Okay, you're getting what you want. We're going to test it on human volunteers."

"We'll keep it going until the data tells us to stop," he said, using one of his favorite expressions that he had often repeated.

"We couldn't ask for anything more than that commitment," Newton says. "We believed in our compound and none of us wanted the company to put money in a loser."

While Roger Newton was actively involved in the Phase I clinical test, the baton was passed to David Canter, who would be running the critical later clinical tests. "Testing on animals is a guide," Canter asserts. "If we used the rat as our only model to discover atorvastatin, it would not have been discovered. That's because the rat's liver can compensate so rapidly that there is no drop in cholesterol. So this class of drug would not have been discovered if rats were all that was available to test it on. This is true with other diseases too—tests reveal effects on tumors and various parts of the stomach of rodents that have no parallel in humans. Over time we have learned to understand what can be a guide and what might turn out to be a red herring.

"There are big enough differences between various species of animals and humans that when we have inconclusive evidence, we have to decide on whether we should test a drug on humans, and it becomes a judgment call. This was one of those calls, and Roger's presentation was quite compelling. It's enormously valuable for a drug to have a champion, and certainly Roger was Lipitor's champion. When it's a close call like this one, it takes such a champion to be the tiebreaker."

The first test on humans consisted of twenty-four Warner-Lambert employees who volunteered to take Lipitor. Like all intial tests on humans, these individuals were be carefully monitored. "One of the really good things about testing a statin drug is that it only takes a couple of weeks to see if it lowers LDL," Roth states. "If it were a drug for a disease such as Alzheimer's, we wouldn't be able to determine its effects for years. But with Lipitor, we could measure LDL lowering and know how it compared with other available drugs early on. And we were fortunate that we found out very quickly that Lipitor had remarkable efficacy in lowering LDL for humans."

Of 24 employee-volunteers, at 10 milligrams, LDL dropped 38 percent. That was as good or better than competing compounds at their recommended maximum doses. At 80 milligrams, LDL dropped 58 percent—about 40 percent more than any other statin at any dose.

Dr. Donald Black, vice president of clinical research at Warner-Lambert, says, "You could tell immediately that this was something really different. This was the real deal."

Black headed up the clinical research team, and, as with every drug, this is by far the most expensive part of its development. The Phase I test on twenty-four patients ran about a million dollars. The Phase II and Phase III clinical trials generally run into the hundreds of millions of dollars, involving thousands of people and taking years to complete. The impressive results from the human tests dictated that the company should go forward and make the huge investment. Even now, it's a risky business. Twenty-four patients is a very small number, and with a much larger patient population, there is always a chance that something could go drastically wrong. For example, twenty-four people may not have any serious side effects, but even if one person in fifty or one hundred did, that could spell disaster—especially if a fatality occurred.

With Bristol-Myers Squibb Pravachol and Merck's Zocor enjoying brisk sales by 1992 and still more companies on the verge of receiving FDA approval for statins, Black devised an all-or-nothing strategy for the trials he believed were needed to win FDA approval: Parke-Davis would test 10 milligrams as a starting dose and 80 milligrams for patients with extremely high cholesterol levels. "It allowed you to go for a strategy that essentially took the competition out," says Cresswell. "We were going to beat them at LDL even with your lowest dose. I credit Dave Canter for coming up with this strategy. We decided to go with a low dosage so it would be evident that our drug would make a real medical difference in comparison to the other statins that were available. By starting at a lower level that would deliver a bigger impact on the reduction of LDL than our competition, we'd be putting everyone on notice that we had a superior product."

There wasn't any assurance at the time that the market would want a supercharged low-dose pill. Indeed, because of studies in the 1980s linking low cholesterol with an increased risk of death from non-heart-related illnesses, many doctors in the early 1990s were wary of aggressive treatment. Cresswell himself, who had had open-heart surgery a few years previously, was modestly reducing his own LDL levels by taking a Merck statin then and had been advised by his heart doctor that the market didn't need a more potent pill. The 80-milligram strategy was risky too. If it turned out to have unacceptable side effects, it could taint the drug even at low doses and leave the company with only a 10-milligram table to take to the market.

But results of larger studies vindicated Black's strategy. In October 1994, he and his colleagues made the first public presentation of human trial data of atorvastatin at a scientific conference in Montreal. The results were so stunning a senior Merck official stood up to suggest the drug be called "turbostatin."

In another Phase III study, the company conducted a head-to-head clinical trial against the leading statins already on the market. The company's marketing people requested this study. It was a risky tactic and one not often done in the industry, because had Lipitor failed to perform significantly better than the competition, it would have been a tough sale for Warner-Lambert sales reps to convince physicians to switch patients over to the new drug. To the company's good fortune, Lipitor passed the test with flying colors.

In 1995, Cresswell had personally enrolled in a compassionate-use program to get the drug before the FDA had approved it and, at 20 milligrams a day, his LDL fell from 160 to 90—below the established goal for people with heart ailments. "My cardiologist at the University of Michigan hospital had previously said to me, 'Why is your company coming out with a new statin?' " Cresswell says. "I wanted him to know that my LDL level was now at 90, so I faxed the results to him. He sent a fax back to me saying, 'You've got a winner.' "

Around the same time, Edward Ludwig, chief operating officer of Warner-Lambert, attended a monthly new-products committee meeting held in Ann Arbor, and he too was participating in a Lipitor clinical trial. "I just got the results today," Ludwig proudly announced to everyone. "My LDL was 180 and it's now 100."

Canter, who was present, took out his pen and started calculating on the back of an envelope, noting that Ludwig had reduced his LDL by 40 percent.

"I hate to tell you," Canter said, "but half the people who take the drug do better than you."

"Say that again," Canter says Ludwig questioned. Canter answered: "I said, 'That's a 40 percent lowering. That is exactly the average response we get with 10 milligrams.' "

Canter recalls from the look on Ludwig's face that for the first time it had dawned on him what 40 percent lowering really meant. "Yes, he had been experiencing what he thought was a tremendous benefit," Canter says, "and when he thought about my remark, he simply said, 'Oh. I see what you really mean by this lowering.' It was one of those 'ah ha' moments, because he personally realized that what he considered was a phenomenal result was in reality a medium impact."

Canter made a decision that the company would not conduct a long-term placebo control trial. "I had a problem with the ethics of using a placebo when it had been established that taking a statin reduced heart disease. It would be wrong to have some people with high LDL in a long-term clinical test to be taking an active pill while others were on a sugar pill. Of course this creates a problem that left us with groups of patients who wanted that high risk, and we'd have to study a lot of them for a long time to get enough events that would determine if we were making any difference. Consequently we had to do some very imaginative thinking. Our prime concern was to come up with a way that we could persuade the FDA that our compound deserved a 'fast-track' review, a status reserved for products that fill an unmet medical need and can shorten the time to market by at least six months.

"In early 1993, we went to the FDA and we said, 'We think this drug is really very good. And because it is so good, we would like to put in our labeling comparative data against other drugs in the class.'

"This comment caused a lot of eyes to roll and heads to shake. They said, 'We don't do that.'

"I said, 'We think we are good enough. So what do you need us to demonstrate?'

" 'This is what you have to do,' we were told. 'You need to do studies that have comparisons that you are significantly different.'

"What they requested was a huge burden. We simply said, 'Thank you.' Then in a cheeky way, we added, 'We would like to put in our labeling comparative data against other drugs in the class.' This time their response was laughter.

" 'Well, you come back and show that you can reduce the death [from] heart disease.' They knew that was an impossible demand at the time. Then they added, 'Or if you show that it works in familial hyper-cholesterolemia.' "

Familial hypercholesterolemia is a rare genetic disorder that strikes one in a million. People who have it lack the gene that makes the LDL receptor, and it impairs their ability to clear cholesterol from their bodies. For children born with two copies of the defective gene—one from each parent—the condition is particularly severe, and these children's cholesterol levels generally exceed six hundred. Such children die of heart disease by the time they are ten, and if they survive to their teens, they suffer heart attacks or require bypass surgery. Without treatment, their average life expectancy is fourteen years. Studies have shown that the disease occurs mostly in Quebec, Lebanon, and South Africa.

"We looked at each other, and then I spoke out, 'Let's get this clear. If we could show this drug works in familial hypercholesterolemia, you will give us the priority review? Is this correct?'

" 'Yes we will,' they replied.

" 'And if we can do this, we would like to be put on the fast-track,' I added.

" 'Yes, if you do that, you'll deserve to be on the fast-track,' an FDA official answered. I'm sure he was thinking that there wasn't much chance of that happening.

"Afterward, we contacted an investigator in South Africa who told us that he could do the study on four children under his care. We treated those four children and the results were favorable. We took our data of these results back to the FDA and requested to make an application for a treatment idea. A treatment idea is a special application that would allow us to treat a very select people, usually ones with a rare disease, and actually be permitted to have the patients pay for the treatment. We had no intentions of charging anyone, but we did want to file an Investigational New Drug application (IND). Two and a half weeks later, the FDA approved the IND but said we needed to test it on more than four patients. They told us forty patients would be a sufficient number, and we said we would do it. We went to Quebec and South Africa, where they had patients with the disease, and shortly thereafter doctors started treating these young children with Lipitor."

Canter stands from behind his desk and walks to his credenza to retrieve a photograph of a group of children. He points to the photo and says in a soft voice, "When we finished the study, we took the children in the study who came from all over the world to Disney World. It was our way of thanking them for what they did for us. Some of the children in this photo have since died." Pointing to the photograph, he says, "This little boy is only three years old. And this one has had several heart attacks and bypass surgery. We weren't able to cure all of them, but because of Lipitor they could live a little longer. Prior to Lipitor, no drugs made any difference. We were able to lower their LDL cholesterol by 20 to 25 percent."

The familial hypercholesterolemia study provided the researchers with a better understanding on the biology aspects of cholesterol. In these incidences heart disease was a result of high cholesterol levels at a young age, whereas the norm is that people with heart disease are middle-aged and older and its causes are not only genetic but also one's weight, lifestyle, and so on.

The company gambled when it first did human tests on Lipitor and it was a risk that paid off with a big return. Not only did the Phase I tests show that the drug worked on humans; as events turned out, it worked substantially better than any other drug when lowering LDL. Equally impressive, Lipitor worked better at a low dose than any of the competitions' drugs at a high dose. "Obviously this told us that we had something that's different," Roth states.

Lipitor was on the FDA fast track and the company submitted a new drug application in June 1996. It was approved six months later, on December 19.

Canter sums up the outcome of the clinical trials by saying, "There's an expression that industry people have about clinical trials. They say, 'For a difference to be a difference, it must make a difference.' Well, had Lipitor shown a 1 or 2 percent drop in LDL, it wouldn't have made much of a difference. In the case of Lipitor, the proof was in the pudding."

MAKING IT

Before the FDA approves a new drug, a company must demonstrate that it has the capability to manufacture it on a large scale. The company must show convincing evidence that it will be able to make the medicine and have enough inventory of it so when a physician prescribes it to a patient, the prescription will available to be filled. If this cannot be done, even the best miracle medicine will not be approved. So while clinical tests were being conducted, concurrently other work was being done by company employees to make Lipitor.

"It's one thing to make a compound in an academic lab," Roth says, "and another to be able to produce it on a large scale so it makes economic sense. I liken it to going to a fancy French restaurant that serves a sophisticated, delicious meal. But could its chef prepare the same quality meal for a huge banquet with a one-thousand-person seating? This is the challenge we have in the pharmaceutical industry. If we can only make a drug in the lab but can't mass-produce it, what good is it? We've got to be able to make it in large quantities."

A big hurdle had to be cleared in order to mass-produce Lipitor. Roth's initial Lipitor had what chemists describe as both left-handed and right-handed sides. But only the left-handed portion latched onto targets in the body, thereby blocking enzymes and causing a reduction in cholesterol. The inactive, right-handed side amounted to a glove that wouldn't fit.

Roth and his colleagues worried that this would leave their synthetic compound less potent than rivals from Merck and Bristol-Myers, which are natural molecules with no inactive components. Moreover, a lot of inactive material could cause unwanted side effects and even jeopardize approval at the FDA. As Roth explains, "It forces patients to metabolize 50 percent of material that is of no value to them."

During the third quarter of 1986, the decision was made to separate the left- and right-handed versions of CI-981 to improve its bioavailability. By August 1987, two members on Roth's team, Robert Sliskovic and Tim Hurley, were able to make the separation, an important achievement that was necessary for the drug's overall success. Their achievement significantly contributed to why Lipitor has become the best statin on the market. Although the left-handed glove wasn't evident in the laboratory or during animal tests, in humans it proved to have a longer half-life than other statins, meaning it lingers longer in the body to do its job.

Around the same time, a team was formed that was headed by Roth to develop a commercial manufacturing process. Team members included Robert Sliskovic, Alex Chucholowski, Tim Hurley, Don Butler, and Thomas Nanninga. Their challenge was to produce a left-handed molecule in large quantities. "The chemistry needed to get the right relationship of the atoms was just becoming available," says Jim Zeller, a chemist in the company's Holland, Michigan, facilities, where the scale-up work was done. He and his colleagues spent months experimenting with various processes, but they kept getting side reactions that produced right-handed gloves.

"I remember the first time our manufacturing people saw the synthesis," Roth recalls. "They said it would be harder than anything they had ever worked on in the history of that site. It took two years to work out a commercially viable synthesis for this compound. There was one critical reaction that was so difficult that Alan Miller, the individual assigned to the task, worked full time for an entire year to get it right. To make a synthesis commercially viable, it is common to take a different synthetic route than the one taken in discovery. Everything changes when you make a compound on a large scale. The kinds of solvents used are different. The safety issues change. There are limitations on the temperatures you can go to. And the kinds of reactors used are not the same. So it gets very complicated. As a chemist, my job normally ends when a compound is no longer in discovery, and typically I move on to the next project—the next compound. In this case, however, I served as an adviser to the people in manufacturing."

After conducting a global search for the right equipment, the scientists hit paydirt by running their reactions at liquid-nitrogen-cooled temperature lower than minus 80 degrees Celsius. A manufacturing process that took three weeks from raw materials to end product yielded a compound that was 100 percent left-handed gloves.

"This was one of those situations where a compound was easy to make in small quantities in the lab," Roth explains, "where we were able to go to a low temperature fairly easily by putting dry ice into isoprophynol or acetone to lower the temperature. We can do things on a small scale that can't be done on a large scale in a plant. This is always a major challenge in chemical development, because if you can't figure out how to translate what's done in the lab to make it by the ton and do it inexpensively, it will never be a viable drug."

Canter likens the manufacturing process for atorvastatin with the making of an automobile. "The most tedious way to make a car is when every piece is assembled one by one as the car moves along the assembly line," he explains. "The most efficient way to make an automobile is by convergence. For example, the engine and transmission can be completely built at one site and separately shipped. Likewise the body, the electronic unit, and other parts can be built at different locations. This way a relatively few number of parts converge at the assembly line versus each and every small piece. Using this analogy, we have third-party contractors make difficult pieces for us, and we assemble the whole molecule here. Carl Wheldon headed our manufacturing site in Holland, Michigan, at the time, and he is credited for getting all the different pieces here in an orderly fashion and then assembling everything into the final product.

"We started building the manufacturing site two years prior to the date that Lipitor was approved by the FDA. In addition to the cost of the site, we spent large sums of money on materials, packaging, and distribution, so everything would be ready to be shipped to pharmacies when the FDA gave its approval. When the final tally was in, the company had invested more than $200 million in manufacturing, materials, and inventory before the first prescription was filled starting in January 1997, when Lipitor was launched."

EXCEEDING EXPECTATIONS

Bruce Roth remembers a red-headed woman in marketing from the old Warner-Lambert company coming up to him at a conference and saying, "I wish someday you guys would give us something we could sell." The encounter was sometime in the early 1990s, just after the results were in from the first human tests. "I wish I could remember her name so I could ask her what she thinks now that we gave her Lipitor to sell," he says with a smile.

Even after the results from those first human tests, nobody was predicting the success that Lipitor would someday enjoy. "We got a 60 percent reduction in LDL cholesterol at the 80-milligram dose," Roth says, "which was greater than any other statin. Still, our marketing guys were projecting worldwide sales of $300 million."

From the beginning Warner-Lambert wanted to do a codevelopment deal with another pharmaceutical company. Shortly before the human tests were conducted, David Canter, Roger Newton, and a handful of other executives traveled to Philadelphia to meet with senior management at Rohm & Haas. "We knew about their compound, dalvastatin, that was in its early stages of development, but we thought they might like to team up with us with our statin. They politely passed on atorvastatin, telling us that they'd stick with their own statin. Only a few weeks later the results of our human volunteer data were made public. Meanwhile Rohm & Hass ran into some trouble with dalvastatin (the company eventually terminated it) and said they'd like to meet with us again. We told them that they were too late and that our offer was no longer on the table."

Warner-Lambert wanted to partner with another pharmaceutical company, and in particular with one that had a strong marketing organization. When the word got out that the company was looking for a partner, several companies expressed interest, but Pfizer was chosen because it had what was considered to be the industry's premier sales force. "There were still internal skeptics who didn't think Lipitor would be a big seller because the statin market had been saturated by 1997. And some were calling calling atorvastatin another 'me-too' drug," says Roth. "And internally, our marketing people never dreamed it would ever hit $1 billion in annual sales. So when our executives negotiated a colicensing agreement with Pfizer, it was structured to give the lion's share of the profits to Warner-Lambert, and when sales exceeded $1 billion, a higher percentage of the profits would go to Pfizer. At the time, our management team believed they made a 'deal of a lifetime,' thinking that they had really pulled the wool over Pfizer's eyes. As it turned out, Lipitor had hit the billion-dollar mark faster than any other drug in the history of the pharmaceutical industry."

The timing for Lipitor's launching in early 1997 couldn't have been better. Major studies conducted by Merck and Bristol-Myers Squibb had convinced doctors that statins worked; the general public had been educated on the fact that low cholesterol reduces heart disease. Pfizer had also priced Lipitor at highly competitive prices, and coming out with better results at lower doses was a convincing sales pitch that got the attention of physicians. Additionally, many published articles had rave reviews of Lipitor. Consequently, many doctors were presold on Lipitor before even meeting with their Pfizer sales rep. At the time of Lipitor's launching, one sales rep called on a physician, and at beginning of his presentation took out some sample packs. "The doctor grabbed a box, opened it up, took out a pill, and popped it in his mouth. 'I've been waiting for this drug to arrive for months,' he said. 'I need this drug myself.' "

*   *   *

A common practice in the pharmaceutical industry is for sales reps to give samples of drugs to physicians, who, in turn, give them to their patients. The purpose of giving away free samples is to get a patient promptly started on a new medication, and at the same time, the doctor can monitor its efficacy. To kick off Lipitor, a five hundred thousand one-month sample inventory was given to sales reps. "All of the samples had been given out within the first three weeks of the launching," Canter explains. "I was still the project leader, and I suddenly realized that we had tested the drug on five thousand patients during the clinical trials, and now five hundred thousand patients would be on the drug. Now, testing five thousand patients was a huge effort, but going from five thousand to five hundred thousand in a matter of a few weeks, well, I felt an enormous sense of responsibility. It is a holding of your breath when you make a gigantic jump, because what if there was some kind of rare side effect, say, one in fifty thousand that we wouldn't have seen in the five thousand? Now, you have ten cases that you find out about. If you had ten serious cases in a short span of time, it would be cause to pull the drug. To our good fortune, that didn't happen. The patients on the Lipitor samples did very well."

Lipitor's inventor, Bruce Roth, comments that he too was holding his breath when the five hundred thousand samples went out. "With the clinical trials, there were only a few thousand people, and you hope that the data will allow you to predict what will happen in a large population. But the clinical trials are done under fairly controlled conditions. Patients are carefully monitored. Once a drug is available to the masses, people and physicians aren't as cautious. Nor are they as educated about the use of the drug. People are on different kinds of medication and that complicates matters. And with millions of people that are using a drug for the first time, it's hard to predict until it's been on the market for a couple of years what may happen."

Roth worked on the compound during the discovery period and afterward served as an adviser to the manufacturing people. "That's the way this business works," he explains. "Once a compound gets out of discovery, as a chemist, I'm on to my next project or projects. No more stress with the old project. Of course, with a medication like Lipitor, I have a vested interest in its success, so I'm rooting for it to be a big success and benefit millions of patients."

*   *   *

Projected sales in 1994 for Lipitor were $250 million annually by its fifth year on the market. That forecast had not been revised when the drug was launched. Sales were $850 to $860 million in its first calendar year, and for its first full twelve months, over $1 billion—the first drug to ever exceed the one-billion-dollar mark in a twelve-month period.

"Imagine what could have gone wrong with such a missed forecast," Canter states. "One of our greatest success stories is how our manufacturing unit was able to stay a few hours ahead of the last package available on the shelves. To manufacturing's credit, there was a time when we were within one shift of exhausting our inventory. For weeks and weeks, sales were climbing so rapidly, we were just sitting about with less than a day away from being back ordered."

To exhaust its inventory would not bode well with the FDA, but even worse, such a deficiency would certainly deal a damaging blow to a pharmaceutical company's customer loyalty. As Canter emphasizes, "No company wants a doctor to be told by a patient, 'You gave me this prescription, but I can't get it at my pharmacy.' "

Also caught off guard was the competition. The word never leaked out in the industry or to the media that the company was applying for a priority review. As a result, they were not prepared with a strategy on how to deal with the rave reviews that Lipitor was getting. "A funny thing happened," Canter explains. "When the other companies' reps talked about their own product, they'd also talk about Lipitor. So when our reps made their sales calls, doctors would say to them, 'Oh, the rep from such-and-such company talked about Lipitor and I am intrigued. Please tell me more.' It's a funny thing, but our competitors helped to spark interest in Lipitor."

THE ACQUISITION

Shareholders of Warner-Lambert were rewarded for their patience by holding on to their stock during the early 1990s when its price was flat. They received a wonderful return on their investment that came with the tremendous success of Lipitor. However, too much success can bring about disaster when investors expect a company's prosperity to continue

and a time comes when it does not. This can happen in the pharmaceutical industry when a blockbuster drug goes off patent and the generic
manufacturers start knocking it off and selling it at steeply discounted
prices. Lipitor's patent was issued in 1993, which meant that it would go
off patent at the end of 2010.

"In 1999 we went through an exercise," explains Canter, "where the
question was posed, 'How could Warner-Lambert remain independent
when Lipitor went off patent?' Our concern was that the huge success
of Lipitor could conceivably mean the company's ultimate destruction.
At a meeting attended by senior management, we concluded that if Lipitor was no more than 25 percent of the company's total annual sales,
we could survive. At that point, our annual sales were $5.5 billion.
Lipitor had generated $1 billion in 1997 and $2.2 billion in 1998. Lipitor
was available in 50 countries and it had a 34 percent share of the entire cholesterol-lowering new prescription market in the U.S. When
the question was raised on how high its annual sales might go before peaking, someone said, 'I think it's possibly going to go as high as
$4 billion.'

" 'We've been wrong so often with Lipitor and have underestimated
its potential,' another executive said, 'so let's put in a real fudge factor and
say sales hit $6 billion.'

"This brought some laughs around the table. 'Well, you could put
in $6 billion for this exercise, but the chances of that happening are
pretty low.'

" 'If we use our rule of 25 percent, that means we need to be selling
$24 billion worth of drugs by the time Lipitor goes off patent. Where is
that $18 billion going to come from?'

"There was a calm in the room. We knew we had gone from a $2.2
billion pharmaceutical company in 1996, and by 1999, our total revenues
climbed to $5.5 billion. Looking at these numbers that were only 11 years
away, and considering our current R&D investment, we realized that
our success with Lipitor had forever altered our company. It was this
thinking that forced us to consider merging with another company."

In 1999, Lipitor sales were approaching $4 billion and sales were pro-
jected to hit $10 billion before 2010. Lipitor was now more than 60 per-
cent of Warner-Lambert's total revenues. When it became obvious that
Warner-Lambert needed to find another company to merge with, talks
were started with Pfizer and American Home Products. In a bidding war,

Pfizer acquired Warner-Lambert on February 2, 2000, at a price of $90 billion, making it the pharmaceutical industry's largest acquisition ever. The combined sales of the two companies totaled $28 billion.

"We had already had a partnership with Pfizer with Lipitor, which I believe was the best thing we ever did," Canter emphasizes, "and because we had an existing relationship with them, the transition went smoothly. Pfizer definitely had a way of thinking that was different. What was different? Theirs was a bigger, more dynamic way of thinking."

As a footnote, Lipitor's annual sales in 2005 were $12 billion, representing 22 percent of Pfizer's annual revenues of $54 billion, making it the largest pharmaceutical company in the world. The company's R&D budget for 2006 is estimated at $8 billion.

WHAT'S NEXT?

Roger Newton, Lipitor's acclaimed codiscoverer and product champion, is a scientist who marches to a different drummer. Remember, this is that product champion who got down on one knee to make a convincing plea to an executive committee to shell out $1 million for funding the first human test on Lipitor. It was Newton's sheer conviction that swayed Warner-Lambert management to make that crucial decision—a veto would have lead to the demise of the company's statin program and Lipitor would not exist today. His presentation was compelling because his passion for his work was so unmistakable. Newton is a man with strong beliefs—beliefs that he will not compromise.

Newton's unyielding beliefs are what led him to leave Warner-Lambert in July 1998 to form Esperion Therapeutics Inc., a start-up biotech company based in Ann Arbor. When asked what prompted his decision to venture out on his own, he says, "I felt I was put in a compromised position at Warner-Lambert because I believed that the company should focus on a drug that would increase HDL levels after the launching of Lipitor. It was my opinion that an HDL program was the next logical step, and that's the direction where our atherosclerosis drug discovery program should be headed. I approached management three times to discuss my views, and each time, I got turned down. Abiding by the three-strike rule, I resigned and started my own company that would focus on making compounds to raise HDL levels. I had spent eighteen years with Warner-Lambert, and it was a great place to be. It was just time for me to move on, and I parted on good terms. Mike Pape, Tom Rea, and Charlie Bisgaier were three of my associates from the atherosclerosis group that came with me. We raised $16 million in venture capital and we were off and running. Our goal was to become a fully integrated pharmaceutical company."

Two years later, in August 2000, Esperion did an initial public offering. At the time, the company didn't have a product on the market, or for that matter, a single drug in a clinical trial. Investors bought shares in the company purely on promise and speculation.

Esperion's macro-molecular discovery program focused on identifying and developing new treatments for acute coronary syndrome patients using HDL therapy that employed recombinant proteins and peptides mimicking apoA-I complexed to phospholipid. One particular drug being developed by Esperion is ETC-216, which contains recombinant apoA-I Milano, complexed to phospholipids to mimic newly secreted HDL particles from the liver and intestine. This variant of apoA-I was discovered approximately three decades earlier in a group of forty healthy individuals who lived in Limone Sul Garda in Northern Italy. Despite having very low levels of HDL cholesterol, these villagers enjoyed excellent health, whereas typically it would have put them at risk of having heart disease. Studies conducted on them revealed a single amino acid substitution to form the variant protein now called apoA-1 Milano. Its name comes from the laboratory in Milan where the discovery work was conducted by Italian doctors Cesare Sirtori and Guido Franceschini.

In a small study conducted by the Cleveland Clinic for Esperion, intravenous doses of ETC-216, the company's recombinant version of apoA-I Milano, were given to a randomized group of acute coronary syndrome patients in a study that, according to Newton, "demonstrated for the first time ever that it is possible to rapidly cause regression of atherosclerosis after five weekly doses in just five six weeks." By enhancing the removal of cholesterol from plaques in artery walls, and promoting a process known as reverse lipid transport, HDL therapy may provide an innovative approach to the treatment of atherosclerosis.

Following the Pfizer acquisition and Lipitor's enormous success, a change of heart occurred. The cholesterol-lowering team began focusing on developing a combination drug that would lower LDL levels while raising HDL levels. Says Newton, "My associates and I had kept in touch with our former colleagues at Warner-Lambert and had kept them abreast on what we were doing and vise versa. When we made public the major results from the ETC-216 study at the Cleveland Clinc, Pfizer became interested in our portfolio of HDL reverse cholesterol transport therapy that we were developing, because it complemented what they were doing with atorvastatin and torcetrapib combination."

When asked what motivated him to sell Esperion to Pfizer, Newton, who is now president and CEO of Espersion, explains, "We had a fiduciary responsibility to our shareholders. Pfizer offered us $1.3 billion, which was a 55 percent premium over our 20-day average stock price at the time. We were looking out for our shareholders. The deal was announced on December 21, 2003, and closed in early February 2004."

After a brief pause, Newton adds: "What other company could be such a perfect fit for us? I knew a lot of people there at both Pfizer and Warner-Lambert because I worked with a group from both companies when Lipitor was launched. Besides, Pfizer has great brainpower, extensive development resources, and deep pockets to take this project forward. Being the world's leader in cardiovascular drugs certainly added significantly to the potential for an ensuing success and a return on investment to Pfizer shareholders."

While on the subject of deep pockets, a drug called torcetrapib is being developed in combination with Lipitor, and by the time the Phase III studies are completed, it's estimated that Pfizer will have spent $800 million on the clinical trials. It's also estimated that 25,000 people will have been tested. "The $800 million spent on the clinical trials is more than the entire R&D budget for some pharmaceutical companies and most biotech companies," Roth exclaims. "Our budget for the clinical tests for Lipitor at Warner-Lambert was only a fraction of that. Quite a difference, isn't it?"

When LDL cholesterol is lowered by Lipitor, it enhances the effectiveness of a patient's HDL therapy. The combination of reducing the volume of atherosclerosic plaques and preventing its progression or even promoting further regression had the promise of providing a major beneficial effect of reducing the morbidity and mortality of heart disease. Patients treated by statins will take a daily pill; torcetrapib will be taken orally on a weekly basis. With Lipitor, torcetrapib, and ETC-216 in its arsenal of cholesterol medicines, Pfizer's market-share leadership is destined to remain intact.

THE JOY OF JOB SATISFACTION

In 2003, Bruce Roth was the recipient of the Esselen Award, one of the most prestigious honors provided by the Northeastern Section of the American Chemical Society. A letter written to support his nomination stated that Lipitor has the potential to save more lives than any other medication in the history of the pharmaceutical industry. The letter maintained that this statement was based on the tens of millions of people that take Lipitor. Roth says, "This is something you never think about when you go about your daily work, focused on figuring out how to make a compound, and trying to get your little drug through the system successfully, and continually asking yourself if it's ever going to make it to the market. You lose track of the big picture, which is, of course, if what you do succeeds, having large numbers of people benefiting from it."

With 2005 annual sales of $12 billion, Lipitor is the world's best-selling drug. It's a success story that came so close to not happening again and again during the course of its perilous journey. In this respect, it is representative of the pharmaceutical industry, a business with enormous risks, and for the handful of drugs that do succeed there can be commensurate monetary rewards.

Yet in the world of medical research, it is not the money that drives men and women who toil long hours in laboratories to discover and develop drugs. It's about doing something truly important that saves lives and provides good health. Roger Newton, for example, enjoyed considerable financial gain when Pfizer acquired Esperion. At the time of the acquisition he could have retired at a young age and lived a live of luxury and leisure. However, he did not. Instead, Newton continues to put in long hours as a senior vice president and director of Esperion. His motivation for getting up and going to work every day is exactly the same as it has always been: he enjoys the challenge of discovering and developing new medicines that can benefit others.

Today, Roger Newton now has another passion—it's a family foundation he established that focuses on human potential, health, and the environment. He put 25 percent of the gross proceeds that he received from the sale of Esperion into the foundation. In effect, the foundation is an extension of his work as a scientist—he is a man who believes that he was put on this earth to contribute to the well-being of others:

"It's that old adage that reminds us that it's not the pot of gold at the end of the rainbow," Newton tells, "it is the journey that you take and the people that you meet. That is the legacy that you have in anything you do in life. And to me, it's the respect I have for the people I work with and those who helped make the successes that we've had. That is our legacy. I feel awfully lucky to be a part of this success, to work with so many exceptional people, and to have received the support from management that was needed to make it happen.

"To do what we accomplished with Lipitor was truly a team effort. No single individual could have done it," Newton emphasizes. "No man is an island here. Again, to paraphrase an old adage, 'Success has many fathers, failure has none.' The job satisfaction of working with so many fine people is what I consider the real reward. It's also the human aspect of the daily struggle that we experience in this line of work. There are more failures in the pharmaceutical industry than any other industry in the world. People don't know how passionate scientists have to be to stay here late at night, weekends, and to be driven to accomplish something that's going to affect the lives of other people."

"Having said that," he continues, "what truly gives our work meaning and what drives us to put in all those extra hours while working against tremendous odds is when a person on one of our drugs expresses his appreciation for what it's meant to him personally. This happened to me in early 1998 when I was speaking to a group of three hundred physicians in a large hotel ballroom in Sydney at the time of our Australian launch of Lipitor. Afterward, a teary-eyed man and his wife came up to me and he gave me a big bear hug. He explained that he was forty-five years old and both his parents died in their forties of heart disease. His cholesterol had been off the charts, but after taking Lipitor his LDL came down close to normal levels.

" 'I was on Lipitor during the clinical studies here in Sydney,' he explained, 'and my doctor told me you were speaking, so that's why I'm here. I had to shake your hand and thank you personally.

" 'You know, sir, I never saved a penny for retirement because I figured I'd be dead at an early age, just like my parents. Then I started taking Lipitor, and now I'm saving my money for retirement. And I met this beautiful woman who is now my wife. I can't tell you how much this drug has changed my life.'

"When he said that, I started welling up inside and almost started crying," Newton says in a soft voice. "Suddenly, the clarity of all the hard work, the long weekends, and the late nights all made sense. It just takes one person and you can put a face on it."

AFTERWORD

After conducting extensive research for this book, I have concluded that the men and women working at the seven pharmaceutical companies featured herein are driven by their strong desire to do the right thing for humankind. This is what motivates them to go to their jobs each morning and spend long hours doing tedious work, often working for years in their quest to serve the public. The odds against their succeeding are immense, as are the financial risks taken by the companies they work for.

These individuals work in an unusual environment in which they have a responsibility not only to shareholders but also to serve millions of men and women whose health and welfare depend on the medicines they make. While the news media have been critical of the large profits made by pharmaceutical companies, it is essential that these companies prosper and continue to make new discoveries. Without profits, funding of research and development is not possible. So while we are prone to complaining about the high costs of medicine, we must realize that medical cures do not come cheaply. As you have read in this book, a high percentage of the molecules that do beat the high odds and make it through discovery still fail along the way. Even after hundreds of millions of dollars have been spent, some drugs fail during the final stages of the clinical tests. Remember, too, that it takes tens of millions of man-hours to bring out a new drug, and there is a limited time frame available within which a company can recoup its investment, which can often exceed the billion-dollar mark.

For example, Pfizer's Lipitor is currently the world's bestselling prescription drug. The company's scientists started their research with statins in 1982, and in 1998, sixteen years later, Lipitor was launched. Years before, the company filed its Lipitor patent; consequently, Lipitor will become a generic drug in 2011, giving it only thirteen years on the market before its patent expires. Then, generic drug manufacturers—which had no research and development investment—will be able to copy what Pfizer scientists spent years discovering and making. Meanwhile, highly able scientists at competitive pharmaceutical companies are working overtime in their efforts to come up with better drugs. Of course, so are Pfizer scientists. They are working in high gear to come out with a statin that will raise the levels of HDL, the good cholesterol.

The pharmaceutical industry is a fiercely competitive and fast-changing field. An army of brilliant scientists are hard at work in search of new discoveries that will improve current cures and heretofore incurable diseases. Change is constant. It's reminiscent of the question a Princeton student posed to his professor, Albert Einstein: "Why are you giving us the identical test as you did last year?" The luminous scientist answered, "Because this year, the answers are different." So, too, do the answers differ as new scientific advances are made in the pharmaceutical field. In our ever-changing world of science and industry, what worked in the past is not assured to work in the future. New medicines will be discovered that will cure diseases that today are untreatable.

We live in an exciting era in which we can expect many major scientific breakthroughs in the pharmaceutical industry. We can anticipate even bigger and more impressive advances than ever before. However, a word of caution: these changes can only occur in an environment that promotes harmony among science, industry, and government. As these seven stories show, miracle medicines don't just happen. They develop over long periods and are a result of the combined efforts of many people. To assure that more miracle medicines make it to the market, our pharmaceutical companies must remain healthy and vibrant. They must because it is in our best interest—yours, mine, our children's, and our children's children's.

ACKNOWLEDGMENTS

Having written fifty previous books, I was under the impression that writing books was not so difficult after all. But after starting this one, I realized that it depended on the subject matter. From start to finish, this was by far my most difficult book to write. In short, I quickly discovered just how complex and technical the pharmaceutical field is. It was a constant struggle, but a worthy venture. I am hopeful that this book will have a positive influence on its readers, and if so, all the hard work and long hours were worthwhile. To my good fortune, I had many people help me along the way—without them, this book could not have been written.

First and foremost, I am grateful to the many men and women at the seven pharmaceutical companies who took time from their busy schedules so that I could conduct extensive interviews with them. These individuals included brilliant and dedicated researchers, chemists, pharmacologists, physicians, physiologists, and other scientists and executives. Many of them spent extra hours with me explaining detailed scientific information that I, as a layperson, was unable to comprehend the first time around. Consequently, numerous follow-up interviews were required and again, they graciously volunteered their time. At all times, they were courteous and accommodating. I sensed they wanted people outside the pharmaceutical industry to have a better understanding of what they do, and therefore it was important to them to tell their story. Their names are not included in these acknowledgments because their stories appear throughout the book; they and the reader will know who they are. I am deeply beholden to each and every one of them.

Three Columbus, Ohio, physicians—Bryan Feldman, Bruce Meyer, and Alan Weinberg—advised me during the research and writing of my manuscript. They answered the many medical questions I had. I am especially indebted to Bryan, who read my early chapter drafts; he made corrections and even did minor editing along the way. My wife, Elinor, and my daughter-in-law Melissa proofread the manuscript. They, too, were terrific.

My longtime agent and dear friend, Al Zuckerman, encouraged me during some challenging times when I had begun to think that I had bitten off more than I could chew. I am grateful for everything he has done to enhance my writing career over the twenty-five-year period that he has represented me.

Bill Beausay, an excellent author, helped with the research and writing of several of the company profiles. Claire Zuckerman, a fine editor, assisted me with the book proposal and the book's first two chapters, as did Ingrid Wickelgren, a notable science writer. Debbie Watts had the exacting job of transcribing all of the interviews; as always, she was exceptional and dependable. Millard Cummins, a good friend and a very smart man, advised me throughout the writing of my manuscript. My heartfelt thanks to all of you.

I am very grateful to the men and women who work at PhRMA, the pharmaceutical industry's association. They opened many doors at the pharmaceutical companies that I approached so I could determine which medicines should be featured in my book. These people are: Billy Tauzin, Ken Johnson, Ed Belkin, Mark Grayson, and Arturo Silva. Whenever I needed advice, Ken and Arturo were always there for me. I admire their dedication and professionalism. And I appreciate their support and friendship.

Other people within the pharmaceutical industry who contributed to this book are: Cathy Babbington, Melissa Brotz, Steve Collens, Elizabeth Hoff, Rick Moser, Jim Schwartz, Jennifer Smoter, Carla Burigatto, Terri Ford, Laura King, Martha Lichtensteiger, Luke Mette, Jim Minnick, David Nicoli, Pat Razzano, Mary Sphar, Sally Dorset, Scott MacGregor, Ed Sagebiel, John Swanton, Nancy Pekarek, Gaile Renegar, Peg Falko, Elizabeth King, Pat Molino, Chris Molineaux, Gloria Stone, Samina Bari, Laura Glick, Andrew McCormick, Kate Robins, Candice Sue, and Rebecca Tillet.

I am also fortunate to have a very talented group of people at Penguin to work with. It is my good fortune that Adrian Zackheim made the decision to publish *Miracle Medicines*. Having known Adrian for many years, I am one of his biggest fans. He is recognized as one of the premier non-fiction publishers in the book business and a delightful person to work with. Penguin's editorial team included Jillian Gray, who joined the team with an impressive background as a medical writer. Jill had the demanding job that required her to tediously edit the contents of my working manuscript, page by page, word by word. Penguin's marketing executive, Will Weisser, did outstanding work, starting with the design of the book jacket (people do judge books by their covers) to getting the word out that *Miracle Medicines* is available to purchase.

Last but not least, I am grateful to my son, RJ Shook, who is also a professional writer as well as founder and CEO of The Winner's Circle Organization, a leading research firm in the securities industry. Time and again I sought RJ's advice during the course of writing this book (to the point where I relied on it). I am blessed to have such a fine and caring son, who is also an astute businessperson. For most of RJ's life, I was his main source of advice; the tables have turned, and nowadays he is the first person I turn to when I seek advice. This is indeed one of the great joys of fatherhood.

NOTES

CHAPTER 1—ABBOTT INC.
The Fight Against AIDS

9   *Born on a rocky farm near Bridewater, Vermont*   Herman Kogan, *The Long White Line: The Story of Abbott Laboratories* (New York: Random House, 1963), p. 5.

9   *Dr. Abbott's Tooth Ache Drops, Rock Candy Cough Syrup, Blackberry Balsam* Ibid., p. 10.

10   *a physician to give small, frequent doses of the pure, isolated alkaloid*   *The Abbott Almanac* (Elmsford, NY: Benjamin Company, Inc., 1988), p. 15.

10   *His production guides were old copies*   Ibid., p. 19.

11   *DOCTOR, WE'VE A NUGGET OF GOLD FOR YOU!*   Kogan, *The Long White Line*, p. 25.

12   *"We have no salesmen, therefore we cannot camp"*   Ibid., p. 42.

14   *It was discovered in 1937 when a young graduate student*   *The Abbott Almanac*, p. 139.

15   *with a staff of more than 65,000*   *Abbott 2005 Annual Report*.

17   *no apparent danger of contagion for nonhomosexuals*   L. K. Altman, "Rare Cancer Seen in 41 Homosexuals," *New York Times*, July 3, 1981.

17   *in children and in transfusion recipients*   D. McGinn, "MSNBC: AIDS at 20: Anatomy of a Plague; an Oral History," *Newsweek* Web Exclusive, June 1982.

18   *The officers were concerned they could bring the bug home*   "San Francisco Seeks to Combat Fear of AIDS," *New York Times*, May 22, 1983.

18   *Landlords evicted individuals with AIDS*   R. Enlow, " 'Special Session,' in *Acquired Immune Deficiency Syndrome, Annuals of the New York Academy of Sciences*, vol. 437, I. J. Selikoff, A. S. Teirstein, and S. Z. Hirschman, eds. (New York: New York Academy of Sciences, 1984), p. 291.

18   *By the end of 1984, the United States had 7,699 reported AIDS cases*   "Acquired Immunodeficiency Syndrome (AIDS) Weekly Surveillance Report—United States," AIDS Activity, Center for Infectious Diseases, Centers for Disease Control and Prevention, December 31, 1984.

19   *"Once the virus was discovered"*   Interview with Gerald Schochetman, Ph.D., Abbott's director of infectious disease diagnostics, April 29, 2005.

20   *AZT was originally designed in the 1960s for the treatment of leukemia*   Neville Hodgkinson, "The Cure That Failed," *Sunday Times*, April 4, 1993.

21   *"Having been trained to make molecules"*   Interview with Dale Kempf, April 28, 2005.

23   *"Even though all your work theoretically might have made some scientific contributions"*   Interview with Dan Norbeck, April 29, 2005.

23   *"What we did was atypical"*   Interview with Dale Kempf, April 28, 2005.

24   *"As soon as we put it into rats for the first time"*   Ibid.

25   *"It was an exciting period"*   Interview with John Leonard, April 29, 2005.

25   *"There were times when we'd ask ourselves"*   Interview with Dan Norbeck, April 29, 2005.

26   *"This was a time when many experts were declaring that AIDS"*   Interview with John Leonard, April 29, 2005.

28   *"What we saw was something we did not expect"*   Ibid.

28   *"It was as if I had been following HIV around"*   Interview with Eugene Sun, May 13, 2005.

29   *"We were the underdog"*   Ibid.

30   *Like a Swiss army knife*   Ibid.

31   *"I've been waiting a long time for this moment"*   Interview with Dale Kempf, April 28, 2005.

32   *"It's like a person running on a treadmill"*   Interview with David Ho, May 16, 2005.

33   *"In order to win against HIV"*   Interview with Eugene Sun, May 13, 2005.

33   *"All of us were determined to find another compound"*   Interview with Dale Kempf, April 28, 2005.

34   *"There was no placebo"*   Interview with Eugene Sun, May 13, 2005.

35   *"The big question when we went into this trial"*   Ibid.

41   *"We hope to have a vaccine [against HIV] ready for testing"*   Office of Technology Assessment, "Review of the Public Health Service's Response to AIDS," U.S. Congress, Washington, D.C., February 1985, p. 29.

CHAPTER 2—ASTRAZENECA COMPANY
A New Lease on Life

42   *"We are starting a new company"*   Bob Lehrman, "Overseas Multinationals Invest in the United States," *Fortune*, May 29, 2000, special section p. 4.

43   *Astra's principals were an impressive and experienced group*   *International Directory of Company Histories* (Farmington Hills, MI: St. James Press, 2005), p. 55.

43 *Sweden's new socialist government*   Ibid., p. 56.

44 *The discovery of Xylocaine*   Ibid., p. 57.

44 *By the 1970s Astra had formed separate divisions*   Ibid.

47 *Zeneca had catapulted into the top twenty pharmaceutical companies world-wide*   Ibid.

49 *In general terms, 10,000 new ideas*   John King, "Top 10 Pipelines," *R&D Directions,* January 2004, p. 3.

49 *works to ensure access to lifesaving medication*   Internet Web site, www .astrazeneca.com/content/corporateResponsibility/corporateCitizenship

51 *Most individuals who migrated to the New World*   Gerald N. Grob, *The Mad Among Us* (New York: Free Press, 1994), p. 8.

51 *Cotton Mather, an eminent Puritan minister*   Ibid., p. 9

52 *Kraepelin postulated that there is a specific brain*   Wikipedia, online encyclopedia, at http://en.wikipedia.org/wiki/Emil_Kraepelin.

55 *Schizophrenia, the most serious, complicated*   See www.schizophrenia.com/ history.htm.

55 *The evidence that schizophrenia*   Ibid.

55 *Doctors treat 3.2 million people in this country suffering from schizophrenia*   Scott Allen, "Schizophrenia Drugs Fare Poorly in Major New Study," *Wall Street Journal,* September 20, 2005, p. A16.

56 *patients with schizophrenia were 2.4 times more likely*   American Journal of Public Health, 1995.

56 *Even with treatment, 85 percent of schizophrenics*   Allen, "Schizophrenia Drugs Fare Poorly," p. A16.

57 *Atlas was a small company whose philosophy*   Interview with Cyrus Ohnmacht, July 29, 2005.

59 *"Roughly speaking, a high degree of dopamine"*   Interview with Wayne MacFadden, July 11, 2005.

60 *"Think of a receptor as if it were a lock and a key"*   Interview with Jeffrey Goldstein, July 11, 2005.

60 *"When we were Zeneca before the merger"*   Interview with Georgia Tugend, July 12, 2005.

60 *"It was a crowded field"*   Interview with Jim Minnick, July 11, 2005.

60 *"We were competing with other drugs within the company"*   Interview with Georgia Tugend, July 12, 2005.

61 *"When you have a drug to treat a disorder of the brain"*   Interview with Jeffrey Goldstein, July 11, 2005.

61 *"Picture a group of business executives sitting around the table"*   Interview with David Brennan, July 11, 2005.

62 *"In the case of Seroquel"*   Ibid.

63 *"At the time, the company wasn't well known in the CNS area"*   Interview with Jeffrey Goldstein, July 11, 2005.

65 *"No longer can a company make small quantities of a medicine"*   Interview with Ken Murtha, July 19, 2005.

66 *"While a pharmaceutical company can't sell or promote"* Interview with David Brennan, July 11, 2005.

66 *"At first, the company wasn't sure"* Interview with Georgia Tugend, July 12, 2005.

67 *"We wanted experienced people"* Interview with Michael Hickey, June 5, 2005.

68 *"This was a risky and expensive venture"* Interview with Jim Blessington, June 17, 2005.

68 *"We set financial targets"* Interview with Don Beamish, July 11, 2005.

69 *"Our salespeople were true believers"* Interview with Georgia Tugend, July 12, 2005.

70 *"It's not uncommon for a pharmaceutical company"* Interview with Tony Zook, August 10, 2005.

70 *"Back in 1997, Seroquel's market share"* Interview with Henry Nasrallah, September 28, 2005.

70 *"There's a lot of competition out there"* Interview with David Brennan, July 7, 2005.

71 *There was a very definitive statement made by senior management* Interview with David Brennan, July 11, 2005.

72 *"What it all boils down to is customer satisfaction"* Interview with Don Beamish, July 11, 2005.

72 *"In all my years in this business"* Interview with Tony Zook, August 10, 2005.

73 *"Patients' testimonials inspire us"* Interview with David Brennan, July 12, 2005.

73 *"It's important for the men and women"* Interview with Ken Murtha, July 19, 2005.

73 *"If you cannot give a drug to a family member"* Interview with Henry Nasrallah, September 28, 2005.

73 *The first documentary filmed and directed by someone living with the disease* Home Box Office, 2005.

74 *"I've heard voices ever since I was a little girl"* Interview with Geri Hanson, October 12, 2005.

77 *"Once you go out there with your label"* Interview with David Brennan, July 11, 2005.

79 *"The physicians had to figure out"* Interview with Don Beamish, July 11, 2005.

80 *"There is a tendency to underestimate a new drug"* Interview with David Brennan, July 11, 2005.

80 *"One of the biggest challenges with bipolar disorder"* Interview with Johan Hoegstedt, July 11, 2005.

81 *"Many bipolar disorder patients self-medicate"* Interview with Jim Blessington, June 17, 2005.

82 *NAMI is a nonprofit, grassroots, self-help support* See www.nami.org.

83 *This organization fosters an understanding* See www.dbsalliance.org.

85   *"I've been in this industry for thirty years"*   Interview with David Brennan, July 11, 2005.

CHAPTER 3—ELI LILLY
The Better-Than-Nature Insulin

86   *Drugstores a century ago*   Roscoe Collins Clark, *Threescore Years and Ten: A Narrative of the First Seventy Years of Eli Lilly and Company* (Indianapolis: Eli Lilly and Company, 1946), p. 6.

87   *"Save the Republic" furor*   Ibid., p. 13.

88   *Lilly's first product catalog*   Ibid., p. 28.

89   *Lilly helped found the Commercial Club*   James H. Madison, *Eli Lilly: A Life, 1885–1977* (Indianapolis: Indianapolis Historical Society, 1989), pp. 4–5.

89   *the popularity of an old Creek Indian recipe*   Madison, *Eli Lilly: A Life*, p. 27.

89   *Josiah K. Lilly, his only son*   Clark, *Threescore Years and Ten*, p. 41.

91   *"The sun never sets on the Red Lilly"*   Clark, *Threescore Years and Ten*, p. 65.

92   *more than half the polio vaccines*   *International Directory of Company Histories* (Farmington Hills, MI: St. James Press, 2005), p. 113.

94   *Today Lilly employs over 44,000 people worldwide*   *Lilly 2004 Annual Report.* Lilly product brand names with their generic designations:

Alimta (pemetrexed, Lilly)
Amytal (amobarbital, Lilly)
Ceclor (cefaclor, Lilly)
Cialis (tadalafil, ICOS), Lilly ICOS LLC
Cymbalta (duloxetine hydrochloride, Lilly)
Evista (raloxifene hydrochloride, Lilly)
Forteo (teriparatide of recombinant DNA origin, Lilly)
Humalog (insulin lispro of recombinant DNA origin, Lilly)
Humulin (human insulin of recombinant DNA origin, Lilly)
Iletin (insulin, Lilly)
Keflin (sodium cephalothin, Lilly)
Prozac (fluoxetine hydrochloride, Lilly)
Strattera (atomoxetine hydrochloride, Lilly)
Symbyax (olanzapine/fluoxetine hydrochloride, Lilly)
V-Cillin (penicillin V, Lilly)
Vancocin (vancomycin hydrochloride, Lilly)
Xigris (drotrecogin alfa [activated], Lilly)
Zyprexa (olanzapine, Lilly)

95   *"a melting down of flesh and limbs into urine"*   E. McGrew Roderick, *Encyclopedia of Medical History,* (New York: McGraw-Hill, 1985), p. 90.

96   *more than 18 million Americans have diabetes*   Betsy McKay, "Stopping Diabetes Before It Happens," *Wall Street Journal,* July 12, 2005, p. D1.

96 *somehow, the absence of the pancreas had caused diabetes* Michael Bliss, *The Discovery of Insulin* (Chicago: University of Chicago Press, 1982), p. 26.

97 *As soon as it was realized that the pancreas controls diabetes* Ibid., p. 28.

98 *At the time Allen introduced what came to be called* Ibid., p. 35.

99 *"It was one of those nights when I was disturbed"* Ibid., p. 12.

100 *developed the method of preparing the extracts* Clark, *Threescore Years and Ten*, p. 57.

100 *the three scientists reported on their research* Madison, *Eli Lilly: A Life*, p. 55.

101 *From the first meeting in Toronto* Ibid., p. 58.

101 *In exchange for providing free insulin* Interview with former Eli Lilly marketing vice president Larry Ellingson, June 30, 2005.

102 *The price stayed the same for nearly 60 years* Ibid.

103 *the exact mode in which the fifty-one amino acids* A. Tiselius, "The Nobel Prize in Chemistry, 1958," *Nobel Lectures, Chemistry, 1942–1962* (Amsterdam: Elsevier Publishing Company, 1964).

104 *type 2 adult-onset diabetes, largely brought on* Betsy McKay, "Stopping Diabetes Before It Happens," *Wall Street Journal*, July 12, 2005, p. D1.

105 *"Insulin is a hormone from the pancreas that is vital"* Interview with Ronald Chance, May 18, 2005.

106 *"Lilly was the primary manufacturer of insulin"* Interview with James Anderson, May 19, 2005.

107 *"When I came to Lilly, I had the opportunity"* Interview with Bruce Frank, May 18, 2005.

108 *"What attracted me to Lilly"* Interview with Richard DiMarchi, June 15, 2005.

109 *when Humulin was injected after a meal* Interview with Ronald Chance, May 18, 2005.

111 *"There we were"* Interview with Bruce Frank, May 18, 2005.

111 *"Insulin that the body produces is a miraculous substance"* Interview with Richard DiMarchi, June 15, 2005.

112 *"We actually removed a part"* Interview with Ronald Chance, May 18, 2005.

112 *"In basic research, concepts are created"* Interview with Bruce Frank, May 18, 2005.

114 *"I spent my Christmas vacation"* Interview with Ronald Chance, May 18, 2005.

115 *"I assure you that what we did"* Interview with Richard DiMarchi, June 15, 2005.

115 *Bill Lacefield, a review board member* Interview with Bruce Frank, July 21, 2005.

117 *"Once management gave its approval"* Interview with James Anderson, May 19, 2005.

120 *"This was comforting to hear"* Interview with James Anderson, May 19, 2005.

120 *"Back in the 1970s when I was in undergraduate school"* Interview with Jeff Baker, May 19, 2005.

122 *"In the manufacturing process during development"* Interview with Bruce Frank, July 18, 2005.

126 *"What it boils down to"* Interview with Jeff Baker, May 19, 2005.

127 *was responsible for coordinating* Interview with Cathy Lawrence, May 19, 2005.

129 *"Having the right education was a requirement"* Interview with Larry Ellingson, June 30, 2005.

130 *"When Humalog was introduced"* Ibid.

131 *There is a story about two clinical investigators* Interview with Ronald Chance, May 18, 2005.

131 *"I had lunch with them"* Interview with Larry Ellingson, June 30, 2005.

132 *"Don't limit yourself"* Interview with Nicole Johnson Baker, March 21, 2006.

136 *"My friend participated in a clinical trial"* Interview with Jeff Baker, May 19, 2005.

CHAPTER 4—GLAXOSMITHKLINE
Clearing the Airways

138 *"charming old man with very little [sic] brains"* See David Passey, www.nzedge.com/josephwardnathan.

139 *"don a tail coat and silk hat and travel by horse and gig to boost sales"* Ibid.

139 *"Mr. Nathan joined to his integrity a cool brain, untiring energy"* Ibid.

140 *In 1919 it hired pharmacist Harry Jephcott* International Directory of Company Histories (Farmington Hills, MI: St. James Press, 2002), p. 202.

141 *"Men without labs are as soldiers without arms"* See www.swan.ac.uk/egypt/infosheet/Wellcome.htm.

142 *Wellcome was an irrepressible showman and entertainer* See www.swan.ac.uk/egypt/infosheet/Wellcome.htm.

142 *"their discoveries concerning prostaglandins and related biologically active substances"* Timeline: Highlights in the History of GlaxoSmithKline, GlaxoSmithKline, p. 15.

143 *"Worth a guinea a box"* Ibid., p. 4.

144 *It was a broad-spectrum penicillin* Ibid., p. 13.

145 *all orders received in the morning would be shipped by no later than that afternoon* Ibid., p. 6.

145 *It was in the first generation of "central nervous system" drugs* Hoover Business Press, 2005, p. 144.

146 *a multimillion-dollar research collaboration with the company Human Genome Sciences* See www.us.gsk.com/timeline.

146 *GSK has an estimated 7 percent share of the world pharmaceutical market* GlaxoSmithKline Annual Report, 2004.

146 *Around 35,000 employees work at 82 manufacturing sites in 37 countries* www.contractpharma.com, July/August 2004.

148   *The term* asthma *comes from the Greek word* panos   Paul J. Hanna-
      way, M.D., *The Asthma Self-Help Book* (Rocklin, CA: Prima Publishing, 1992),
      p. 8.
148   *A description by the Greek physician Aretaeus*   Christopher H. Fanta, M.D.,
      Lynda M. Cristiano, M.D., and Kenan E. Haver, M.D., *The Harvard Medical
      School Guide to Taking Control of Asthma* (New York: Free Press, 2003), p. 4.
150   *Considerable progress has been made*   Ibid., p. 73.
151   *The airways of people with asthma are abnormal*   American Lung Association
      Asthma Advisory Group with Norman H. Edelman, M.D., *Family Guide to
      Asthma and Allergies* (Boston: Little, Brown, 1998), p. 21.
151   *The muscles surrounding the airways known as bronchial tubes*   *Healthwise
      Handbook* (Boise: Healthwise, Incorporated, 1997).
152   *One of the first cases of the use of environmental controls*   Edelman, *Family
      Guide*, p. 20.
152   *Asthma can be inherited, but it does not always follow*   Hannaway, *The Asthma
      Self-Help Book*, p. 11.
152   *The world's hotbed, Tristan da Cunha*   Ibid.
154   *"An advantage in being a very large pharmaceutical company"*   Interview with
      Dr. Tachi Yamada, September 25, 2005.
156   *"When I came here, I worked for Glaxo"*   Interview with Malcolm Johnson,
      September 23, 2005.
158   *"I think that there are some people"*   Interview with Dr. Tachi Yamada, Sep-
      tember 25, 2005.
159   *"I believe I can do more good helping millions"*   Interview with Kathleen Ric-
      kard, September 15, 2005.
161   *"We never anticipated that by putting the two drugs together"*   Interview with
      Dr. Tachi Yamada, September 25, 2005.
161   *"Advair is an inhaled corticosteroid and a long-acting bronchodilator"*   Inter-
      view with Darrell Baker, October 12, 2005.
162   *three distinct classes of steroids*   Hannaway, *The Asthma Self-Help Book*,
      p. 82.
163   *"In our field, we call this corticophobia"*   Interview with Malcolm Johnson,
      September 23, 2005.
164   *"All steroids have some side effects that you want to avoid"*   Interview with
      Darrell Baker, October 12, 2005.
164   *"Inhaled steroids have been proven to be a good idea"*   Interview with Mal-
      colm Johnson, September 23, 2005.
165   *An 1859 article in Scotland's* Edinburgh Medical Journal *read*   Hannaway,
      The Asthma Self-Help Book, p. 98.
166   *For example, oral ephedrine works well*   Ibid., p. 90.
167   *In 1973, upon receiving a degree in product design*   Interview with Paul Rand,
      September 16, 2005.
168   *"One of the strengths of the Diskus"*   Interview with Andrew Grant, Septem-
      ber 16, 2005.

168 *"The Diskus had to be precisely constructed"* Interview with Paul Rand, September 16, 2005.

169 *"The challenge was to get a consistent and reliable delivery"* Interview with Andrew Grant, September 16, 2005.

170 *"We also spent a lot of time"* Interview with Paul Rand, September 16, 2005.

170 *During a 1989 job interview in Glaxo's drug development department* Interview with Elaine Jones, September 15, 2005.

173 *"We had to invent the manufacturing process"* Interview with Andrew Grant, September 16, 2005.

173 *"We prepared for nearly two months for this all-day affair"* Interview with Elaine Jones, September 15, 2005.

174 *"When Advair was launched"* Interview with Darrell Baker, October 12, 2005.

174 *"The FDA regulates everything that goes on here"* Interview with Will Boykin, September 15, 2005.

176 *"Asthma was relatively easy to test"* Interview with Darrell Baker, October 12, 2005.

177 *"Over a period of time, the standard of practice evolved"* Interview with Dr. Tachi Yamada, September 23, 2005.

177 *"As recently as the 1990s"* Interview with Malcolm Johnson, September 23, 2005.

178 *"It's quite obvious when you have asthma"* Interview with Elaine Jones, September 15, 2005.

CHAPTER 5—JOHNSON & JOHNSON
A Miracle Biotech Medicine

180 *At the youthful age of sixteen* Lawrence G. Foster, *Robert Wood Johnson* (State College, PA: Lillian Press, 1999), p. 11.

181 *chemicals, paints, perfumes* Ibid., p. 12.

181 *The Chinese, for example* Ibid., p. 16.

181 *He'd work for hours with a hot iron* Lawrence G. Foster, *A Company That Cares: One Hundred Year Illustrated History of Johnson & Johnson* (New Brunswick, NJ: Johnson & Johnson, 1986), p. 12.

182 *"invisible assassins"* Ibid., p. 15.

182 *the German kitgut, meaning "fiddle"* See http://20.1911encyclopedia.org/C/CA/CATG.

183 *The first products were improved medicinal plasters* Brief History of Johnson & Johnson (New Brunswick, NJ: Johnson & Johnson, 2004), p. 2.

183 *One of the company's most innovative early products* Interview with Elisabeth King, August 23, 2005.

185 *"you can't get well without Johnson & Johnson"* See Susan Warner, http://www.jnj.com/news/in_the_news/pdf/nyt_41005.pdf.

186 *He had an easy rapport with the workers* Foster, *Company That Cares*, p. 70.

187 *"Washington is a magnet for mediocrity"* Ibid., p. 104.

187 *We are responsible* See full credo at Johnson & Johnson Web site, http://www.jnj.com/our_company/our_credo/index.htm.

189 *"improve the healthcare of the nation"* Foster, *Company That Cares*, p. 135.

189 *"a patriot whose love for America was as deep as his love for people"* Ibid., p. 135.

190 *The leadership at Johnson & Johnson provided unprecedented access* Ibid., p. 154.

190 *"Johnson & Johnson has effectively demonstrated how a major business ought to handle a disaster"* See Johnson & Johnson Web site, http://www.jnj.com/our_company/history/history_section_3.htm.

190 *With more than 220 operating units around the world* Carol Hymowitz, "The 50 Women to Watch, 2005," *Wall Street Journal*, October 31, 2005, p. R8.

193 *"A collection of technologies that capitalize"* D. Eramian, L. Dry, D. Strickland, et al., and the BIO communications staff, editors, and reporters, *Guide 2003–2004: Biotechnology, A New Link to Hope*, 7th ed. (Washington, D.C.: Biotechnology Industry Organization, 2003), pp. 1–5.

193 *"it also refers to the type of manufacturing process"* U.S. Food and Drug Administration, Drugs@FDA glossary of terms. Available at: http://www.fda.gov/cder/drugssatfda/glosssary.htm. Accessed March 31, 2005.

193 *"medical products derived from living sources"* U.S. Food and Drug Administration, *FDA Consumer Magazine: 100 Years of Biologics Regulation*. Available at: http://www.fda.ogv/fdac/features/2002/402–bio.html. Accessed March 31, 2005.

196 *Centocor used its limited cash reservoir to piggyback* International Directory of Company Histories, volume 14 (Detroit: St. James Press, 1996), p. 98.

196 *"Early on we recognized that we couldn't do everything on our own"* Interview with John Ghrayeb, February 13, 2006.

197 *"I had never heard of the company"* Interview with Harlan Weisman, December 5, 2005.

200 *"My aspiration was to be a physical therapist"* Interview with David Holveck, December 12, 2005.

201 *"The interesting thing about antibodies"* Interview with Harlan Weisman, December 5, 2005.

201 *"In the early days of Centocor"* Interview with David Holveck, December 12, 2005.

203 *In 1985, Centocor embarked* Hubert J.P. Schoemaker and Anne Faulkner Schoemaker, "The Three Pillars of Bioentrepreneurship," *Nature Biotechnology*, 1998, p. 13.

203 *Sepsis is the most common cause of death* Robert Shulman, "Current drug treatment of sepsis," *Hospital Pharmacist*, April 2002, p. 97.

203 *HA-1A was developed in 1985 by Dr. Henry Kaplan* Gina Kolata, "Halted at the Market's Door: How a $1 Billion Drug Failed," *New York Times*, nytimes.com, February 12, 1993.

203 *"We had faith in our game plan"* Interview with Harlan Weisman, December 5, 2005.

204 *"Centoxin looked so good"* Interview with David Holveck, December 12, 2005.

204 *Dr. Jay Siegel, who reviewed Centocor's license application* Kolata, "Halted at the Market's Door."

205 *$50 million for a 5 percent stake in the company* International Directory of Company Histories, volume 14, p. 99.

205 *On January 18, 1993, the company abruptly halted* Kolata, "Halted at the Market's Door."

205 *"Centocor missed an important cue"* Schoemaker and Schoemaker, "The Three Pillars of Bioentrepreneurship," p. 14.

206 *"We were down and it was hurtful to see that cartoon"* Interview with David Holveck, December 12, 2005.

206 *"I joined the company in January 1990"* Interview with Harlan Weisman, December 5, 2005.

206 *"Honest to truth, I never had it"* Interview with David Holveck, December 12, 2005.

209 *"We recoiled and refocused"* James Bamford, "How a Near-Death Experience Forced Centocor into Strategic Alliances," *Financial World*, April 11, 1995, p. 68.

209 *"The bane the of exploration industry is choices"* Interview with David Holveck, December 12, 2005.

210 *"Our focus was mainly on manufacturing"* Interview with Harlan Weisman, December 5, 2005.

211 *"Centoxin is often referred to as a failed drug"* Interview with David Holveck, December 12, 2005.

212 *"If you look up optimist in the dictionary"* Linda Loyd and Sally A. Downey, "Chemist Who Helped Found Pa. Biotech Industry dies at 55," *Philadelphia Inquirer*, January 4, 2006.

213 *"Our researchers initially thought Remicade"* Interview with Julie McHugh, December 7, 2005.

214 *"We realized early on that Remicade"* Interview with John Ghrayeb, February 13, 2006.

214 *"Sepsis is a systemic infection that can cause"* Interview with Thomas Schaible, January 16, 2006.

215 *"When Dave [Holveck] took over as Centocor's CEO"* Interview with Joe Scodari, December 12, 2005.

217 *"Since Remicade is specific for human TNF"* Interview with Thomas Schaible, January 16, 2006.

217 *"We wanted to hear the results firsthand"* Interview with Joe Scodari, December 12, 2005.

220 *"He had heard about the results"* Interview with John Ghrayeb, February 13, 2006.

220 *"Van Deventer wrote an article about his success"* Interview with Thomas Schaible, January 16, 2006.

221 *A healthy immune system is the body's best ally* Kher Unmesh, "New Ways to Intervene When the Body Attacks Itself," *Time*, January 15, 2001, p. 76.

221 *There's one thin layer of cells* Josh Fischman, "Vital Signs," *U.S. News & World Report*, October 7, 2002, p. 64.

222 *It is socially disabling* Interview with Jay Siegel, December 19, 2005.

222 *"We were concurrently in Phase II development"* Interview with Julie McHugh, December 7, 2005.

222 *"We learned a valuable lesson with Centoxin"* Interview with Joe Scodari, January 12, 2006.

223 *Traditional treatments at the time had included* "First Treatment Approved for Crohn's Disease," *FDA Consumer*, November/December 1998, p. 3.

223 *"In the case of a drug like Lipitor"* Interview with Thomas Schaible, January 16, 2006.

224 *The ATTRACT trial was a double-blind, placebo-controlled* "The FDA Recommends Approval of Remicade (Infliximab) with Methotrexate for Rheumatoid Arthritis Joint Damage," P\S\L Consulting Group Inc., 1999.

225 *"We designed ATTRACT as a rolling trial"* Interview with Thomas Schaible, January 16, 2006.

226 *"What we do here is known as large-molecule manufacturing"* Interview with Remo J. Colarusso Jr., January 16, 2006.

227 *"It's a clean room operation"* Interview with Robert Sheroff, January 26, 2006.

228 *"Depending [on] what stage the batch is in"* Interview with Remo J. Colarusso Jr., January 16, 2006.

229 *"When we go to that container and take out our cell line"* Interview with Robert Sheroff, January 26, 2006.

229 *"At that particular time"* Interview with David Holveck, December 12, 2005.

230 *"If you think Las Vegas is a gamble"* Interview with Thomas Schaible, January 16, 2006.

232 *"Fortunately, Remicade is such a powerful drug"* Interview with Harlan Weisman, December 5, 2005.

232 *"In some instances, patients received their first infusion of Remicade"* Interview with Julie McHugh, December 7, 2005.

233 *"In January 1999, a few months after we launched the product"* Interview with Joe Scodari, December 12, 2005.

233 *"It's an amazing medicine that transforms lives"* Interview with Julie McHugh, December 7, 2005.

233 *"With rheumatoid arthritis, it is best that patients"* Interview with Thomas Schaible, January 16, 2006.

234 *"Crohn's disease was uncharted territory"* Interview with Julie McHugh, December 7, 2005.

235 *"Rather than recruiting, training, and paying an idle sales force"* Interview with Joe Scodari, December 12, 2005.

235 *"Some of the first reps we hired were nurses"* Interview with Julie McHugh, December 7, 2005.

236 *"Once we made the decision"* Interview with David Holveck, December 12, 2005.

237 *"We identified J&J as our preferred white knight"* Interview with Joe Scodari, December 12, 2005.

238 *"One of the benefits I see that has happened"* Interview with Julie McHugh, December 7, 2005.

238 *"We've remained a fully integrated company"* Interview with Chris Molineaux, November 29, 2005.

238 *"The people at Centocor have a lot of pride"* Interview with David Holveck, December 12, 2005.

240 *"Why do I drive an hour and ten minutes"* Interview with David Holveck, December 12, 2005.

241 *"Most companies would be happy"* Interview with John Ghrayeb, February 13, 2006.

241 *"It's a privilege to be part of a company"* Interview with Julie McHugh, December 7, 2005.

CHAPTER 6—NOVARTIS
A Designer Medicine that Targets Cancer Cells

242 *"World's Leading Life Sciences Company"* See Wikipedia online encyclopedia at www.en.wikipedia.org/wiki/novartis.

242 *"materials, chemicals, dyes and drugs of all kinds"* See Novartis corporate Web site at www.novartis.com/about_novartis/en/3companies.html.

243 *his family was able to marry into the lucrative silk manufacturing establishment of Switzerland* International Directory of Company Histories (Farmington Hills, MI: St. James Press, 2005), p. 632.

244 *Their original plant was built on an 11,000-square-foot tract along the Rhine River* Ibid.

244 *their dye production rose from 13,000 kilograms of 6 different dyes to 380,000 kilograms of 28 different dyes* Ibid., p. 671.

245 *because of labor shortages in Switzerland* Ibid., p. 632.

246 *specialists in industrial cleansers, soaps, softening agents, bleaches, fungicides, herbicides, insecticides, and rodenticides* Ibid., p. 672.

246 *an alkaloid distilled from a fungus* Ibid.

246 *Sandoz focused on LSD's role in experimental psychiatry* See Wikipedia online encyclopedia at http://en.wikipedia.org/wiki/LSD.

248 *Sandoz, invited the "grand old man" of Swiss pharmacy* Daniel Vasella, M.D., Magic Cancer Bullet (New York: HarperBusiness, 2003), p. 58.

248 *"In our case, we need both kinds of people"* Interview with Daniel Vasella, July 5, 2005.

249 *Syngenta, the world's first global agrichemical business* Hoover's Handbook of World Business (Austin, TX: Hoover's Inc., 2005), p. 47.

250 *Its well-stocked pipeline* Contract Pharma, Washington, D.C. July/August 2004, p. 74

252 *This discovery marked the first time* Vasella, Magic Cancer Bullet, p. 37.

253 *"I read nearly every book about scientists"* Interview with Alex Matter, May 11, 2005.

255 *Kinases are enzymes that play a major role* Interview with cell biologist Dr. Elisabeth Buchdunger, June 6, 2005.

256 *"a real intellectual bulldozer"* Vasella, *Magic Cancer Bullet*, p. 39.

256 *"He genuinely believed that, based on the work"* Ibid., p. 41.

256 *"Based on this concept"* Interview with Alex Matter, May 11, 2005.

257 *in 1986 and 1987 when Dr. David Baltimore and Dr. Owen N. White* Vasella, *Magic Cancer Bullet*, p. 37.

257 *"There are twenty different amino acids"* Interview with Alex Matter, May 11, 2005.

258 *"From the time I was a medical student"* Interview with Brian Druker on July 13, 2005.

260 *Until their conversation, Lydon* Vasella, *Magic Cancer Bullet*, p. 47.

261 *"When I came here"* Interview with Juerg Zimmermann, June 18, 2005.

266 *When Juerg Zimmermann arrived at work* Vasella, *Magic Cancer Bullet*, p. 51.

269 *"We must do something with the compound"* Ibid., p. 56.

271 *"As the CEO, I knew"* Interview with Daniel Vasella, July 5, 2005.

272 *he had muscle that allowed him* Vasella, *Magic Cancer Bullet*, p. 59.

273 *"All of my concerns are gone"* Interview with Daniel Vasella, July 5, 2005.

273 *"The more I got to know Alex Matter"* Ibid.

273 *"The way things turned out, the Gleevec team"* Interview with David Epstein, June 9, 2005.

275 *"We can always find a commercial solution"* Vasella, *Magic Cancer Bullet*, p. 62.

275 *"It doesn't matter that there was a liver toxicity problem"* Interview with Brian Druker, July 13, 2005.

276 *"Inhibiting a tyrosine kinase"* Interview with Brian Druker, July 13, 2005.

276 *"The best scientific progress doesn't mean much"* Interview with Daniel Vasella, July 5, 2005.

276 *Human trials have to be very exacting* Vasella, *Magic Cancer Bullet*, p. 69.

277 *"I was the principal investigator"* Interview with Brian Druker, July 13, 2005.

278 *All sorts of things could happen* Vasella, *Magic Cancer Bullet*, p. 73.

278 *The patient had to have CML* Ibid., p. 75.

278 *"We ended up having about forty to fifty patients in Oregon"* Interview with Brian Druker, July 13, 2005.

279 *"The immediate response from Gleevec"* Interview with Alex Matter, May 11, 2005.

279 *"The first feedback showed"* Interview with Juerg Zimmerman, June 18, 2005.

280 *The data were astonishing* Vasella, *Magic Cancer Bullet*, p. 89.

281 *"How could we gear up our resources"* Ibid., p. 91.

281 *"Routinely, our strategy at Novartis"* Ibid., p. 93.

282 *Her physician told her* Interview with Suzan McNamara, August 22, 2005.

285 *"When the ASH attendees heard about the hematologic responses"* Interview with Laurie Letvak, June 9, 2005.

285 *"Literally within an hour after Dr. Druker's presentation"* Interview with Barbara Kennedy, June 9, 2005.

288 *The results from the follow-up data* Interview with Laurie Letvak, June 9, 2005.

288 *"We enrolled these patients in record time"* Interview with David Epstein, June 9, 2005.

290 *"We made the decision to launch this medicine"* Ibid.

291 *"I loved working at IBM"* Interview with Hugh O'Dowd, June 9, 2005.

291 *"This kind of selling"* Interview with Deborah Dunsire, June 9, 2005.

292 *"In addition to the other formal training"* Interview with Hugh O'Dowd, June 9, 2005.

293 *"At a press conference"* Interview with David Epstein, June 9, 2005.

293 *Secretary Thompson noted that the drug* Vasella, *Magic Cancer Bullet,* p. 162.

295 *"PAP was set up here in the U.S."* Interview with Hugh O'Dowd, June 9, 2005.

295 *She takes one 400-milligram pill a day* Interview with Suzan McNamara, August 22, 2005.

296 *"As it turns out, we probably can't kill"* Interview with Brian Druker, July 13, 2005.

296 *It is a tumor that generally forms* U.S. Food and Drug Administration, *FDA Talk Paper,* February 1, 2002.

297 *"The fight against cancer continues"* Interview with Daniel Vasella, July 5, 2005.

CHAPTER 7—PFIZER
How the World's Bestselling Drug Nearly Didn't Happen

298 *Though they came from well-to-do families* *Celebrating Pfizer: 150 Years of Innovation, 1849–1999* (New York: Pfizer Inc., 1999), p. 5.

298 *when life was not only more primitive* Jeffrey L. Rodengen, *The Legend of Pfizer* (Fort Lauderdale: Write Stuff Syndicate, 1999), p. 13.

299 *By 1860, the Pfizer line had expanded to include iodine preparations* Ogden Tanner, *25 Years of Innovation: The Story of Pfizer Central Research* (Lyme, CT: Greenwich Publishing Group, Inc., 1966), p. 24.

300 *naval blockades and a cartel of Italian citrus growers put a stranglehold* Rodengen, *The Legend of Pfizer,* p. 13.

302 *In 1928, when bacteriologist Alexander Fleming* *Celebrating Pfizer,* p. 8.

302 *When these firms were selected* Gladys L. Hobby, *Penicillin, Meeting the Challenge* (New Haven: Yale University Press, 1985), p. 172.

303 *Pfizer produced 90 percent of the penicillin* *Celebrating Pfizer,* p. 9.

304 *Generically, the compound, now known as oxytetracycline* Tanner, *25 Years of Innovation,* p. 22.

307 *a record-breaking earthquake rocked Sumatra* *Pfizer 2004 Annual Review,* p. 36.

310 *For transport to and from the cells*   Robert Langreth, "Blood Feud—Competitors Are Gunning for Pfizer and Its Champion Cholesterol Drug, Lipitor," *Forbes*, February 5, 2001, p. 66.

314 *was born on a farm in the snowy north of Japan*   Peter Landers, "How One Scientist Intrigued by Molds Found First Statin," *Wall Street Journal*, January 9, 2006, p. A1.

316 *"We didn't make it because we had an interest in insecticides"*   Interview with Bruce Roth, November 16, 2005.

317 *"I had been reading a book on atherosclerosis and cholesterol"*   Interview with Roger Newton, November 17, 2005.

319 *"I was a project leader"*   Interview with David Canter, November 17, 2005.

320 *Sankyo granted Merck access to its data and methods*   Landers, "How One Scientist Intrigued by Molds Found First Statin," p. A1.

321 *"The first thing we did"*   Interview with Bruce Roth, November 16, 2005.

323 *"As a research biologist"*   Interview with Roger Newton, November 17, 2005.

324 *"Roger and Bruce were a great combination"*   Interview with David Canter, November 17, 2005.

324 *"Before computers, the chemists did far more trial-and-error work"*   Interview with Daniel Ortwine, November 16, 2005

325 *"When we started our statin project"*   Interview with Bruce Roth, November 16, 2005.

326 *"We'd study what the other companies did"*   Interview with David Canter, November 17, 2005.

326 *"After our program was underway"*   Interview with Bruce Roth, November 16, 2005.

328 *"Consequently we had to terminate our plans"*   Interview with Bruce Roth, November 21, 2005.

330 *"Parke-Davis had just launched Quinapril"*   Interview with Roger Newton, November 17, 2005.

331 *"I wanted to make sure there would be large quantities"*   Interview with Ronald Cresswell, January 25, 2006.

333 *"It was a somber atmosphere"*   Interview with Bruce Roth, November 16, 2005.

333 *"That is a good thing"*   Interview with Roger Newton, November 17, 2005.

335 *at 10 milligrams, LDL dropped 38 percent*   Ron Winslow, "The Birth of a Blockbuster: Lipitor's Route Out of the Lab," *Wall Street Journal* Online, January 24, 2000.

335 *"It allowed you to go for a strategy"*   Interview with Ronald Cresswell, January 25, 2006.

336 *Around the same time, Edward Ludwig*   Interview with David Canter, November 17, 2005.

337 *"I had a problem with the ethics of using a placebo"*   Ibid.

340 *"It's one thing to make a compound in an academic lab"*   Interview with Bruce Roth, November 21, 2005.

341 *"The chemistry needed to get the right relationship"* Winslow, "The Birth of a Blockbuster: Lipitor's Route out of the Lab."

342 *"The most efficient way to make an automobile"* Interview with David Canter, November 17, 2005.

342 *a red-headed woman in marketing* Interview with Bruce Roth, November 16, 2005.

343 *"We knew about their compound"* Interview with David Canter, November 16, 2005.

343 *"There were still internal skeptics"* Interview with Bruce Roth, November 16, 2005.

344 *"All of the samples had been given out"* Interview with David Canter, November 17, 2005

344 *"With the clinical trials"* Interview with Bruce Roth, November 21, 2005.

345 *"Imagine what could have gone wrong"* Interview with David Canter, November 17, 2005.

346 *"In 1999 we went through an exercise"* Ibid.

347 *"I felt I was put in a compromised position"* Interview with Roger Newton, November 16, 2005.

349 *"The $800 million spent on the clinical trials"* Interview with Bruce Roth, November 21, 2005.

350 *"This is something you never think about"* Interview with Bruce Roth, November 16, 2005.

351 *"It's that old adage that reminds us"* Interview with Roger Newton, November 16, 2005.

INDEX

molecules (*continued*)
  designer, 296
  growth factors, 259
  leads, 2–3
  structure of, 23
Molineaux, Christopher, 238, 239
Moniz, Egas, 53
monoclonal antibodies, 195–96, 197–99, 211, 213, 215
Montagnier, Luc, 18
Moores and Ross Milk Company, 13
Moret, Marc, 248, 270
Morton, Oliver P., 87
Mueller, Paul, 246
Muller-Pack, Johann, 243
Murphy, Robert, 35, 36
Murtha, Ken, 65, 73
music, healing properties of, 50
Myoscint, 202

NAMI (National Alliance of the Mentally Ill), 82, 83
Nanninga, Thomas, 321, 341
Nasrallah, Henry, 70, 73
Nathan, Alex, 140
Nathan, Joseph E., 138–40, 147
National Cancer Act (1971), 251
nelfinavir (Viracept), 34, 36
Nembutal, 13–14
neuroleptics, 58
Neuronyx, 212
Newton, Roger, 316, 317–18, 323–24, 327, 330–34, 342, 347, 350–52
Nexium, 47–48, 80
Nixon, Richard M., 251
NMHA (National Mental Health Association), 84
NMR (nuclear magnetic resonance), 23
Norbeck, Dan, 23, 25–26, 31
Norcliff Thayer, 144
Norvasc, 307
Norvir, 15, 40
  clinical trials of, 26–29, 30
  development of, 28
  FDA approval of, 30–31
  and Kaletra, 33–34
  name of, 31
  saquinavir combined with, 32–33

Novartis:
  agrochemical business of, 47, 249
  company profile, 242–50
  corporate culture in, 242, 274, 281
  formation of, 247, 248–50, 269, 271
  GIPAP program of, 249, 295
  and Gleevec, *see* Gleevec
Nowell, Peter, 252

obesity, 104, 107
O'Dowd, Hugh, 290–92, 295
Ohnmacht, Cyrus, 56–57, 58
OHSU (Oregon Health and Science University), 268–69
oncogenes, 202, 254–55; *see also* Bcr-Abl oncogene
Opie, Eugene Lindsay, 97
Orphan Drug Act, 294
Ortho Biotech, 211
Orthoclone OKT3, 211
Ortho Pharmaceuticals, 188
Ortwine, Daniel, 324–25
Ostelin, 140
oxytetracycline, 304

Palmer, James, 156, 157, 165
pancreas:
  and diabetes, 97, 104
  insulin secreted by, 96, 97, 105, 107, 111
Panorex, 209
PAP (patient assistance program), 295
Pape, Mike, 348
Parke-Davis:
  and Adrenalin, 150
  and penicillin, 302
  Pfizer acquisition of, 306
  and Quinapril, 330
  and statins, 317, 320, 331–32, 335
Pasteur, Louis, 141, 253–54
patent medicines, 182
pathognomonic symptoms, 52
Patient Zero, 16
PCP (pneumocystis carinii pneumonia), 17
PDGF-R (platelet-derived growth factor), 296
Peacock, Bruce, 212
Pearl, Laurence, 21